**OPERATING SYSTEMS
THEORY**

Prentice-Hall
Series in Automatic Computation

George Forsythe, editor

AHO, editor, *Currents in the Theory of Computing*
AHO AND ULLMAN, *Theory of Parsing, Translation, and Compiling, Volume I: Parsing;*
  Volume II: Compiling
(ANDREE)[3], *Computer Programming: Techniques, Analysis, and Mathematics*
ANSELONE, *Collectively Compact Operator Approximation Theory*
  and Applications to Integral Equations
ARBIB, *Theories of Abstract Automata*
BATES AND DOUGLAS, *Programming Language/One*, 2nd ed.
BLUMENTHAL, *Management Information Systems*
BRENT, *Algorithms for Minimization without Derivatives*
COFFMAN AND DENNING, *Operating Systems Theory*
CRESS, et al., *FORTRAN IV with WATFOR and WATFIV*
DAHLQUIST, et al., *Numerical Methods*
DANIEL, *The Approximate Minimization of Functionals*
DEO, *Graph Theory with Applications to Engineering and Computer Science*
DESMONDE, *Computers and Their Uses*, 2nd ed.
DESMONDE, *Real-Time Data Processing Systems*
DRUMMOND, *Evaluation and Measurement Techniques for Digital Computer Systems*
EVANS, et al., *Simulation Using Digital Computers*
FIKE, *Computer Evaluation of Mathematical Functions*
FIKE, *PL/1 for Scientific Programmers*
FORSYTHE AND MOLER, *Computer Solution of Linear Algebraic Systems*
GAUTHIER AND PONTO, *Designing Systems Programs*
GEAR, *Numerical Initial Value Problems in Ordinary Differential Equations*
GOLDEN, *FORTRAN IV Programming and Computing*
GOLDEN AND LEICHUS, *IBM/360 Programming and Computing*
GORDON, *System Simulation*
HARTMANIS AND STEARNS, *Algebraic Structure Theory of Sequential Machines*
HULL, *Introduction to Computing*
JACOBY, et al., *Iterative Methods for Nonlinear Optimization Problems*
JOHNSON, *System Structure in Data, Programs, and Computers*
KANTER, *The Computer and the Executive*
KIVIAT, et al., *The SIMSCRIPT II Programming Language*
LORIN, *Parallelism in Hardware and Software: Real and Apparent Concurrency*
LOUDEN AND LEDIN, *Programming the IBM 1130*, 2nd ed.
MARTIN, *Design of Man–Computer Dialogues*
MARTIN, *Design of Real-Time Computer Systems*
MARTIN, *Future Developments in Telecommunications*
MARTIN, *Programming Real-Time Computing Systems*
MARTIN, *Security, Accuracy and Privacy in Computer Systems*
MARTIN, *Systems Analysis for Data Transmission*
MARTIN, *Telecommunications and the Computer*

MARTIN, *Teleprocessing Network Organization*

MARTIN AND NORMAN, *The Computerized Society*

MATHISON AND WALKER, *Computers and Telecommunications: Issues in Public Policy*

MCKEEMAN, et al., *A Compiler Generator*

MEYERS, *Time-Sharing Computation in the Social Sciences*

MINSKY, *Computation: Finite and Infinite Machines*

NIEVERGELT, et al., *Computer Approaches to Mathematical Problems*

PLANE AND MCMILLAN, *Discrete Optimization: Integer Programming and Network Analysis for Management Decisions*

PRITSKER AND KIVIAT, *Simulation with GASP II: a FORTRAN-Based Simulation Language*

PYLYSHYN, editor, *Perspectives on the Computer Revolution*

RICH, *Internal Sorting Methods Illustrated with PL/1 Programs*

RUSTIN, editor, *Algorithm Specification*

RUSTIN, editor, *Computer Networks*

RUSTIN, editor, *Data Base Systems*

RUSTIN, editor, *Debugging Techniques in Large Systems*

RUSTIN, editor, *Design and Optimization of Compilers*

RUSTIN, editor, *Formal Semantics of Programming Languages*

SACKMAN AND CITRENBAUM, editors, *On-Line Planning: Towards Creative Problem-Solving*

SALTON, editor, *The SMART Retrieval System: Experiments in Automatic Document Processing*

SAMMET, *Programming Languages: History and Fundamentals*

SCHAEFER, *A Mathematical Theory of Global Program Optimization*

SCHULTZ, *Spline Analysis*

SCHWARZ, et al., *Numerical Analysis of Symmetric Matrices*

SHERMAN, *Techniques in Computer Programming*

SIMON AND SIKLOSSY, editors, *Representation and Meaning: Experiments with Information Processing Systems*

STERBENZ, *Floating-Point Computation*

STERLING AND POLLACK, *Introduction to Statistical Data Processing*

STOUTEMYER, *PL/1 Programming for Engineering and Science*

STRANG AND FIX, *An Analysis of the Finite Element Method*

STROUD, *Approximate Calculation of Multiple Integrals*

TAVISS, editor, *The Computer Impact*

TRAUB, *Iterative Methods for the Solution of Polynomial Equations*

UHR, *Pattern Recognition, Learning, and Thought*

VAN TASSEL, *Computer Security Management*

VARGA, *Matrix Iterative Analysis*

WAITE, *Implementing Software for Non-Numeric Application*

WILKINSON, *Rounding Errors in Algebraic Processes*

WIRTH, *Systematic Programming: An Introduction*

OPERATING SYSTEMS THEORY

EDWARD G. COFFMAN, JR.
Pennsylvania State University

PETER J. DENNING
Purdue University

PRENTICE-HALL, INC.

ENGLEWOOD CLIFFS, NEW JERSEY

Library of Congress Cataloging in Publication Data

COFFMAN, EDWARD GRADY.
    Operating systems theory.

    (Prentice-Hall series in automatic computation)
    Includes bibliographical references.
    1. Electronic digital computers—Programming.
2. Algorithms. I. Denning, Peter J., joint author.
II. Title.
QA76.6.C62   001.6'42   73–18
ISBN 0–13–637868–4

10 9 8 7 6 5 4

Printed in the United States of America

PRENTICE-HALL INTERNATIONAL, INC., *London*
PRENTICE-HALL OF AUSTRALIA, PTY. LTD., *Sydney*
PRENTICE-HALL OF CANADA, LTD., *Toronto*
PRENTICE-HALL OF INDIA PRIVATE LIMITED, *New Delhi*
PRENTICE-HALL OF JAPAN, INC., *Tokyo*

CONTENTS

PREFACE   xi

1 INTRODUCTION   1

1.1. Operating Systems   1
1.2. Resources   3
1.3. Concurrent Processes   7
   1.3.1. Process Coordination   10
   1.3.2. Task System Scheduling   11
   1.3.3. Probability Models of Schedulers   12
1.4. Memory Management   15
   1.4.1. Auxiliary Storage and Buffer Problems   19
   1.4.2. Paging Algorithms   21
   1.4.3. Program Behavior and Multiprogramming   23

2 CONTROL OF CONCURRENT PROCESSES   31

2.1. Introduction   31
2.2. Determinacy of Task Systems   35
2.3. Deadlocks   44
   2.3.1. Introduction   44
   2.3.2. Prevention   51
   2.3.3. Detection   53
   2.3.4. Avoidance   55
2.4. Mutual Exclusion   59
   2.4.1. Introduction   59
   2.4.2. Primitives for Implementing Mutual Exclusion   62
   2.4.3. Solution of the General Problem   64
2.5. Synchronization   68

3 DETERMINISTIC MODELS OF PROCESSOR
SCHEDULING   83

3.1. Introduction   83
3.2. Optimal Schedules for Two-Processor Systems   87
3.3. Optimal Schedules for Tree-Structured Precedence Graphs   94
3.4. Scheduling of Independent Tasks   100
3.5. List Scheduling   106
3.6. Scheduling with Preemptions and Processor Sharing   112
3.7. Systems of Different Processors   123
3.8. Scheduling to Minimize Mean Flow Time   128

4 PROBABILITY MODELS OF COMPUTER
SEQUENCING PROBLEMS   144

4.1. Introduction   144
    4.1.1. Basic Definitions   144
    4.1.2. The Arrival Process   146
    4.1.3. The Service Mechanism   150
    4.1.4. Performance Measures   151
4.2. Basic Queueing Results   152
    4.2.1. The M/M/1 Queueing System   152
    4.2.2. The M/G/1 Queueing System   157
    4.2.3. Waiting Times   161
    4.2.4. The Busy-Period Distribution   165
4.3. State-Dependent Arrival and Service Times in Poisson Queues 166
4.4. The Round-Robin Service Discipline   169
4.5. Nonpreemptive Priority Queues   175
4.6. The Shortest-Elapsed-Time Discipline   178
4.7. The Shortest-Remaining-Processing-Time Discipline   182
4.8. Comparison of Processing Time Priority Disciplines   186

5 AUXILIARY AND BUFFER STORAGE MODELS   198

5.1. Introduction   198
5.2. Minimization of Rotational Latency Effects   201
5.3. Minimization of Seek-Time Effects   209
5.4. Models of Interacting Input/Output and CPU Queues   218
5.5. Buffer Storage Allocation Problems   224

6 STORAGE ALLOCATION IN PAGING SYSTEMS   241

6.1. Introduction   241
6.2. Paging Algorithms   243
6.3. Optimal Paging Algorithms   246
  6.3.1. Cost Function   246
  6.3.2. Optimal Replacement Policies   249
6.4. Stack Algorithms   254
  6.4.1. Introduction   254
  6.4.2. Priority Algorithms   257
  6.4.3. Procedure for Determining the Cost Function   263
6.5. The Extension Problem   265
6.6. The Independent Reference Model   268
6.7. The LRU-Stack Model   275

7 MULTIPROGRAMMED MEMORY MANAGEMENT   285

7.1. Introduction   285
7.2. Locality   286
7.3. Working Set Model   287
  7.3.1. Assumptions About Reference Strings   288
  7.3.2. Definitions   290
  7.3.3. Properties   292
  7.3.4. Distribution of Working Set Size   295
7.4. Relation between LRU Paging and Working Sets   298
7.5. Fixed versus Variable Partitioning   299

APPENDIX

A TRANSFORMS, THE CENTRAL LIMIT THEOREM, AND MARKOV CHAINS   313

A.1. Generating Functions   313
A.2. Laplace Transforms and the Central Limit Theorem   315
A.3. Markov Chains   317

APPENDIX

B RECURRENCE TIMES   320

INDEX   323

PREFACE

Motivations for Studying Operating Systems Theory

In the years since 1969, the study of computer systems has assumed a role nearly equal in importance to "theory of computation" and "programming" in computer science curricula. In contrast, the subject of computer operating systems was regarded as recently as 1965 as being inferior in importance to these two traditional areas of study. This is a significant change in attitude. The first signs of the change are evidenced in ACM's *Curriculum 68*,† and the speed of its development is evidenced in the report of Task Force VIII of the COSINE (computer science in engineering) Committee of the Commission on Education of the National Academy of Engineering, *An Undergraduate Course on Operating Systems Principles* (June 1971).‡ There are several important reasons for this change.

First, three practical objectives—improving existing and future designs, building systems whose correctness and behavior can be determined a priori, and solving the resource allocation and performance evaluation problems—have stimulated increasing amounts of research in computer system modeling. A principal result of this effort has been the emergence of a "theory" of computer operating system design and analysis. This in turn is having an almost immediate impact on curricula: The traditional "case-study" approach to teaching operating systems concepts, which never proved to be an outstanding success, is giving way rapidly to the "modeling and analysis" approach.

Second, the problems of designing complex software systems have traditionally been considered of less intellectual interest than "theory of com-

†*Comm. ACM.* March 1968.
‡Commission on Education, National Academy of Engineering, 2102 Constitution Avenue, Washington, D.C. 20418.

putation" and "programming." The so-called software problem, i.e., reducing the high cost of software development and improving quality control over software packages, has been found to be increasingly severe. As a result, tradition is being reversed, there is rising interest in software system design as a deep intellectual problem. Much of "computer system theory" is related in one way or another to understanding and managing complexity in software systems.

Third, there is an ever widening appreciation of the view that the world we live in has become a real-time system whose complexity is beyond the reach of the unaided human mind to understand. Again and again we see decisions taken in business systems, economic systems, social systems, and urban systems—all real-time information systems—which, despite the best of intentions, often turn out to have effects quite unlike those intended. This phenomenon is not new in the experience of operating systems designers. Since computer-system "theorists" are deeply involved in the problems of managing complex real-time information systems in order to get them behaving as intended, this subject material appears destined ultimately to have an impact not restricted to the computer industry.

PURPOSE OF THIS BOOK

The principal object of this book is studying algorithms arising in the design of computer operating systems. The study includes specifically sequencing and control algorithms designed to avoid various types of failures in systems supporting concurrent processes, scheduling algorithms designed to minimize total execution times and mean flow times, algorithms for allocating processors among multiprogrammed tasks, algorithms for using input/output devices, and algorithms for managing storage. These algorithms are studied from a formal view. In studying a given problem, for example, we shall discuss methods of devising mathematical models for the system and algorithms of interest; we shall then work out analyses whose goals are proofs of optimality, derivations of performance measures, or demonstrations that the systems or algorithms have certain desirable properties.

Consistent with this theme, our educational goal is presenting in one place, in as simple a form as possible, the most important formal methods that have been applied to the study of operating systems algorithms. Our interest is explicating the nature of the results, the essence of the analysis, and the power and limitations of the methods. In many cases we have chosen the simplest form extant of a model; we have done this whenever the additional generality would have multiplied the complexity of analysis beyond the value of whatever additional insight would have been gained. The book will succeed in its basic purpose to the extent that a reader moderately experienced in operating system design is enabled to examine a given operating system and successfully to execute a project of (formal) modeling and analysis with respect to that system.

There are two broad subject areas that we have consciously avoided in our treatment: heuristic and experimental methods. (Indeed, the inclusion of these topics and the corresponding results would surely have doubled the size of the book.) Our exclusion of heuristic and exhaustive search methods for combinatorial problems in scheduling is largely justified by their excellent treatment in Conway, Maxwell, and Miller.† Our exclusion of experimental results relating to storage management is justified by their extensive coverage in the literature.

Experimental work concerned with simulation studies and statistical analysis of system performance (and program behavior) interfaces directly with the content of this book and would constitute a book on its own right. However, our use of models of program and computer-use behavior proceeds only as far as it is necessary to study the properties of specific algorithms. Important and well-known work in modeling program behavior includes graph models of parallelism and locality models of storage referencing. In the course of the book we shall have numerous occasions to reference the various engineering studies that support the assumptions made in the mathematical models.

We have arranged the presentation to be useful both to professionals as a reference and to students as a text. The reader is assumed to be familiar with the concepts, systems, and techniques acquired in the core of a computer science curriculum. For this reason we have omitted lengthy motivations for the models devised and extensive interpretation of the results obtained. The reader is expected to have a mathematical maturity corresponding roughly to a senior undergraduate or beginning graduate student. More specifically, a basic facility with formal systems is assumed along with a knowledge of the elements of applied probability theory and Markov chains. We have included a brief review of the latter material in an appendix.

Unfortunately, one or both of these latter assumptions is very frequently not valid when and where it should be. If it is agreed that a major part of computer science education is the study of algorithms—how to design and write them clearly, how to design optimal or efficient algorithms, and how to assess their performance—it follows from the nature and applicability of probability models that the student must have achieved some competence in applied probability theory and combinatorics. Until he acquires such skills, the student will not generally be capable of designing nontrivial algorithms and communicating to others precisely what he has done—in particularly designing proofs that show his algorithm to have certain properties and

†R. W. Conway, W. L. Maxwell, and L. W. Miller, *Theory of Scheduling* (Reading, Mass.: Addison–Wesley), 1967.

derivations of measures that can be used to judge the effectiveness and performance of his algorithm.

At the end of each chapter we have included a selection of problems relating to extensions or modifications of the material in that chapter. In the majority of cases these are *problems*, rather than *exercises*. It is especially important that the reader examine them, for their purpose is not only to improve the understanding of material in the text, but also to fill out the coverage of the book. There are many problems that extend the methods treated in the various chapters to different but closely related applications not otherwise discussed.

PLAN OF THE BOOK

According to the COSINE report there are six aspects of computer system modeling in which useful abstractions and theoretical developments have evolved:

Procedures and their implementation
Management of named objects
Protection
Concurrent processes
Management of memory hierarchies
Resource allocation

Of these six sets of concepts, the first three tend to be more descriptive in nature, i.e., the abstractions do not involve any mathematics and are used by designers for immediate guidance in implementations. The last three sets of concepts do, however, rely on mathematical analysis before they produce useful results. Accordingly, we have restricted attention to these three sets of abstractions in this book.

One can identify additional areas in which modeling and analysis is highly desirable; as of 1972, however, there are few results of practical interest available, so we have omitted any treatment of them. They include system reliability and integrity, system performance evaluation, and design methodologies.

The book consists of seven chapters. A brief description of each follows.

Chapter 1. Introduction is an outline of the physical properties of the systems in which the results of our analyses in later chapters can be applied. This includes a discussion of the relevant properties of processor and memory devices; of the implementation features of virtual memory, especially paging; of the general aspects of the memory management and processor scheduling problems; and of the motivations for using concepts of parallelism, scheduling, paging, resource pooling, and program behavior in systems design.

Chapter 2. Control of Concurrent Processes contains a formalism for studying the important problems of controlling parallel processes, viz., determinacy, deadlock, mutual exclusion, and synchronization. We have been able to formulate and study these problems in the context of a single model, a partially-ordered system of tasks. While this model is by no means the most general studied previously, it exhibits the properties one would expect and desire in a practical system. The results of this chapter are: a) the task system model allows a uniform discussion of the four control problems, making evident the differences and similarities among them; b) the task system model permits simple proofs of the determinacy results; c) the deadlock results extend those available in the literature; and d) the synchronization results are all new and demonstrate the generality and power of the synchronizing primitives.

Chapter 3. Deterministic Models of Processor Scheduling is a nearly complete treatment of the results presently available on this subject. Given an *n*-task system in which the execution time of each task is known, and given *k* processors, the problem is finding a schedule (assignment of tasks to processors) that completes in minimum time, or minimizes mean flow time, and is consistent with the precedence constraints among tasks. Problems of this type are important not only in the classical job-shop environment, but also in future environments where, for example, task systems of the type studied in Chapter 2 will be implemented.

Chapter 4. Probability Models of Computer Sequencing Problems contains a review of basic queueing processes and their application to scheduling tasks in multiprogramming systems. We have attempted to present a selfcontained treatment in as short a space as possible. A major goal achieved in this chapter is an analysis of the basic computer priority queues.

Chapter 5. Auxiliary and Buffer Storage Models treats problems arising particularly in connection with input or output processes. The methods developed in Chapter 4 are used extensively. The chapter includes a study of the good (and bad) points of "shortest-latency-time-first" policies for serving queues on rotating storage devices (disks, drums). It includes an analysis of the buffering problem, showing the tremendous advantages inherent in pooled buffers as opposed to private buffers. These results have important implications with respect to any pooled resource, especially the partitioning of main memory among tasks under multiprogramming. The chapter includes a treatment of cyclic queue networks.

Chapter 6. Storage Allocation in Paging Systems is a fairly complete treatment of the results known for controlling and analyzing the page traffic resulting from given demand paging algorithms managing a single program in a fixed memory space. All the known results about optimal algorithms are included, as well as a new treatment of the important "stack algorithm" concept. The relation between these results and multiprogramming is studied.

Chapter 7. Multiprogrammed Memory Management specifically deals with the properties of program-behavior models that exhibit "locality of reference" and their implications with respect to multiprogrammed memory management. The properties of fixed and variable partitioning strategies of multi-programming are treated. The "working set model" is studied in its own right, various important relations among working set size, paging rate, and page reference patterns being obtained.

ACKNOWLEDGMENTS

There are many people whose help and guidance were instrumental in the preparation of this book. Two in particular to whom we must express our special gratitude are the Prentice-Hall Computer Science Series Editor Karl V. Karlstrom, for his continuing patience and encouragement, and Richard R. Muntz, for the many corrections and helpful suggestions resulting from a painstaking reading of the manuscript.

Others whom we should like to acknowledge for their constructive criticisms of portions of the manuscript are Robert Butler, Robert M. Keller, Stephen R. Kimbleton, W. Frank King III, John E. Pomeranz, Barbara Ryan, John Bruno, Vincent Shen, and Jeffrey R. Spirn.

Very special thanks are due Miss Doris Rice whose speed and efficiency made the clerical aspects of preparing this book almost routine. Thanks are due also to Mrs. Hannah Kresse for help in this regard.

Finally, the Pennsylvania State University and Princeton University are to be acknowledged for their implicit support and for stimulating environments in which to write this book. The National Science Foundation under grant GJ-28290 provided partial financial support.

EDWARD G. COFFMAN, JR.

PETER J. DENNING

OPERATING SYSTEMS
THEORY

1 INTRODUCTION

1.1. OPERATING SYSTEMS

The era of electronic computing has been characterized as a series of "generations" [1], the first covering the period 1946–1950, the second covering the period 1950–1964, and the third covering the period since 1964. Although the term generation was intended originally to suggest differences in hardware technology, it has come to be applied to the entire hardware-software system rather than the hardware alone [2]. The development of general-purpose complex software systems did not begin until the third generation and has motivated the development of theoretical approaches to design and resource allocation.

As will be discussed in detail later, the term "process" is used to denote a program in execution. A computer system may be defined in terms of the various supervisory and control functions it provides for the processes created by its users:

1. Creating and removing processes.

2. Controlling the progress of processes, i.e., ensuring that each logically enabled process makes progress and that no process can block indefinitely the progress of others.

3. Acting on exceptional conditions arising during the execution of a process, e.g., arithmetic or machine errors, interrupts, addressing errors, illegal or privileged instructions, or protection violations.

4. Allocating hardware resources among processes.

5. Providing access to software resources, e.g., files, editors, compilers, assemblers, subroutine libraries, and programming systems.

6. Providing protection, access control, and security for information.

7. Providing interprocess communication and synchronization.

These functions must be provided by the system since they cannot always be handled correctly or adequately by the processes themselves. The computer system software that assists the hardware in implementing these functions is known as the *operating system.*

There is an enormous diversity among types of computer systems and the views programmers or designers hold about them. Despite this, these systems have a great deal in common. The common characteristics result from three general design objectives: providing programmers with an efficient environment for program development, debugging, and execution; providing a range of problem-solving facilities; and providing low-cost computing by sharing resources and information. The most important characteristics include

1. *Concurrency,* the existence or potential existence of simultaneous parallel activities, or processes.

2. *Automatic resource allocation mechanisms,* provided by the system because programmers tend to be shielded from machine details by programming languages, because demands in a system supporting concurrent activities are likely to be unpredictable, and because a central resource allocator is able to monitor the entire system and satisfy objectives of both good service and system efficiency.

3. *Sharing,* the simultaneous use of resource types by more than one process (irrespective of whether individual units of that type are sharable) or the simultaneous use of information by more than one process.

4. *Multiplexing,* a technique according to which time is divided into disjoint intervals and a unit of resource is assigned to at most one process during each interval.

5. *Remote conversational access* to system resources or processes.

6. *Asynchronous operation,* i.e., unpredictability in the order of occurrence of events.

7. *Long-term storage* of information, especially in the form of a file system.

The abstractions underlying these seven common characteristics can be grouped into two broad categories: *processes* and *memory management.* Our purpose in this book is studying the theoretical bases for these two broad classes of abstractions. We shall emphasize the study of *algorithms* for managing, coordinating, and scheduling processes; for managing main and auxiliary memory devices; and for managing the flows of information among the various devices in a computer system. Our study of processes encompasses three subareas: the theory of coordination of processes, optimal scheduling of processes on devices when the execution times are known; scheduling of processes on devices when the execution times are unknown or must be estimated; and scheduling to achieve desirable waiting or flow time distributions. These subareas are the subjects of Chapters 2, 3, and 4. Our study of memory management encompasses three subareas: policies for managing auxiliary storage devices, buffer areas, and interdevice information flows; policies for determining which portions of a program's instruction and data code should reside in main memory; and policies for allocating main memory among many programs (multiprogramming). These subareas are the subjects of Chapters 5, 6, and 7. The goal of the book is to expose the important problems and formal analysis techniques without attempts at complete generality.

1.2. RESOURCES

The results of this book are applicable across a wide range of computer systems. These systems will be assumed to satisfy certain general assumptions about the nature of hardware resources (devices), as described below.

By a *processor* we mean any device which performs transformations on information or carries out the steps of a process. The usual concept of an arithmetic processor, or central processing unit, which executes instructions and performs arithmetic operations on data, falls within the scope of this definition. The less familiar concept of an input/output processor, or channel, is also included in the scope of this definition.

By a *memory* we mean any device which is used for storage of information; examples include semiconductor, core, disk, drum, and tape memories. The *capacity* of a memory device is the number of words (or bytes) of information that it can store. The *access time* of a memory device is the average interval between the receipt and completion of a request, queueing delays neglected. An *address* is a name for the storage site of a word in a given memory device. A memory device is *positionally addressed* if a mechanical motion is generally required, such as moving a read/write head to the site addressed or moving the storage medium so that the site addressed is adjacent to the read/write heads. In such memories the access time of a word depends on its position in the storage medium. A memory device is *random access* if the access time of each storage site is the same. Disks, drums, and tapes are examples of the former; semiconductor and core memories are examples of the latter.

Computer systems have always included a variety of different types of storage media organized into at least two levels, *main memory* and *auxiliary memory*. Information must reside in main memory, which typically is random access with very short access time, in order to be immediately accessible for processing; otherwise it may reside in auxiliary memory, which typically is positionally accessed with relatively longer access times. Most random access memories use some form of electronic switching to address a storage site, access times thus being very short; a typical value of access time for a semi-conductor memory is 100 nanoseconds, and for a core memory 1 microsecond (the memory cycle time). Most positionally accessed memories have typical access times in the range from 10 milliseconds for the fastest drums to over 200 milliseconds for disks. The desire for large amounts of storage has always forced a compromise between access times and the quantities of main and auxiliary memory.

The accessing properties of main and auxiliary memory devices, which are important in Chapters 5, 6, and 7, will be reviewed now. It is customary to use *blocks*, rather than individual words, as the units of memory allocation and transfer. A block has a unique name and consists of some number of words whose addresses are contiguous. If the blocks are all of the same size, they are called *pages*. A request to reference a word in main memory is presented (by a processor) either in the form of an absolute address or a pair (b, r), wherein b is a block number and r is an address relative to the base of block b. Requests to auxiliary memories typically involve the movement of blocks (rather than accessing words in them); they take the form of a pair (p, l) where p is the position of the initial address of the desired block and l is its length.

The organization of a magnetic *drum memory* is shown in Fig. 1.2-1. It consists of a cylindrical drum rotating at constant speed, one rotation each T time units; a typical value of T is 30 milliseconds. The storage sites for words are at coordinate points (t, θ) on the drum, where t is a *track index* and θ is an angular position. Each site passes beneath the read/write heads once per revolution, and so each word is accessible only once every T time units.

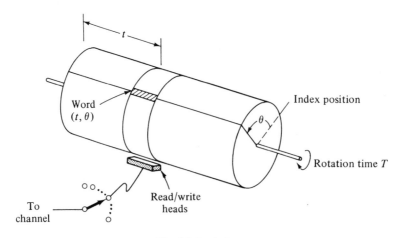

Fig. 1.2-1   A drum.

A *track* is the set of storage sites around a band of the drum as shown in Fig. 1.2-1. (There is usually a small time associated with switching the transmission channel between tracks; this time is normally sufficiently small that we may ignore it in our analyses.) A request for a block on the drum thus takes the form (t, θ, l), where the block length l does not exceed the number of words on a track. In the case of paging (Fig. 1.2-2), where all blocks are of the same size, l is understood, the angular positions are given as *sector indices*, and a request takes the simpler form (t, θ). Figure 1.2-3 shows the delays experienced by a request for the drum: The queueing delay represents the time the request waits in queues, the latency delay represents the time for the drum to rotate to the desired angular position, and the transfer delay represents the time to transmit the words of the block requested.

The organization of a magnetic *disk memory* is shown in Fig. 1.2-4. A number of circular plates (disks) are mounted on a common shaft, which rotates at constant speed with one revolution each T time units; a typical value of T is 60 milliseconds. There is a movable arm which can be moved among k positions in a single dimension of motion. Each storage site has a coordinate (t, d, ω), where t is a track index, d a disk surface index, and ω an angular position. A *track* is the set of words at a given arm position on a given disk surface and a *cylinder* is the set of words at a given arm position. Note that the properties of a disk when the arm is positioned at a given cylinder are logically identical to those of a drum. In fact, some manufacturers' drums are implemented as disks without movable arms, there being instead arms positioned permanently at each cylinder. One may regard such

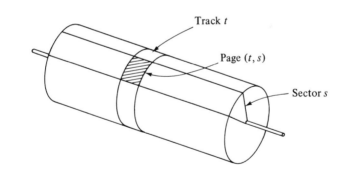

Fig. 1.2-2 Paged drum.

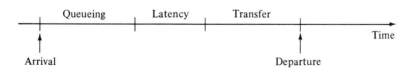

Fig. 1.2-3 Timing diagram for drum.

units as defining a series of concentric drums. Figure 1.2-5 shows a timing
diagram for a request; as suggested above, there is a pair of additional delays
prefixed to those of the drum (Fig. 1.2-3), the *seek time* being the time required
to position the arm at the requested cylinder. A typical range of seek times for
a given disk unit is 120 milliseconds for the shortest (nonzero) seek to 250
milliseconds for the longest; therefore seek times dominate latency times.

The foregoing discussion has dealt with the important characteristics of
hardware devices of interest to the readers of this book. In our treatment of
resource allocation problems in Chapter 2, we shall use the term "resource"
in a sense much more general than hardware resources such as described

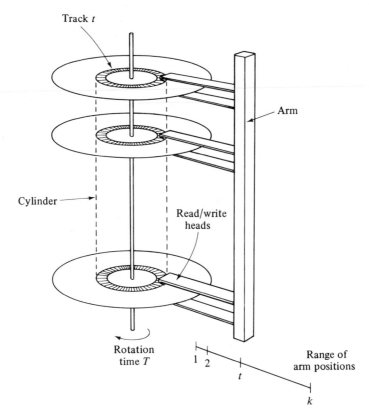

Fig. 1.2-4   A disk.

Fig. 1.2-5   Timing diagram for a disk.

above. By adopting a very general view of resources, it is possible to treat many operating-systems problems as resource allocation problems, with meaningful results. According to this view, the set of objects which a process may use, and on which its progress depends, is called the set of *resources* required by the process. The system provides a variety of resource *types*, and there is generally a limited number of *units* of each type available. Examples of resource types include processors, memory, peripheral devices, data files, procedures, and messages. Examples of resource units include a processor, a page of memory, a disk or drum track, a file, a procedure, or a message. Some resource types have immediate realizations in terms of hardware (e.g., processor, memory, peripherals), whereas others have realizations in software only (e.g., files, procedures, messages). Some resource types are *reusable*, a unit of that type being reassignable after its release; in contrast, other types are *consumable*, ceasing to exist after use (e.g., a message, or the activation record of a called procedure) [3]. All resources have internal "states" which convey information to their users; if the state of a resource is modified during use, a unit of that type is said to be "restricted to exclusive control" by at most one process at a time.

When preempting a resource from a process it is necessary to save the state of the resource; the resource may later be restored to that process by causing the state of that resource to become what it was at the time of preemption. Associated with each unit of resource is a *preemption cost function*, representing the cost of preempting that unit from the process using it at time t. If the cost at time t exceeds a certain threshold, the unit is considered nonpreemptible at that time; otherwise it is considered preemptible. The preemption cost would be considered high if loss of input, output, or progress would result from preemption, or more generally if a considerable effort would be required to save the resource state. Typically, there will be a sequence of times t_i such that the resource unit is preemptible at times t_i but not otherwise: for example, the t_i for a processor correspond to the ends of instruction-executions, for a drum to the departures of requests, or for a line printer to the completions of printings. In some cases the t_i will be known a priori (e.g., for processors); in other cases a process itself must signal that the unit is preemptible (e.g., when it releases the resource).

1.3. CONCURRENT PROCESSES

The development of third-generation computer systems has led to a new aspect of designing programs: *concurrent* (parallel) *programming*. The reasons for this include:

1. The demand for rapid response time and efficient utilization of resources has led to various forms of multiprogramming and has created a need for

specifying the "states" and resource requirements of each program dynamically.

2. The desire for efficient utilization of equipment has led further to the widespread use of concurrent activity among the central machine and its peripheral devices.

3. The desire to share information and communicate among executing programs has created a need for specifying synchronization at the software level.

4. It has been found useful to regard an operating system as a control program that coordinates various concurrent activities.

Even though the hardware technology allows for the realization of concurrent activity, it remains the task of the operating-systems designer to write the programs that bring it into being. It is the purpose of Chapters 2, 3, and 4 to study the important models of concurrent activity.

The term *process* as the abstraction of the activity of a processor appears to have emerged in several projects during the early 1960s (e.g., Multics and TSS/360), so that the concept of a "program in execution" could be meaningful at any instant of time, irrespective of whether a processor was executing instructions from the program at that instant. In these systems, a process was distinguished from a program by noting that a program is a sequence of instructions, whereas a process is the sequence of actions performed by a program: A program is static; a process is dynamic. The original purpose of this distinction was to allow for preempting and restarting programs without affecting the result of a computation. The idea of *parallel processes* can be interpreted to mean that, at any given time, more than one program may be observed between its initiation and termination points. Processes may or may not be progressing simultaneously; at a given time, for example, we may observe one process running on the central processor while a second is suspended, awaiting its turn, and a third is running on an input/output channel. Processes may interact in two ways: indirectly, by competing for the same resources, and directly, by sharing or communicating information. When processes are logically independent they interact indirectly, and control of concurrency is normally delegated to the underlying system; but when they may interact directly, control of concurrency must be expressed explicitly in their implementations.

Unfortunately, the literature is filled with many alternative, and some conflicting, definitions of process. There is, for example, "locus of control within an instruction sequence," offered by Dennis and Van Horn [4]. There is "program in execution on a pseudo-processor," offered by Saltzer [5]. There is "clerk carrying out the steps of a procedure," offered by Van Horn [6]. There is "sequence of program states," offered by Horning and Randell [7]. There are "program in execution" and "a program is a sequence of instructions, a process the sequence of actions performed by the program," as offered above. There is "a process is a program status block," as used on some IBM System/360 installations.

One result of all these attempts to define *process* is that the term has come to assume a very general meaning, denoting any computational activity whatever in a system. Another result of all this: It is nearly impossible to adopt a single definition which is consistent with all the foregoing notions. Accordingly, we have adopted a more neutral term, *task*, for use in all our formal discussions. We shall continue to use "process" in general or informal discussions. A task will be taken to be an atomic unit of computation, whose terminal behavior is specified but whose internal operation is unspecified and of no interest to a discussion. Depending on the application, a task can be an instruction, a procedure, or even an entire system.

Suppose that $P(\mathbf{x}, t)$ is a predicate making an assertion about the values of the system variables $\mathbf{x}$ at time t. If the validity of P is supposed to cause some special action by the system, then "P is true" defines an *exceptional condition* in the system [4]. The beginning of an interval during which P is true is the "occurrence" of condition P. Examples of exceptional conditions include an attempt to execute an illegal instruction, arithmetic overflow, addressing snags, or the completion of a peripheral device transaction. Some exceptional conditions are detected by hardware (such as the above), but they may also be detected by software (such as interprocess messages or the programmed interrupts of PL/I). Many terms of often conflicting meanings have been used for exceptional conditions: exceptions, interrupts, faults, traps. The term *fault* is most often used for an exceptional condition arising as a result of actions by the task being run on a given processor. The term *interrupt* is most often used for an exceptional condition arising from a task different from the one being run on a given processor. The term *trap* is most often used to denote the action taken in response to an exceptional condition. For each exceptional condition the system recognizes, there is a task, called the *handler* of that condition, which is supposed to be invoked within a short time after the condition occurs; each handler may be implemented as a process which is to be "awakened," or as a subroutine which is to be called. Most systems incorporate a combination of special interrupt hardware and software for preempting the process running on a processor and assigning the processor to the proper interrupt-handler task. To guarantee the correct operation of a handler task, a processor is placed into *uninterruptible mode* ("interrupts are masked off") during the time such a task is being run. Thus the action of a handler task is "indivisible" with respect to other actions in the system. In some systems, the exceptional conditions are assigned priorities (based on the relative importance of responding to the conditions promptly); the occurrence of a condition whose priority is higher than that of the handler presently in operation will cause it to be interrupted in favor of the higher-priority condition. Upon completion of a handler task, the system scheduler will reactivate some other task—priority being given, of course, to pending handler tasks—and the processor will be placed in interruptible mode only after all handler tasks have been completed.

1.3.1. Process Coordination

Chapter 2 contains a treatment of four related process control problems. These problems are stated in terms of a system of tasks with intertask precedence constraints specified. They are:

1. *Determinacy*. The result of a computation performed by a system of tasks on common data is to be independent of the relative speeds of the tasks.

2. *Deadlocks*. The following situation is to be avoided: A collection of parallel tasks is stuck in "circular wait," each waiting for another to release its claim on certain resources.

3. *Mutual exclusion*. Certain tasks must be programmed so as not to be in execution at the same time; e.g., one task may not write a file while another is reading it.

4. *Synchronization*. Certain tasks must be stopped at a given point until some event under the control of another task has occurred.

One of the first problems to receive a great deal of attention in the literature was the determinacy problem. Whenever two or more processes cooperate in the solution of a single problem, it is possible that the outcome of the computation can depend on their relative speeds. Since multiprogramming systems must tolerate both process interruption at arbitrary times and concurrent peripheral activity of arbitrary speed, it is necessary to constrain cooperating processes so that the computation is speed-independent, or *determinate*. It is interesting that investigations of speed-independent logic circuits had been carried out by Muller [8] in the period 1955–1960 but that their applications for programming were not appreciated until nearly a decade later [9, 10].

More recently, further problems of interprocess interaction (including deadlocks, mutual exclusion, synchronization, message sending) have received a great deal of attention. The solutions have led to improvements in resource allocation procedures and most particularly in input/output control and interrupt systems. Solutions to the mutual exclusion problem were first given by Dijkstra [12] and Knuth [104]. The treatment of synchronization problems was inherent in Karp and Miller's [105] work in abstract models of parallelism; Dijkstra [11] dealt later with synchronization in concrete programming terms, creating the well-known P and V operations for application in operating systems. Examination of the deadlock problem began with Dijkstra [11], Habermann [13], Havender [14], Shoshani [106], and Murphy [15].

It should be noted that a rather extensive body of mathematical knowledge on parallelism has been developing in the period beginning in 1960. There are, for example, the asynchronous nets of Petri [16]; the parallel program schemata of Karp and Miller [17], Luconi [18], and Slutz [19]; and the program-graph theory of Rodriguez [20] and the marked-graph theory of Holt and Commoner [21]. All these works go to much greater depth than we can afford to treat here.

1.3.2. Task-System Scheduling

Chapter 3 contains a treatment of results in the scheduling of a partially ordered set of tasks (using the task-system model of Chapter 2) whose execution times τ_i are known, given that there are m (identical) processors available to execute tasks. Two performance measures for schedules are considered: time until the last task is completed and average turnaround (flow) time. The first measure is of interest owing to its relation to processor utilization; indeed, if a given schedule finishes in time T, the utilization factor of the processors by the schedule is

$$u = \frac{1}{mT} \sum_i \tau_i$$

Evidently, minimizing T maximizes u. The second measure is of interest because it relates to the performance of the system as experienced by users and because it frequently minimizes the average number of incomplete tasks. The reader will discover that it is often difficult to find a schedule that does well, simultaneously, with respect to both measures. He will also discover that simple (nonenumerative) procedures for generating optimal schedules exist only for very restricted assumptions on task systems—e.g., all execution times are identical, or the tasks are arranged in a tree structure—and even in these special cases the proofs that the procedures do in fact generate optimal schedules are arduous.

It can be argued that results of the type presented in Chapter 3 are of limited applicability in today's systems; in particular, it is not ordinarily possible to know a priori the task execution times $\{\tau_i\}$ and one would at best have only probability distributions for the τ_i. The counterargument to this is, of course, that these results allow us to determine just how well practical scheduling procedures do in comparison to the optimal. Many of the results in Chapter 3 state ratios between two types of schedules. For example, in one context to be analyzed the ratio of the length of an arbitrary schedule to that of an optimal schedule cannot exceed $(2m - 1)/m$, on m processors with an arbitrary task system. This tells the system designer that a practical scheduler can do no worse than $m/(2m - 1)$ of the processing efficiency of an optimal schedule; it gives him guidance in improving his scheduler.

The class of scheduling problems considered in Chapter 3 is quite old, predating its interest to computer science by some years. These problems were first observed in the classic job-shop or assembly-line problems of long-standing interest to operations researchers. One of the earliest works of significance is the now-classic study of two- and three-stage assembly-line problems by Johnson in 1954 [22]. There was a considerable body of work in management science and operations research circles on partially ordered sets of tasks of interest to job shops; this work dealt with analyses of "critical paths" (longest ordered sequences of task execution times) and of sensitivity to changes in precedence structure, resource availablity or cost, and task execution times. Representative texts include the 1952 book on Gantt charts by Clark [23] and the 1964 text by Moder and Phillips on PERT analysis [24].

Efforts to obtain simple results concerning optimal schedules have been spotty. There is Johnson's work, cited above. In 1959 McNaughton published a result concerning independent task schedules, with preemptions, to meet deadlines [25]. In 1961, Hu published a now well-known result for optimally scheduling tree-structured sets of tasks with equal execution times [26]. In 1967, Manacher published an engineering study concerning the control of anomalous behavior in schedules [27]: it is possible for the optimal schedule's length to *increase* if, for example, task execution times are decreased or the number of processors increased. In 1969, Graham published bounds on the effects of such anomalies [28]. In 1969, Fujii et al. published a result for finding optimal schedules for the case of any partially ordered set of tasks with equal execution times on two processors [29]; their algorithm employs maximal matching of bipartite graphs and, for an n-task system, requires time proportional to at least n^3 to compute an optimal schedule. In 1972, Coffman and Graham published an n^2 algorithm for the same problem [30]. In 1970, Muntz and Coffman published results for optimal preemptive scheduling of arbitrary task systems [31]. Interest in preemptive schedules has risen in recent years owing to its applicability in multiprogramming contexts.

The scarcity of results for these problems derives from the difficulty of finding fast, nonenumerative algorithms producing optimal schedules; Conway, Maxwell, and Miller discuss this in detail in their excellent 1967 text [32], which contains a sizable bibliography on the subject. In 1971, Krone derived some heuristic techniques for efficiently producing near-optimal schedules [33].

1.3.3. Probability Models of Schedulers

Chapter 4 continues the study of scheduling procedures. Fundamental to the work of Chapter 3 is the assumption that the execution times of tasks are known in advance and that all tasks are available for execution at once; Chapter 4 studies the properties of scheduling techniques when only probability statements can be made in these respects.

During the early and mid-1960s, a great many systems designers adopted the idea of *priority scheduling*: At each moment of time each task has a priority number; whenever a processor becomes idle, either by a preemption or by a task's releasing it, the scheduling procedure will assign the processor to that available task whose priority number is highest. Some systems use "time slicing" to prevent any task from holding a processor unduly long. In this case, the scheduler will load an "interval timer" clock with a time quantum; if the task has not released the processor of its own accord by the expiration of the quantum, the clock will generate an interrupt which will cause the task to be preempted and a new task assigned. This philosophy of scheduling was summarized by Lampson in 1968 [34]. The priorities of tasks may be fixed during tasks' residence in the system, or they may be recomputed from time to time based on observed task behavior [35].

Our treatment in Chapter 4 begins with a review of the fundamental concepts and techniques of queueing theory: the exponential distribution and its properties, the FIFO (first-in-first-out) queueing system, Little's formula relating waiting time to queue length, and the Pollaczek-Khintchine formula relating queue length to the parameters of the input and output distributions. The remaining part of the chapter presents analyses of several important classes of queues:

1. *Round-robin.* These were the queues used in the earliest time-sharing systems. A task joins a FIFO queue. Each time it reaches the front of the queue, it executes on the processor for a maximum time of one "quantum." If it has not completed, it is preempted and placed at the end of the queue.

2. *Simple priority queues.* Each task has a fixed priority number, assigned on its arrival. Whenever the processor is free, it runs the task of highest priority. Some systems use preemptions; i.e., the arrival of a task of higher priority than the one running causes the latter to be preempted and replaced by the former.

3. *Shortest-elapsed-time and shortest-processing-time queues.* These queues attempt to favor tasks with short execution times by giving priority to the task which has used the processor the least since arriving or which has the least execution time. The arrival of a task will cause preemption of the running task.

Our analysis of the third class is straightforward, because these queues can be modeled as priority queues with preemption and the techniques of the other two classes employed in the analysis. This class includes the well-known multilevel queue as reported in 1962 by Corbato et al. for the CTSS scheduler [36]. All results are expressed in terms of a quantum size Q; the case $Q \rightarrow \infty$ corresponds to the nonpreemptive case, and the case $Q \rightarrow 0$ to the so-called processor-sharing case.

Queueing theory began in the period 1909–1918 when Erlang published a series of papers showing that telephone systems can be modeled by Markov processes whose states represent the number of active calls, the interarrival and service times of calls being exponentially distributed. The works of Pollaczek and of Khintchine in the early 1930s added further to the growing body of knowledge on *stochastic service systems*. During the 1950s there was literally an explosion of interest in stochastic service systems by operations researchers; these models were found useful in analyzing such problems as automobile traffic congestion, waiting lines in industry and commerce, and inventories in businesses. The early 1960s witnessed the first serious attempts to apply these results to computer scheduling problems. These attempts were not always as successful as their proposers had hoped, primarily because computer scheduling methods involved finite source populations, unconventional queueing structures, systems with several congestion points or different types of processors, and preemptive scheduling—none of these things having received much attention previously.

The first analysis of significant interest to computer engineers was Kleinrock's treatment in 1964 of the round-robin queue for an infinite source population [37]. Also in 1964 was Coffman and Krishnamoorthi's treatment of the same problem for the more realistic assumption of a finite source population [38]. In 1966, Krishnamoorthi and Wood presented a comprehensive treatment of time-sharing scheduling methods for interarrival and service times exponentially distributed [39]. As noted above, Corbato et al. proposed a multilevel feedback queue for CTSS in 1962, the purpose of which was to control the overhead of swapping in the system; this queueing system was analyzed in 1965 by Schrage [40] with variations studied by Coffman and Kleinrock [41]. In 1965, Scherr demonstrated that the performance of CTSS could be predicted quite reliably using the classic machine-repair model of queueing theory [42].

Although the study of priorities in queueing systems is not new (see Cobham, 1954 [43]), interest in their applications to computers has been generated by the widening use of priority scheduling methods. As system designers gained more experience with, and confidence in, processor multiplexing techniques (such as the round-robin), there arose considerable interest in the (limiting) behavior of systems for extremely short time quanta; this is known as the "processor-sharing" limit. This interest stemmed mainly from the analytical simplifications achieved by eliminating the parameter Q. Most of the analyses cited above pointed out the limiting values of expected waiting time and queue length as the quantum size vanishes. However, waiting time distributions for two basic processor-sharing queues were obtained by Schrage [40] and by Coffman et al. [44], and the waiting time distribution for round-robin systems has been obtained recently by Muntz [45]. A comprehensive and much more detailed review and bibliography of this history of computer scheduling methods has been given by McKinney [46]. A good many of the more modern refinements and extensions of time-sharing algorithms have been examined by Adiri et al. [47–49].

A limitation of the preemptive scheduling techniques used in many priority queues is the cost of preemptions. Specifically, it is infeasible to use extremely short quanta in these systems because the overhead due to preemptions would consume all the processing resources available. No theoretical treatments of optimal scheduling with preemption costs taken into consideration have appeared by the time of this writing. Some preliminary work by Mullery and Driscoll [50] indicates that the round-robin technique generates the highest possible preemption cost for a given quantum size and that other policies exist with much lower preemption costs and more desirable response time distributions.

1.4 MEMORY MANAGEMENT

Since the earliest days of electronic computing, computer memory systems have always been organized into at least two levels, and the *memory management problem*—i.e., deciding how to distribute information among the levels and when to move it about—has always been a problem of first importance. The objective of a memory management policy is providing fastest possible execution speed, by maintaining in main memory those parts of a program with the greatest likelihood of being referenced. A memory management policy comprises three subpolicies [51, 52]:

1. *The fetch policy* determines when a block is to be moved from auxiliary to main memory, either in advance of need or on demand.
2. *The placement policy* determines that unallocated region of main memory into which an incoming block is to be placed.
3. *The replacement policy* determines which blocks, and when, will be removed from main memory.

Figure 1.4-1 shows the structure of a two-level memory system. The system provides *move commands* (for moving specified blocks between main and auxiliary memories), by which the three subpolicies may be implemented. In the earliest computers, the programmer had to solve the memory management problem for himself, organizing his instruction and data code into blocks and inserting the appropriate move commands into the program text. This approach was known as the *overlay solution* to the memory management problem.

The introduction of higher-level programming languages during the late 1950s gave programmers the ability to construct ever more complicated programs; as the complexity of their programs grew, so grew the magnitude

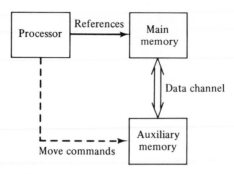

Fig. 1.4-1   Two level memory system.

of the overlay problem. (Sayre estimates that solutions to the overlay problem accounted for 25 to 40 percent of programming costs [53].) Thus was motivated the search for automated procedures for solving the overlay problem.

One set of techniques for relieving the programmer of the overlay problem involved the compiler of a program. According to these techniques, the compiler would analyze a program's structure, organize the program into blocks, and insert the appropriate move commands into the compiled program text. Despite a considerable degree of initial interest in this approach, it never progressed very far; interest was diverted by the success of dynamic storage allocation techniques and by virtual memory techniques. The proceedings of a 1961 ACM Symposium on Storage Allocation [54] and a paper by Ramamoorthy in 1966 [55] pretty well summarize compiler-generated solutions to the overlay problem. Knuth has an excellent treatment of the various important techniques for dynamic storage allocation [56, pp. 435ff.].

Our attention in this book will focus on analyses of virtual memory techniques for memory management. We have done this for three reasons. First, in 1969 Sayre published a significant paper demonstrating that virtual memory techniques are competitive, and in terms of overall costs potentially superior to, overlay techniques [53]. Second, virtual memory techniques appear to be most appealing in terms of simplicity of implementation and are becoming widespread. Third, virtual memory techniques provide the most challenging, interesting, and general problems in memory management, the analyses being applicable to many aspects of other approaches to dynamic storage allocation.

A virtual memory can be regarded as the main memory of a simulated (or virtual) computer. It is described in terms of three abstractions: address (or name) space, memory (or location) space, and an address map. The *address space* of a task is the set of addresses that can be generated by a processor as it executes the task. Most systems are designed to accommodate more than one address space (multiprogramming systems, for example). When it is desired to protect one task's information from access by another, each such task will normally have a private address space; when tasks may share information, they may share the same address space. The *memory space* of the system is the set of locations in the physical main memory. The *address map* is a (partial) function $f: N \longrightarrow M$ from address space N into memory space M, $f(x)$ being defined as y at a given time if the item of N with address x is stored in main memory at location y at that time, and $f(x)$ being undefined otherwise. An attempt by the processor to reference an x for which $f(x)$ is undefined will cause a fault condition and interrupt the task. The fault handler will arrange for the missing item to be placed in main memory (some other item may be displaced in the process), update the address map f, and reactivate the stopped task.

The physical interpretation of address mapping is suggested in Fig. 1.4-2. The processor generates addresses from N only. These addresses are intercepted by the "mapper," which has access to a table describing f. If $f(x)$ is defined and equal to y, the mapper presents the address y to M. Otherwise, the mapper initiates the appropriate move commands and adjusts the table describing f.

It is important to note that the address space is an abstraction of main memory, just as process is an abstraction of processor. The overlay problem is solved because the address space can be made sufficiently large that no overlaying within it is warranted. Moreover, the task will be able to execute regardless of the size of M, because N does not depend on prior assumptions about M. Among the important analysis problems to be considered are the choices of fetch, placement, and replacement policies and the effect of memory size on performance. Complete discussions of the motivations for, and limitations of, virtual memory systems have been given by Denning [1, 52].

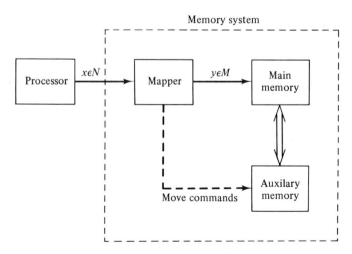

Fig. 1.4-2 Virtual memory system.

If, as suggested in Fig. 1.4-3, one monitors the channel between the processor and the memory system, one will observe a task generating a sequence of addresses, or *address trace*, $x_1 x_2 \ldots x_t \ldots$; for $t \geq 1$, x_t of N is the address referenced at time t. (Time is measured discretely, in references.) We noted earlier that most auxiliary memory devices are block-oriented as well, since a table f with separate entries for each x in N would be intolerably large. [In a block-oriented map, $f(b)$, if defined, would denote the base address of block b in M; an address x would be transformed to a pair (b, w) composed of the number b of the block containing x and the address w of x relative to the base of b. The mapper would compute $y = f(b) + w$ for presentation to M.] Since blocks are the units of allocation and transfer of information, an address trace is more detailed than necessary for analysis. Accordingly, we define the task's *reference string* $r_1 r_2 \ldots r_t \ldots$ such that r_t is the number of the block containing address x_t, $t \geq 1$. In our analyses of memory management policies, we shall use the reference string as the basis for our models of program behavior.

All our results about memory management are stated in terms of *paging*; i.e., all blocks are of the same, uniform size. If each page consists of p words, then the (block-number) pair corresponding to an address x of N is

$$(b, w) = \left(\left[\frac{x}{p} \right], x \bmod p \right)$$

where $[x/p]$ denotes the largest integer not exceeding x/p and $x \bmod p$ denotes the residue of x modulo p. In most machines, address computations are performed using binary arithmetic and $p = 2^q$ for some $q > 0$, whereupon the computation of (b, w) from x is trivial (see Fig. 1.4-4). Since we shall be assuming paged memory systems, reference strings will be sequences of page numbers. The restriction to paging admittedly sacrifices some generality in the analyses; nonetheless, one could reformulate the analyses using variable block sizes together with a probability distribution over block sizes and would find that many results do not change significantly in nature.

All virtual memory systems derive from the "one-level store" used on the Atlas machine prior to 1960 [57]; this was a paging machine. The techniques of paging are widely used today, particularly the techniques of demand paging (in which the fetch policy is purely demand), because of their great simplicity of implementation [52]. The techniques of virtual memory using variable block size (known as segmentation) have been used successfully on a few

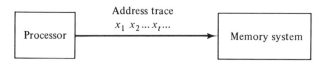

Fig. 1.4-3   Address trace.

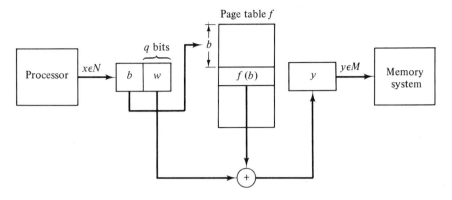

Fig. 1.4-4   Address formation in paging.

machines, notably the Borroughs B5000 and later series [51]. A combination of both segmentation and paging, as was described in a well-known paper by Dennis [58], has been implemented on only a few computers, notably Multics [59]. A comparison of these three techniques—paging, segmentation, both—has been given by Denning [52].

Most implementations of virtual memory store the mapping tables of tasks in main memory. During the computation of locations from name-space addresses, therefore, there is a potential speed degradation of a factor of 2 or more (depending on the number of levels of tables that constitute the address map) owing to the necessity of accessing mapping tables. Most virtual memory mappers therefore incorporate a small associative memory, which contains the most recently used mapping table entries. During address formation, the given address x is transformed into a pair (b, w) as described above; if some associative register contains the entry $(b, f(b))$, the memory address $y = f(b) + w$ can be computed immediately without the extra access to the table f. (Of course, if no such entry is present in the associative memory, the extra access to f would be required.) Schroeder has reported that in Multics, which uses three levels of mapping tables, the speed degradation with a 16-cell associative memory does not exceed 3.5 percent over what it would be if all mapping table entries could be accessed in zero time [60]; therefore the performance of a virtual memory is dominated by the fetch, placement, and replacement policies—not by the mapping mechanism.

1.4.1.   Auxiliary Storage and Buffer Problems

Chapter 5 contains a treatment of several important auxiliary memory problems. Since most auxiliary memory device access times are significantly longer than the access time of other memory devices in the system, these devices tend to become congestion points in the system. The policies of managing these devices are, therefore, concerned primarily with maximizing their throughput rates. We have placed our treatment of these problems before that on main memory management problems because the analysis techniques are direct applications of the probability models developed in Chapter 4.

The first problem considered in Chapter 5 is the analysis of the paging drum (cf. Fig. 1.2-2), which is used extensively in paged memory systems. If requests to use the drum are sorted into queues, one for each sector, and if the drum services the request at the head of a given queue as the corresponding sector passes beneath the heads, the drum will behave according to a *shortest-access-time-first* (SATF) policy. Since an SATF policy minimizes the total accumulated latency time, it is optimal with respect to maximizing the throughput of a drum. In fact, a paging drum with n sectors will have a throughput approximately $n/2$ times greater than a drum system using a single FIFO queue for all requests. Although the paging drum has been commercially available since the early 1960s, the first attempts at analyzing it were not completed until the mid-1960s. Denning discussed it in 1965 [61], and Weingarten in 1966 [62]; Coffman presented the first complete analysis of its behavior in 1969 [63]. Subsequent work by Abate and Dubner in 1969 [64], Burge and Konheim in 1971 [65], Greenberg in 1971 [66], and Denning in 1972 [67] has provided a good understanding of this drum system.

Attempts to analyze the behavior of moving arm disks (cf. Fig. 1.2-4) have not proved quite as successful. The problem is that the SATF scheduling policy—which in practice reduces to a *shortest-seek-time-first* (SSTF) policy—tends to discriminate against requests at the extreme inner and outer cylinders. Although the overall throughput rate may be maximized, requests for inner and outer cylinders can receive service so poor that the performance of the entire system (of which the disk unit is a component) can suffer seriously. In 1967, Denning proposed an arm-control policy called SCAN [68], which causes the arm to use an SSTF policy in a given direction of arm motion, the arm not being allowed to reverse its direction until there are no requests ahead of it in the given direction. This policy achieves a practical compromise between the SSTF policy and the nondiscriminatory (but low throughput) FIFO policy. We have included an analysis of it in Chapter 5. Other analyses include the one in 1966 by Seaman et al. [69] and the one in 1972 by Teorey and Pinkerton, which is a comprehensive study of known disk-scheduling policies [70]. Their results show that SCAN behaves well. Their results show also that no one policy is suitable over the entire range of load conditions.

Since all transfers between auxiliary or input/output devices (remote and local) and main memory use buffers, we have included analyses of certain pertinent buffer problems. The results indicate that shared (pooled) buffers are considerably more efficient (in terms of storage utilization) than individual buffers, one for each process. For the shared buffer, additional analyses give the buffer occupancy and overflow probability in terms of the parameters of the input and output processes and the request-size distribution. Since main memory can be regarded as a (shared) buffer under multiprogramming, these results find immediate application in multiprogrammed memory management. Among the earliest analyses of buffer problems is Wolman's 1965 treatment of optimum cell size for a buffer area where variable-length messages are stored using some number of fixed-size blocks [71]; these results are applicable to a certain extent in the optimal page-size problem, wherein variable-size segments or files must be stored as sets of pages. Some early work on comparing pooled versus private buffers was given in 1968 by Denning [72]; the most important work was presented in 1971 by Gaver and Lewis [73], and this work motivated our treatment of the material here. In 1972, Coffman and Ryan applied similar techniques to multiprogramming [74].

All the queueing and probability models treated to this point give insight into the behavior of particular subsystems without regard to the behavior of the exterior computer system which serves as the environment. Each of these models was a single congestion point, i.e., contained one server. These models fail to predict the behavior of the entire computer system, which normally contains many points of congestion. For this reason, we have included a treatment of important results by Jackson [75] and Gordon and Newell [76], which allows for the analysis of arbitrary closed networks of servers, under the assumption that each server in the network has exponentially distributed service time and that the total number of active tasks in the network is fixed. We believe these results to be of special future significance, since 1971 work by Baskett [77, 78] and Kimbleton and Moore [79, 80] demonstrates that a queueing network, each of whose servers is replaced by an exponential server having the same mean service time, will predict the behavior of the original (real-world) system with surprising accuracy. These results suggest that it is far more important for a model to reflect the true system structure rather than the detailed behavior of the individual servers in the system. It is worth noting in closing that the 1971 work of Buzen [81] and the recent work of Chandy [107], which treats resource allocation as a problem of optimizing the flows in such networks, promises to yield useful insights into the general resource allocation problem.

1.4.2. Paging Algorithms

Chapter 6 turns attention toward the problems of main memory management, where the objective is usually related to maximum execution speed of programs. By restricting attention to paging, we eliminate the effect of a placement policy on performance and simplify the analyses; by restricting the greater part of our attention to demand paging, we eliminate the effect of a fetch policy on performance. (Under these two restrictions, the performance of a memory management policy is governed by the replacement policy.) The restrictions are not unnecessarily severe, inasmuch as paging and demand paging are widely used and many results would not change qualitatively if we catered for variable-size blocks in our analyses.

The results of Chapter 6 deal with the case of a single n-page program (described by its reference string) operating under demand paging in an m-page memory, $1 \leq m \leq n$. Questions of page size, or of distributing information among pages, are represented in the problems. Questions relating to multiprogramming, or to allocating a program a variable amount of space, are deferred to Chapter 7.

Two aspects of paging algorithm behavior are treated in Chapter 6. First are the matters of optimal paging algorithms and principles of optimal page replacement. It will be shown that when the cost function measures the number of pages moved into memory during the course of a program's execution, every paging algorithm can be improved by converting it to a demand paging policy. This result was discovered by Mattson et al. in their well-known 1970 paper [82]. It will be shown that, when the paging policy is permitted to look ahead in a program's reference string, the optimal demand paging policy replaces the page not to be reused for the longest time. This policy was proposed in 1966 as the MIN algorithm by Belady [83], proofs of its optimality being discovered independently in 1970 by Mattson et al. [82] and Aho et al. [84]. (The principle of operation of this algorithm closely resembles that of the index register allocation algorithm proposed in 1966 by Horwitz et al. [85]). When the paging policy is not permitted to look ahead into the future, the rule "replace the page not expected to be reused for the longest time" is a good heuristic; there are cases for which this rule is known to produce an optimal policy, such as the independent-reference model, in which the page reference string is treated as a stationary sequence of independent random variables [84], and the so-called LRU-stack model [74, 82, 86].

The second aspect of the treatment in Chapter 6 concerns the behavior of two important, equivalent classes of demand paging algorithms, the *priority algorithms* and the *stack algorithms*. These algorithms were proposed in 1970 by Mattson et al. [82]. Most paging policies of practical interest are stack algorithms, including policies whose rule is "replace the lowest priority page according to a given priority list." The importance of these algorithms derives from their being well behaved (i.e., free of anomalies) and their being relatively easy to analyze. It will be shown also that, given only the sequences of (fetch, replacement) pairs generated by a stack algorithm in a given size memory, one can predict the sequence of (fetch, replacement) pairs for any larger memory. This is known as the *extension problem*, which was first considered by Coffman and Randell in 1971 [87].

1.4.3. Program Behavior and Multiprogramming

Chapter 7 presents analyses relating to optimal memory management in multiprogrammed memory systems. Most of the analyses of Chapter 6 do not extend in any natural way to multiprogramming, mainly because they deal with the behavior of given paging algorithms for given reference strings, whereas multiprogramming strategies must be designed to work only with probabilistic assumptions about reference strings and behavior.

We take *locality* as the basic property of program behavior. A reference string satisfies this property if, during any interval of time, the program's pages are referenced nonuniformly, and the page reference densities change slowly in time. The prediction of future reference patterns based on past reference patterns is clearly more reliable for programs exhibiting greater locality in page referencing. The property of locality has been observed in programming for years; it appears to derive from the programmer's natural tendency to concentrate on small parts of large problems for moderately long intervals before switching attention to other parts of the problem. It has consistently been observed in empirical program behavior studies, the best known of which include the one in 1966 by Fine et al. [88], the one in 1966 by Belady [83], the one in 1968 by Coffman and Varian [89], and the one in 1970 by Kuck and Lawrie [90]. A pair of works by Brawn and Gustavson in 1968 and 1970 [91, 92] have established that, with but a modicum of effort, a programmer can improve the locality properties of his programs so significantly that a paging mechanism can compete in terms of performance with the most carefully planned, hand-nurtured overlay scheme; this conclusion was corroborated and emphasized by Sayre in 1969 [53]. Other works dealing with the properties of programs under locality include the 1969 treatment of dynamic space sharing by Belady and Kuehner [93], the 1969 description of organizing matrices and matrix manipulation procedures for maximum locality by McKellar and Coffman [94], and the 1970 analysis by Kernighan showing how to distribute code among pages to maximize locality [95].

One may define the *working set* of a task to be the smallest subset of its pages that must be in main memory at any given time in order to guarantee the task a specified level of processing efficiency. A practical technique of measuring a task's working set—as the set of pages observed within a given sized window extending backward into the past—was proposed in a 1968 paper by Denning [96]. The utility of this measure as a predictor of a task's immediate future memory demand derives from locality: Any page in the working set at a given time is likely to remain there for the immediate future. The *working set principle* of memory management asserts that a task may be designated as "processable" only if its working set is present in main memory. This principle's utility has been demonstrated in practice, in such systems as

Multics, IBM's TSS/360 [97], BBN's TENEX System on the PDP-10 [98], and RCA's Spectra 70/46 [99, 100]. The principle has been shown to control the problem of *thrashing*, i.e., performance collapse occasioned by attempted overcommitment of main memory [52, 101]. We have included in Chapter 7 a treatment of techniques for modeling locality and the analysis of the working set model for reference strings having locality. The results of the analyses include relations among working set size, paging rate, and page interreference-interval distributions and of methods of implementing working set memory management using the *least-recently used* (LRU) paging technique. These analyses follow along the lines of work reported in 1972 by Denning and Schwartz [102]; the results of these analyses have been corroborated in 1972 by Rodriguez-Rosell [103]. In 1972, Denning et al. postulated a program model which embodies the properties of locality; they showed that the working set model defines a near-optimal memory management strategy for this model [86].

Under the assumptions of locality, one can demonstrate that the size of a task's working set tends to be normally distributed. For those tasks obeying locality, this is a significant result, for it means that the vast literature on Gaussian processes can be applied to the study of memory management (the memory demands of tasks being taken as Gaussian processes). This result is reported by Denning and Schwartz [102] and agrees with the experiments of Coffman and Ryan [74]. Rodriguez-Rosell gives examples of programs which do not obey the properties of locality; their working set processes also do not tend to be Gaussian [103].

Suppose that it is desired to map address spaces of tasks T_i into a single memory space M. According to the *fixed-partition* strategy, each task T_i is assigned a block of a static partition of M and some paging algorithm determines which subset of its address space resides in that block at any given time. According to the *variable-partition* strategy, each task T_i is assigned an amount of space at a given time sufficient to hold its working set at that time; this defines a dynamic partition. By a modification of the buffer analysis of Chapter 5, under the assumption that task working sets as functions of time are Gaussian processes, we are able to compare the performance of the two strategies with respect to the measures *overflow probability* and *expected total amount of overflow*. For typical parameters, the variable partition strategy (the working set principle) is decidedly superior. These results follow those presented in 1972 by Coffman and Ryan [74].

REFERENCES

1. DENNING, P. J., "Third generation computer systems." *Computing Surveys 3*, 4 (Dec. 1971), 175–216.

2. ROSEN, S., "Electronic computers: An historical survey." *Computing Surveys 1*, 1 (Mar. 1969), 7–36.

3. HOLT, R. C., "On deadlock in computer systems." Ph.D. thesis, Dept. of Computer Science, Cornell Univ., Ithaca, N.Y., TR–71–91 (1971).

4. DENNIS, J. B., and E. G. VAN HORN, "Programming semantics for multi-programmed computations." *Comm. ACM 9*, 3 (Mar. 1966), 143–155.

5. SALTZER, J. H., "Traffic control in a multiplexed computer system." M.I.T. Project MAC report MAC–TR–30, M.I.T., Cambridge, Mass. (1966).

6. VAN HORN, E. C., "Computer design for asynchronously reproducible multi-processing." M.I.T. Project MAC report MAC–TR–34, M.I.T., Cambridge, Mass. (1966).

7. HORNING, J. J., and B. RANDELL, "Structuring complex processes." IBM, T. J. Watson Research Center report RC-2459, Yorktown Heights, N.Y. (May 1969).

8. MULLER, D. E., and W. S. BARTKY, "A theory of asynchronous circuits." *Proc. Int'l Symp. Thy. Sw., An. Comp. Lab. Harv. U. 29*, Pt I (1959), 204–243.

9. ACM. Record of the project MAC conference on concurrent systems and parallel computation. Wood's Hole, Mass. (June 1970).

10. BERNSTEIN, A. J., "Analysis of programs for parallel programming." *IEEE Trans. Comp. EC-15*, 5 (1966), 757–762.

11. DIJKSTRA, E. W., "Cooperating sequential processes," in *Programming Languages* (F. Genuys, ed.). Academic Press, New York (1968), 43–112.

12. DIJKSTRA, E. W., "Solution of a problem in concurrent programming control." *Comm. ACM 8*, 9 (Sept. 1965), 569.

13. HABERMANN, N., "Prevention of system deadlock." *Comm. ACM 12*, 7 (July 1969), 373–377.

14. HAVENDER, J. W., "Avoiding deadlock in multitasking systems." *IBM Sys. J. 7*, 1 (1968), 74–84.

15. MURPHY, J., "Resource allocation with interlock detection in a multitask system." *AFIPS Conf. Proc. 33* (1968 FJCC), 1169–1176.

16. PETRI, C. A., "Communication with automata." Suppl. 1 to RADC-TR-65-377 (Vol. 1) Griffis AFB, Rome, N.Y. (1966). [Original in German, Univ. of Bonn (1962).]

17. KARP, R. M., and R. E. MILLER, "Parallel program schemata." *J. Comp. Sys. Sci. 3*, 2 (May 1969), 147–195.

18. LUCONI, F., "Asynchronous control structures." M.I.T. Project MAC report MAC-TR-49, M.I.T., Cambridge, Mass. (1968).

19. SLUTZ, D. R., "The flow graph schemata model of parallel computation." M.I.T. Project MAC report MAC-TR-53, M.I.T., Cambridge, Mass. (1968).

20. RODRIGUEZ, J., "A graph model for parallel computation." M.I.T. Project MAC report MAC-TR-64, M.I.T., Cambridge, Mass. (1969).

21. HOLT, A. W., and F. COMMONER, "Events and conditions." *Rec. Pr. MAC Conf. on Concur. Sys. Par. Comp.* (June 1970) [9].

22. JOHNSON, S. M., "Optimal two and three stage production schedules with set-up times included." *Nav. Res. Log. Quart. 1*, 1 (Mar. 1954).

23. CLARK, W., *The Gantt Chart* (3rd ed.). Sir Isaac Pitman & Sons Ltd., London (1952).

24. MODER, J. J., and C. R. PHILLIPS, *Project Management with CPM and PERT.* Van Nostrand Reinhold, New York (1964).

25. McNAUGHTON, R., "Scheduling with deadline and loss functions." *Manag. Sci. 12*, 1 (Oct. 1959).

26. HU, T. C., "Parallel sequencing and assembly line problems." *Opns. Res. 9*, 6 (Nov. 1961), 841–848.

27. MANACHER, G. K., "Production and stabilization of real-time task schedules." *J. ACM 14*, 3 (July 1967), 439–465.

28. GRAHAM, R. L., "Bounds on multiprocessing time anomalies." *SIAM J. Appl. Math. 17*, 2 (Mar. 1969), 416–429.

29. FUJII, M., T. KASAMI, and K. NINOMIYA, "Optimal sequencing of two equivalent processors." *SIAM J. Appl. Math. 17*, 4 (July 1969), 784–789.

30. COFFMAN, E. G., JR., and R. L. GRAHAM, "Optimal scheduling for two-processor systems." *Acta Informatica 1*, 3 (1972), 200–213.

31. MUNTZ, R. R., and E. G. COFFMAN, JR., "Preemptive scheduling of real-time tasks on multiprocessor systems." *J. ACM 17*, 2 (Apr. 1970), 324–338.

32. CONWAY, R. W., W. L. MAXWELL, and L. W. MILLER, *Theory of Scheduling.* Addison-Wesley, Reading, Mass. (1967).

33. KRONE, M., "Heuristic programming applied to scheduling problems." Ph.D. thesis, Dept. of Electrical Engineering, Princeton Univ., Princeton, N.J. (Sept. 1970).

34. LAMPSON, B. W., "A scheduling philosophy for multiprocessing systems." *Comm. ACM 11*, 5 (May 1968), 347–359.

35. COFFMAN, E. G., JR., and L. KLEINROCK, "Computer scheduling methods and their countermeasures." *AFIPS Conf. Proc. 32* (1968 SJCC), 11–21.

36. CORBATO, F. J., M. M. DAGGETT, and R. C. DALEY, "An experimental time sharing system." *AFIPS Conf. Proc. 21* (1962 FJCC), 335.

37. KLEINROCK, L., "Analysis of a time shared processor." *Nav. Res. Log. Quart. 11*, 10 (March 1964), 59–73.

38. COFFMAN, E. G., JR., and B. KRISHNAMOORTHI, "Preliminary analyses of time-shared computer operation." Technical report SP-1719, Systems Development Corp., Santa Monica, Calif. (Aug. 1964).

39. KRISHNAMOORTHI, B., and R. C. WOOD, "Time-shared computer operations with both interarrival and service time exponential." *J. ACM 13*, 3 (July 1966), 317–338.

40. SCHRAGE, L. E., "The queue M/G/1 with feedback to lower priority queues." *Manag. Sci. 13* (1967), 466–474.

41. COFFMAN, E. G., JR., and L. KLEINROCK, "Feedback queueing models for time-shared systems." *J. ACM 15*, 4 (Oct. 1968), 549–576.

42. SCHERR, A. L., *An Analysis of Time-Shared Computer Systems*. M.I.T. Press, Cambridge, Mass. (1966).

43. COBHAM, A., Priority assignment in waiting line problems." *Opns. Res. 2* (Feb. 1954), 70–76.

44. COFFMAN, E. G., JR., R. R. MUNTZ, and H. TROTTER, "Waiting time distributions for processor sharing systems." *J. ACM 17*, 1 (Jan. 1970), 123–130.

45. MUNTZ, R. R., "Waiting time distribution for round-robin queueing systems." *Proc. Symp. Comp.-Commun.*, *Networks*, *Teletraffic*, Microwave Research Institute, Polytechnic Institute of Brooklyn (Apr. 1972).

46. MCKINNEY, J. M., "A survey of analytical time sharing models." *Computing Surveys 1*, 2 (June 1969), 105–116.

47. ADIRI, I., and B. AVI-ITZHAK, "A time-sharing queue." *Manag. Sci. 15*, 11 (1969), 639–657.

48. ADIRI, I., "A dynamic time-sharing queue." *J. ACM 18*, 4 (Oct. 1971), 603–610.

49. ADIRI, I., "A note on some mathematical models of time-sharing systems." *J. ACM 18*, 4 (Oct. 1971), 611–615.

50. MULLERY, A. P., and G. C. DRISCOLL, "A processor allocation method for time-sharing." *Comm. ACM 13*, 1 (Jan. 1970), 10–14.

51. RANDELL, B., and C. KUEHNER, "Dynamic storage allocation systems." *Comm. ACM 11*, 5 (May 1968), 297–306.

52. DENNING, P. J., "Virtual memory." *Computing Surveys 2*, 3 (Sept. 1970), 153–189.

53. SAYRE, D., "Is automatic folding of programs efficient enough to displace manual?" *Comm. ACM 12*, 12 (Dec. 1969), 656–660.

54. ACM. Proceedings of a symposium on storage allocation. *Comm. ACM 4*, 10 (Oct. 1961).

55. RAMAMOORTHY, C., "The analytic design of a dynamic look ahead and program segmentation system for multiprogrammed computers." *Proc. 21st Nat'l ACM Conf.* (1966), 229–239.

56. KNUTH, D. E., *The Art of Computer Programming* (Vol. 1). Addison-Wesley, Reading, Mass. (1968).

57. KILBURN, T., D. B. G. EDWARDS, M. J. LANIGAN, and F. H. SUMNER, "One-level storage system." *IRE Trans. EC-11* (Apr. 1962), 223–238.

58. DENNIS, J. B., "Segmentation and the design of multiprogrammed computer systems." *J. ACM 12*, 4 (Oct. 1965), 589–602.

59. BENSOUSSAN, A., C. T. CLINGEN, and R. C. DALEY, "The Multics virtual memory." *Proc. 2nd ACM Symp. Op. Sys. Princ.* (Oct. 1969), 30–42.

60. SCHROEDER, M. D., "Performance of the GE-645 associative memory while Multics is in operation." *Proc. ACM Symp. Sys. Perf. Eval.* (Apr. 1971), 227–245.

61. DENNING, P. J., "Queueing models for file memory operations." M.I.T. Project MAC report MAC-TR-21, M.I.T., Cambridge, Mass. (Oct. 1965).

62. WEINGARTEN, A., "The Eschenbach drum scheme." *Comm. ACM 9*, 7 (July 1966), 509–512.

63. COFFMAN, E. G., JR., "Analysis of a drum input/output queue under scheduled operation in a paged computer system." *J. ACM 16*, 1 (Jan. 1969), 73–90.

64. ABATE, J., and H. DUBNER, "Optimizing the performance of a drum-like storage." *IEEE Trans. Comp. C-18*, 11 (Nov. 1969), 992–996.

65. BURGE, W. H., and A. G. KONHEIM, "An accessing model." *J. ACM 18*, 3 (July 1971), 400–404.

66. GREENBERG, M. L., "An algorithm for drum storage management in time sharing systems." *Proc. 3rd ACM Symp. Op. Sys. Princ.* (Oct. 1971).

67. DENNING, P. J., "A note on paging drum efficiency." *Computing Surveys 4*, 1 (Mar. 1972), 1–3.

68. DENNING, P. J., "Effects of scheduling on file memory operations." *AFIPS Conf. Proc. 30* (1967 SJCC), 9–21.

69. SEAMAN, P. H., R. A. LIND, and T. L. WILSON, "Analysis of auxiliary storage activity." *IBM Sys. J. 5*, 3 (1966), 158–170.

70. TEOREY, T. J., and T. B. PINKERTON, "A comparative analysis of disk scheduling policies." *Comm. ACM 15*, 3 (Mar. 1972), 177–184.

71. WOLMAN, E., "A fixed optimum cell-size for records of various lengths." *J. ACM 12*, 1 (Jan. 1965), 53–70.

72. DENNING, P. J., "A model for console behavior in multiuser computers." *Comm. ACM 11*, 9 (Sept. 1968), 605–612.

73. GAVER, D. P., JR., and P. A. W. LEWIS, "Probability models for buffer storage allocation problems." *J. ACM 18*, 2 (Apr. 1971), 186–198.

74. COFFMAN, E. G., JR., and T. A. RYAN, "A study of storage partitioning using a mathematical model of locality." *Comm. ACM 15*, 3 (Mar. 1972), 185–190.

75. JACKSON, J., "Job shop-like queueing systems." *Manag. Sci. 10*, 1 (1963), 131–142.

76. GORDON, W. J., and G. F. NEWELL, "Closed queueing systems with exponential servers." *Opns. Res. 15*, 2 (Apr. 1967), 254–265.

77. BASKETT, F., "Mathematical models of multiprogrammed computer systems." TSN-17, Computation Center, Univ. of Texas at Austin (Jan. 1971).

78. BASKETT, F., "The dependence of computer system queues upon processing

time distribution and central processor scheduling." *Proc. 3rd ACM Symp. Op. Sys. Princ.* (Oct. 1971).

79. KIMBLETON, S. R., and C. G. MOORE III, "A limited resource approach to system performance evaluation." Dept. of Industrial Engineering, Univ. of Michigan, Ann Arbor, TR-71-2 (June 1971).

80. MOORE, C. G., III, "Network models for large scale time sharing systems." Dept. of Industrial Engineering, Univ. of Michigan, Ann Arbor, TR-71-1 (Apr. 1971).

81. BUZEN, J., "Analysis of system bottlenecks using a queueing network." *Proc. ACM Symp. Sys. Perf. Eval.* (Apr. 1971), 82–103.

82. MATTSON, R. L., J. GECSEI, D. R. SLUTZ, and I. L. TRAIGER, "Evaluation techniques for storage hierarchies." *IBM Sys. J. 9*, 2 (1970), 78–117.

83. BELADY, L. A., "A study of replacement algorithms for virtual storage computers." *IBM Sys. J. 5*, 2 (1966), 78–101.

84. AHO, A. V., P. J. DENNING, and J. D. ULLMAN, "Principles of optimal page replacement." *J. ACM 18*, 1 (Jan. 1971), 80–93.

85. HORWITZ, L. P., R. M. KARP, R. E. MILLER, and S. WINOGRAD, "Index register allocation." *J. ACM 13*, 1 (Jan. 1966), 43–61.

86. DENNING, P. J., J. E. SAVAGE, and J. R. SPIRN, "Models for locality in program behavior." Dept. of Electrical Engineering, Princeton Univ., Princeton, N.J., Computer Science technical report TR-107 (May 1972).

87. COFFMAN, E. G., JR., and B. RANDELL, "Performance predictions for extended paged memories." *Acta Informatica 1*, 1 (1971), 1–13.

88. FINE, G. H., C. W. JACKSON, and P. V. MCISAAC, "Dynamic program behavior under paging." *Proc. 21st Nat'l. ACM Conf.* (1966), 223–228.

89. COFFMAN, E. G., JR., and L. C. VARIAN, "Further experimental data on the behavior of programs in a paging environment." *Comm. ACM 11*, 7 (July 1968), 471–474.

90. KUCK, D. J., and D. H. LAWRIE, "The use and performance of memory hierarchies—A Survey," in *Software Engineering* (Vol. I) (J. T. Tou, ed.). Academic Press, New York (1970), 45–78.

91. BRAWN, B., and F. GUSTAVSON, "Program behavior in a paging environment." *AFIPS Conf. Proc. 33* (1968 FJCC), 1019–1032.

92. BRAWN, B., and F. GUSTAVSON, "Sorting in a paging environment." *Comm. ACM 13*, 8 (Aug. 1970), 483–494.

93. BELADY, L. A., and C. J. KUEHNER, "Dynamic space sharing in computer systems." *Comm. ACM 12*, 5 (May 1969), 282–288.

94. McKELLAR, A. C., and E. G. COFFMAN, JR., "Organizing matrices and matrix operations for paged memory systems." *Comm. ACM 12*, 3 (Mar. 1969), 153–164.

95. KERNIGHAN, B. W., "Optimal sequential partitions of graphs." *J. ACM 18*, 1 (Jan. 1971), 34–40.

96. DENNING, P. J., "The working set model for program behavior." *Comm. ACM 11*, 5 (May 1968), 323–333.

97. DOHERTY, W., "Scheduling TSS/360 for responsiveness." *Proc. AFIPS Conf. 37*, (1970 FJCC), 97–112.

98. BOBROW, D. G., J. D. BURCHFIEL, D. L. MURPHY, and R. S. TOMLINSON, "TENEX—A paged time sharing system for the PDP-10." *Comm. ACM 15*, 3 (Mar. 1972), 135–143.

99. OPPENHEIMER, G., and N. WEIZER, "Resource management for a medium scale time sharing operating system." *Comm. ACM 11*, 5 (May 1968), 313–322.

100. WEIZER, N., and G. OPPENHEIMER, "Virtual memory management in a paging environment." *AFIPS Conf. Proc. 34* (1969 SJCC), 249–256.

101. DENNING, P. J., "Thrashing: Its causes and prevention." *AFIPS Conf. Proc. 33* (1968 FJCC), 915–922.

102. DENNING, P. J., and S. C. SCHWARTZ, "Properties of the working set model." *Comm. ACM 15*, 3 (Mar. 1972), 191–198.

103. RODRIGUEZ-ROSELL, J., "Experimental data on how program behavior affects the choice of scheduler parameters." *Proc. 3rd ACM Symp. Op. Sys. Princ.* (Oct. 1971).

104. KNUTH, DONALD E., "Additional comments on a problem in concurrent programming." *Comm. ACM 9*, 5 (May 1966), 321–323.

105. KARP, RICHARD M., and RAYMOND E. MILLER, "Properties of a model for parallel computations: determinacy, termination, and queueing." *SIAM J. Appl. Math. 14*, 6 (Nov. 1966), 1390–1411.

106. SHOSHANI, A., and E. G. COFFMAN, JR., "Sequencing tasks in multi-process multiple resource systems to avoid deadlocks." *Proc. 11th Symp. Switching and Automata Theory* (Oct. 1970), 225–233.

107. CHANDY, K. M., "Local balance in queueing networks with interdependent servers with applications to computer systems." *Proc. 10th Allerton Conf.*, U. of Ill., Urbana (Oct. 1972).

2 CONTROL OF CONCURRENT PROCESSES

2.1. INTRODUCTION

Concurrently executing processes can interact in a number of undesirable ways if resources are improperly shared or there is faulty communication of results (signals) between processes. In general terms, the problem is always one of timing. Thus corresponding performance failures are manifested by the overwriting of information before it has been properly used, the execution of a process that should be dormant, two processes hung-up in "after-you, after-you" loops each waiting for the other to proceed, and so forth.

In this chapter we shall identify four problems of sequence control: determinacy, deadlocks, mutual exclusion, and synchronization. Before describing these problems we shall present the basic definitions that provide the framework of our study of these problems. To begin with we need a sufficiently general definition of *process* and the mechanism by which a process may arise.

A *task* will constitute the unit of computational activity in the sequencing problems of this and the next chapter. A task will be specified in terms of its external behavior only, e.g., the inputs it requires, the outputs it generates, its action or function, and its execution time. The internal operation of a task will be unspecified and of no concern to a discussion. Associated with a task there are two events: *initiation* and *termination*. If T is a task, we denote the initiation of T by $\bar{T}$ and the termination of T by $\underline{T}$. (An overbar is used to suggest "starting up," and an underbar, "closing down.") Letting $t(\cdot)$ denote the time of occurrence of an event, we assume that $t(\underline{T}) - t(\bar{T})$ is nonzero and finite as long as all resources required by T are available.

We shall subsequently be concerned with sequences of initiation and termination events from a given set of n tasks. The theory which we shall develop assumes nothing about the particular operation of any given task; that is, the tasks are *uninterpreted*. (A task might, for example, be a job, a program, or an instruction.) The results will therefore be applicable to any system of tasks consistent with the definitions. Another purpose of studying uninterpreted systems of tasks is to emphasize that the results concern control and sequencing of arbitrary tasks, not their particular functions.

In a physical system on which tasks are performed, there is a set S of states representing the system configurations of interest. For the purposes of defining system states, it is convenient to imagine that the system is partitioned into a set of *resources*, the partitioning and precise definition of resources being dependent on the problem under investigation. In general, however, a resource will be any (not necessarily physical) device which is used by tasks in performing certain functions. Resources may include control and input/output devices (tape and disk drives, channels, card readers, etc.), processors, storage media (core, drum, disk, tape, etc.), programs, procedures, and data files. In a similar fashion, the definition and interpretation of a system state will reflect not only the particular system of interest but also our particular purpose in studying the related model of parallel computation. The functions of tasks as well as system capabilities will be made explicit by sets of allowable state transitions $s \longrightarrow s'$ $(s, s' \in S)$, defined for the initiation and termination events of tasks.

In the above terms an initiation event corresponds to a state transition which reflects: 1) the acquisition or assignment of resources, 2) the initialization of the resource state, and 3) the reading of input values. A termination event corresponds to a state transition which reflects: 1) the release or discontinued use of resources, 2) the writing of output values, and 3) if values or internal states are associated with resources, a termination event may also correspond to "saving" resource states. With these preliminaries we turn now to the definition of a computation model which provides for parallelism in task executions.

Let $\mathfrak{I} = \{T_1, \ldots, T_n\}$ be a set of tasks, and let $<$ be a partial order (precedence relation) on $\mathfrak{I}$. The pair $C = (\mathfrak{I}, <)$ is called a *task system*. The partial order represents operational precedence; i.e., $T < T'$ means that task T is to be completed before task T' is begun.†

Structures more general than partial orders could be considered for task systems. In fact, however, we could have formulated the problems of this chapter using only sets of independent tasks, i.e., task systems $C = (\mathfrak{I}, <)$ for which $< = \varnothing$. In the next chapter we shall exploit the full generality of

---

†Here, as in the literature, the term "partial order" is being abused somewhat in terms of the reflexive property. The expression $T < T$ is meaningless in our context and is best ruled out.

partial orders in our treatment of scheduling problems. Although they are not essential in this chapter, it will occasionally be a decided convenience to have structures more general than sets of independent tasks.

The nature of the foregoing definition is clarified by introducing a graphical representation for task systems. The *precedence graph* corresponding to task system C has $\mathfrak{I}$ as its vertices and the following set of directed edges. The edge (T, T') from T to T' is in the graph if and only if $T \prec T'$ and there exists no T'' such that $T \prec T'' \prec T'$. This definition ensures that redundant specifications of precedence do not appear in the graph. Thus the set of edges may also be defined as the smallest relation on $\mathfrak{I}$ whose transitive closure is $\prec$. An example is shown in Fig. 2.1-1. When there is no danger of ambiguity we shall frequently shorten the terms *task system* and *precedence graph* to simply *system* and *graph*, respectively.

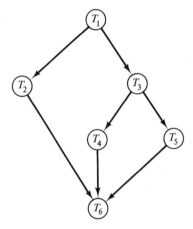

Fig. 2.1-1 A precedence graph.

Consider a (directed) *path* $(x_1 x_2)(x_2 x_3) \cdots (x_{k-1} x_k)$ passing through vertices (tasks) $x_1 \cdots x_k$ in the graph C. The *length* of this path is k, i.e., the number of vertices in the path. For i and j such that $1 \le i < j \le k$, x_j is a *successor* of x_i and x_i a *predecessor* of x_j. If $j = i + 1$, we shall use the terms *immediate successor* and *immediate predecessor*, respectively. A task with no successor is a *terminal* task, and one with no predecessors is an *initial* task. If task T is neither a successor nor predecessor of T', then T and T' are *independent*. Since we are interpreting $\prec$ as a (temporal) precedence ordering on tasks, T and T' may be concurrent if and only if they are independent (otherwise, T and T' must occur temporally in some fixed order). A nonterminal task is at *level k* in C if a longest path from it to a terminal task is of length k. The level of a terminal task is defined to be 1.

An *execution sequence* of an n-task system $C = (\mathfrak{I}, \prec)$ is any string $\alpha = a_1 a_2 \cdots a_{2n}$ of task initiation and termination events satisfying the precedence constraints of C. Stated precisely,

1. For each T in $\mathfrak{I}$ the symbols $\bar{T}$ and $\underline{T}$ appear exactly once in α.
2. If $a_i = \bar{T}$ and $a_j = \underline{T}$, then $i < j$.
3. If $a_i = \underline{T}$ and $a_j = \bar{T}'$, where $T < T'$, then $i < j$.

Two valid execution sequences for Fig. 2.1-1 are

$$\bar{T}_1\underline{T}_1\bar{T}_2\underline{T}_2\bar{T}_3\underline{T}_3\bar{T}_4\underline{T}_4\bar{T}_5\underline{T}_5\bar{T}_6\underline{T}_6$$

and

$$\bar{T}_1\underline{T}_1\bar{T}_2\bar{T}_3\underline{T}_3\bar{T}_4\bar{T}_5\underline{T}_5\underline{T}_4\underline{T}_2\bar{T}_6\underline{T}_6$$

A *partial* execution sequence is any prefix of an execution sequence. Clearly, the set of execution sequences for C is the set of all event sequences according to which the tasks of C can be carried out subject to the precedence constraints imposed by $<$. Task T is *active* after a partial execution sequence $\alpha = a_1 \cdots a_k$ if for some $i \leq k$, $a_i = \bar{T}$ but $a_j \neq \underline{T}$ for all $j \leq k$.

Given a state space S for the computer system of interest, the *state sequence* corresponding to an execution sequence $\alpha = a_1 a_2 \cdots a_{2n}$ is denoted $\sigma = s_0 s_1 s_2 \cdots s_{2n}$, $s_i \in S(0 \leq i \leq 2n)$, where s_0 is a given initial state and $s_{i-1} \rightarrow s_i$ is the state transition defined for event a_i. A transition for the state-event pair (s, a) will be defined only if event a is possible when the system is in state s.

It is sometimes convenient to suppose that a task system has a unique initial task and a unique terminal task. A task system will be called *closed* if it satisfies this property. Figure 2.1-1 is an example of a closed task system. If an n-task system C is not closed, we can construct a closed system C' by introducing "dummy" tasks T_0 and T_{n+1}, where T_0 is a predecessor of every initial task of C and T_{n+1} is a successor of every terminal task of C. Every execution sequence of C' is of the form $\bar{T}_0\underline{T}_0\alpha\bar{T}_{n+1}\underline{T}_{n+1}$ for some execution sequence α of C. Assuming that T_0 and T_{n+1} are introduced only for the closure of a task system, the systems C and C' will be equivalent in terms of the functions they perform.

Suppose that C_1 and C_2 are closed task systems. The graph of a new (closed) system $C_1 \cdot C_2$, the *concatenation* of C_1 and C_2, is formed by adding an edge from the final task of C_1 to the initial task of C_2. An execution sequence of $C_1 \cdot C_2$ is any string α such that $\alpha = \alpha_1\alpha_2$ for some execution sequences α_1 of C_1 and α_2 of C_2.

Suppose that C_1 and C_2 are systems having no tasks in common. The new system $C_1 \| C_2$, the *parallel combination* of C_1 and C_2, is simply the union of C_1 and C_2. The graph of $C_1 \| C_2$ has the graphs of C_1 and C_2 as disjoint subgraphs; since C_1 and C_2 have no tasks in common, every task of C_1 is independent of every task of C_2. Therefore an execution sequence of $C_1 \| C_2$

can be formed by merging an execution sequence of C_1 with one from C_2. More precisely, if $c_1 c_2 \cdots c_{2(m+n)}$ is an execution sequence of $C_1 \| C_2$, then there exist sequences $a_1 a_2 \ldots a_{2m}$ of C_1 and $b_1 b_2 \ldots b_{2n}$ of C_2 such that

1. c_1 is either a_1 or b_1.
2. If $a_1 \cdots a_i$ and $b_1 \cdots b_j$ are the elements of $c_1 \cdots c_{i+j}$, $i + j < 2(m + n)$, then c_{i+j+1} is either a_{i+1} or b_{j+1}.

The notion of parallel combination arises frequently in systems design. It provides the principal motivation for studying the control problems of this chapter; even though the problems may be solvable with a given task system by ad hoc methods, a general solution is required to account for the parallel combination of arbitrary systems.

Many operating systems support task systems that may be reinitiated arbitrarily often. A simple but typical example is a program in a loop producing lines of output for a line printer. We shall not attempt to model such systems directly, because some of our results depend on the acyclic property of precedence graphs. However, we can model k iterations or cycles of a closed task system C by the k-fold concatenation C^k. An execution sequence α of C^k is then of the form $\alpha_1 \alpha_2 \cdots \alpha_k$, where α_i is the execution sequence from the ith iteration of C. We shall call a system *cyclic* if it has the form C^k for $k > 1$ or if it is a parallel combination of *closed* systems at least one of which is cyclic. The execution sequences of a cyclic system will also be called cyclic.

We are now prepared to introduce and analyze the sequence control problems that can arise in systems of concurrent processes.

2.2. DETERMINACY OF TASK SYSTEMS

When a collection of tasks cooperating toward a common goal can be executed in parallel, we are frequently interested in ensuring the uniqueness of the results despite variations in task execution rates and the order of task executions. A task system satisfying this property is said to be functional, speed-independent, or determinate. A task system will be non-determinate if the results produced by independent tasks depend on the order in which these tasks are executed. This will frequently be the case, for example, when independent tasks read and write common storage locations. The problem of nondeterminacy can be solved simply by introducing the proper precedence constraints between previously independent tasks. In this section our main goal will be to establish necessary and sufficient conditions for determinate task systems.

For the determinacy problem, the physical system on which task systems are executed is represented by an ordered set $M = (M_1, \ldots, M_m)$ of *memory cells.* Each cell M_i can contain any value in the set V, the *value set* of the system. Our terminology is motivated by recent literature and by what appears to be the most important application of determinacy problems in studies of operating systems. However, it will become apparent that the elements of M can be regarded as resources of any type whose state can be read (used) or written (changed) by a task system. More abstractly, M is also called a *name space* associated with tasks.

System states will be defined by the configuration of values in the memory cells. More precisely, let $\alpha = a_1 a_2 \cdots a_{2n}$ and $\sigma = s_0 s_1 \cdots s_{2n}$ be an execution sequence and corresponding state sequence for a given n-task system. Let $M_i(k)$ be the value denoted by (contained in) M_i just following the kth event. Then the state s_k is defined as

$$s_k = [M_1(k), \ldots, M_m(k)]$$

The set of all possible states can therefore be written as $S = V^m$.

To define the state transitions $s_k \longrightarrow s_{k+1}$ we must first formalize the effect task executions have on the memory state. With each task T of a system C are associated two, possibly overlapping, ordered subsets of M, the *domain* D_T and *range* R_T. When T is initiated it reads the values stored in its domain cells, and when it terminates it writes values into its range cells. That is, associated with each task T is a mapping $f_T \colon V^d \longrightarrow V^r$, where $d = |D_T|$ and $r = |R_T|$. Executing the task T is to be regarded as "performing" or implementing the mapping f_T. Accordingly, for a given initial state s_0 and a given execution sequence α the corresponding state sequence $\sigma = s_0 s_1 s_2 \cdots s_{2n}$ is defined as follows. Let $D_T = (M_{x_1}, \ldots, M_{x_d})$ and $R_T = (M_{y_1}, \ldots, M_{y_r})$:

    1. If $a_{k+1} = \bar{T}$, then $M_i(k+1) = M_i(k)$, $1 \leq i \leq m$.
    2 If $a_{k+1} = \underline{T}$ and $a_l = \bar{T}$ $(l \leq k)$, then

$$[M_{y_1}(k+1), \ldots, M_{y_r}(k+1)] = f_T([M_{x_1}(l), \ldots, M_{x_d}(l)])$$

and

$$M_i(k+1) = M_i(k) \text{ for all } M_i \notin R_T$$

In other words, no state change occurs ($s_{k+1} = s_k$) if a_{k+1} is an initiation event; otherwise, if a_{k+1} denotes the termination of T, then s_{k+1} can differ from s_k only in the range cells R_T, the new values in R_T being determined by f_T on the basis of the domain values just prior to the initiation event for T. We may display the state sequence $\sigma = s_0 s_1 s_2 \cdots s_{2n}$ resulting from an execution sequence in the form of an m by $(2n + 1)$ array, called the *history array*, whose rows correspond to cells of M and whose columns correspond to states, as suggested in Fig. 2.2-1.

In the following it is more convenient to deal with the sequences of values written by a task system into individual memory cells. For this reason we

$$C = (\{T_1, T_2\}, \phi) \qquad\qquad M = (M_1, M_2) = D_{T_1} = D_{T_2} = R_{T_1} = R_{T_2}$$

Interpretations

Tasks	I	II
T_1	$(M_1, M_2) \leftarrow (1, M_2)$	$(M_1, M_2) \leftarrow (M_1 + M_2, M_2)$
T_2	$(M_1, M_2) \leftarrow (2, M_2)$	$(M_1, M_2) \leftarrow (M_1, M_1 + M_2)$

History arrays

	α:	$\overline{T_1}$	$\underline{T_1}$	$\overline{T_2}$	$\underline{T_2}$		α':	$\overline{T_2}$	$\underline{T_2}$	$\overline{T_1}$	$\underline{T_1}$	
I	M_1	1	1	1	1	2		1	1	2	2	1
	M_2	2	2	2	2	2		2	2	2	2	2
II	M_1	1	1	3	3	3		1	1	1	1	4
	M_2	2	2	2	2	5		2	2	3	3	3

Value sequences

	I		II	
	α	α'	α	α'
M_1	(1, 1, 2)	(1, 2, 1)	(1, 3, 3)	(1, 1, 4)
M_2	(2, 2, 2)	(2, 2, 2)	(2, 2, 5)	(2, 3, 3)

Fig. 2.2-1 Examples of non-determinate task systems.

define the *value sequence* $V(M_i, \alpha)$ of cell M_i to be the sequence of values written by terminations of tasks T for which $M_i \in R_T$ appearing in (partial) execution sequence α. To put this precisely, let ϵ denote the empty string and let us adopt a vector notation for value sequences; e.g., $V(M_i, \alpha) = (v_1, \ldots, v_s)$. Let $\alpha = a_1 a_2 \cdots a_{2n}$ and $\sigma = s_0 s_1 s_2 \cdots s_{2n}$ be an execution sequence and corresponding state sequence. For the corresponding value sequences we have

$$V(M_i, \epsilon) = M_i(0)$$

$$V(M_i, a_1 \cdots a_k) = \begin{cases} (V(M_i, a_1 \cdots a_{k-1}), M_i(k)) & \text{if } a_k = \underline{T}, M_i \in R_T \\ V(M_i, a_1 \cdots a_{k-1}) & \text{otherwise} \end{cases}$$

Note that $V(M_i, \alpha)$ and $V(M_j, \alpha)$ need not be of the same length, for M_i need not be in the range of as many tasks as M_j. If $V(M_i, \alpha) = (v_1, \ldots, v_s)$, we define the *final value* $F(M_i, \alpha) = v_s$. According to our definitions, it is readily verified that if $\alpha = a_1 \cdots a_k$, then $s_k = [F(M_1, \alpha), \ldots, F(M_m, \alpha)]$.

Suppose that the partial order $\prec$ and the ranges and domains for each task are all that is known for a task system $C = (\mathfrak{I}, \prec)$. Then C (and each task in $\mathfrak{I}$) is said to be *uninterpreted*. Accordingly, an *interpretation* for a task system is a specification, for each task T, of the task function f_T. For the sake of generality we shall be considering properties of task systems which ensure determinacy irrespective of the specific task functions f_T. Consequently, our subsequent results will be stated in terms of uninterpreted task systems.

Definition 2.1

> Task system C is determinate if for any given initial state s_0, $V(M_i, \alpha) = V(M_i, \alpha')$, $1 \leq i \leq m$, for all execution sequences α and α' of C. That is, the cell-value sequences depend uniquely on the initial values in s_0.

Perhaps a more intuitive definition of determinacy is the weaker requirement $F(M_i, \alpha) = F(M_i, \alpha')$; as will be seen later, however, the constraint on the task system for determinacy implies this stronger condition.

Example

Figure 2.2-1 shows a two-task system with memory cells M_1 and M_2 and interpretations I and II. History arrays and value sequences are shown. Interpretation I is nondeterminate because tasks T_1 and T_2 are in a race to write cell M_1. Interpretation II is nondeterminate because one task writes a value in a cell read by the other.

It is obvious from this example that nondeterminate systems may result whenever a task's range intersects with the domain or range of another, independent task. Intuitively, it is impossible for a system containing tasks whose ranges do not intersect with domains or ranges of independent tasks to be nondeterminate. This leads to the following definition, which in turn will lead to necessary and sufficient conditions for determinate systems.

Definition 2.2

> Tasks T and T' are *noninterfering* if either
>
> 1. T is a successor or predecessor of T', or
> 2. $R_T \cap R_{T'} = R_T \cap D_{T'} = D_T \cap R_{T'} = \varnothing$.
>
> $\mathfrak{I} = \{T_1, \ldots, T_n\}$ is said to contain mutually noninterfering tasks if T_i and T_j are noninterfering for all i and j $(i \neq j)$.

The following lemma provides the induction step for Theorem 2.1, which proves the determinacy of systems comprising mutually noninterfering tasks.

Lemma 2.1

Let C be an n-task system consisting of mutually noninterfering tasks, and let T be a terminal task of C. If $\alpha = \beta_1 \bar{T} \beta_2 T \beta_3$ is an execution sequence of C, then $\alpha' = \beta_1 \beta_2 \beta_3 \bar{T} T$ is an execution sequence of C for which $V(M_i, \alpha) = V(M_i, \alpha')$ for all i, $1 \le i \le m$.

Proof. Since T has no successors in C, α' satisfies the precedence constraints of C and so must be an execution sequence. Because T writes cells in R_T only and because $R_T \cap D_{T'} = \varnothing$ for any T' initiated in β_3, each such T' finds the same domain values in α' as it did in α. Therefore $V(M_i, \alpha) = V(M_i, \alpha')$ for $M_i \notin R_T$.

Now for any $M_j \in D_T$, $V(M_j, \beta_1) = V(M_j, \beta_1 \beta_2 \beta_3)$ since no T' in $\beta_2 \beta_3$ writes into D_T (i.e., $R_{T'} \cap D_T = \varnothing$). Therefore $F(M_j, \beta_1) = F(M_j, \beta_1 \beta_2 \beta_3)$ for all $M_j \in D_T$, and T writes the same value into each $M_i \in R_T$ in α' as it did in α. Letting v denote the value written into $M_i \in R_T$ by T in α, it follows that

$$
\begin{aligned}
V(M_i, \alpha) &= V(M_i, \beta_1 \bar{T} \beta_2 T) &&(\text{no } T' \text{ in } \beta_3 \text{ writes into } R_T) \\
&= (V(M_i, \beta_1 \bar{T} \beta_2), v) &&(T \text{ writes } v \text{ into } M_i) \\
&= (V(M_i, \beta_1), v) &&(\text{no } T' \text{ in } \beta_2 \text{ writes into } R_T) \\
&= (V(M_i, \beta_1 \beta_2 \beta_3), v) &&(\text{no } T' \text{ in } \beta_2 \beta_3 \text{ writes into } R_T) \\
&= V(M_i, \beta_1 \beta_2 \beta_3 \bar{T} T) &&(T \text{ writes } v \text{ into } M_i) \\
&= V(M_i, \alpha')
\end{aligned}
$$

which completes the proof. ∎

A straightforward induction argument will now establish that mutually noninterfering tasks are a sufficient condition for determinacy.

Theorem 2.1

Task systems consisting of mutually noninterfering tasks are determinate.

Proof. We proceed by induction on the number of tasks in a system. The assertion is trivially true for single-task systems. Assume that the assertion holds for systems with fewer than n tasks, and let $C = (\mathfrak{I}, <)$ be an n-task system.

C is trivially determinate if it has but one execution sequence. Therefore suppose that α_1 and α_2 are distinct execution sequences of C. Let T be a terminal task of C and form α'_1 and α'_2 according to Lemma 2.1. We have

$$\alpha'_1 = \alpha''_1 \bar{T} T; \qquad V(M_i, \alpha_1) = V(M_i, \alpha'_1) \quad 1 \leq i \leq m$$
$$\alpha'_2 = \alpha''_2 \bar{T} T; \qquad V(M_i, \alpha_2) = V(M_i, \alpha'_2) \quad 1 \leq i \leq m$$

But α''_1 and α''_2 are execution sequences of the $(n-1)$-task system $C' = (\mathfrak{I} - \{T\}, <')$, where $<'$ is obtained from $<$ by eliminating all precedence constraints involving T. It follows from the induction hypothesis that $V(M_i, \alpha''_1) = V(M_i, \alpha''_2)$, $1 \leq i \leq m$. Therefore the domain values used by T are the same in α'_1 and α'_2; i.e., $F(M_j, \alpha''_1) = F(M_j, \alpha''_2)$ for $M_j \in D_T$. It follows that T writes the same value v into $M_i \in R_T$ in both α'_1 and α'_2. Hence for $M_i \notin R_T$

$$
\begin{aligned}
V(M_i, \alpha_1) &= V(M_i, \alpha'_1) && \text{(Lemma 2.1)} \\
&= V(M_i, \alpha''_1) && (M_i \notin R_T) \\
&= V(M_i, \alpha''_2) && \text{(induction hypothesis)} \\
&= V(M_i, \alpha'_2) && (M_i \notin R_T) \\
&= V(M_i, \alpha_2) && \text{(Lemma 2.1)}
\end{aligned}
$$

and for $M_i \in R_T$

$$
\begin{aligned}
V(M_i, \alpha_1) &= V(M_i, \alpha'_1) && \text{(Lemma 2.1)} \\
&= (V(M_i, \alpha''_1), v) && (T \text{ writes } v \text{ into } M_i) \\
&= (V(M_i, \alpha''_2), v) && \text{(induction hypothesis)} \\
&= V(M_i, \alpha'_2) && (T \text{ writes } v \text{ into } M_i) \\
&= V(M_i, \alpha_2) && \text{(Lemma 2.1)}
\end{aligned}
$$

This establishes the determinacy of C. ∎

Noninterference is also a necessary condition for determinacy provided

1. All tasks have nonempty ranges; for otherwise a task T with $R_T = \varnothing$ can be interfered with, but there is no way ever to detect this by observing the contents of cells.

2. Determinacy must hold for all possible interpretations of an (uninterpreted) system.

Theorem 2.2

Let C be a system in which for every task T, f_T is unspecified but D_T and $R_T \neq \varnothing$ are given. Then C is determinate for all interpretations of its tasks only if these tasks are mutually noninterfering.

Proof. Suppose that T and T' interfere; then T and T' are independent and there exist execution sequences

$$\alpha = \beta_1 \bar{T} \underline{T} \bar{T}' \underline{T}' \beta_2$$
$$\alpha' = \beta_1 \bar{T}' \underline{T}' \bar{T} \underline{T} \beta_2$$

Suppose that $M_i \in (R_T \cap R_{T'})$. We can choose f_T and $f_{T'}$ so that T writes u into M_i and T' writes v, where $u \neq v$ (see Fig. 2.2-1 for an example). But then

$$V(M_i, \beta_1 \bar{T} \underline{T} \bar{T}' \underline{T}') = (V(M_i, \beta_1), u, v)$$
$$V(M_i, \beta_1 \bar{T}' \underline{T}' \bar{T} \underline{T}) = (V(M_i, \beta_1), v, u)$$

contradicting the determinacy of C. Therefore $R_T \cap R_{T'} = \varnothing$ must hold.

Suppose that $M_j \in (R_{T'} \cap D_T)$ and let $M_i \in R_T$ (since $R_T \neq \varnothing$). We can choose $f_{T'}$ so that $F(M_j, \beta_1) \neq F(M_j, \beta_1 \bar{T}' \underline{T}')$; i.e., T reads different values in α and α'. Therefore we can choose f_T so that T writes u in α and v in α', where $u \neq v$ (see Fig. 2.2-1 for an example). But then

$$V(M_i, \beta_1 \bar{T} \underline{T} \bar{T}' \underline{T}') = V(M_i, \beta_1 \bar{T} \underline{T}) \quad (R_T \cap R_{T'} = \varnothing)$$
$$= (V(M_i, \beta_1), u)$$
$$V(M_i, \beta_1 \bar{T}' \underline{T}' \bar{T} \underline{T}) = (V(M_i, \beta_1 \bar{T}' \underline{T}'), v)$$
$$= (V(M_i, \beta_1), v) \quad (R_T \cap R_{T'} = \varnothing)$$

Since $u \neq v$, the determinacy of C is contradicted. (Note that if $R_T = \varnothing$, it is possible for $M_j \in (R_{T'} \cap D_T)$ without arriving at this contradiction.) Finally, by symmetry we see that $R_T \cap D_{T'} = \varnothing$ must also hold. ∎

A useful application of Theorems 2.1 and 2.2 concerns the maximum parallelism [26] of task systems in which precedence constraints are to be determined only by the requirements of determinacy. To develop this application we shall first formalize the notions of maximum parallelism and the equivalence between task systems.

By Definition 2.1, to each determinate task system and given initial state there corresponds exactly one value sequence for each memory cell M_i. Two task systems having the same set of tasks are said to be *equivalent* if they are determinate and if, for the same initial state, they produce the same value sequences. A task system C and its graph G are called *maximally parallel* if C is determinate and if the removal of any arc (T, T') from G would cause T and T' to become interfering. Thus, if (T, T') is an arc of a maximally parallel graph, then

$$(2.2.1) \qquad (R_T \cap R_{T'}) \cup (R_T \cap D_{T'}) \cup (R_{T'} \cap D_T) \neq \varnothing$$

Given a determinate task system C, we are interested in constructing an equivalent, maximally parallel system C'.

Theorem 2.3

From a given determinate task system $C = (\mathfrak{I}, <)$ construct a new system $C' = (\mathfrak{I}, <')$, where $<'$ is the transitive closure of the relation

$$X = \{(T, T') \in\ < \mid (R_T \cap R_{T'}) \cup (R_T \cap D_{T'}) \cup (R_{T'} \cap D_T) \neq \varnothing\}$$

Then C' is the unique maximally parallel system equivalent to C.

Proof. Let G' denote the precedence graph corresponding to X and hence $<'$. (The example in Fig. 2.2-2 illustrates that in general $G' \subset X \subset <'$.) Suppose that we remove an arc (T, T') from G'. Since there can be no other path from T to T' (by definition of precedence graphs) and since T and T' satisfy (2.2.1) by the definition of $X \supset G'$, we see that T and T' become interfering. Hence G' will be maximally parallel if we can show that C' is determinate.

Since C is determinate, we must have $T < T'$ or $T' < T$ for every pair of tasks T and T' satisfying (2.2.1). It follows from the definition of X that we must also have $T <' T'$ or $T' <' T$. Hence all tasks in C' are mutually non-interfering, and by Theorem 2.1, C' is determinate.

Every precedence constraint of C' is in C; hence every execution sequence of C is generated by C'. Let α' be an execution sequence of C' which is not generated by C, and let α be an execution sequence common to C and C'. The determinacy of C' implies that $V(M_i, \alpha') = V(M_i, \alpha)$, $1 \leq i \leq m$, for a given initial state. Therefore C' has the same cell-value sequences as C and we can conclude that C and C' are equivalent.

Finally, it can be seen that $T <' T'$ if and only if there exists a chain $T = T_{i_1} < T_{i_2} < \cdots < T_{i_k} = T'$ $(k > 1)$ in which every pair of tasks T_{i_j} and $T_{i_{j+1}}$ $(1 \leq j < k)$ satisfies (2.2.1). It can be readily verified that this must be true of any maximally parallel task system equivalent to C. Hence C' is unique. ∎

Figure 2.2-2 illustrates the construction of G' (see Problem 2.10). After computing the relation X the corresponding graph is drawn. G' is produced from this graph by eliminating redundant arcs. [An arc (T, T') is redundant if there is another path from T to T' containing more than one arc.] Note that the computation of X is simplified somewhat by the task indexing: $T_i < T_j$ implies that $i < j$ (see Problem 2-11). Thus X is constructed by considering only the pairs (T_i, T_j) for $i = 1, 2, \ldots, n$ and $j = i + 1, \ldots, n$, placing (T_i, T_j) in X whenever (2.2.1) holds for this pair of tasks.

Determinacy results have appeared in many different contexts, but an informal treatment relating to the environment of operating systems has been

$$M = \{M_1, M_2, M_3, M_4, M_5\}$$ (Tasks denoted by their indices)

Cell	In domain of tasks	In range of tasks
M_1	1, 2, 7, 8	3
M_2	1, 7	5
M_3	3, 4, 8	1
M_4	3, 4, 5, 7	2, 7
M_5	6	4, 6, 8

X: (1, 3) (1, 4) (1, 5) (1, 8)
       (2, 3) (2, 4) (2, 5) (2, 7)
       (3, 7) (3, 8)
       (4, 6) (4, 7) (4, 8)
       (5, 7)
       (6, 8)

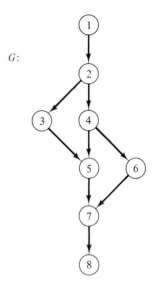

G:

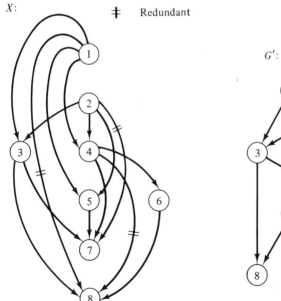

X: ╪ Redundant

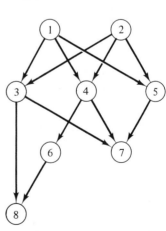

G':

Fig. 2.2-2 Computing a maximally parallel graph.

given by Bernstein[1]. Bernstein also shows that the general problem of decomposing a program (expressed in Algol, say) into tasks executable in parallel is recursively unsolvable. The approach of the proof is typical of decidability results but falls outside the scope of our presentation. Baer[2] has given an extensive survey covering many aspects of parallelism, for example, detection of program blocks which can be executed in parallel, other models for parallelism, hardware implementations of parallelism, and program linguistic methods for expressing parallelism (see also Problems 2-12 and 2-14).

2.3. DEADLOCKS†

2.3.1. Introduction

A system $C = C_1 \| C_2 \| \cdots \| C_n$ is deadlocked if its progress is blocked indefinitely because a subset of the C_is are concurrently active, each holding nonpreemptible resources that must be acquired by some other system in the set in order to proceed. In this chapter a nonpreemptible resource is one that can be released only by the task system holding it.

For the purposes of studying the deadlock problem, the physical system consists of m *resource types* $R_1, \ldots, R_m$, with $w_1, \ldots, w_m$ units of the respective types. The vector $\mathbf{w} = (w_1, \ldots, w_m)$ represents the system *capacity*. Each resource unit of a given type is indistinguishable from other units of the same type. Examples of resource types include processors, pages of memory, tape units, disk tracks, and so forth, but they may also include resources having no direct physical realization in terms of hardware devices, such as data files, message buffers, or system tables. Nonpreemptibility of a resource may result simply from the system's not being designed to preempt the given resource, or it may result from inherent limitations. Examples of the latter include data files in the process of being updated and input/output units with mechanical positioning.

To illustrate the conditions under which deadlocks can occur, we consider a simple example[4]. There are two systems C_1 and C_2 and one unit each of resource types R_1 and R_2. For each system the number of instructions completed since its initiation is used as a measure of its progress, and a pair of such values defines a point in a two-dimensional *progress space*, as illustrated in Fig. 2.3-1. The joint progress of C_1 and C_2 is represented by a sequence of discrete points $(x_1, y_1)(x_2, y_2) \ldots (x_k, y_k) \ldots$ in this space; clearly, $x_k \leq x_{k+1}$ and $y_k \leq y_{k+1}$ (i.e., progress is irreversible). Each such sequence of progress points originating at $(0, 0)$ will be called a joint progress path of C_1 and C_2.

Not every joint progress path is feasible. As shown in Fig. 2.3-1, the progress points corresponding to simultaneous use of R_1 are disallowed,

†A survey on this subject is given in [3].

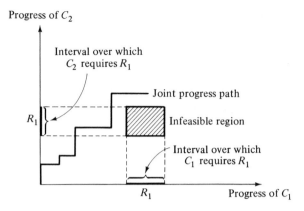

Fig. 2.3-1   Progress space.

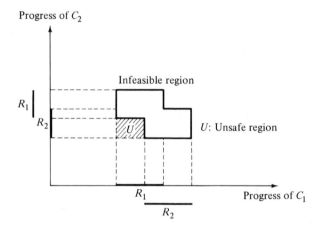

Fig. 2.3-2   Progress space with unsafe region.

since only one unit of R_1 is available. To be valid, every progress path must circumvent the infeasible region.

Now consider Fig. 2.3-2, which shows a larger infeasible region resulting from the union of the R_1 region and the R_2 region. If ever a joint progress path enters the region U—the "unsafe region"—the irreversibility of progress guarantees the eventual occurrence of deadlock. Specifically, the progress of both tasks must stop permanently at the upper right corner of U. Three conditions are necessary for the unsafe region to exist:

1. *Mutual exclusion.* Each task system claims exclusive control of the resources it uses.

2. *Nonpreemption.* A task system does not release resources it holds until it completes its use of them.

3. *Resource waiting.* Each task system holds resources while waiting for the others to release resources.

The deadlock itself is defined by an unresolvable *circular wait* condition, the unresolvability being guaranteed by the mutual exclusion and nonpreemption conditions. After formalizing the notions of *progress*, *deadlock*, and *safeness*, we shall consider three approaches to dealing with deadlocks:

1. *Prevention.* One or more of the above three necessary conditions are precluded, either by constraining the system design or by suitably restricting resource usage.

2. *Detection and recovery.* The operating system monitors the joint progress of all task systems; if and when it observes deadlocks, it takes special action to correct the situation and recover at minimum cost.

3. *Avoidance.* On the basis of advance information about resource usage, the operating system controls resource allocation so that the next increment in a joint progress path will not enter an unsafe region.

In formalizing deadlock problems we shall consider only task systems consisting of *chains* of tasks [5]. In the system of chains $C_1 \| C_2 \| \cdots \| C_n$ we shall denote the ith chain $C_i = T_i(1)T_i(2) \cdots T_i(p_i)$, $p_i \geq 1$. With respect to the nature of deadlocks our simplification to chains of tasks is a very convenient one that incurs no essential sacrifice in generality. A key assumption will be that the resource usage of a chain is constant during the execution of a task but varies from one task to the next. This property effectively defines the task decomposition of the program or job being modeled by the chain.

Each task is characterized by a request prior to its initiation for resources over and above those already held by the chain and by a release after its termination of those resources not to be passed on to the next task of the chain. Therefore we associate with task $T_i(l)$ the *request vector* $\mathbf{q}_i(l) = (q_{i1}(l), \ldots, q_{im}(l))$ in which $q_{ij}(l)$ represents the number of additional units of R_j required to initiate $T_i(l)$, and the *release vector* $\mathbf{r}_i(l) = (r_{i1}(l), \ldots, r_{im}(l))$ in which $r_{ij}(l)$ represents the number of units of R_j released by $T_i(l)$ on termination. In general, we may have $\mathbf{q}_i(l) = \mathbf{0}$ or $\mathbf{r}_i(l) = \mathbf{0}$, where $\mathbf{0}$ is an m-tuple of zeros. The assumption that the resource usage of chain C_i changes from $T_i(l)$ to $T_i(l+1)$ is equivalent to

$$\mathbf{r}_i(l) \neq \mathbf{q}_i(l+1) \quad 1 \leq l < p_i$$

Let us first define states and state transitions under the assumption that a single chain C_i is to be executed. The chain C_i has the unique execution sequence $\alpha = \bar{T}_i(1)\underline{T}_i(1) \ldots \underline{T}_i(p_i) = a_1 \ldots a_k \ldots a_{2p_i}$. We wish to specify the corresponding state sequence, $\sigma = s_0 s_1 \ldots s_k \ldots s_{2p_i}$. These states will be defined to specify the subsets of resources allocated to and requested by the chain after each event in α. Since the study of deadlocks does not concern the functions performed by the tasks, the internal states of resources are of no concern. Therefore the state s_k is specified completely by the pair of vectors $\mathbf{P}_i(k) = (P_{i1}(k), \ldots, P_{im}(k))$ and $\mathbf{Q}_i(k) = (Q_{i1}(k), \ldots, Q_{im}(k))$, where $P_{ij}(k)$ and $Q_{ij}(k)$ denote, respectively, the number of units of R_j held and requested by chain C_i after the event a_k in α. The vectors $\mathbf{P}_i(k)$ and $\mathbf{Q}_i(k)$ are defined in terms of $\mathbf{q}_i(l)$ and $\mathbf{r}_i(l)$ as follows:

$$
\begin{array}{lll}
& \mathbf{Q}_i(0) = \mathbf{q}_i(1) & \mathbf{P}_i(0) = \mathbf{0} \\
(2.3.1) & \mathbf{Q}_i(k) = \mathbf{0} & \mathbf{P}_i(k) = \mathbf{P}_i(k-1) + \mathbf{Q}_i(k-1) \quad \text{if } a_k = \bar{T}_i(l) \\
& \mathbf{Q}_i(k) = \mathbf{q}_i(l+1) & \mathbf{P}_i(k) = \mathbf{P}_i(k-1) - \mathbf{r}_i(l) \qquad\quad \text{if } a_k = \underline{T}_i(l)
\end{array}
$$

It is assumed that the final allocation of resources, $\mathbf{P}_i(2p_i)$, satisfies

$$
(2.3.2) \qquad\qquad \mathbf{P}_i(2p_i) = \sum_{l=1}^{p_i} [\mathbf{q}_i(l) - \mathbf{r}_i(l)] = \mathbf{0}
$$

(i.e., a chain eventually releases every resource it requests). According to (2.3.1), the additional resources requested by a task must all be allocated at once, and the termination event $\underline{T}_i(l)$ is associated with both the releasing of resources by $T_i(l)$ and the (immediate) requesting of resources by $T_i(l+1)$. It is only for convenience that we have chosen an initial state in which all resources are available. The definitions and results to follow are trivially extended to take into account a more general initial state. Figure 2.3-3 shows a chain C_1 comprising three tasks and the request/release vectors (demands) of the tasks. The state sequence corresponding to C_1's execution sequence is shown also.

	C_1	q_1	r_1
$T_1(1)$		$(0, 1, 2, 0)$	$(0, 0, 2, 0)$
$T_1(2)$		$(1, 0, 0, 1)$	$(0, 0, 0, 1)$
$T_1(3)$		$(0, 0, 2, 0)$	$(1, 1, 2, 0)$

System: $\mathbf{R} = (R_1, R_2, R_3, R_4)$, $\mathbf{w} = (3, 3, 3, 3)$

Execution sequence	$\bar{T}_1(1)$	$\underline{T}_1(1)$	$\bar{T}_1(2)$	$\underline{T}_1(2)$	$\bar{T}_1(3)$	$\underline{T}_1(3)$
$P_1(k)$: (0000)	(0120)	(0100)	(1101)	(1100)	(1120)	(0000)
$Q_1(k)$: (0120)	(0000)	(1001)	(0000)	(0020)	(0000)	(0000)

states

Fig. 2.3-3 Example chain and execution sequence.

We can now define states and state transitions assuming that the system $C = C_1 \| C_2 \| \cdots \| C_n$ is to be executed. Generalizing the discussion above, each state s_k of the system is described by a pair $[P(k), Q(k)]$ of matrices, in which

$$P(k) = \begin{bmatrix} \mathbf{P}_1(k) \\ \cdot \\ \cdot \\ \cdot \\ \mathbf{P}_n(k) \end{bmatrix} \qquad Q(k) = \begin{bmatrix} \mathbf{Q}_1(k) \\ \cdot \\ \cdot \\ \cdot \\ \mathbf{Q}_n(k) \end{bmatrix}$$

If $\alpha = a_1 \ldots a_k \ldots$ is an execution sequence of the system C, then the corresponding state sequence $s_0 s_1 \ldots s_k \ldots$ is defined by applying (2.3.1) to the appropriate row of the matrices $P(k)$ and $Q(k)$. In these matrices, the interpretation of $\mathbf{Q}_i(k) \neq \mathbf{0}$ is that chain C_i is awaiting the allocation of one or more resources. Also, $\mathbf{P}_i(k) \neq \mathbf{0}$ and $\mathbf{Q}_i(k) = \mathbf{0}$ implies that C_i is executing or is prepared to continue execution. A chain C_i for which $\mathbf{P}_i(k) + \mathbf{Q}_i(k) \neq \mathbf{0}$ is *active*. An example of a task system with two chains is shown in Fig. 2.3-4.

Our model lacks full generality in the sense that task chains can neither be added nor removed from the set of chains under consideration. As will be seen, it is easy to account for the arrival and departure of new chains by

	C_1			C_2	
	q_1	r_1		q_2	r_2
$T_1(1)$	$(0, 1, 2, 0)$	$(0, 0, 2, 0)$	$T_2(1)$	$(2, 0, 2, 2)$	$(0, 0, 0, 2)$
$T_1(2)$	$(1, 0, 0, 1)$	$(0, 0, 0, 1)$	$T_2(2)$	$(1, 0, 1, 0)$	$(3, 0, 3, 0)$
$T_1(3)$	$(0, 0, 2, 0)$	$(1, 1, 2, 0)$			

$$\text{System:} \quad \mathbf{R} = (R_1, R_2, R_3, R_4), \quad \mathbf{w} = (3, 3, 3, 3)$$

Execution sequence	α	$\overline{T}_1(1)$	$\underline{T}_1(1)$	$\overline{T}_2(1)$	$\underline{T}_2(1)$	$\overline{T}_2(2)$	$\underline{T}_2(2)$
$P(k)$:	0000 0000	0120 0000	0100 0000	0100 0000	0100 2022	0100 2020	0100 3030	0100 0000
$Q(k)$:	0120 2022	0000 2022	1001 2022	1001 0000	1001 1010	1001 0000	1001 0000

	$\overline{T}_1(2)$	$\underline{T}_1(2)$	$\overline{T}_1(3)$	$\underline{T}_1(3)$
	1101 0000	1100 0000	1120 0000	0000 0000
	0000 0000	0020 0000	0000 0000	0000 0000

Completion

Fig. 2.3-4 Example for $C = C_1 \| C_2$.

adding or deleting rows from the matrices P and Q. In particular, when a new chain C_{n+1} is added to the set of active chains, the row $\mathbf{P}_{n+1} = \mathbf{0}$ is appended to matrix P and the row $\mathbf{Q}_{n+1} = \mathbf{q}_{n+1}(1)$ is appended to matrix Q. Since this is a straightforward extension to our development and does not affect in any essential way our definitions and results, we shall not consider it further.

An initiation transition (one corresponding to a task initiation) is said to be *allowable* if the resources requested of each type R_j do not exceed the amount of R_j available at the time. Define the *available resource vector* $\mathbf{v}(k) = (v_1(k), \ldots, v_m(k))$ in which

$$v_j(k) = w_j - \sum_{i=1}^{n} P_{ij}(k), \quad 1 \le j \le m$$

Assuming that the initiation of $T_i(l)$ is the next event pending in chain C_i, the state transition corresponding to the event $a_{k+1} = \bar{T}_i(l)$ is allowable if $\mathbf{Q}_i(k) \le \mathbf{v}(k)$†. An execution sequence is *valid* if all its initiation transitions are allowable. That valid execution sequences always exist is demonstrated as follows. Recall that no chain may ever request resources in excess of the system's capacity; accordingly, it is possible to execute the chains to completion in an arbitrary but serial order (e.g., C_1 then C_2 then C_3, etc.) and so define a valid execution sequence. Consequently, there are at least $n!$ valid execution sequences for each task system consisting of n independent chains.

There are two definitions central to the treatment of the deadlock problem; the first is useful in connection with deadlock detection, and the second in connection with deadlock avoidance.

Definition 2.3

Let $C = C_1 \| C_2 \| \cdots \| C_n$, where each C_i ($1 \le i \le n$) is a chain. Let $\alpha = a_1 \ldots a_k$ be a partial execution sequence of C and let $\sigma = s_0 s_1 \ldots s_k$ be the corresponding partial state sequence. Suppose that there exists a nonempty set D of chain indices such that for each i in D,

(2.3.3) $$\mathbf{Q}_i(k) \not\le \mathbf{v}(k) + \sum_{j \notin D} \mathbf{P}_j(k)$$

Then σ is said to be *deadlocked* (or, alternatively, s_k contains a deadlock). Also, each chain C_i for i in D is said to be deadlocked.

This definition has the following interpretation. Observe that (2.3.3) can hold only if for each i in D, $\mathbf{Q}_i(k) \ne \mathbf{0}$, which in turn can hold only if the next event pending in chain C_i is the initiation of some task $T_i(l)$; (2.3.3) asserts that the initiation transition $a_{k+1} = \bar{T}_i(l)$ is not allowable for all $i \in D$. Thus this definition states that a deadlock exists if there is a nonempty subset of the

---

†If $\mathbf{x} = (x_1, \ldots, x_m)$ and $\mathbf{y} = (y_1, \ldots, y_m)$, then $\mathbf{x} \le \mathbf{y}$ implies that $x_i \le y_i$ for each i; $\mathbf{x} < \mathbf{y}$ means that $\mathbf{x} \le \mathbf{y}$ and $x_i < y_i$ for at least one i.

active chains which cannot commence execution of their next task, *irrespective* of the future resource usage of the remaining active chains. Specifically, we can assume from (2.3.3) that, even if all chains not deadlocked release all the resources in their possession, there will still be insufficient resources for any one of the deadlocked chains to proceed. Since we have assumed that no chain ever requests more that the system's capacity in any resource, we note that a deadlock must involve at least two chains; i.e., D contains at least two chains if it is nonempty.

	C_1			C_2	
	q_1	r_1		q_2	r_2
$T_1(1)$	(0, 1, 2, 0)	(0, 0, 2, 0)	$T_2(1)$	(2, 0, 2, 2)	(0, 0, 0, 2)
$T_1(2)$	(1, 0, 0, 1)	(0, 0, 0, 1)	$T_2(2)$	(1, 0, 1, 0)	(3, 0, 3, 0)
$T_1(3)$	(0, 0, 2, 0)	(1, 1, 2, 0)			

System: $\mathbf{R} = (R_1 R_2 R_3 R_4)$, $\mathbf{w} = (3, 3, 3, 3)$

α	$\bar{T}_1(1)$	$\underline{T}_1(1)$	$\bar{T}_2(1)$	$\underline{T}_2(1)$	$\bar{T}_1(2)$	$\underline{T}_1(2)$
$P(k)$ 0000 / 0000	0120 / 0000	0100 / 0000	0100 / 2022	0100 / 2020	1101 / 2020	1100 / 2020
$Q(k)$ 0120 / 2022	0000 / 2022	1001 / 2022	1001 / 0000	1001 / 1010	0000 / 1010	0020 / 1010
s_0	s_1	s_2	s_3	s_4	s_5	s_6
$v(k)$ (3333)	(3213)	(3233)	(1211)	(1213)	(0212)	(0213)

Deadlock

Fig. 2.3-5 Example of deadlock.

A simple example of a deadlocked process is shown in Fig. 2.3-5 for the chains and system of the previous examples. It is easily verified that every initiation transition defined by the partial execution sequence

$$\alpha = \bar{T}_1(1)\underline{T}_1(1)\bar{T}_2(1)\underline{T}_2(1)\bar{T}_1(2)\underline{T}_1(2)$$

is valid. After the event $\underline{T}_1(2)$, both $\mathbf{Q}_1(k) \not\leqslant v(k)$ and $\mathbf{Q}_2(k) \not\leqslant v(k)$ so that $\bar{T}_1(3)$ and $\bar{T}_2(2)$ are not allowable with respect to $v(k)$. The interpretation of the deadlock is, of course, that neither C_1 nor C_2 can proceed beyond the final event in α unless resources are forcibly preempted from one of them.

Definition 2.4

Let $\sigma = s_0 s_1 \ldots s_k$ be the state sequence corresponding to the partial execution sequence $\alpha = a_1 \ldots a_k$. If there exists at least one valid, complete execution sequence having α as a prefix, then s_k is called a *safe* state; otherwise it is *unsafe*.

It is evident that a state can be proved safe only if the resource usage of chains is known in advance. The final (deadlocked) state of a deadlocked process is obviously unsafe, but a state may be unsafe without being deadlocked. This is illustrated by s_5 in Fig. 2.3-5; from this state no possible remaining execution sequence (satisfying precedence constraints) is the suffix of a valid complete execution sequence. Indeed, once the system gets into an unsafe state it must remain in unsafe states, and a deadlock is inevitable.

A number of graphical methods have been introduced as means of representing deadlocks and the resource states s_k[5, 6, 7]. Although the use of graphs is not essential for our purposes, they do help in visualizing and simplifying the properties of a formal resource allocation model. The simplest graphical representation defines a directed graph G_k as a set of m vertices corresponding to the resource types $R_1, \ldots, R_m$ and a set of edges defined as follows. G_k contains the edge (R_{j_1}, R_{j_2}) if and only if there exists a chain C_i such that $P_{ij_1}(k)$ and $Q_{ij_2}(k)$ are both nonzero; i.e., just after the kth event C_i holds resources of type R_{j_1} and is requesting resources of type R_{j_2}.

Now suppose that D is a set of deadlocked chains in s_k. Because of the deadlock, a chain C_{i_1} in D must require resources of some type R_{j_1} held by another deadlocked chain C_{i_2} in D. Similarly, C_{i_2} must require resources of some type R_{j_2} held by another chain C_{i_3} in D, which in turn requires resources of some type R_{j_3} held by C_{i_4} in D, and so forth. From the definition of G_k we can conclude

Proposition 2.1

If the state s_k contains a deadlock, then G_k contains a circuit, i.e., a directed loop or cycle of one or more vertices.

A circuit in G_k is not generally a sufficient condition for the existence of a deadlock, for chains represented in a circuit of G_k need not be controlling all the resources of a given type. For example, the chain C may be represented in a given circuit only because it requires a resource of type R_j held by some other chain represented in the circuit. However, if $w_j > 1$, then a currently unavailable resource of type R_j may be subsequently released by another chain not represented in the given circuit. Thus C need not be deadlocked in s_k. As a special case, however, it is clear that if a circuit in G_k consists of the vertices $R_{j_1}, R_{j_2}, \ldots, R_{j_n}$ and there is only one unit of each of these types ($w_{j_1} = w_{j_2} = \cdots = w_{j_n} = 1$), then a deadlock must exist.

2.3.2. Prevention

As stated earlier, deadlocks may be prevented if one or more of the necessary conditions (mutual exclusion, nonpreemption, and circular wait) cannot hold. The mutual exclusion condition cannot normally be denied because of the physical or logical properties of resources. The nonpreemption condition can be denied in certain special cases, as can the circular wait condition. We shall consider each below.

Suppose that all chains are constrained so that, in any partial execution sequence, $\mathbf{Q}_i(k) \neq \mathbf{0}$ implies that $\mathbf{P}_i(k) = \mathbf{0}$ for all k and all chains C_i. It follows that the right-hand side of (2.3.3) reduces to $\mathbf{w}$, the system capacity. By assumption, all task initiations are allowable with respect to $\mathbf{w}$, and so deadlocks are impossible under this constraint. This constraint denies the nonpreemption simply by requiring that each chain have no resources to preempt whenever it is requesting additional resources.

The constraint above will hold if, whenever a chain holding certain resources is being denied a further request, the chain is required to release its original resources and request them together with the additional ones. The general application of this technique would imply the untenable assumption that every resource is preemptible.

Another way to implement the above constraint is to grant each chain its maximum possible request at the outset. This has the disadvantage that resource utilization may suffer because certain resources allocated to a chain may remain idle for long periods.

A technique that is frequently applicable involves a constraint on resource usage that denies the circular wait condition implied by Proposition 2.1 [9]. This constraint takes the form of a linear ordering $\ll$ of resource types which has the following property. Assume for convenience that the resource types are indexed so that $R_1 \ll R_2 \ll \cdots \ll R_m$. Whenever a chain holds resources of type R_i and requests resources of type R_j, then $R_i \ll R_j$. We shall say that chains are restricted to an *ordered resource usage* whenever such a linear order exists.

Now suppose that there exists a circuit in graph G_k which contains the sequence of vertices $R_{j_1}, R_{j_2}, \ldots, R_{j_n}$. If the chains represented in G_k are restricted to an ordered resource usage, then (R_i, R_j) can be an edge of G_k only if $R_i \ll R_j$. Thus the given circuit implies that $R_{j_1} \ll R_{j_2} \ll \cdots \ll R_{j_n} \ll R_{j_1}$, and the transitivity of the linear ordering implies the following contradiction: $R_{j_i} \ll R_j$ and $R_j \ll R_{j_i}$ for all resource types R_{j_i} and R_j in the circuit. Hence we have

Proposition 2.2

No state sequence corresponding to the execution of a set of chains restricted to an ordered resource usage can be deadlocked.

As a means of deadlock prevention, ordered resource usage is particularly appropriate when chains require resources in some serial order, such as that required by an input-execute-output sequence of operations.

When the foregoing strategies for preventing deadlock are only partially applicable it is clearly possible to use a combination of them in a given system and also to implement them either by embodying the constraints in the design of the system or by insisting that all task systems including system components follow certain conventions in requesting resources.

2.3.3. Detection

The detection problem will be solved if we can devise an algorithm that uses the information contained in a state s_k to decide whether or not a deadlock exists. The simple algorithm below is based directly on Definition 2.3 and is designed to reveal a deadlock by simulating the execution of chains until a set remains for which the final value of the available resources is insufficient.

Algorithm D1

1. Initialize: $D \leftarrow \{1, 2, \ldots, n\}$ and $\mathbf{V} \leftarrow \mathbf{v}(k)$.
2. Search for a chain index i in D such that $\mathbf{Q}_i(k) \leq \mathbf{V}$. If none is found, terminate the algorithm.
3. $D \leftarrow D - \{i\}$; $\mathbf{V} \leftarrow \mathbf{V} + \mathbf{P}_i(k)$; go to step 2.

The important observation to make about Algorithm D1 is that the available resources vector $\mathbf{V}$ is always monotonically nondecreasing over the successive passes of the algorithm, irrespective of the sequence in which executable chains are completed (if in fact more than one sequence is valid). Thus any chain executable on pass i must be executable on pass j for any $j > i$. Conversely, since the final value of the available resource vector is insufficient for every chain in the (final) set D, it follows that this set is precisely the set of deadlocked chains. Note that the algorithm does not check to see whether entire chains can be completed but only whether one more task on each chain can be completed.

In the worst case, Algorithm D1 searches the entire set D at the ith pass, a set of $n - i + 1$ chains. Thus the running time of the algorithm is proportional to $m \sum_{i=1}^{n} (n - i + 1) = \Theta(m \cdot n^2)$.† By using a more elaborate representation for resource states, a detection algorithm can be designed whose running time is $\Theta(m \cdot n)$ [6].

The principle of this faster algorithm is as follows. Let the available resources vector $\mathbf{V} = (V_1, \ldots, V_m)$, the current request matrix $\mathbf{Q}$, and the current resource allocation matrix $\mathbf{P}$ be given. For each column j, mark entry Q_{ij} if $Q_{ij} \leq V_j$. If all the entries in row i are marked, it follows that $\mathbf{Q}_i \leq \mathbf{V}$ and the initiation of the next task in chain C_i is allowable with respect to $\mathbf{V}$. Assuming that C_i eventually completes, its current resource holdings ($\mathbf{P}_i$) will eventually be returned, so we can continue marking entries in $\mathbf{Q}$ with the

---

†The notation $\Theta(f(n))$, "of order $f(n)$," denotes a quantity whose magnitude is less than or equal to some constant times $|f(n)|$ for all n.

new available resources vector $\mathbf{V}' = \mathbf{V} + \mathbf{P}_i$. Since $Q_{ij} \leq V_j \leq V'_j$, all the entries previously marked remain marked. Continuing this process, we eventually mark all the entries of $\mathbf{Q}$, or there is some subset D of row indices for which at least one entry in these rows is unmarked. This implies that, for each j in D, the granting of $\mathbf{Q}_j$ is not allowable with respect to

$$\mathbf{V} + \sum_{i \notin D} \mathbf{P}_i$$

and that the chains whose indices are in D are deadlocked.

To streamline the marking procedure, we define a vector $\mathbf{x} = (x_1, \ldots, x_n)$ such that at any point in the marking procedure x_i is the number of unmarked entries in row i of $\mathbf{Q}$. Initially, $\mathbf{x} = (m, \ldots, m)$. Whenever Q_{ij} is marked, we reduce x_i by 1, and if $x_i = 0$, we add $\mathbf{P}_i$ to $\mathbf{V}$. To improve the procedure further, we need to make the search for an unmarked $Q_{ij} \leq V_j$ in column j more efficient. To do this, we arrange the entries in column j in the form of a queue

$$E_j = (Q_{i_1 j}, Q_{i_2 j}, \ldots, Q_{i_n j})$$

such that $Q_{i_1 j} \leq Q_{i_2 j} \leq \cdots \leq Q_{i_n j}$. The search procedure in column j will consist of inspecting the entry at the head of E_j, Q_{hj}, to see whether $Q_{hj} \leq V_j$. If so, we decrease x_h by 1 and delete Q_{hj} from E_j. Evidently, the running time of this algorithm is proportional to the time required to empty the queues $E_1, \ldots, E_m$, which is $\Theta(mn)$. A more formal specification of this algorithm is given below. For convenience we define for any string $\omega = z_1 z_2 \ldots z_r$, $\mathbf{head}(\omega) = z_1$ and $\mathbf{tail}(\omega) = z_2 \ldots z_r$.

Algorithm D2

> $D \longleftarrow \{1, 2, \ldots, n\}$; $\mathbf{V} \longleftarrow \mathbf{v}(k)$; $\mathbf{x} \longleftarrow (m, \ldots, m)$; $done \longleftarrow$ **false**;
> **while not** $done$ **do**
> $\quad done \longleftarrow$ **true**;
> $\quad$ **for** $j = 1, 2, \ldots, m$ **do**
> $\quad\quad$ **while** E_j nonempty **and** $\mathbf{head}(E_j) \leq V_j$ **do**
> $\quad\quad\quad h \longleftarrow$ index of chain whose request is in $\mathbf{head}(E_j)$
> $\quad\quad\quad E_j \longleftarrow \mathbf{tail}(E_j)$
> $\quad\quad\quad x_h \longleftarrow x_h - 1$
> $\quad\quad\quad$ **if** $x_h = 0$, **then** $\{\mathbf{V} \longleftarrow \mathbf{V} + \mathbf{P}_h(k)$; $D \longleftarrow D - \{h\}$;
> $\quad\quad\quad\quad done \longleftarrow$ **false**$\}$

When Algorithm D2 stops, the set D (if nonempty) will contain the indices of the deadlocked chains. In practice, it is not necessary to delete entries from the various queues E_j; instead, one needs to maintain a series of pointers into the lists E_j, advancing them as the search proceeds.

It should be noted that, although the time to execute Algorithm D2 when $E_1, \ldots, E_m$ are given is proportional to mn, there is a hidden cost of maintaining $E_1, \ldots, E_m$ in order of increasing demand. In practice, the request matrix need not be retained as a separate entity when these sorted queues are maintained. As compensation for the additional complexity of Algorithm D2, the sorted request queues have the additional important advantage of providing a simple means for determining which tasks can be activated whenever resources are released and made available to waiting chains. In particular, it is only necessary to scan the queues corresponding to the resources which have been made available and to reduce the counts x_i for all those chains C_i whose requests are now satisfiable. Any chain whose count has been reduced to zero can now have its next task initiated.

Given a deadlock detection mechanism, perhaps the simplest approach to recover from a deadlock situation would involve aborting each of the deadlocked chains or, less drastically, aborting them in some sequence until sufficient resources become free to remove deadlocks in the set of remaining chains. Obviously, we could also design an algorithm that searches for a minimal set of chains which, if aborted, would remove the deadlock. A more general technique has been devised [8] which assigns a fixed cost c_j to the removal (forced preemption) of a unit of resource of type R_j from a deadlocked task which is being aborted; the recovery algorithm searches for a minimum cost set of tasks to abort.

2.3.4. Avoidance

By our definition of avoidance techniques, advance information is required on the resource usage of chains. This information is in the form of a specification of the request and release vectors $\mathbf{q}_i(l)$ and $\mathbf{r}_i(l)$ of each task step $T_i(l)$.

The function of an algorithm for avoiding deadlocks is controlling the sequence of events so that the system state is safe at all times (see Definition 2.4). Such algorithms, therefore, must be called each time a chain requests or releases resources. Suppose that the state $s_k = [P(k), Q(k)]$ is known to be safe and that the avoidance algorithm is trying to determine whether the transition $s_k \longrightarrow s_{k+1}$ is both allowable and safe. Two cases are possible, viz., $a_{k+1} = T_i(l)$ or $a_{k+1} = \bar{T}_i(l)$ for some i and l. In the first case, the state s_{k+1} is defined by

$$\mathbf{P}_i(k+1) = \mathbf{P}_i(k) - \mathbf{r}_i(l) \qquad \mathbf{Q}_i(k+1) = \mathbf{q}_i(l+1), \quad l < p_i$$
$$\mathbf{P}_h(k+1) = \mathbf{P}_h(k) \qquad \mathbf{Q}_h(k+1) = \mathbf{Q}_h(k), \qquad h \neq i$$
$$\mathbf{v}(k+1) = \mathbf{v}(k) + \mathbf{r}_i(l)$$

State s_{k+1} is safe since $\mathbf{v}(k) \leq \mathbf{v}(k+1)$ and s_k was safe. Even though a termination transition is both allowable and safe, the avoidance algorithm has an important role to play here such that requests $q_j(T)$ ($j \neq i$) granted in β have corresponding releases $r_j(T) \geq q_j(T)$, since the increase in available resources may render one or more initiation transitions allowable where they were not so before.

In the second case, the transition into s_{k+1} is allowable if $\mathbf{q}_i(l) \leq \mathbf{v}(k)$, and s_{k+1} is defined by

$$\begin{aligned}
\mathbf{P}_i(k+1) &= \mathbf{P}_i(k) + \mathbf{Q}_i(k) & \mathbf{Q}_i(k+1) &= \mathbf{0} \\
\mathbf{P}_h(k+1) &= \mathbf{P}_h(k) & \mathbf{Q}_h(k+1) &= \mathbf{Q}_h(k), \quad h \neq i \\
\mathbf{v}(k+1) &= \mathbf{v}(k) - \mathbf{Q}_i(k)
\end{aligned}$$

Even though this transition into s_{k+1} may be allowable, s_{k+1} may not be safe. Thus the avoidance algorithm must incorporate some procedure for testing the safeness of a state entered by an initiation transition.

In general, a procedure for settling the safeness question amounts to an enumerative search of all possible sequences of remaining events that might occur for the active chains. Such sequences are called *completion* sequences. The objective of the search procedure is a completion sequence having only allowable initiation transitions, assuming that $\mathbf{v}(k+1)$ provides the initially available resources.

A completion sequence is any suffix of an execution sequence. If $a_1 \ldots a_k a_{k+1} \ldots a_{2r}$ ($r = p_1 + \cdots + p_n$) is an execution sequence of the parallel combination of chains $C_1, \ldots, C_n$, then $a_{k+1} \ldots a_{2r}$ is a completion sequence for state s_k. A partial completion sequence is any prefix of a completion sequence. A partial completion sequence is *valid* if every initiation transition in it is allowable. The following results are useful when devising efficient search procedures for valid completion sequences.

Proposition 2.3

Suppose that s_k and all allocations not for C_i in β are safe and that $a_{k+1} = \overline{T}(l)$ is allowable. If $\beta \underline{T}_i(p_i)$ is a valid partial completion sequence for s_{k+1}, then s_{k+1} is safe.

To verify this, suppose that s_{k+1} is not safe. Since s_k is safe, granting the request $\mathbf{q}_i(l)$ must inevitably lead to a deadlock in which C_i is one of the deadlocked chains. The partial completion sequence $\beta \underline{T}_i(p_i)$ shows, however, that C_i is not deadlocked.

Under the assumptions of Proposition 2.3, if at any point in developing a trial completion sequence for s_{k+1} we discover that the last task of chain C_i can be completed, we may terminate the algorithm immediately with the decision that s_{k+1} is safe. A related result can be given which states that if for any state s_k the chains holding resources can be completed without deadlock, then s_k is safe. Clearly, after completing these chains the remaining chains can always be executed in an arbitrary (serial) order. We state this result in the form of

Proposition 2.4

Let $A = \{C_i \mid \mathbf{P}_i(k) > \mathbf{0}\}$ be the set of chains holding resources according to s_k. If β is a valid partial completion sequence containing all termination events $\underline{T}_i(p_i)$ for C_i in A, then s_k is safe. (Therefore the search for valid completion sequences can be restricted to events in chains holding resources.)

Further improvements in search times can be provided by the following result [5].

Proposition 2.5

Let s_k be a safe state. Let β be a valid partial completion sequence for s_k and suppose that for all tasks $T_i(l)$ initiated in β we have $\mathbf{q}_i(l) \leq \mathbf{r}_i(l)$. Then β is the prefix of a valid completion sequence.

Proof. Assuming that s_k is safe, there exists a valid completion sequence θ. Let β' be formed by suffixing to β (in any order) all termination events in θ for tasks initiated but not terminated in β. Since β is valid and since termination events are always allowable, β' must also be valid. Let β'' be the subsequence of θ containing all those events not contained in β'. We claim that $\theta' = \beta'\beta''$ is a valid completion sequence (obviously containing β as a prefix). Since β' is known to be valid, it remains to verify that β'' is valid.

Let $\bar{T}$ be a task initiation in β''. The event $\bar{T}$ is preceded in θ' by all those events preceding $\bar{T}$ in θ. In general, it will also be preceded in θ' by other task initiations and terminations which succeed $\bar{T}$ in θ. But by definition of β', for each such initiation $\bar{T}'_i$ there must exist a succeeding termination event $\underline{T}'_i$ in β' which releases at least as many resources as $\bar{T}'_i$ acquired; i.e., $\mathbf{q}'_i \leq \mathbf{r}'_i$ must hold for the request/release vectors of T'. Note that any other task terminations preceding $\bar{T}$ in θ' but not θ can only increase the resources available to $\bar{T}$ in θ'. Hence the amount of resources available prior to $\bar{T}$ in θ' must be at least as great as the amount prior to $\bar{T}$ in θ. ∎

The implication of this result is easily described. When searching for a valid completion sequence for s_k, one tries to find a maximal length valid partial completion sequence β containing only task initiations for which the corresponding terminations release at least as many resources as the initiations acquire. In particular, if a completion sequence is found not to be valid, there is no need to back up the search procedure to try other completion sequences not having β as a prefix.

Despite the techniques we have outlined for improving the search for completion sequences, we are unable to design algorithms which are not essentially enumerative [7] (e.g., those whose execution time can be expressed as a polynomial in the number of events in a completion sequence, rather than being exponential in this number). We shall not consider such algorithms further because, so far, we have been dealing with a model for avoiding dead-locks which assumes complete, prior information on resource usage. In practice, this will not generally be a feasible assumption; not only is it a potentially heavy burden on programmers, but it is quite impossible in those cases when resource usage is not known until some time after a computation has begun (e.g., when resource usage is data-dependent). Thus a model which assumes that only the maximum (or an upper bound on) resource usage is assumed known beforehand is more practical. We call this the *MRU* (maximum resource usage) *system* [10].

In a formal treatment of the MRU system we examine deadlock avoidance under the assumption that the only prior information associated with each chain C_i is the vector $\mathbf{M}_i = (M_{i1}, \ldots, M_{im})$ in which M_{ij} is the maximum amount of R_j that C_i will ever require. In terms of C_i's tasks, $\mathbf{M}_i$ is given by

$$M_{ij} = \max_{1 \le l \le p_i} \{q_{ij}(l) + \sum_{h=1}^{l-1} (q_{ij}(h) - r_{ij}(h))\}$$

Since we now have only partial information on resource usage, we must consider a more restrictive notion of safe state in order to guarantee avoidance of deadlocks. In particular, consideration must be given to the fact that, with the MRU system, the task composition of chains is not known until after execution.

With this in mind consider the avoidance problem in the MRU system: The system is in state s_k and a request in $Q(k)$ is being examined to determine whether it can be granted safely. As before, if the request were granted, then the new state s_{k+1} would differ from s_k only in $\mathbf{Q}_i(k+1) = \mathbf{0}$ and $\mathbf{P}_i(k+1) = \mathbf{P}_i(k) + \mathbf{Q}_i(k)$. Given that s_k is such that deadlock can be avoided, we want to determine those conditions under which the (hypothetical) new state s_{k+1} would also have this property so that we can indeed grant the request being examined.

This question must be resolved under the constraint that we know only the maximum requirements $\mathbf{M}_i$. Thus, to guarantee absolutely that deadlock can be avoided according to s_{k+1} we must assume the worst possible resource requirements for whatever tasks remain in the active chains. The worst case will be achieved if the remainder of each active chain C_i releases none of the resources allocated in s_{k+1} [i.e., in $\mathbf{P}_i(k+1)$] but subsequently requires its maximum allocation prior to completion. Now for C_i to acquire its maximum demand it must request $\mathbf{M}_i - \mathbf{P}_i(k+1)$ additional resources. Thus the worst case, on which the deadlock avoidance decision must be founded, can be modeled by the following simple problem. Let the active chains in s_{k+1} be denoted $C_{i_j}, j = 1, \ldots, a$. With an initial resources vector $\mathbf{v}(k+1)$ find a valid execution sequence of (independent) tasks $T'_1, \ldots, T'_a$, where the request and release vectors for the T'_j are given by

$$(2.3.4) \qquad \begin{aligned} \mathbf{q}'_j &= \mathbf{M}_{i_j} - \mathbf{P}_{i_j}(k+1) \\ \mathbf{r}'_j &= \mathbf{M}_{i_j} \end{aligned} \qquad (1 \leq j \leq a)$$

Evidently, the task T'_j models the remainder of chain C_{i_j}. C_{i_j} will generally have more than one remaining task, according to our definition of task decomposition. But for our worst-case assumption no subsequent requests can be made, since the maximum $\mathbf{M}_{i_j}$ is already held and none are released (until the completion of C_{i_j}). Hence the assumption of only a single remaining task is consistent with our requirement that a new task can appear only if resources are released by a chain, new resources requested, or both.

From Definition 2.3 and Algorithms D1 and D2 we have the following result.

Proposition 2.6

Given the state s_{k+1}, define for $1 \leq i \leq n$

$$\begin{aligned} \mathbf{Q}'_i(k+1) &= \mathbf{M}_i - \mathbf{P}_i(k+1) \qquad \text{if } \mathbf{P}_i(k+1) + \mathbf{Q}_i(k+1) > \mathbf{0} \\ &= \mathbf{0} \qquad\qquad\qquad\qquad \text{otherwise} \end{aligned}$$

and take $Q'(k+1)$ to be the matrix with rows $\mathbf{Q}'_i(k+1)$. The state s_{k+1} is safe according to Definition 2.4 if the state $[P(k+1), Q'(k+1)]$ does not contain a deadlock.

According to our earlier discussion and the properties of Algorithm D1 (and D2 if states are appropriately structured), the state $[P(k+1), Q'(k+1)]$ will have a deadlock if and only if we cannot find a valid execution sequence of the tasks $T'_1, \ldots, T'_a$ defined above by (2.3.4). It follows that since the tasks T'_j were constructed to model the worst case, we have a sufficient condition for a safe state. However, with only partial information the price we must pay is that the condition is not a necessary one. Thus we shall in general be rejecting (postponing) requests because the worst case would create a deadlock, whereas in reality deadlock need not be inevitable in granting the given request.

On the other hand, we have gained considerably in the efficiency (complexity) of the deadlock avoidance procedure. In particular, from Proposition 2.6 we may avoid deadlocks by use of Algorithm D2, an algorithm whose running time is linearly related to n.

2.4. MUTUAL EXCLUSION

2.4.1. Introduction

The discussion in this and the next section concerns programming tools for implementing process control and synchronization. Tasks may interact in two ways: indirectly, by competing for the same resources, and directly, by sending or waiting for messages. When independent tasks are in execution, the responsibility for controlling their progress may rest with an underlying system, as we have just seen in the deadlock problem. However, when tasks may interact directly, mechanisms for controlling their progress must appear explicitly in their programming. The tools that we shall discuss for mutual exclusion and synchronization are of the latter type†.

The mutual exclusion, or arbitration, problem concerns the control of a reusable resource‡ so that it is never in use by more than one task at a time. Examples of such a resource include a processor, a page of memory, a line-oriented input/output device, or even a data base. From the point of view of the correct operation of tasks, it is necessary that the resource be granted to at most one task at a time since tasks modify the state of the resource during their use of it; but since they initialize the state of the resource before using it, the order in which they use it is immaterial. Therefore any solution to the mutual exclusion problem which imposes prior constraints on the order in which tasks must use the resource is undesirable. Moreover, it may not be possible to tell a priori which tasks will want to use a given resource or how many units of a given resource type will be available when tasks request it, in which case imposing prior precedence constraints among tasks may not be done in a way that assures efficient utilization of resources.

Implementing mutually exclusive use of resources is not really a problem if resource usage is under the centralized control of an operating system, for then the only questions from the viewpoint of task design are those concerning the conventions used by tasks for signaling the operating system that specific resources are requested or released. We shall say more about such conventions later; for the present we shall assume that mutual exclusion must be implemented by the tasks themselves, using globally accessible variables for intertask communication. Tasks (or more properly segments of code) to be executed mutually exclusively are called *critical sections* in the literature.

The problem of finding a desirable solution to the mutual exclusion problem is decidedly nontrivial as a result of possible race conditions and the varying (finite but nonzero) speeds of tasks executing on different processors. Thus, for example, one must be concerned with the possibility that two tasks T_1 and T_2 on different processors may recognize and act on the availability of a desired resource R before either has had sufficient opportunity to block the other from using the resource. This would be the case, for instance, if, in an

---

†Wirth [11] proposes two kinds of programming language features for expressing concurrency: In addition to those dealing with direct interactions among existing tasks, he suggests those for declaring that certain pieces of code may potentially be in execution by distinct tasks. Linguistic mechanisms of this type are intended primarily to provide compilers or operating systems with more flexibility in making resource allocation decisions.

‡One whose internal state is modified during use but can be initialized on assignment to another task.

attempt to solve the problem, we defined a single, global variable to be used by T_1 and T_2 to signal each other the availability of R. After T_1 has tested the variable and found R available, T_2 may do the same thing before T_1 gets a chance to change the variable to a value indicating that R is in use. Note that the arbitration of references to main memory for such global variables is an example of mutual exclusion at the hardware level [12]; although several requests may arrive together, the hardware services them in some order, one at a time.

In our study of the mutual exclusion problem we shall make the simplifying assumption that there exists only one resource R which is to be used by at most one task at a time. A more general treatment allowing for several resources can be easily obtained by extending the analysis below.

It is a simple matter to formalize mutual exclusion in terms of the notation developed earlier.

Definition 2.5

Let $\alpha = a_1 a_2 \ldots a_k$ be a partial execution sequence of the task system $C = (3, <)$. Task T is said to be *active* after α if $a_i = \bar{T}$ for some $i \leq k$ and $a_j \neq \underline{T}$ for all j, $i < j \leq k$. Tasks T and T' are *mutually excluded* in α if and only if at most one of T and T' is active after every prefix of α.

For obvious reasons we should like the following additional condition to be satisfied by our implementation of mutual exclusion; it complicates our problem considerably and it is not so easily formalized. Quite simply, the condition is that no individual task requesting the use of R can be blocked indefinitely by other tasks requesting or using R. In other words, under no circumstances should our solution become vacuous in the sense that mutual exclusion is achieved by completely blocking the use of R from any one or more of the tasks requiring it. For example, the solution must avoid those situations in which tasks hang-up in "after-you, after-you" loops. Since this is related to the concept of safeness introduced in the previous section on deadlocks, we shall call a solution *safe* if it avoids indefinite blocking.

Since we are dealing with finite systems and execution sequences, the satisfaction of this condition will be straightforward except when we are considering cyclic task systems. In this case, we adopt the following interpretation of "blocked indefinitely." Consider the execution sequences of the cyclic system

$$(2.4.1) \qquad\qquad C = C_1^{m_1} || C_2^{m_2} || \cdots || C_k^{m_k}$$

and let n_i $(1 \leq i \leq k)$ denote the number of tasks in C_i. Then we shall regard the absence of indefinite blocking (the safe condition) as meaning that the time a task in any system C_i spends waiting for the use of R is bounded by a function only of the numbers n_i $(1 \leq i \leq k)$. (By waiting time we mean the number of events intervening in an execution sequence between a termination and subsequent initiation of a cyclically executing task.) For a given specification of the C_is this means in particular that no matter how large the m_is, the time any task is blocked is less than some fixed constant.

Before treating the general problem we shall examine simplified techniques for implementing mutual exclusion when certain restrictive assumptions can be made. This treatment will be informal and will help motivate the more subtle aspects of the general problem.

2.4.2. Primitives for Implementing Mutual Exclusion

The design of tasks implementing mutual exclusion can be simplified considerably if we can assume that certain operations with the global variables are indivisible; i.e., at most one of these can be in execution at any point in time, and one must complete before another begins. As an illustration we shall present a mechanism devised by Knuth [13] for implementing mutual exclusion. The operations to be assumed indivisible are significantly more elaborate than the single reads and writes to storage that constitute the only indivisible operations on global variables in the general problem. Thus instead of completely solving a mutual exclusion problem we are, to a large extent, passing it on to the hardware designer, who is responsible for implementing the mutual exclusion of the necessary indivisible operations.

Consider a task system C comprising the tasks $T_1, \ldots, T_n$, and suppose that at least two of these tasks are to be mutually excluded because they require the use of resource R. We shall modify C so that the mutual exclusion of these tasks is guaranteed. (Clearly, it is guaranteed already if no two of the tasks using R are independent.) In particular, for each task T_i using R we introduce new tasks S_i and U_i, which immediately precede and follow T_i, respectively. The modification is suggested by Fig. 2.4-1. Although the T_i will remain uninterpreted (except for their known use of R), the S_i and U_i will be

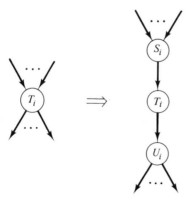

Fig. 2.4-1 Introduction of auxiliary tasks S_i and U_i.

completely specified. This specification of S_i and U_i (and the global variables they use) will effectively constitute the solution to the mutual exclusion problem.

We shall design task S_i so that it will terminate (thereby enabling T_i to initiate) if and only if each of the other S_js is prohibited from terminating. The principal function of U_i is to signal the other tasks that T_i's use of R is done. Thus by manipulating the global variables the task S_i is to control the events following S_i in an execution sequence so that subsequences of the form $\dots S_i \dots S_j \dots \bar{U}_i \dots$ are disallowed for all j. Also included in S_i and U_i will be a mechanism for queueing requests for the use of R. For future reference we shall let C' denote the system C augmented by the tasks S_i and U_i, for each T_i using R.

$$S_i: \left\{ \begin{array}{ll} i1: & Q[p] \leftarrow i; \, p \leftarrow i; \\ \\ i2: & \text{if } Q[0] \neq i \text{ then go to } i2; \end{array} \right.$$

$$U_i: \qquad i3: \quad \begin{array}{l} \text{if } p \neq i \text{ then } Q[0] \leftarrow Q[i] \\ \qquad \text{else} \{ p \leftarrow 0; \; Q[0] \leftarrow 0 \} \end{array}$$

Fig. 2.4-2　Auxiliary task programming.

The specifications for S_i and U_i are given in Fig. 2.4-2, where the global variables are the $(n + 1)$-element integer array $Q[0], \dots, Q[n]$ and the integer variable p. The purpose of the array Q is to store in FIFO (first-in-first-out) order the list of tasks waiting to use R. This is done by storing the index of the task at the head of the queue, in $Q[0]$, and if S_i is waiting, storing the index of the task following S_i in the queue in $Q[i]$. Thus the queue is stored as a simple linked list in Q. The integer p is the index of the tail task of the queue, i.e., that waiting task which was last to enter the queue. The condition $p = 0$ and $Q[0] = 0$ signifies an empty queue and will be assumed as the initial condition.

The task S_i signals the intent of T_i to use R, enters T_i into the queue Q, and then waits at step $i2$ until T_i becomes the head of the queue. The task U_i removes T_i from the queue and sets the next task to execute at the head of the queue; if T_i was the last task in the queue ($p = i$ when U_i executes), then the variables p and $Q[0]$ are reset to signal an empty queue.

The description thus far has not taken into account the possible interference between tasks S_i and S_j or S_i and U_j executing concurrently. Noninterference can be assured by stipulating that the appropriate steps in S_i and U_i are in fact indivisible. However, let us first consider the nature of the problems making these assumptions necessary.

Suppose that $p = Q[0] = 0$ and that S_j commences execution. Suppose that, after S_j executes $Q[p] \leftarrow j$ but before it sets $p = j$ in step $j1$, task S_k comes along and succeeds in executing (at high speed) both assignments in step $k1$. Clearly, T_k can execute immediately, but the request for T_j has been "lost," since $Q[0]$ was overwritten by S_k. This possibility of interference is eliminated if we assume that step $i1$ is indivisible so that only one S_i at a time can be executing in step $i1$. It is natural to express such an operation in the form of a *primitive*, **enqueue**(i), where i is the task-index parameter supplied by the task S_i invoking the primitive. The word "primitive" calls attention to the fact that the corresponding operation is implemented at a lower level not accessible to the task programmer. (In general, however, a primitive is not to be assumed indivisible unless this property is explicitly stated, as above.)

Assuming that the indivisible primitive **enqueue**(i) is adopted, we can still have problems arising from the task U_i. For example, suppose that p has been tested by U_i in step $i3$ and found to be equal to i. Before p and $Q[0]$ are reset to zero by U_i, S_k comes along and executes the primitive **enqueue**(k); but before step $k2$ is executed, U_i succeeds in resetting p and $Q[0]$. Evidently, T_k will never execute. Proceeding as before we can eliminate interference by assuming that step $i3$ constitutes an indivisible primitive, say **remove**(i), which is mutually excluded from the primitive **enqueue**(j) for any j. In fact, with these primitives for steps $i1$ and $i3$ it is readily verified that we have a safe solution to the mutual exclusion problem.†

Some comments on resource utilization are appropriate at this point. In the procedure we have described, waiting tasks (S_i) occupy processors and thus can cause inefficient processor utilization in systems where a relatively large number of tasks compete for R. This has been called "the busy form of waiting"; not only are processors tied up but memory interference results from repeated accesses to common variables. In a system of autonomous computers not subject to central control, we would want the loop in step $i2$ to be incorporated in the interrupt systems of the individual computers, thus enabling these computers to reallocate their CPU for productive use during periods of waiting for R.

For multiprocessor systems the busy form of waiting is but one instance of the basic argument for a centralized control of resources by an operating system. With the appropriate operating system the tasks S_i and U_i amount to no more than supervisor calls; the system carries out the functions of Fig. 2.4-2 along with processor reallocation and general resource scheduling functions.

2.4.3. Solution of the General Problem

In the next section on synchronization problems, we shall introduce different primitives that can be adapted to the functions of **enqueue**(i) and **remove**(i). It should also be noted that the design of primitives can be modified

---

†Our arguments regarding program properties (e.g., those of S_i and U_i) will be largely informal in this section and the next. Techniques can be developed for formalizing these arguments [14, 15]; however, the exclusion of a more rigorous approach is justified by the additional mechanism it would require and by the convincing nature of the informal discussion.

to implement a priority sequencing rule other than the FIFO rule. The remainder of this section will be devoted to the implementation of mutual exclusion when a centralized control of resources is not feasible and the only indivisible operations with global variables are single reads and writes to storage.

The problem solution will be expressed as before: We shall design the tasks S_i and U_i to implement the mutual exclusion. S_i will terminate if and only if all other active S_js are prohibited from terminating. The principal difficulty of the design arises from our requirement of a safe solution guaranteeing no indefinite blocking.

We define the global variables to consist of an integer array $c[1:n]$ (the "control") and an integer r. Initially, $c[i] = 0$ for all i. The design of the tasks S_i and U_i is shown in Fig. 2.4-3. The vector c contains a 1 in the ith position only if S_i is active. If a task T_i is using R, then $r = i$ and $c[i] = 2$. If no T_i is using R, then $r = j + 1$ (or 1 if $j = n$), where T_j was the last task to use R.

$$
S_i \left\{
\begin{array}{l}
\text{1. } c[i] \leftarrow 1 \\[4pt]
\text{2. for } j = r \text{ step 1 until } n, \text{ 1 step 1 until } n \text{ do} \\
\quad \text{if } j = i \text{ then go to 3 else if } c[j] \neq 0 \text{ then go to 2} \\[4pt]
\text{3. } c[i] \leftarrow 2 \\[4pt]
\text{4. for } j = 1 \text{ step 1 until } n \text{ do} \\
\quad \text{if } (j \neq i) \text{ and } (c[j] = 2) \text{ then go to 1} \\[4pt]
\text{5. } r \leftarrow i
\end{array}
\right.
$$

$T_i \qquad \text{6. } \{\text{Use of } R\}$

$$
U_i \left\{
\begin{array}{l}
\text{7. } r \leftarrow \text{if } i = n \text{ then 1 else } i + 1 \\[4pt]
\text{8. } c[i] \leftarrow 0
\end{array}
\right.
$$

Fig. 2.4-3   Programming of auxiliary tasks for T_i.

In the proof that the algorithms in Fig. 2.4-3 provide a safe solution we suppress notation and concentrate on showing that S_i and U_i cooperate (communicate) in the desired fashion. Following the proof an example is described in detail which illustrates fully the subtleties involved in producing a safe solution. Although it is not necessary in following the proof, if may be helpful to study this example while going through the latter part of the proof. The arguments parallel those of Dijkstra [16] and Knuth [13] and it seems appropriate to present the result in the form of

Theorem 2.4

Consider task systems requiring a resource R which is to be used by at most one task at a time. Suppose that the tasks S_i and U_i have been introduced as above. The programs defined for S_i and U_i in Fig. 2.4-3 constitute a safe solution to the mutual exclusion problem.

Proof. In a given system C let $T_1, \ldots, T_n$ be independent tasks requiring R. The first thing to show is that at most one of the tasks $T_1, \ldots, T_n$ can be active at a time. This follows directly from the fact that a task S_i sets $c[i] = 2$ in step 3 before testing the other elements of c in step 4. Thus, if S_i reaches step 5 at the same time $c[j] = 2$ for any $j \neq i$, it must be true that S_i completed step 3 before S_j, and hence S_j will encounter $c[i] = 2$ and return to step 1. Consequently, at most one task T_i can be active at a time.

It is implied above that two or more tasks can in fact be executing concurrently in steps 3 and 4. To see this, suppose that S_i commences execution of step 2. For the given value of r let $(r, r+1, \ldots, r-1)$ denote the cyclic permutation of $(1, 2, \ldots, n)$ with r in the first position. At step 2, S_i inspects $c[r], c[r+1], \ldots, c[i-1]$ according to the ordering $(r, r+1, \ldots, r-1)$ and it reaches step 3 if and only if each of these c values was zero at the moment it was tested. Thus a task S_k may reach step 3 together with S_i if k precedes i in the ordering $(r, r+1, \ldots, r-1)$ but S_k did not complete step 1 until after S_i found $c[k] = 0$.

To show safeness, we must show that no single task can cycle endlessly through steps 1–4. First we show that no set of two or more tasks can be doing this. Suppose that $S_{i_1}, \ldots, S_{i_k}$ are found to be cycling within steps 1–4. Without loss of generality we may suppose that i_1 precedes $i_2 \cdots$ precedes i_k in the ordering $(r, r+1, \ldots, r-1)$. After a finite time interval each of the S_{i_j}s must execute step 2. According to the operation of step 2, S_{i_j} tests the c-values in the order specified by $(r, r+1, \ldots, r-1)$; it follows that every task except S_{i_1} must hang-up in step 2. Since the c values for tasks other than the S_{i_j} are zero, S_{i_1} eventually reaches step 5 and T_{i_1} initiates. It follows that a *set* of two or more tasks can never be blocked indefinitely from using R. We use this to show that no specific task can be blocked from using R.

Let us suppose that S_i is blocked indefinitely from using R. Since no set of two or more tasks can ever be blocked indefinitely, there must exist another task, say S_k, which is initiating arbitrarily often. Now, S_k can pass step 2 arbitrarily often while $c[i] \neq 0$ only if some task has set r in such a way that k precedes i in $(r, r+1, \ldots, r-1)$. The task which sets r must be distinct from S_k, for otherwise S_k would set $r = k+1$ (or 1 if $k = n$) on its last visit to step 7 and would search at step 2 according to an ordering in which i precedes k. This shows that there must exist a task S_l which initiates arbitrarily often and for which l precedes k and follows i in $(r, r+1, \ldots, r-1)$. However, if we suppose, as we may, that k is the first successor of i with this property, we have a contradiction. ∎

Using the preceding argument, further insight into the possible race conditions of the mutual exclusion problem is provided by the following general example, which shows how long the waiting time of a task can be in unfavorable circumstances. To simplify the explanation let us say that a task *takes a turn* (using R) whenever control passes from step 5 through step 8 of Fig.

2.4-3. Also, we shall say that a task is *at position i* if it has just completed step i in Fig. 2.4-3. Over every time interval we assume that we are completely free to choose the relative rates at which tasks execute.

Suppose that we have n tasks $T_1, \ldots, T_n$ competing for R and that the initial condition for our example is $r = n$, that S_1 is at position 1, and that tasks $S_2, \ldots, S_n$ are all at position 2. We choose the following sequence of actions:

1. After S_n proceeds to position 5, T_n (very quickly) takes a turn (leaving $r = 1$ and $c[n] = 0$). At this point S_n would not be able to pass step 2 since $r = 1$ and $c[r] = 1$. Thus we assume that, before S_1 sees the present value of r,

2. S_{n-1} proceeds to position 5 and T_{n-1} takes a turn (leaving $r = n$, $c[n-1] = 0$). It is now possible for S_n to pass step 2 so the action chosen is

3. S_n proceeds to position 5 and then T_n takes another turn (leaving $r = 1$ and $c[n] = 0$). At this point S_{n-1} and S_n cannot proceed past step 2, and so before S_1 sees the present value of r,

4. S_{n-2} proceeds to position 5 and T_{n-2} takes a turn (leaving $c[n-2] = 0$, $r = n-1$). According to the logic of step 2 and because $c[n-1] = c[n] = 0$, it is now possible to stipulate that

5. S_n and S_{n-1} proceed, in that order, to position 2. We are now in position to iterate actions 1–3 above so that

6. T_n takes two more turns and T_{n-1} takes one according to 1–3 above (leaving $r = 1$, $c[n-1] = c[n] = 0$). To proceed and keep T_1 from using R, we must assume (similar to 4 above) that S_1 misses the present value of r and that

7. S_{n-3} proceeds to position 5 and T_{n-3} takes a turn (leaving $r = n-2$, $c[n-3] = 0$).

The pattern now should be clear; at this point S_{n-2}, S_{n-1}, and S_n proceed to position 2 and 1–6 above are iterated so that T_n receives four, T_{n-1} receives two, and T_{n-2} receives one more turn. Eventually, we shall reach a point as represented in 4 and 7 above where we have exhausted the initial set of tasks, $r = 1$, and $T_2, \ldots, T_n$ cannot take their next turn (i.e., $S_2, \ldots S_n$ cannot pass step 2) until T_1 receives the turn for which it has been waiting. At this point T_1 has waited for T_2 to take one turn, T_3 to take two turns, T_4 to take four turns, $\ldots$, and T_n to take 2^{n-2} turns ($n \geq 2$). In particular, T_n has taken every second turn beginning with the first, T_{n-1} every fourth turn starting at the second, T_{n-2} every eighth starting at the fourth, etc. Thus T_1 must wait a total of $\sum_{i=2}^{n} 2^{i-2} = 2^{n-1} - 1$ turns before receiving its first turn. If $n = 5$, for example, the sequence $T_5 T_4 T_5 T_3 T_5 T_4 T_5 T_2 T_5 T_4 T_5 T_3 T_5 T_4 T_5$ indicates the turns and the relative ordering for which T_1 must wait.†

---

†At the expense of a somewhat more elaborate algorithm, the worst-case wait by any task can be reduced [27, 28], the least being linearly related to n.

2.5. SYNCHRONIZATION

The implementation of the requirement that certain task executions be ordered in time is called *task synchronization*. The concept is precisely the same when we consider the synchronization of systems of tasks. Broadly speaking, the problems of synchronization encompass the timing and sequencing problems already treated in this chapter. However, as illustrated later in this section, we shall also want synchronization constraints to include those situations in which the number of task completions in certain cyclic systems is made to depend on the number of task completions in other, concurrently executing cyclic systems.

A synchronization requirement is made explicit in the precedence graphs of task systems. Our treatment of the determinacy problem concerned one of the reasons why precedence, and hence synchronization, constraints have to be imposed. Deadlock prevention can also be responsible for precedence among tasks because of the competition for resources. Although mutual exclusion also represents a synchronization problem, it differs in that it does not require an orientation for precedence relations; i.e., mutually excluded tasks must be ordered (disjoint) in time but the precise ordering need not be specified.

Our goals in this section are to present so-called *synchronization primitives*, whereby tasks requiring synchronization can effect it in their own programming, and to discuss their use in the class of so-called *producer-consumer* synchronization problems arising in operating system design. Like the **enqueue** and **remove** primitives in the preceding section, these primitives will operate on global communication variables.

The global variables through which tasks communicate consist simply of integer variables known as *semaphores*. The two primitives, **wait**(s) and **send**(s), are defined for the manipulation of the semaphore s.† These operations are defined in Fig. 2.5-1. At the time they are created, semaphores are initialized to a value which is determined by the type of synchronization being implemented.

As in the preceding section more than one assumption can be made regarding the execution of the primitives. They could be built (at least in part)

wait(s):

$$s \leftarrow s - 1$$

$L:$ if $s < 0$ then go to L

send(s): $s \leftarrow s + 1$ **Fig. 2.5-1** Synchronization primitives.

†These operations were originally called P and V operations by Dijkstra [4]; unfortunately, the mnemonic value of these symbols is in Dutch, not English.

into the hardware; they could be executed by an operating system routine invoked by the tasks; and they could be executed by the tasks themselves. However, we must be assured that certain operations are indivisible. In particular, under the assumption that single reads and writes to storage are the only indivisible operations it is possible for two tasks to interfere in their manipulation of a semaphore s. For example, suppose that two tasks are executing $s \leftarrow s + 1$. In general, it may be possible for them both to read the old value of s before either writes the augmented value back. In this event, after both have completed execution, s will be changed to $s + 1$ instead of $s + 2$. Thus we require that the assignments $s \leftarrow s - 1$ and $s \leftarrow s + 1$ in **wait** (s) and **send**(s), respectively, be indivisible.

A simple application of these operations is provided by the problem of implementing the precedence relations of a given task system C. Let us define a semaphore s_j for each task T_j which is not an initial task in the graph G of C. Given the programs for each task T_i we form new tasks T_i' as follows. We prefix each noninitial task T_j with the primitive **wait**(s_j) and suffix each non-terminal task T_j with a primitive **send**(s_k) for each immediate successor T_k of T_j. The initial value of s_j is set at $-(d_j - 1)$, where d_j is the number of immediate predecessors of T_j. An example is shown in Fig. 2.5-2. Note that when **wait**(s_j) is executing in step L the absolute value of s_j is equal to the number of as yet incomplete predecessors of T_j. Each of these predecessors must execute the primitive **send**(s_j) before T_j can commence execution. (See also Problem 2-15.)

The problems of resource utilization resulting from the busy form of waiting apply to the **wait** primitive as well as to the tasks S_i discussed in the preceding section. Solutions to the problems are the same as well. In par-

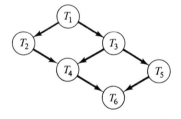

T_1': T_1, send(s_2), send(s_3)

T_2': wait(s_2), T_2, send(s_4)

T_3': wait(s_3), T_3, send(s_4), send (s_5)

T_4': wait (s_4), T_4, send (s_6)

T_5': wait (s_5), T_5, send (s_6)

T_6': wait (s_6), T_6

Fig. 2.5-2 Implementing precedence constraints.

ticular, it may be possible to implement the wait loop of the **wait** primitive in an interrupt system, or it may be feasible to have a centralized system routine coordinating intertask communications through semaphore variables.

Another important application of synchronization occurs in connection with cyclic task systems executing in a producer-consumer relationship. For example, the system C_1 may produce output commands, placing them in an N-cell buffer; concurrently, C_2 removes output commands from the buffer and executes them. Evidently, C_1 must be blocked from attempting to place commands into a full buffer, and C_2 must be blocked from attempting to remove commands from an empty buffer. Stated more abstractly, the number of completions of C_2 must not exceed that of C_1, and C_2 must not lag behind C_1 by more than N completions. These properties are easily formalized in terms of execution sequences.

Definition 2.6

Define $C = C_1^m \| C_2^n$ ($m \geq 1$, $n \geq 1$) and let α be an execution sequence of C. In any prefix β of α let $N_i(\beta)$ denote the number of termination events of the terminal task of C_i. For a given k we say that C_1 is k-synchronized to C_2 in α if $N_1(\beta) = 0$ or $N_1(\beta) \leq N_2(\beta) + k$ for all prefixes β of α.

To illustrate this definition with the previous example, suppose that the output buffer of size N is initially empty. Then in every execution sequence, C_1 must be N-synchronized to C_2 in order that no attempt is ever made to write into a full buffer. Similarly, C_2 must be 0-synchronized to C_1 in order that no attempt is ever made to read from an empty buffer. We have here a form of *mutual* synchronization; we shall return to this property later.

We note immediately the unsymmetrical nature of Definition 2.6 and the fact that no α with the desired property will exist if $m > n + k$. We note also that for a given α, C_1 being k-synchronized to C_2 is not the same as C_2 being $(-k)$-synchronized to C_1. In particular, if k is nonnegative, then the k-synchronization of C_1 to C_2 in α means that over all prefixes of α the number of completions of C_1 never exceeds by more than k the number of completions of C_2. On the other hand, if k is negative, then the k-synchronization of C_2 to C_1 in α means that over all prefixes of α the number of completions of C_2 is either zero or at least $-k$ less than those of C_1. That is, if C_2 has executed at all, it must lag behind C_1 by at least $-k$ completions. As will be seen, the applications discussed in this section will involve only synchronization with nonnegative parameters.

The problem now is to consider primitives which, when properly incorporated into two task systems, ensure the appropriate synchronization properties. For the parallel combinations of the newly defined task systems we want the desired synchronization properties to hold for all valid execution sequences. This can be accomplished by using the **wait** and **send** primitives.

Suppose that C_1 and C_2 are two closed systems and let x denote a semaphore variable. We define the new (closed) system $C_1' = [\textbf{wait}(x); C_1]$ to denote the system C_1 prefixed by a new initial task containing the single operation $\textbf{wait}(x)$. Similarly, we let $C_2' = [C_2; \textbf{send}(x)]$ denote the new closed system consisting of C_2 suffixed by the new terminal task $\textbf{send}(x)$.

Next, consider the valid execution sequences for $C = (C_1')^m \| (C_2')^n$ and let the initial value of x be k. Clearly, a cycle of C_1' can only begin when $x \geq 0$ at the time it is tested in the $\textbf{wait}(x)$ operation. Since $\textbf{send}(x)$ increases x by one and $\textbf{wait}(x)$ decreases x by one, it is clear that in any valid partial execution sequence for C the number of completed cycles of C_1' cannot exceed those of C_2' by more than k if $k \geq 0$ and must be at least $-k$ less than those of C_2' if $k < 0$. We summarize this property in

Proposition 2.7

Let C_1, C_2, C_1', and C_2' be as defined above and let k be the initial value of semaphore x. Define $C = (C_1')^m \| (C_2')^n$, where $m \geq 1$ and $n \geq 1$, and let E denote the set of valid execution sequences for C. Then, in every $\alpha \in E$, C_1' is k-synchronized to C_2'. Moreover, E is nonempty if and only if $m \leq n + k$.

Let us now return to the notion of mutual synchronization.

Definition 2.7

Let $C = C_1^m \| C_2^n$ ($m \geq 1, n \geq 1$) and let α be an execution sequence for C. We say that C_1 and C_2 are (k, l)-*synchronized* in α if C_1 is k-synchronized to C_2 in α and C_2 is l-synchronized to C_1 in α.

For an execution sequence to exist having the above property, the integers k, l, m, and n must satisfy certain constraints. These are as follows.

Proposition 2.8

Let C_1, C_2, and C be given as in Definition 2.7. Let E be the set of execution sequences in which C_1 is k-synchronized to C_2 and C_2 is l-synchronized to C_1. E is nonempty if and only if

(2.5.1) $k + l \geq 1$ and $-l \leq m - n \leq k$

To verify this result, suppose that β is a prefix of some execution sequence in E. Then

(2.5.2) $N_1(\beta) \leq N_2(\beta) + k$

and

(2.5.3) $N_2(\beta) \leq N_1(\beta) + l$

Adding these inequalities gives us $k + l \geq 0$. It remains to show that $k + l = 0$ is not possible. But if we assume that $k = -l$, it is not difficult to see that *all* prefixes β would have to satisfy $N_1(\beta) = N_2(\beta) + k$, and this is an obvious impossibility. Hence $k + l \geq 1$. Finally, choosing $\beta = \alpha$ in (2.5.2) and (2.5.3) gives us $-l \leq m - n \leq k$. The "if" part of the result can be provided by a simple algorithm for constructing an appropriate execution sequence. The details are omitted.

Note that the special cases ($k = 0, l = 1$) and ($k = 1, l = 0$) correspond to requirements whereby the completions of C_1 and C_2 must alternate; the first completion is of C_1 if ($k = 1, l = 0$) and of C_2 if ($k = 0, l = 1$). We shall now describe the use of **wait** and **send** operations in implementing mutual synchronization. By a symmetric application of Proposition 2.7 we obtain the following result in a straightforward manner.

Proposition 2.9

Let C'_i be given as in Proposition 2.7 and define $C''_1 = [C'_1; \mathbf{send}(y)]$ and $C''_2 = [\mathbf{wait}(y); C'_2]$. Let E be the set of execution sequences for $C = (C''_1)^m \| (C''_1)^n$. Let k and l be the initial values of the semaphores x and y, respectively. Then in all $\alpha \in E$, C''_1 and C''_2 are (k, l)-synchronized.

Figure 2.5-3 shows the pattern of **wait** and **send** operations used in the mutual synchronization of C_1 and C_2.

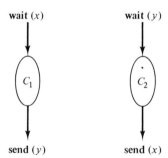

Fig. 2.5-3   Mutually synchronized task systems.

Let us now consider in somewhat more detail the producer-consumer problem illustrated by the earlier example. This important application of mutual synchronization is a model for intertask communications in general as well as for input/output buffering in particular. Suppose that B is a buffer of N places. A task (i.e., a single-task system) called the producer places items into the buffer, and a task called the consumer removes them. The items are to be removed in the order of placement. The programming for these two tasks is shown in Fig. 2.5-4. Let *in* and *out* be integer variables with $in = out = 1$ initially. There are two operations defined on B:

$$input(w): \quad B[in] \longleftarrow w; \ in \longleftarrow \text{ if } in = N \text{ then } 1 \text{ else } in + 1$$

$$output(w): \quad w \longleftarrow B[out]; \ out \longleftarrow \text{ if } out = N \text{ then } 1 \text{ else } out + 1$$

Producer:	**produce** (w)	Consumer:	**wait** (x)
	wait (y)		**output** (w)
	input (w)		**send** (y)
	send (x)		**consume** (w)
	goto Producer		**goto** Consumer

Fig. 2.5-4   The producer-consumer problem.

The semaphore x has the initial value 0, and its value at any time indicates the number of used positions in the buffer. The semaphore y has initial value N, and its value at any time indicates the number of unused positions in the buffer. Proposition 2.9 can be used to conclude that the producer is blocked from attempting to insert into a full buffer and that the consumer is blocked from attempting to remove from an empty buffer. To complete the proof of correctness of the two tasks, it is necessary to show that the producer and consumer do not attempt to access the same cell in the buffer concurrently. This can happen only if $in = out$, and the condition $in = out$ holds if and only if the value of x is 0 or the value of y is 0; in either case, one task or the other is blocked.

It is not difficult to conceive of generalizations to synchronization properties concerning more than two task systems. For example, we could generalize to the mutual synchronization of n tasks with $n(n - 1)$ parameters (a pair for each pair of tasks). However, such generalizations appear to be mainly of theoretical interest. (See Problem 2-2.) One generalization of practical interest is the producer-consumer problem when there is more than one producer or more than one consumer. In this case the desired synchronization property can be stated informally as follows: The sum of the numbers of completions for the producer tasks cannot be more than N greater than the corresponding sum for the consumer tasks. Also, the former sum can never be less than the latter sum.

To implement a solution to the multiple producer-consumer problem we must use primitives such as **enqueue** and **remove** which include a queueing mechanism. To adapt these primitives to the present purpose it is only necessary to introduce the global variable (array) Q as an additional parameter. However, to be consistent with the **wait** primitive, let us combine the wait loop in step $i2$ of Fig. 2.4-2 with the **enqueue** primitive in step $i1$. As shown in Fig. 2.5-5, we shall define the new primitive **enter**(i, Q) to consist of steps $i1$ and $i2$ and extend the **remove** primitive to include Q as a parameter. Using these primitives, we program the ith producer and the jth consumer as shown in Fig.

$$\text{enter } (i, Q): \quad i1: \quad Q[p] \leftarrow i; \ p \leftarrow i;$$
$$i2: \quad \text{if } Q[0] \neq i \text{ then goto } i2;$$

$$\text{remove } (j, Q): \quad \text{if } p \neq j \text{ then } Q[0] \leftarrow Q[j]$$
$$\text{else } \{p \leftarrow 0; \ Q[0] \leftarrow 0\} \ ;$$

Fig. 2.5-5   Definition of **enter** and **remove**.

Producer i:	**produce** (w)	Consumer j:	**enter** $(j, Q2)$
	enter $(i, Q1)$		**wait** (x)
	wait (y)		**output** (w)
	input (w)		**send** (y)
	send (x)		**remove** $(j, Q2)$
	remove $(i, Q1)$		**consume** (w)
	goto producer i		**goto** consumer j

Fig. 2.5-6 Multiple producer-consumer problem.

2.5-6. Note that in general a task must first wait to gain access to the buffer and then wait for an empty or nonempty cell depending on whether it is a producer or consumer, respectively.

It is be reemphasized that the extent to which the operations denoted by the primitives in Fig. 2.5-6 are carried out by the tasks themselves will depend on the use and availability of the appropriate hardware or operating system. However, we must continue to assume that the operations on the global variables are indivisible, for otherwise we shall need an algorithm similar to that given for the general mutual exclusion problem of the last section.

We have restricted our treatment of synchronization to the primitives **wait** and **send**. Many other sets of synchronizing primitives have been defined and studied [17, 18, 19]. Problem 2-13 considers some examples.

PROBLEMS

2-1. Let us consider the problem of "communication deadlocks" in which "resources" such as messages, card images, and data are *consumable* rather than reusable, as assumed in the text [6]. Assume a set of tasks each of which either produces consumable resources, uses (consumes) them, or both. Naturally, the subset of tasks that produces resources must be nonempty. Assume that no limit is placed on the amount of any given resource that can be produced; i.e., *assuming that a producer task can execute* (not currently waiting for resources from other tasks), then it can produce as many resources as desired. Interaction between tasks is now explicit and specified with respect to the resources required by each task from every other task. The problem is to model such resource systems, being careful to identify the essential differences from reusable resource systems, and to give an appropriate definition of deadlock. In terms of this definition provide an algorithm for detecting deadlocks and consider the prevention and avoidance questions.

2-2. Consider an arbitrary set of independent, cyclic tasks $T_1, \ldots, T_n$. For each i and j there exists an integer k_{ij} such that T_j must be k_{ij}-synchronized to T_i. These constraints may be represented graphically as follows. We define a graph (called a synchronization graph) whose nodes are the tasks T_i $(1 \leq i \leq n)$ and which has arcs from each task to every other task labeled with the appropriate synchronization parameters; i.e., the arc from T_i to T_j carries the label k_{ij}. Note that $k_{ij} = \infty$ implies that T_j is not constrained by T_i.

Suppose that there exists a valid execution sequence $\beta\alpha$ satisfying all synchronization constraints such that each task is executed at least once in α and that $\beta\alpha^n$ is valid for all $n \geq 1$. Then the synchronization graph is said to be *consistent*. Show that a synchronization graph is consistent if and only if the sum of the labels on the arcs of each circuit in the graph is greater than or equal to 1.

The consistency question is similar to the "termination" question of parallel program schemata [22] and the "liveness" question of marked graphs [23]. We may generalize the above problem to include

a. P and V operations by which arbitrary integers can be subtracted and added, respectively, to semaphores, and

b. the case where semaphores may be "shared variables"; more than one task may execute P-operations or V-operations on a given semaphore.

These generalized models are easily seen to be realizations of those studied by Karp and Miller [22, 24]. A treatment based directly on semaphore systems under generalization (a) above can be found in [25].

2-3. The following, alternative graph representation of resource states can be used to study the deadlock problem [6]. The nodes of a state graph G now consist of both the set of task chains $C_1, \ldots, C_n$ and the set of resource types $R_1, \ldots, R_m$. G contains an arc from chain C_i to resource type R_j for each unit of type R_j that C_i is currently requesting. There is an arc from R_j to C_i for every unit of type R_j that is currently allocated to C_i. Thus the sum of the currently available resources of type R_j and the number of arcs incident out of R_j is constant at w_j—the total of type R_j available in the system. Note that G is *bipartite* in the sense that all arcs incident out of (into) nodes in the set $R_1, \ldots, R_m$ are incident into (out of) nodes in the disjoint set $C_1, \ldots, C_n$.

A state graph G is said to be *expedient* if no chain has a resource request that can be granted with currently available resources. (Note that all arcs from C_i to R_j must be removed at once; no partial satisfaction of requests is possible.) A set of nodes in G is said to constitute a *knot* if every node in the set has at least one successor but no successors outside the set. Show that a knot in an expedient graph is a sufficient condition for deadlock and that a circuit is a necessary condition.

Suppose that the system is constrained so that tasks can have a **total** request outstanding of at most one resource unit. Show that, under these circumstances, the existence of a knot in an expedient state graph is both necessary and sufficient for deadlock.

2-4. Define the system C to be *weakly determinate* if for any given intitial state s_0, $F(M_i, \alpha) = F(M_i, \alpha')$ $(1 \leq i \leq m)$ for all execution sequences α and α' of C. Show that the existence of interfering tasks does not imply that a task system must fail to satisfy the property of weak determinacy. Consider the example of tasks T_1, T_2, and T_3, a partial order containing only $T_2 \prec T_3$, and the following domains and ranges:

$$D_{T_1} = (M_1), \qquad R_{T_1} = (M_2), \qquad D_{T_2} = (M_2), \qquad R_{T_2} = (M_3),$$
$$D_{T_3} = (M_4), \qquad R_{T_3} = (M_3).$$

2-5. In Section 2.2 the values written by a task T were made to depend on the domain values that existed at the time T was initiated. Suppose that we modify the definition of state transitions so that the values written in R_T by the event $a_{k+1} = T$ depend only on the domain values as given in the state s_k. With respect to the determinacy question, do we still have a meaningful model? If so, what changes, if any, must be made in the basic results?

2-6. Suppose that we have m identical copies of a resource but that each copy must be in use by at most one task at a time. Extend the solutions to the mutual exclusion problem given in the text to take into account this more general system. Of course, efficient utilization of the given resource is to be obtained; no copy of the resource can be idle indefinitely unless no tasks are waiting for this resource.

2-7. We want to consider an extension to the MRU model for deadlock avoidance. Suppose that each time a chain makes a request the maximum requirement of the remainder of the chain is known for each resource type [8]. (No further information on resource usage can be assumed known.) Clearly, in this "dynamic" MRU system the maximum *remaining* requirements at any time are (for each resource) less than or equal to the maximum requirements for the entire chain (which is the only information assumed known in the MRU system). Investigate deadlock avoidance algorithms for the new system and compare resource utilization in the two systems, subject to deadlock avoidance. Also compare resource utilization in the dynamic MRU system with that in the model assuming complete information about resource usage.

2-8. In working out a solution to the mutual exclusion problem suppose that we have available a so-called test-and-set primitive operation, denoted **test** (A, a) and defined as follows. The variable named A is set to zero by **test** (A, a), and if A was originally nonzero, control is transferred to the statement labeled a; otherwise, the next statement in sequence is executed. Construct an efficient algorithm and define appropriate global communication variables which amount to a solution to the mutual exclusion problem, assuming that **test** (A, a) is the only indivisible operation apart from single reads or writes to storage.

2-9. Consider a bipartite precedence graph G whose disjoint sets of vertices contain n_1 and $n_2 = n - n_1$ vertices. What is the maximum number of edges that G can have? Show that this number is maximum at $n^2/4$, when $n_1 = n_2 = n/2$. Show that *no* precedence graph of n vertices can have more than $n^2/4$ edges.

2-10. Consider the n-task system $C = (\mathfrak{I}, <)$. Suppose that $<$ is represented by an n by n Boolean matrix Z whose elements are defined by $Z_{ij} = 1$ if and only if $T_i \prec T_j$. Design an efficient algorithm for finding the precedence graph G for C. Do this by producing a matrix Z' for which $Z'_{ij} = 1$ if and only if $(T_i, T_j) \in G$. (See Moyles and Thompson [20].)

Suppose that the graph G is known and that $\prec$ is to be computed. Design an efficient algorithm for finding Z assuming that Z' is given. (See Warshall [21].)

2-11. Let G be a precedence graph whose vertices are $\mathfrak{I} = \{T_1, \ldots, T_n\}$. Give a constructive proof that an ordering $(T_{i_1}, T_{i_2}, \ldots, T_{i_n})$ of $\mathfrak{I}$ exists which has the property $(T_{i_j}, T_{i_k}) \in G$ implies that $j < k$. [The process of producing such orderings from G is called *topological sorting* (see Knuth [15], for example).]

2-12. This and the following problem consider some "linguistic aspects" of parallelism, i.e., the methods of expressing parallel tasks in programming languages. The reader is referred to Dijkstra [4], Dennis and Van Horn [17], and Wirth [11] for more detailed treatments.

The execution of the statement

fork $(L1, L2)$

causes a new task to be initiated at statement $L2$ and the original task to continue at statement $L1$. The execution of the statement

join $(x, L1)$

causes the action $x \leftarrow x - 1$; if $x > 0$ the task is terminated, and if $x = 0$ it is continued at statement $L1$. The variable x can be initialized by the programmer or computed by some task.

a. Verify that every task system $C = (\mathfrak{I}, \prec)$ can be implemented using the **fork-join** constructions.

b. Verify that there exist programs using **fork-join** constructions which cannot be represented as partially ordered systems of tasks; in particular, loops and conditional statements containing **fork-join** constructions may not be logically equivalent to any partially ordered system of tasks.

2-13. Shown below are three sets of primitives:

Set 1	Set 2	Set 3
lock x	**disable**	**wait**(s)
unlock x	**enable**	**send**(s)
fork $(L1, L2)$	**block**	
join $(y, L1)$	**wakeup**(j)	

Assume that **disable** turns off the interrupts, and **enable** turns them on again. The operation of **wait** and **send** has been defined in the text; the operation of **fork** and **join** has been defined in Problem 2–12. If x is a binary variable, **lock** and **unlock** are defined as:

> **lock:** L: [**if** $x = 1$ **then** $x \leftarrow 0$ **else goto** L]
>
> **unlock:**   [$x \leftarrow 1$]

where the actions enclosed in brackets constitute an indivisible sequence. The operation of **block** by task j is intended to stop task j, releasing the processor, until another task executes a corresponding **wakeup**(j); task j is then to resume at the next statement following **block**. We require that **block** turns on the interrupts if they are off and that **block** and **wakeup**(j) are indivisible operations.

a. Suppose that, with each task i, there must be associated a *wakeup-waiting switch* s_i. The operation **wakeup**(i) sets s_i to 1; in task j, **block** examines s_j, stops if $s_j = 0$, or otherwise does not stop and sets s_j to 0. Show how omission of the wakeup-waiting switch can cause incorrect operation of **block** and **wakeup**.

b. Investigate the equivalence of sets 2 and 3 for the purposes of implementing mutual exclusion.

c. Show whether or not sets 1 and 2 are equivalent.

2-14. Let us consider some generalizations to *closed* task systems. Define the special tasks given in Figs. P2-14(a)–P2-14(d).

> *Wye:*   Initiate; terminate immediately, thus enabling successors with respect to the precedence relations shown.
>
> *Junction:*   Initiate when both immediate predecessors terminate, then terminate immediately.
>
> *Decider:*   Initiate; test condition A; if A is true, initiate successor task T_1; if A is false, initiate successor task T_2. Note that *only one* of T_1 and T_2 is initiated.
>
> *XOR:*   Initiate when either immediate predecessor terminates, then terminate immediately.

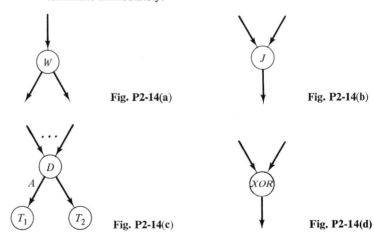

Fig. P2-14(a)

Fig. P2-14(b)

Fig. P2-14(c)

Fig. P2-14(d)

a. Suppose that C_1 and C_2 are closed task systems. Verify that the new
    system [Fig. P2-14(e)] is determinate if and only if C_1 and C_2 are determi-
    nate and their memory cells are disjoint, except for cells that are read-
    only in both C_1 and C_2.

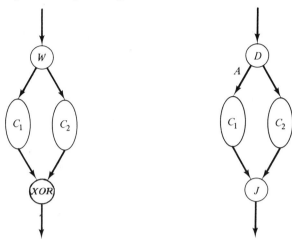

Fig. P2-14(e)   Fig. P2-14(f)

b. Suppose that C_1 and C_2 are closed task systems. Show that the new
    system [Fig. P2-14(f)] is determinate if and only if both C_1 and C_2 are
    determinate and that the memory cells of C_1 and C_2 need not be dis-
    joint. The condition A is some Boolean function of the values in the
    union of the memory cells of C_1 and C_2. Note that this construction is
    analogous to the construction **if** A **then** C_1 **else** C_2.

c. Suppose that C is a closed task system. Show that the new system [Fig.
    P2-14(g)] is determinate if and only if C is determinate. The condition
    A is a Boolean function defined over the memory cells of C. Note that
    this construction is analogous to the statement **while** A **do** C.

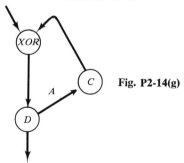

Fig. P2-14(g)

d. Suppose that we define a class $\mathcal{C}$ of task systems to contain all closed
    systems formed from individual tasks by a finite number of applications
    of constructions A, B, and C. Discuss the conditions under which every
    system in $\mathcal{C}$ is determinate.

2-15. In Fig. 2.5-2 it was shown how to implement a closed n-task system using exactly $n - 1$ semaphores.

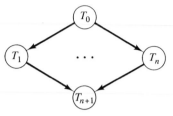

Fig. P2-15

    a. Show how the task system in Fig. P2-15 can be implemented using just two semaphores.

    b. Define a complexity measure of a task-system implementation to be the sum of the number of semaphores, the number of **wait** operations, and the number of **send** operations. Show that the complexity of a closed n-task system implemented according to Fig. 2.5-2 is $2(n - 1) + e$, where e is the number of edges in the precedence diagram. Show that a solution for Fig. P2-15 can be obtained with complexity $n + e + 3$. Note that the complexity of a chain of n tasks must be at least $3(n - 1)$.

    c. Is it possible to implement all closed n-task systems with complexity less than $2(n - 1) + e$?

2-16. Suppose that the semaphore queueing discipline is last-in-first-out. Nonetheless, we wish to implement safe mutual exclusion of a certain critical section for a set of n cycling tasks, where *safe* means that no one task can be blocked indefinitely from entering the critical section by other tasks cycling through arbitrarily often. For example, T_1 and T_2 can block T_3 indefinitely if T_3 arrives second and T_1 and T_2 cycle through the critical section alternately.

    Consider an n-leaf binary tree, each of whose internal nodes (and root) is labeled by a distinct semaphore. Tasks $T_1, \ldots, T_n$ desire to use a certain critical section. Suppose that the path from leaf j to the root is labeled by semaphores $s_{j1}, \ldots, s_{jp_j}$. The programming within task T_j for use of the critical section is

$$\textbf{wait}(s_{j1}); \ldots ; \textbf{wait}(s_{jp_j})$$

$$\text{use of critical section}$$

$$\textbf{send}(s_{jp_j}); \ldots ; \textbf{send}(s_{j1})$$

    a. Show that this solution is safe.

    b. Discuss the effects of the structure of the tree on the speed of operation of the system of tasks.

REFERENCES

1. BERNSTEIN, A. J., "Analysis of programs for parallel processing." *IEEE Trans. Comp. EC-15*, 5 (Oct. 1966), 757–762.

2. BAER, J. L., "A survey of some theoretical aspects of multiprocessing." *Computing Surveys 5*, 1 (March 1973).

3. COFFMAN, E. G., JR., M. J. ELPHICK, and A. SHOSHANI, "System deadlocks." *Computing Surveys 2*, 3 (June 1971), 67–78.

4. DIJKSTRA, E. W., "Cooperating sequential processes," in *Programming Languages* (F. Genuys, ed.). Academic Press (1968), 43–112.

5. SHOSHANI, A., and E. G. COFFMAN, JR. "Sequencing tasks in multi-process, multiple resource systems to avoid deadlocks." *Proc. 11th Symp. Annual Switching and Automata Theory* (Oct. 1970), 225–233.

6. HOLT, R. G., "On deadlock in computer systems." Ph.D. thesis, Dept. of Computer Science, Cornell Univ., Ithaca, N.Y., TR-71-91 (1971).

7. HEBALKAR, P. G., "A graph model for analysis of deadlock prevention in systems with parallel computations." *Proc. IFIP Congress* (Aug. 1971), 168–172.

8. SHOSHANI, A., "Detection, prevention, and recovery from deadlocks in multiprocess multiple resource systems." Ph.D. thesis, Dept. of Electrical Engineering, Princeton Univ., Princeton, N.J. (Oct. 1969).

9. HAVENDER, J. W., "Avoiding deadlock in multitasking systems." *IBM Sys. J. 7*, 2 (1968), 74–84.

10. HABERMANN, A. N., "Prevention of system deadlock." *Comm. ACM 12*, 7 (July 1969), 373–377.

11. WIRTH, N., "A note on program structure for parallel processing." *Comm. ACM 9*, 5 (May 1966), 320–321.

12. BREDT, T. H., and E. J. McCLUSKEY, "Analysis and synthesis of control mechanisms for parallel processes," in *Parallel Processor Systems, Technologies and Applications* (L. C. Hobbs et al., eds.). (1970), 287–296.

13. KNUTH, D. E., "Additional comments on a problem in concurrent programming." *Comm. ACM 9*, 5 (May 1966), 321–323.

14. FLOYD, R. W., "Assigning meanings to programs." *Proc. Symp. Appl. Math.* (1967), 19–32.

15. KNUTH, D. E., *The Art of Computer Programming* (Vol. I). Addison-Wesley, Reading, Mass. (1968).

16. DIJKSTRA, E. W., "Solution of a problem in concurrent program control." *Comm. ACM 8*, 9 (Sept. 1965), 569.

17. DENNIS, J. B., and E. C. VAN HORN, "Programming semantics for multiprogrammed computations." *Comm. ACM 9*, 3 (Mar. 1966), 143–155.

18. BRINCH HANSEN, P., "The nucleus of a multiprogramming system." *Comm. ACM 13*, 4 (Apr. 1970), 238–241, 250.

19. SPIER, M. J., and E. I. ORGANICK, "The Multics interprocess communication facility." *Proc. 2nd ACM Symp. Op. Sys. Princ.* (Oct. 1969), 83–91.

20. MOYLES, D. M., and G. L. THOMPSON, "An algorithm for finding a minimum equivalent graph of a digraph." *J. ACM 16*, 3 (July 1969), 455–460.

21. WARSHALL, S., "A theorem on Boolean matrices." *J. ACM 9*, 1 (Jan. 1962), 11–12.

22. KARP, RICHARD M., and RAYMOND E. MILLER, "Properties of a model for parallel computations: determinacy, termination, and queueing." *Siam Journal of Applied Math 14*, 6 (Nov. 1966), 1390–1411.

23. COMMONER, F., A. W. HOLT, S. EVEN, and A. PNUELI, "Marked directed graphs." *Journal of Computer and System Sciences 5*, 5 (Oct 1971).

24. KARP, R. M., and R. E. MILLER, "Parallel program schemata." *Journal of Computer and System Sciences 3*, 2 (May 1969), 147–195.

25. BRUNO, J. L., E. G. COFFMAN, JR., and W. H. HOSKEN, "Consistency of synchronization nets using P and V operations." *Proc. 13th Symp. on Switching and Automata Theory* (Oct. 1972), 71–76.

26. KELLER, R. M., "On maximally parallel program schemata." *Proc. 11th Symp. on Switching and Automata Theory* (Oct. 1970), 33–50.

27. EISENBERG, M. A., and M. R. McGUIRE, "Further comments on Dijkstra's concurrent programming control problem." *Comm. ACM 15*, 11 (Nov. 1972), 999.

28. DE BRUIJN, "Additional comments on a problem in concurrent programming control." *Comm. ACM 10*, 3 (Mar. 1967), 137–138.

3 DETERMINISTIC MODELS OF PROCESSOR SCHEDULING

3.1. INTRODUCTION

A number of advantages were attributed to multiprocessor systems in Chapter 1, the one of most importance to a large class of users being the potential decrease in computation times achievable by parallel programming, i.e., concurrently executing independent portions of the same computation. This is especially important in real-time applications and for lengthy computations, such as the many applications involving experimental data reduction, when the results are needed more quickly than they can be provided by single-processor systems. How best to exploit the multiple processor organization in order to obtain maximum performance for these applications is the primary concern of this chapter.

Our specific goal will be the presentation of efficient algorithms for the scheduling of multiprocessor systems under the assumption that the task systems to be scheduled (or estimates of these systems) are known in advance and that all task systems are simultaneously available for scheduling. We shall extend the basic model of Chapter 2 to include the assumption that the execution time (a positive number) of each task is specified. Although restrictions are inherent in the assumption of partially ordered sets of tasks, the large majority of theoretical results in this area apply to these structures or to special cases of them.

In the next five sections of this chapter we shall be studying scheduling problems in which multiprocessor systems are defined to consist simply of $m \geq 2$ identical and independent processors. In Section 3.7 we shall present the few known results for systems containing distinct processors having distinct functions. The basic objective of the algorithms presented in these sections is to schedule task systems so that they execute in minimal time. In

Section 3.8 we shall consider other objectives of importance, but mainly for the single-processor assumption (which has been necessary for a successful theoretical treatment of the related problems). For the remainder of this introductory section we shall develop the notation and basic ideas related to the problem of scheduling on $m \geq 2$ identical processors.

A *schedule* or *assignment* for m processors and a given precedence graph is a description of the work to be done by each processor at each moment of time. The schedule must not violate the given precedence relations, it must not assign more than one processor to a task over any time interval, and it must allocate an amount of processor time equal to the task's execution time. The simplest way of specifying a schedule is to use a Gantt chart [1], which consists of a time axis for each processor with intervals marked off and labeled with the name of the task being processed. In Fig. 3.1-1(a) we have shown

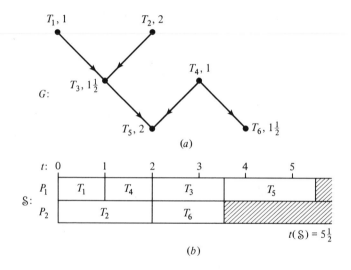

Fig. 3.1-1   Example graph and Gantt chart.

a graph G (or more precisely a task system with graph G), and in Fig. 3.1-1(b) a schedule for G with two processors P_1 and P_2. We use the symbol $\mathbb{S}$ to denote schedules and the symbol $t(\mathbb{S})$ to denote the length of $\mathbb{S}$, i.e., the latest finishing time in $\mathbb{S}$. We use cross-hatching in the figures to represent processor idle periods. We shall also have occasion to say that during an idle period contained in the interval $[0, t(\mathbb{S})]$, a processor executes an empty task, ϕ. The symbol τ_i denotes the execution time of task T_i.

The measure of execution time that we have associated with each task has at least three practical interpretations. First, it may represent the known, deterministic execution time of the task, in which case the schedule constructed will have a precise interpretation. Second, it may specify the maximum possible value of task execution time. Scheduling using these values amounts to a worst-case analysis and is applicable to "hard" real-time problems with strict deadlines that must be observed. Under this interpretation program execution can be controlled according to two basic strategies, once a schedule has been constructed:

1. If a processor P_j is assigned to work on a task T_i over some interval, then the control mechanism will reserve all this interval for T_i on P_j. In the event the execution time of T_i does not achieve its maximum value on a given run the processor may be left idle or devoted to background work of some kind.

2. The control mechanism is constructed to take advantage of shorter execution times on particular runs to reduce the execution time of the task system. One such control mechanism is described in Section 3.5.

Finally, the weight associated with a given task may be the expected value of the task execution time viewed as a random variable. A schedule that allocates an amount of processor time to each task equal to the expected value of the task execution time can be used in the following way. The schedule assigns each task to a particular processor and in a particular sequence relative to other tasks assigned to the same processor. Suppose now that this assignment and sequence is fixed and that tasks are started as soon as all their predecessors in the graph have been completed and all tasks preceding them on the same processor have been completed. Define a new graph G' by adding to the graph G all precedence relations $T_i < T_j$, where T_i is independent of T_j in G and T_i appears prior to T_j in the sequence of tasks assigned to some processor. An optimistic estimate of the mean length of the schedule is the length of a longest path in G'. A reasonable heuristic would consist of finding a minimum length schedule assuming that the expected values are the given execution times and using the corresponding assignments and sequences.

For all the scheduling problems that we shall subsequently define only a finite number of schedules need to be considered in a search for an optimal schedule. Thus these problems are all effectively solvable by enumeration (examination of all possibilities). Dynamic programming, branch and bound, and other techniques [2] from mathematical programming have been applied to many scheduling problems as essentially enumerative methods that have been effectively used for producing standards of comparison in the study of heuristics. For our purposes, however, an "efficient" algorithm for scheduling task systems will mean an essentially nonenumerative one, e.g., one which requires a number of steps that vary as a polynomial in the number of tasks as opposed to being exponential in this number.

We shall be concerned with both *preemptive* and *nonpreemptive* scheduling disciplines. In nonpreemptive scheduling a task once begun must be executed to completion. With preemptive disciplines tasks may be interrupted prior to their completion and removed from the processor in favor of some other task. It is still assumed, of course, that preempted tasks are resumed from the point of interruption and are eventually given sufficient processor time to complete.

From a practical standpoint, it may be useful to consider restricted preemptive disciplines, (e.g., placing a lower bound on the time between preemptions or placing an upper bound on the number of preemptions per unit time). We shall deal here only with unrestricted disciplines.

It is important to note that, with preemptive disciplines, it is never beneficial to introduce idle periods on processors when there are tasks available for execution. That this is not the case with nonpreemptive disciplines is illustrated by the graph and Gantt charts of Fig. 3.1-2. Observe that when P_3 is idle in the (optimal) schedule $\mathcal{S}$ from ϵ to 2ϵ, T_7 is continuously available for assignment. By assigning T_7 to P_3 at $t = \epsilon$ we produce the longer schedule $\mathcal{S}'$.

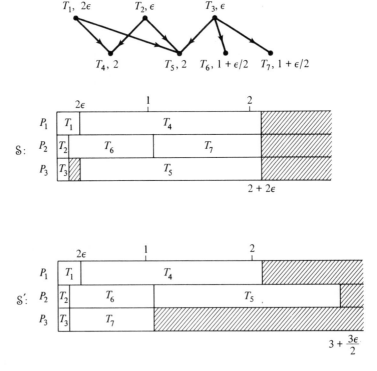

Fig. 3.1-2   Introducing idle time.

3.2. OPTIMAL SCHEDULES FOR TWO-PROCESSOR SYSTEMS [3]

At present the only known case involving arbitrary precedence structures for which optimal nonpreemptive schedules can be computed efficiently requires the assumptions of two processors and equal execution times for all tasks.† The most direct practical application of this system consists of those situations in which computations are decomposed prior to scheduling into approximately equal-size tasks and a corresponding partial ordering. As with the tree-scheduling result of the next section, we shall see in Section 3.6 that the importance of the two-processor result lies mainly in its connection with optimal preemptive scheduling.

The solution for the two-processor problem involves a labeling algorithm which associates with each task in a graph G a positive integer. The scheduling algorithm is correspondingly defined in terms of task labels. For convenience in defining the labeling algorithm we shall introduce the following definition. We linearly order decreasing sequences of positive integers as follows. Let $N = (n_1, n_2, \ldots, n_t)$ and $N' = (n'_1, n'_2, \ldots, n'_{t'})$ be two such sequences; i.e., $n_i > n_{i+1}$ and $n'_j > n'_{j+1}$ for $1 \leq i < t$ and $1 \leq j < t'$. We shall say that $N < N'$ if either

    1. For some i, $1 \leq i \leq t$, we have $n_j = n'_j$ for all j satisfying $1 \leq j \leq i - 1$ and $n_i < n'_i$, or

    2. $t < t'$ and $n_j = n'_j$, $1 \leq j \leq t$.

For example, $(7, 5, 3, 2) < (7, 5, 4, 1)$, $(4, 3, 1) < (5, 1)$, and $(7, 2) < (7, 2, 1)$.

Let n denote the number of tasks in G. The labeling algorithm assigns to each task T an integer label $\alpha(T) \in \{1, 2, \ldots, n\}$. The mapping α is defined recursively as follows. Let $S(T)$ denote the set of immediate successors of T.

    1. An arbitrary task T_0 with $S(T_0) = \varnothing$ is chosen and $\alpha(T_0)$ is defined to be 1.

    2. Suppose for some $k \leq n$ that the integers $1, 2, \ldots, k - 1$ have been assigned. For each task T for which α has been defined on all elements of $S(T)$, let $N(T)$ denote the decreasing sequence of integers formed by ordering the set $\{\alpha(T') \mid T' \in S(T)\}$. At least one of these tasks T^* must satisfy $N(T^*) \leq N(T)$ for all such tasks T. Choose one such T^* and define $\alpha(T^*)$ to be k.

    3. We repeat the assignment in 2 until all tasks of G have been assigned some integer.

Figure 3.2-1 shows an example graph with a valid labeling. Note, for example, that the tasks carrying the labels 10, 11, and 12 can be assigned

†For a treatment of the complexity of the general problem, see [19].

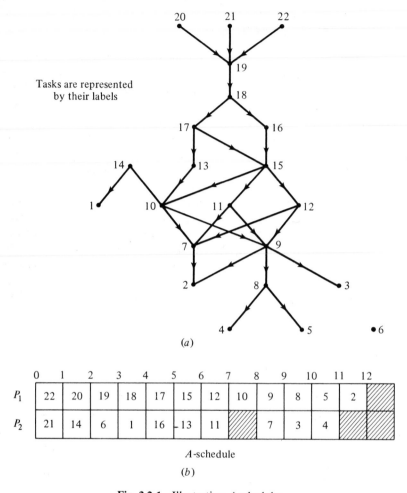

Tasks are represented
by their labels

(a)

	0	1	2	3	4	5	6	7	8	9	10	11	12
P_1	22	20	19	18	17	15	12	10	9	8	5	2	
P_2	21	14	6	1	16	13	11		7	3	4		

A-schedule

(b)

Fig. 3.2-1   Illustrating *A*-schedules.

these integers in any order. The scheduling algorithm based on the above labeling algorithm is defined as follows. *Whenever a processor becomes free assign that task all of whose predecessors have already been executed and which has the largest label among those tasks not yet assigned.* For convenience and without loss of generality we shall adopt the convention that when P_1 and P_2 become available simultaneously in a two-processor system P_1 is always the first processor to be assigned a task by the algorithm. (We shall adhere to this convention extended to an arbitrary number of processors as well.) The schedules produced by the above algorithm (to be called Algorithm A) will be called *A-schedules*. Without loss of generality we shall adopt as the time unit the task execution time. Before examining the rather difficult proof that A-schedules are optimal for $m = 2$ and tasks having equal execution times, we shall discuss some important properties of the labeling algorithm and the corresponding A-schedules.

After a certain amount of reflection on the scheduling problem being considered, one's intuition normally would lead to a labeling algorithm having the following properties:

1. If T is at a higher level than T', then we should have $\alpha(T) > \alpha(T')$; i.e., T should have scheduling priority over T'. See Fig. 3.2-1 for examples.

2. If $S(T') \subset S(T)$, then again $\alpha(T) > \alpha(T')$. For example, in Fig. 3.2-1 it appears that the task labeled 15 should have a higher priority (label) than the task labeled 13.

It is easy to see that the labeling algorithm we have described has property 2. Also, it is not difficult to show that property 1 is a characteristic of our labeling algorithm. A straightforward proof can be constructed by using induction on the number of levels in G (see Problem 3-1).

One might also be inclined to think that if the execution of a task T immediately makes available for execution a large number of tasks, then T should be given a high scheduling priority, even higher in some cases than other tasks at a higher level. This is not the case except under the conditions of property 2, but this property is critically dependent on our assumption that $m = 2$. Examine the graph in Fig. 3.2-2, for example. For $m = 2$ it is easy to verify than an A-schedule is optimal, but as shown in the figure the A-schedule for $m = 3$ is not optimal. The apparent reason is that task T_5 is not given a sufficiently high priority due to its large number of immediate successors.

It is inviting but erroneous to suppose that properties 1 and 2 are sufficient to define an optimal labeling algorithm. Problem 3-4 provides a counter-example which the reader is urged to work through before proceeding further.

Because of the equal (unit) execution times both P_1 and P_2 become available for executing tasks at the same times. Suppose that, at time t, P_1 and P_2 become available for executing new tasks and that T is the unexecuted task whose label is highest of those corresponding to tasks as yet unexecuted at time t. For all T' such that $T' < T$ the labeling produced by Algorithm A is such that $\alpha(T') > \alpha(T)$. Hence at time t all predecessors of T must have been executed and T is ready to be executed. Since by the definition of A-schedules P_1 and P_2 always attempt to execute the unexecuted task with the highest label and since P_1 is assigned tasks before P_2 by convention, we see that T must be the task executed by P_1 in the unit interval beginning at time t. This establishes the following property, which we shall put in the form of a lemma for ease of reference in the proof that A-schedules are optimal.

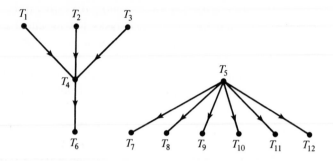

The A-schedule

	0	1	2	3	4	5
P_1	T_1	T_4	T_6	T_9	T_{12}	
P_2	T_2	T_5	T_7	T_{10}		
P_3	T_3		T_8	T_{11}		

The optimal schedule

P_1	T_1	T_3	T_4	T_6	
P_2	T_2	T_7	T_9	T_{11}	
P_3	T_5	T_8	T_{10}	T_{12}	

Fig. 3.2-2   Counterexample for $m = 3$.

Lemma 3.1

Define $t(T)$ as the nonnegative integer representing the time at which task T begins execution in an A-schedule for G. If T is executed by P_1 and $t(T) \leq t(T')$, then $\alpha(T) > \alpha(T')$.

From the above we note also that P_1 is never idle before the latest finishing time (length) of an A-schedule. The principal result now follows.

Theorem 3.1

For an arbitrary graph whose tasks all have the same execution time an A-schedule has minimal length if $m = 2$.

Proof. We begin with some definitions. Suppose that the tasks of G are executed using an A-schedule $\mathcal{S}$. If P_2 is idle from time t to time $t + 1$, we say that P_2 is executing an empty task ϕ and we define $\alpha(\phi) = 0$. We recursively define tasks V_i and W_i as follows:

1. V_0 is defined to be the task executed by P_1 satisfying $t(V_0) = t(\mathcal{S}) - 1$ (i.e., V_0 is the last task to be executed by P_1). Similarly, W_0 is defined to be the (possibly empty) task executed by P_2 with $t(W_0) = t(\mathcal{S}) - 1$.

2. In general, for $k \geq 1$, W_k is defined to be the (possibly empty) task T for which $\alpha(T) < \alpha(V_{k-1})$, $t(T) < t(V_{k-1})$ and $t(T)$ is *maximal*. It follows from Lemma 3.1 that W_k must be executed by P_2. V_k is defined to be the task executed by P_1 satisfying $t(V_k) = t(W_k)$.

If W_1 does not exist, then no processor is idle before time $t(\mathcal{S}) - 1$ and $\mathcal{S}$ is clearly optimal. Hence we may assume that W_1 (and therefore V_1) exists. Suppose that we are only able to define W_k for $1 \leq k \leq r$. Define X_i to be the set of tasks T satisfying $t(V_{i+1}) < t(T) \leq t(V_i)$ but with $T \neq W_i$, $1 \leq i \leq r$. Since V_{r+1} does not exist, X_r is the set of T with $t(T) \leq t(V_r)$ and $T \neq W_r$.

Note that the cardinality of each X_k is odd and that we can set $|X_k| = 2n_k - 1$ for a positive integer n_k, $0 \leq k \leq r$. An example illustrating the above definitions is provided by Fig. 3.2-3. The sets X_k are enclosed in heavy lines.

The heart of the proof of the theorem is contained in the fact that for $0 \leq k \leq r$, if $T \in X_k$, $T' \in X_{k+1}$, then $T' < T$. We proceed to prove this by (double) induction on $t(T)$ and $t(T')$. By the definition of X_k, $T \in X_k$ implies that $\alpha(T) \geq \alpha(V_k)$ and $t(T) \leq t(V_k)$.

First, let $T \in X_k$ with $t(T)$ minimal; i.e., $t(T) = t(V_{k+1}) + 1 = t(V_k) - n_k + 1$. Since

$$\alpha(V_{k+1}) > \alpha(T) \geq \alpha(V_k) > \alpha(W_{k+1})$$

T was considered for P_2 to execute at time $t(V_{k+1})$ but it was not executed. Hence at that time some predecessor T' of T must not have been executed. Thus $t(T') \geq t(V_{k+1})$. But this implies that $\alpha(T') > \alpha(T)$ by the definition of A-schedules. Since T was executed at time $t(T)$, T' must be executed before T and

$$t(T') \leq t(T) - 1 = t(V_{k+1})$$

Therefore $t(T') = t(V_{k+1})$ and $\alpha(T') > \alpha(W_{k+1})$. There is only one possibility for T', namely, $T' = V_{k+1}$. Thus we have $V_{k+1} < T$.

Next, suppose that for a fixed j, $1 \leq j < n_k$, we have shown that $T \in X_k$ and $t(T) \leq t(V_k) - n_k + j$ imply that $V_{k+1} < T$. Let $T' \in X_k$ with $t(T')$

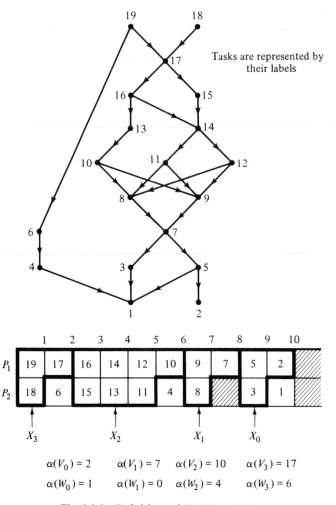

Tasks are represented by their labels

$\alpha(V_0) = 2 \qquad \alpha(V_1) = 7 \qquad \alpha(V_2) = 10 \qquad \alpha(V_3) = 17$

$\alpha(W_0) = 1 \qquad \alpha(W_1) = 0 \qquad \alpha(W_2) = 4 \qquad \alpha(W_3) = 6$

Fig. 3.2-3 Definitions of V_i, W_i, and X_i.

$= t(V_k) - n_k + j + 1$. Since

$$\alpha(V_{k+1}) > \alpha(T') \geq \alpha(V_k) > \alpha(W_{k+1})$$

as before, T' was considered at time $t(V_{k+1})$ for execution by P_2 but it was not ready to be executed. Thus some predecessor T'' of T' had not been executed by this time and we must have $t(T'') \geq t(V_{k+1}) = t(V_k) - n_k$. Also, since $T'' < T'$, $t(T'') \leq t(T') - 1 = t(V_k) - n_k + j$. If $t(T'') = t(V_k) - n_k$, then since $\alpha(T'') > \alpha(T') \geq \alpha(V_k) > \alpha(W_{k+1})$, we must have $T'' = V_{k+1}$ and we obtain $V_{k+1} < T'$ as required. Hence we may assume that $t(T') \geq t(V_k) - n_k$

$+\ 1$. By the induction hypothesis, since

$$t(V_k) - n_k + 1 \leq t(T'') \leq t(V_k) - n_k + j$$

we see that $T'' \in X_k$ and $V_{k+1} \prec T''$. Therefore by the transitivity of the partial order $\prec$ we obtain $V_{k+1} \prec T'$ and the first induction step is completed. This shows that $V_{k+1} \prec T$ for all $T \in X_k$.

Let I_k denote the set of tasks in X_k which *have no predecessors in* X_k. Since $V_{k+1} \prec T$ for all $T \in X_k$, it is not difficult to see that $S(V_{k+1}) \cap X_k = I_k$.

Suppose that now for some j, $0 \leq j \leq n_{k+1} - 2$, we have shown that if $T \in X_{k+1}$ with $t(V_{k+1}) - j \leq t(T) \leq t(V_{k+1})$, then $T \prec U$ for all $U \in X_k$. Let $T' \in X_{k+1}$ with $t(T') = t(V_{k+1}) - j - 1$. Since $T' \in X_{k+1}$, $\alpha(T') > \alpha(V_{k+1})$. Thus we must have $N(T') \geq N(V_{k+1})$, where we recall that $N(T')$ is formed by taking the decreasing sequence of α values of the immediate successors of T'. If there exists $T'' \in S(T') \cap X_{k+1}$, then by the induction hypothesis, since $t(T'') > t(T') = t(V_{k+1}) - j - 1$, i.e., $t(T'') \geq t(V_{k+1}) - j$, $T'' \prec T$ for all $T \in X_k$, and by transitivity, $T' \prec T$ for all $T \in X_k$. Thus let

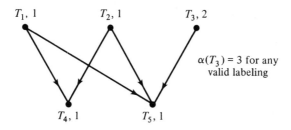

$$\alpha(T_3) = 3 \text{ for any valid labeling}$$

The A-schedule

	0	1	2	3	4
P_1	T_1	T_3		T_5	
P_2	T_2	T_4			

An optimal schedule

	0	1	2	3
P_1	T_3		T_4	
P_2	T_1	T_2	T_5	

Fig. 3.2-4　Counterexample, unequal execution times.

us assume that $S(T') \cap X_{k+1}$ is empty. By Lemma 3.1 $\alpha(T) < \alpha(V_k)$ if $t(T)$ $> t(V_k)$. Also, we have $\alpha(W_k) < \alpha(V_k)$. A moment's reflection now shows that from the definition of A-schedules, if $N(T') \geq N(V_{k+1})$ and T' has no successor in X_{k+1}, then we must have $S(T') \cap X_k = I_k$. This in turn implies that T' $\prec T$ for all $T \in X_k$. This completes the induction step and the proof that if $T \in X_k$ and $T' \in X_{k+1}$, $0 \leq k \leq r$, then $T' \prec T$.

It is now a short step to a proof of the theorem. For an arbitrary schedule, *all* the tasks in X_{k+1} must still be executed before any task in X_k can be started. Since X_{k+1} consists of $2n_{k+1} - 1$ tasks, this will require at least n_{k+1} units of time. Thus to execute G will require at least $\sum_{k=0}^{r} n_k$ units of time, no matter what schedule is used. Since $t(\mathcal{S}) = \sum_{k=0}^{r} n_k$, we have shown that $\mathcal{S}$ has minimal length and the proof is complete. ∎

We have already shown that A-schedules are not always optimal for $m > 2$ (see Fig. 3.2-2). It is also true that A-schedules need not be optimal when the execution times are not all the same. Suppose we assume that tasks can have execution times which are either one or two units in length. Figure 3.2-4 shows a graph containing such tasks which has an A-schedule for two processors that is not optimal. This example points up the obvious fact that the scheduling priority of a task must be made to depend on its execution time, or, more generally, the total execution time represented by the tasks in that path which includes the given task and for which this total is maximal.

3.3. OPTIMAL SCHEDULES FOR
TREE-STRUCTURED PRECEDENCE GRAPHS

In this section we shall consider an important special case of graphs in which the precedence relations define a tree. The number of processors available for scheduling tasks will be assumed to be arbitrary. The remaining assumptions of Section 3.2, including unit execution times for all tasks, will carry over to this section.

The precedence structures with which we shall be concerned in this section are (directed) singly rooted trees in which each vertex, except for the root, has exactly one arc incident out of the vertex. The root will have no such arcs. The trees that we shall consider will be unordered in the sense that no ordering will be assumed for the immediate predecessors of any given vertex (task). An example of these trees is shown in Fig. 3.3-1.

A simple algorithm has been devised [4] for optimally scheduling trees. The algorithm is intuitively very appealing and quite likely to occur to anyone considering this scheduling problem, but the proof of its optimality is more difficult than one might expect. The statement of this algorithm and a proof of its optimality appear below.

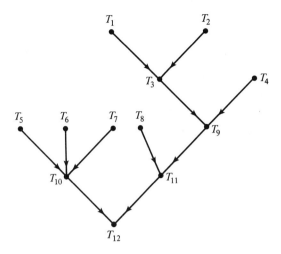

Fig. 3.3-1   A precedence tree.

The algorithm to be described assumes that the set of tasks in the given tree has initially been processed (only one pass is necessary) so that associated with each task T is its level $L(T)$ (see Section 2.1). The scheduling algorithm is described by the following statement: *Whenever a processor becomes free† assign that task (if any) all of whose predecessors have already been assigned and which is at the highest level of those tasks not yet assigned. If there is a tie among several tasks, then an arbitrary one of these tasks is selected.* A schedule produced by this algorithm will be called a *B-schedule*. An example is given in Fig. 3.3-2(a), which shows a *B*-schedule for the tree in Fig. 3.3-1 assuming $m = 3$ processors. In Fig. 3.3-2(b) the schedule is specified by simply enclosing those tasks which are executed during the same time unit. It is worthwhile observing that an *A*-schedule extended in the obvious way to $m > 2$ processors produces a valid *B*-schedule for a tree.

Before proving that *B*-schedules are optimal for trees we shall introduce a useful lower bound for the minimum execution times of arbitrary graphs and an arbitrary number (m) of processors. Subsequently, we shall show that this bound is actually achieved by *B*-schedules for trees (of tasks with equal execution times).

Let $Q(j)$ denote the set of tasks at levels greater than or equal to j, and let $\mathbf{P} = (T_{i_1}, T_{i_2}, \ldots, T_{i_L})$ be a maximum length path in a given graph G. We observe that for any j $(0 \leq j \leq L)$ it is not possible to execute all the tasks whose level exceeds j in less than $|Q(j+1)|/m$ units of time. Since at least j units of time are required for the remainder of the graph we have for

---

†Recall that although in fact more than one processor at a time may be available we shall assume that they are scheduled in the order of their indices—P_i before P_{i+1} before P_{i+2}, etc.

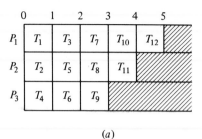

(a)

(b)

Fig. 3.3-2 *B*-schedule for Figure 3.3-1.

the length, $t_{\min}$, of a best schedule

$$(3.3.1) \qquad t_{\min} \geq \max_{0 \leq j \leq L} \left\{ j + \left\lceil \frac{|Q(j+1)|}{m} \right\rceil \right\}$$

where the notation $\lceil x \rceil$ denotes the least integer greater than or equal to x.

Note that we can proceed in a similar fashion to derive a bound on the minimum number of processors required to execute a given graph in t units of time. (L is an obvious minimum for graph execution time and so we must assume that $t \geq L$.) This bound is given by

$$(3.3.2) \qquad m_{\min} \geq \max_{0 \leq j < L} \left\lceil \frac{|Q(j+1)|}{t-j} \right\rceil, \quad t \geq L$$

To simplify the proof that *B*-schedules are optimal it is convenient to dispose first of the following special case.

Lemma 3.2

Suppose that G is a tree having fewer than m initially available tasks (leaf vertices). Then a B-schedule for G on m processors has length L, where L is the length of a longest path in G.

Proof. Let $\S$ be a B-schedule for the given graph G. Let R_i $(0 \leq i \leq t(\S) - 1)$ denote the set of tasks that are available for execution in the $(i + 1)$st time interval of $\S$. Since G is a tree, the sequence $|R_0|, |R_1|, \ldots, |R_{t(\S)-1}|$ is monotonically nonincreasing. This important observation follows from the simple fact that the execution of an available task can cause at most one task to become available for execution in the next time interval. Hence $|R_0| < m$ implies that $|R_j| < m$ for all $j(1 \leq j \leq t(\S))$. Using this fact it is easy to verify that the tasks in R_{j+1} are all at a lower level than the maximum level of those in R_j, $0 \leq j < t(\S)$, for if we assume that this is not the case, then according to the definition of B-schedules a task in R_{j+1} should have been included in R_j since it could have no predecessors in R_j and $|R_j| < m$. Thus, since the number of levels is L, we have $t(\S) \leq L$. Since L is also a lower bound for $t(\S)$, we conclude that $t(\S) = L$. ∎

Theorem 3.2

Let G be a tree and let $\S_0$ be a B-schedule for G on m processors. Then $t(\S_0) \leq t(\S)$ for all valid schedules $\S$ of G on m processors.

Proof. Let L be the number of levels in G. The result of the theorem is trivially true for $L = 1$ and so assume that $L \geq 2$. Let t denote the length of a given B-schedule for G on m processors, and let N_i denote the set of tasks executed in the first i $(1 \leq i \leq t)$ time units of the given schedule. Define p as the least integer such that $|N_{p+1} - N_p| < m$. If $p = 0$, then Lemma 3.2 applies and we are done; therefore suppose that $0 < p < t$. Note that no processor can be idle in $(0, p)$ and that $|N_i|$ is an integral multiple of m for all i, $1 \leq i \leq p$.

Define v_j $(0 \leq j < t)$ as the maximum level occupied by tasks in the tree remaining to be executed after the first $j + 1$ time units. Equivalently, we define v_j as the least integer (level) such that $Q(v_j + 1) \subseteq N_{j+1}$. Figure 3.3-3 illustrates the definitions of p and v_j. Considering the special case $j = p$ we note for future use that, although $Q(v_p + 1) \subseteq N_{p+1}$ and $N_p \subseteq N_{p+1}$, it is not possible for N_p and $Q(v_p + 1)$ to be equal, for if they were equal, then, since $|N_{p+1} - N_p| < m$ implies that the number of levels in the tree remaining at p is one greater than in the tree remaining at $p + 1$, we would have $Q(v_p) \subseteq N_{p+1}$, and this contradicts the definition of v_p.

Now from the definition of p we have from Lemma 3.2 that the tasks

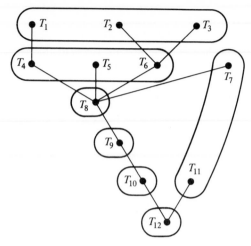

$m = 3$, $t = 7$

$p = 2$, $v_p = 4$, $Q(5) = \{1 - 7\}$

$N_2 = \{1 - 6\}$, $N_3 = \{1 - 7, 11\}$, $N_2 \subset Q(5) \subset N_3$

Fig. 3.3-3   Example for case 1.

remaining after $p + 1$ time units can be completed in v_p time units. Hence

$$t = p + 1 + v_p = v_p + \left\lceil \frac{|N_{p+1}|}{m} \right\rceil$$

To apply (3.3.1) we want to express t in terms of $Q(v_p + 1)$. We need to consider two cases:

Case 1. $N_p \subset Q(v_p + 1)$. [See the example in Fig. 3.3-3.] By definition $Q(v_p + 1) \subseteq N_{p+1}$ and so in this case

$$\left\lceil \frac{|N_{p+1}|}{m} \right\rceil = \left\lceil \frac{|Q(v_p + 1)|}{m} \right\rceil$$

Therefore we have

$$t = v_p + \left\lceil \frac{|Q(v_p + 1)|}{m} \right\rceil \leq \max_{0 \leq j \leq L} \left\{ j + \left\lceil \frac{|Q(j + 1)|}{m} \right\rceil \right\}$$

After applying (3.3.1) we are done.

Case 2. $N_p \not\subset Q(v_p + 1)$. [See the example in Fig. 3.3-4, where $p = 3$ and $v_p = 3$.] Note that this implies that N_p contains tasks at levels lower than $v_p + 1$. We shall consider two subcases:

a. Suppose there exists no integer i, $1 \leq i \leq p$, such that $N_i \subset Q(v_i + 1)$. It is readily verified that this implies for all i, $0 \leq i < p$, that the number of tasks at the highest level executed in the time unit $(i, i + 1)$ is less than m. (For each such i, $N_{i+1} - N_i$ contains at least one task at a level lower than $v_i + 1$.) This in turn means that the maximum level of tasks executed in $(i + 1, i + 2)$ is less than the maximum level of tasks executed in $(i, i + 1)$ for all i, $0 \leq i < p$. Since by definition of p and Lemma 3.2 this statement must also hold for $i \geq p$, it follows that $t = L$, which is the obvious minimum.

b. Now suppose there exists an integer i ($1 \leq i < p$) such that $N_i \subset Q(v_i + 1)$ and let s be the largest such integer. For example, in Fig. 3.3-4 $s = 1$, $v_s = 5$,

$$N_1 = \{T_2, T_3, T_4\} \subset Q(6) = \{T_1, T_2, T_3, T_4\} \subset N_2 = \{T_1 - T_4, T_7, T_8\}$$

Clearly, we can write

$$t = v_p + (p - s) + \left\lceil \frac{|Q(v_s + 1)|}{m} \right\rceil$$

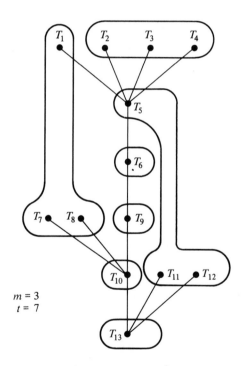

$$m = 3$$
$$t = 7$$

$$p = 3, \quad N_3 = \{1 - 5, 7, 8, 11, 12\}$$
$$N_4 = \{1 - 8, 11, 12\}$$
$$v_p = 3, \quad Q(4) = \{1 - 6\} \quad N_p \not\subset Q(v_p + 1) \subseteq N_{p+1}$$

Fig. 3.3-4   Example for case 2.

But $N_i \not\subseteq Q(v_i + 1)$ for all i $(s \leq i \leq p)$ means that $v_i = v_{i+1} + 1$ for all i $(s \leq i < p)$ and hence that $v_p + (p - s) = v_s$. Thus

$$t = v_s + \left\lceil \frac{|Q(v_s + 1)|}{m} \right\rceil \leq \max_{0 \leq j \leq L} \left\{ j + \left\lceil \frac{|Q(j + 1)|}{m} \right\rceil \right\}$$

whereupon application of (3.3.1) completes the proof. ∎

3.4. SCHEDULING OF INDEPENDENT TASKS

The discovery of scheduling algorithms for sets of independent tasks with arbitrary execution times and an arbitrary number of processors is a classic sequencing problem of wide interest and applicability. It has been conjectured that this superficially very tantalizing problem is not likely to admit of any basically nonenumerative solution [20]. However, because of the importance of the problem, a significant amount of effort has gone into the study and analysis of heuristic methods as well as efficient techniques that in essence search for optimal schedules [5]. This section will be devoted to an interesting result [6] that has been obtained for what is perhaps the most obvious, simple heuristic for nonpreemptive scheduling of independent tasks.

For systems of independent tasks let us define *largest-processing-time* (LPT) scheduling as the result of an algorithm which, whenever a processor becomes free, assigns that task whose execution time is the largest of those tasks not yet assigned. For cases when there is a tie, an arbitrary tie-breaking rule can be assumed. An example is shown in Fig. 3.4-1, where LPT scheduling

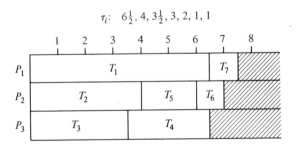

Fig. 3.4-1   An LPT schedule.

actually produces an optimal schedule. The example in Fig. 3.4-2 demonstrates that LPT scheduling is in general not optimal.

The question naturally arises as to just how good LPT scheduling is relative to the optimum. After a certain amount of experimentation to determine the possible shortcomings of LPT schedules one normally arrives at the example shown in Fig. 3.4-3(a) as the simplest, worst-case illustration for

$$\tau_i: 8, 6\tfrac{1}{2}, 6, 4, 3, 2\tfrac{1}{2}, 2\tfrac{1}{2}, 1$$

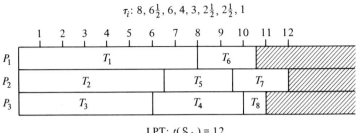

LPT: $t(\mathcal{S}_L) = 12$

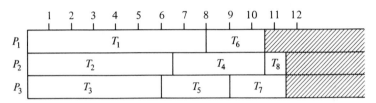

Optimal: $t(\mathcal{S}_{min}) = 11\tfrac{1}{2}$

Fig. 3.4-2 A sub-optimal LPT schedule.

$m = 2$ processors. An extension of this structure to $m = 3$ processors is shown in Fig. 3.4-3(b). Finally, in extending to an arbitrary number of processors we obtain the general example shown in Fig. 3.4-4; letting $\lfloor x \rfloor$ denote the greatest integer less than or equal to x, the task execution times are given by $\tau_i = 2m - \lfloor (i + 1)/2 \rfloor$, $i = 1, 2, \ldots, 2m$, and $\tau_{2m+1} = m$. As can be verified from the figure we have $t(\mathcal{S}_L) = 4m - 1$ and $t(\mathcal{S}_{min}) = 3m$, so that

$$\frac{t(\mathcal{S}_L)}{t(\mathcal{S}_{min})} = \frac{4}{3} - \frac{1}{3m}$$

describes the extent to which LPT scheduling is suboptimal in this case. In fact, as shown by the next theorem, Fig. 3.4-3 illustrates the worst possible performance of LPT scheduling [6].

Theorem 3.3

For a set of independent tasks let t_L denote the length of a corresponding LPT schedule and t_{min} the length of an optimal schedule. We have

(3.4.1)
$$\frac{t_L}{t_{min}} \leq \frac{4}{3} - \frac{1}{3m}$$

Proof. The theorem is trivially true for $m = 1$ and so let $m \geq 2$. Contrary to the theorem assume that we have a set $\mathfrak{I} = \{T_1, T_2, \ldots, T_n\}$ of tasks and

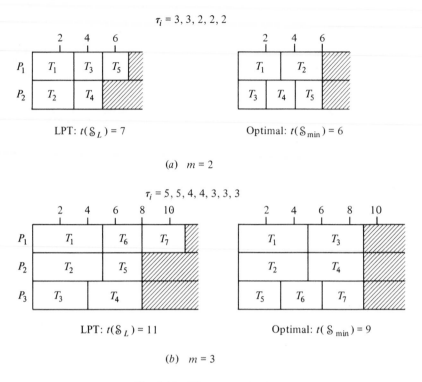

$$\tau_i = 3, 3, 2, 2, 2$$

LPT: $t(\mathcal{S}_L) = 7$

Optimal: $t(\mathcal{S}_{min}) = 6$

(a) $m = 2$

$$\tau_i = 5, 5, 4, 4, 3, 3, 3$$

LPT: $t(\mathcal{S}_L) = 11$

Optimal: $t(\mathcal{S}_{min}) = 9$

(b) $m = 3$

Fig. 3.4-3 Worst-cases for LPT.

execution times $\{\tau_1, \tau_2, \ldots, \tau_n\}$ for which (3.4.1) does not hold, and let us assume, as we may, that there exists no set of fewer tasks for which (3.4.1) does not hold. To simplify the following discussion let us also assume that the tasks are indexed in the order of decreasing execution times (i.e., $\tau_1 \geq \tau_2 \geq \cdots \geq \tau_n$) and that the tie-breaking rule always selects the task with the smallest index. With these assumptions an LPT schedule for $\mathfrak{I}$ always assigns the tasks in the order $T_1, T_2, \ldots, T_n$.

Let $\mathcal{S}_L$ be the LPT schedule for $\mathfrak{I}$ and suppose that T_k $(k \leq n)$ denotes a task with the latest completion time (t_L) in $\mathcal{S}_L$. Since the tasks T_i $(1 \leq i < k)$ are all assigned prior to T_k we observe immediately that the length t'_L of an LPT schedule for $\{T_1, T_2, \ldots, T_k\}$ must also be t_L. On the other hand, the minimal time t'_{min} for scheduling $\{T_1, T_2, \ldots, T_k\}$ must satisfy $t'_{min} \leq t_{min}$. Consequently, according to our assumptions

$$\frac{t'_L}{t'_{min}} \geq \frac{t_L}{t_{min}} > \frac{4}{3} - \frac{1}{3m}$$

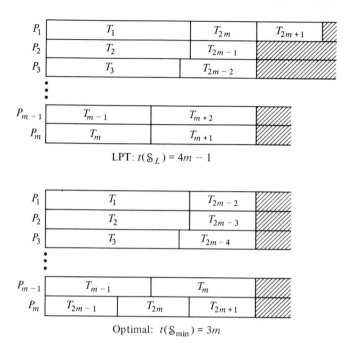

Fig. 3.4-4   The general worst-case.

Thus, if we assume that $k < n$, we have a contradiction in that there exists a set of fewer than n tasks, which violates (3.4.1). Hence we can assume that $T_n \in \mathfrak{J}$ is the only task to have the latest completion time, t_L.

We shall now further restrict our problem by showing that in any optimal schedule for $\mathfrak{J}$ there can never be assigned more than two tasks to a processor. First, we can write for the length of an optimal schedule

(3.4.2)
$$t_{\min} \geq \frac{1}{m} \sum_{i=1}^{n} \tau_i$$

Note that (3.3.1) gives the same expression when the tasks are independent and they all have unit execution times. Now let t_n denote the starting time of T_n in $\mathcal{S}_L$. Since no processor can be idle before T_n begins execution, we have

(3.4.3)
$$t_n \leq \frac{1}{m} \sum_{i=1}^{n-1} \tau_i$$

Hence

$$\frac{t_L}{t_{\min}} = \frac{t_n + \tau_n}{t_{\min}} \leq \frac{\tau_n}{t_{\min}} + \frac{1}{m t_{\min}} \sum_{i=1}^{n-1} \tau_i$$

or

$$\frac{t_L}{t_{\min}} \le \frac{(m-1)\tau_n}{mt_{\min}} + \frac{1}{mt_{\min}} \sum_{i=1}^{n} \tau_i$$

Using (3.4.2) this reduces to

$$\frac{t_L}{t_{\min}} \le \frac{(m-1)\tau_n}{mt_{\min}} + 1$$

Since (3.4.1) is assumed not to hold for $\mathfrak{I}$, it follows that

$$\frac{(m-1)\tau_n}{mt_{\min}} + 1 > \frac{4}{3} - \frac{1}{3m}$$

from which we obtain

$$t_{\min} < 3\tau_n$$

Therefore, since T_n has the least execution time, we conclude that if (3.4.1) is violated, then no processor can execute more than two tasks in an optimal schedule for $\mathfrak{I}$.

Letting $\mathcal{S}_0$ denote such an optimal schedule of length t_0 we shall now show that $\mathcal{S}_0$ can be transformed into a schedule $\mathcal{S}_0^*$ which is no longer than $\mathcal{S}_0$ and which is isomorphic to the LPT schedule, i.e., containing assignment sequences which are the same within a renaming of processors and tasks with equal execution times. Since $t_0^* = t_0$, we have a contradiction that establishes the theorem.

We begin by defining three transformations which when applied to $\mathcal{S}_0$ will not increase the schedule length. The first transformation, which we shall term type 1, is illustrated in Fig. 3.4-5. It is easily seen that if $\tau_i > \tau_j$ and $\tau_{i'} > \tau_{j'}$, then interchanging the assignments for $T_{i'}$ and $T_{j'}$ as shown in the figure will certainly not increase the overall schedule length. A type 2 transformation is shown in Fig. 3.4-6. In this figure if we assume that $\tau_i > \tau_{j'}$, then the transformed schedule clearly has a length no greater than the original schedule. Moreover, the following property of type 1 and type 2 transforma-

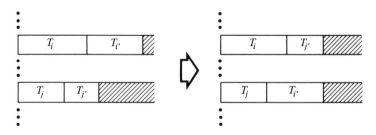

Fig. 3.4-5   Type 1 transformation.

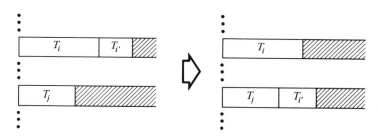

Fig. 3.4-6 Type 2 transformation.

tions is readily verified. If we let I_i and I_i' denote the least times at which P_i becomes idle in S_0 and the transformed schedule S_0', respectively, then

$$\sum_{1 \le i < j \le m} |I_i' - I_j'| < \sum_{1 \le i < j \le m} |I_i - I_j|$$

We conclude that only a finite number of transformations of types 1 and 2 can be applied to S_0.

Finally, a type 3 transformation as illustrated in Fig. 3.4-7 will simply

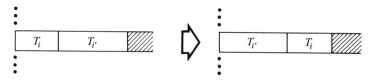

Fig. 3.4-7 Type 3 transformation.

involve an ordering, in decreasing sequence, of those tasks on processors to which two tasks have been assigned. Obviously, this transformation has no effect on schedule lengths. Also, since the number of tasks and the number of processors are finite, only a finite number of consecutive type 3 transformations can be performed on S_0.

It follows from the definitions of the three transformations that after an exhaustive application of these transformations we can obtain by an appropriate reordering of processors the schedule S_0^* illustrated in Fig. 3.4-8. Since no pair of processor assignments is subject to a transformation of type 1, 2, or 3, it must be true that

$$\tau_{k_1} \ge \tau_{k_2} \ge \cdots \ge \tau_{k_r} \ge \tau_{i_1} \ge \cdots \ge \tau_{i_s} \ge \tau_{i_s'} \ge \cdots \ge \tau_{i_1'}$$

In addition, $t_0^* = t_0$ since the transformations have not increased the schedule length and t_0 is optimal. Thus we shall be done if we can show that the apparently LPT schedule S_0^* is indeed just such a schedule. A study of Fig. 3.4-8 reveals that the only way in which S_0^* could differ from an LPT schedule is

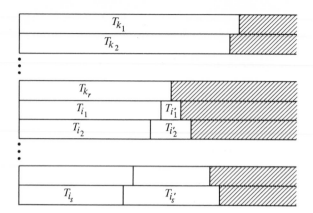

Fig. 3.4-8   The schedule S_0^*.

for two-processor assignments to be as pictured in Fig. 3.4-9 with $\tau_{i_k} > \tau_{i_p}$ $+ \tau_{i_{p'}}$ for some $k < p$. In this case, it is clearly consistent with LPT scheduling to assign $T_{i'_k}$ to P_v following the completion of $T_{i'_p}$. However, this would imply the existence of an optimal schedule in which a processor is assigned more than two tasks. This contradiction proves that S_0^* is indeed an LPT schedule, and this in turn contradicts the assumption that there exists a set of tasks violating (3.4.1).   ∎

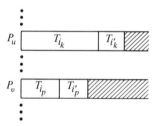

Fig. 3.4-9   Example regarding S_0^*.

3.5. LIST SCHEDULING

In the interests of simplicity or perhaps because task execution times are unknown in advance, it is worthwhile considering a scheduler that uses only a given list of the tasks to be executed and the partial order by which the sequencing of these tasks is constrained. Whenever a processor becomes free the scheduler simply performs a fixed directed scan of the list and assigns to the processor the first task encountered which has not yet been executed and whose predecessors have all been completed. The task lists submitted to this *list scheduler* are usually assumed to be ordered according to some external priority scheme. An example is shown in Fig. 3.5-1 where $\mathcal{L}$ denotes the so-called *priority list* of tasks. We assume that $\mathcal{L}$ is scanned from left to right for the first unexecuted available task, whenever a processor becomes free for assignment.

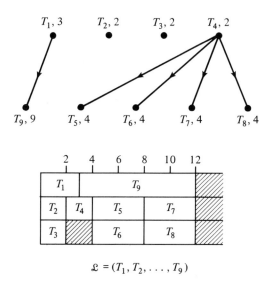

$$\mathcal{L} = (T_1, T_2, \ldots, T_9)$$

Fig. 3.5-1　Anomaly example.

Each of the scheduling algorithms discussed so far can be stated in the form of list scheduling. For example, the algorithm producing A-schedules illustrates a list scheduler in which the priority list orders the tasks so that corresponding labels are in a decreasing sequence. The LPT scheduling algorithm discussed in the last section illustrates list scheduling when the priority list is ordered by execution time. Our objectives in this section will be to expose certain anomalous properties of list scheduling and to derive corresponding bounds for the increases in schedule lengths. Following this we shall briefly outline approaches for coping with these anomalies.

The length of a list schedule depends on the number of processors, the execution time of tasks, the partial order containing precedence constraints, and the priority list used. The anomalous behavior of list scheduling refers to those instances when *increases* in schedule lengths are produced by increases in the number of processors, decreases in execution times, a removal of certain precedence constraints, and the use of different priority lists. Graham [7] has provided a single example which illustrates each of these four anomalies; this is the example shown in Fig. 3.5-1.

First, suppose that we change the number of processors from three to

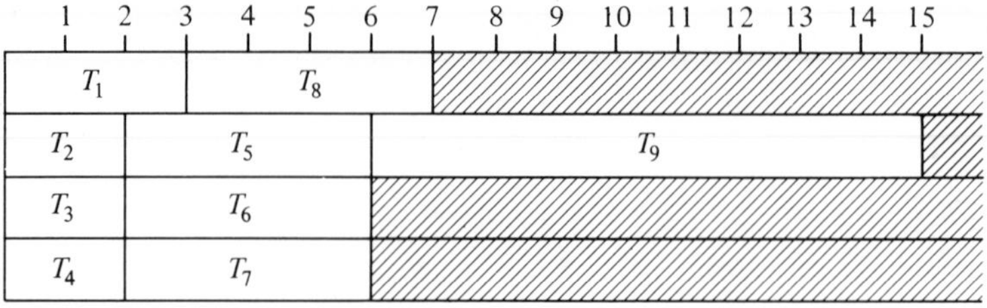

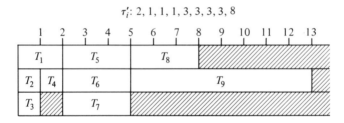

Fig. 3.5-2 Increasing *m* to 4.

four while holding the other parameters of Fig. 3.5-1 constant. As shown in Fig. 3.5-2 we have the counterintuitive result that the schedule length has increased from 12 to 15. Next, redefine the execution times so that the new times are given by $\tau_i' = \tau_i - 1$. Figure 3.5-3 shows that the schedule length has actually increased from 12 to 13.

Figure 3.5-4 demonstrates the anomaly that can arise when the partial ordering is relaxed, i.e., when certain of the precedence constraints are removed. As can be seen, the schedule length increases from 12 to 16 when the

τ_i': 2, 1, 1, 1, 3, 3, 3, 3, 8

Fig. 3.5-3 Decreasing execution times.

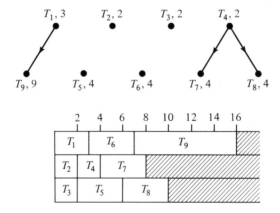

Fig. 3.5-4 Relaxing the partial ordering.

dependence of T_5 and T_6 on T_4 is removed. Finally, suppose that we change the priority list from $\mathcal{L}$ to

$$\mathcal{L}' = (T_1, T_2, T_4, T_5, T_6, T_3, T_9, T_7, T_8)$$

We then have the longer schedule shown in Fig. 3.5-5.

We shall now proceed to derive a general bound on the effects the above anomalies can have on schedule lengths. First, however, it will be convenient

$$\mathcal{L}' = (T_1, T_2, T_4, T_5, T_6, T_3, T_9, T_7, T_8)$$
Fig. 3.5-5 Changing the priority list.

to develop a general property of multiprocessor, list schedules. In particular, we wish to show that for any task system C and a corresponding schedule $\mathcal{S}$ there exists a chain of tasks in C such that whenever a processor is idle in $\mathcal{S}$ one of the tasks in the chain must be executing.

Let $\mathcal{S}$ be a valid schedule for a graph G and let t be the length of $\mathcal{S}$. Consider any task T_{i_1} with the latest completion time in $\mathcal{S}$ and let t_{i_1} be the starting time of T_{i_1} in $\mathcal{S}$. Suppose that at t_{i_1} at least one processor is in an idle period; i.e., there exists an $\epsilon > 0$ such that some processor is idle in $(t_{i_1} - \epsilon, t_{i_1} + \epsilon)$. It must be true that T_{i_1} was not assigned earlier to one of the idle processors only because there exists some task T_{i_2} which finishes at t_{i_1} and which must precede T_{i_1}; i.e., $T_{i_2} < T_{i_1}$.

Now suppose that t_{i_1} is not properly contained in the idle period of some other processor. Let $(t', t' + \epsilon)$, $t' \geq 0$, denote the latest interval of processor idle time short of t_{i_1}. Once again we can state that there must exist a task $T_{i_2} < T_{i_1}$ executing during this interval, for otherwise T_{i_1} or one of its predecessors could have been assigned during this idle period.

Focusing next on T_{i_2} we can similarly argue that if there exists any idle time prior to t_{i_2}, then there must also exist a task $T_{i_3} < T_{i_2}$ executing during this idle period. Inductively, we have the desired chain of tasks as summarized in the following lemma.

Lemma 3.3

Let $\mathcal{S}$ be an arbitrary schedule for a given task system $C = (\mathfrak{I}, <)$. Then there exists a chain of tasks

$$T_{i_1} < T_{i_2} < \cdots < T_{i_s}; \qquad T_{i_j} \in \mathfrak{I} \quad (1 \leq j \leq s)$$

such that whenever a processor is idle in $(0, t(\mathcal{S}))$ one of the other processors is executing a task in the chain.

Using this lemma we can easily establish the following bound on the effects of list-scheduling anomalies.

Theorem 3.4

Let $\mathcal{J} = \{T_1, T_2, \ldots, T_n\}$ be a given set of tasks, let $m, \tau_1, \tau_2, \ldots, \tau_n, \mathcal{L}$, and $<$ denote one choice for the number of processors, execution times, priority list, and partial ordering, respectively, and let $m', \tau'_1, \tau'_2, \ldots, \tau'_n, \mathcal{L}'$, and $<'$ denote another such choice with the restrictions that $\tau'_i \leq \tau_i (1 \leq i \leq n)$ and the partial ordering $<'$ is contained in the partial ordering $<$; i.e., each precedence relation in $<'$ is contained in $<$. Corresponding to these two choices let $\mathcal{S}$ and $\mathcal{S}'$ denote the list schedules for $\mathcal{J}$ and let t and t' denote the respective schedule lengths. Then

(3.5.1)
$$\frac{t'}{t} \leq 1 + \frac{m - 1}{m'}$$

Proof. Let ϕ_i denote the total amount of idle time on processor P_i in the interval $(0, t)$ of $\mathcal{S}$. Similarly, define ϕ'_i for $\mathcal{S}'$. Applying Lemma 3.3 to $\mathcal{S}'$ we arrive at a chain of tasks

(3.5.2)
$$T_{i_1} <' T_{i_2} <' \cdots <' T_{i_s}$$

such that whenever a processor is idle in $\mathcal{S}'$ some task in the chain is executing. We can observe immediately that

(3.5.3)
$$\sum_{i=1}^{m'} \phi'_i \leq (m' - 1) \sum_{k=1}^{s} \tau_{i_k}$$

simply because the total idle time cannot exceed that obtained when it is assumed that all remaining $m' - 1$ processors are idle when one of the T_{i_k} is executing. Now since the partial ordering $<$ contains the partial ordering $<'$, (3.5.2) also implies that

$$T_{i_1} < T_{i_2} < \cdots < T_{i_s}$$

from which we obtain

(3.5.4)
$$t \geq \sum_{k=1}^{s} \tau_{i_k} \geq \sum_{k=1}^{s} \tau'_{i_k}$$

As a result of (3.5.3) and (3.5.4) we can produce from the relation

$$t' = \frac{1}{m'} \left\{ \sum_{j=1}^{n} \tau'_j + \sum_{i=1}^{m'} \phi'_i \right\}$$

the following inequality:

$$t' \leq \frac{1}{m'}[mt + (m' - 1)t]$$

From this inequality (3.5.1) follows directly. ∎

List scheduling has received special emphasis in the problem of scheduling computations in a hard real-time environment, i.e., an environment which imposes deadlines on the completion times. (See Problems 3-11, 3-12, and 3-13). When only maximum values are known for task execution times the appearance of the anomalies arising from reduced execution times is of some importance. Thus, if we design a schedule to meet the deadlines on the basis of maximum execution times, we should like to be assured that smaller, actual execution times do not increase the resulting schedule lengths beyond acceptable deadlines.

$C = (\Im, <\cdot)$ m processors
$\Im = \{T_1, T_2, \ldots, T_{2m-1}\}$, $<\cdot = \phi$ (independent tasks)
$\tau_i = 1$ $(1 \leq i \leq m - 1)$, $\tau_i = m - 1$ $(m \leq i \leq 2m - 2)$, $\tau_{2m-1} = m$
$\mathcal{L}: (T_1, T_2, \ldots, T_{m-1}, T_{2m-1}, T_m, T_{m+1}, \ldots, T_{2m-2})$
$\mathcal{L}': (T_1, T_m, T_{m+1}, \ldots, T_{2m-2}, T_2, T_3, \ldots, T_{m-1}, T_{2m-1})$

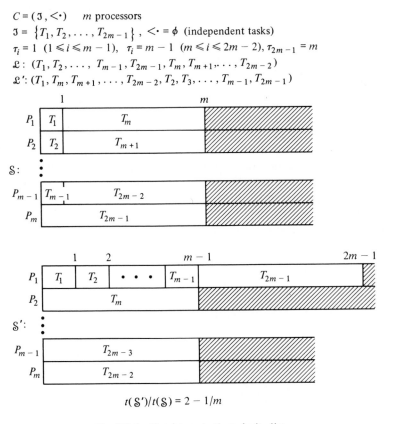

$$t(\mathcal{S}')/t(\mathcal{S}) = 2 - 1/m$$

Fig. 3.5-6 Varying only the priority list.

A direct solution to this problem can be obtained by inserting appropriate precedence relations into the original graph in the following way. Suppose that T_i and T_j are independent in the original graph G but that T_i precedes T_j on a given processor according to a given priority list and the corresponding list schedule that results when maximum execution times are assumed for the tasks. We construct a new graph G' by adding to the partial order for G the precedence constraints $T_i < T_j$ for all such pairs of tasks in G. It is easily verified that with the same priority list the graph G' is free from the anomalies arising from decreased execution times. Another, similar solution to this problem has been described [8] in which a smaller but still sufficient number of precedence relations are added to G, thus allowing for more flexibility.

Examples can be given which show that (3.5.1) is a best possible bound. In fact, the bound can be achieved by varying any *one* of the parameters $\mathcal{L}$, $<$, m, and $\{\tau_i\}$. One such example is shown in Fig. 3.5-6, where the only parameter varied is the priority list. As can be seen, the schedule lengths corresponding to the two lists $\mathcal{L}$ and $\mathcal{L}'$ are such that $t'/t = 2 - 1/m$, the value of (3.5.1) when $m = m'$. Other examples are provided in Problem 3-10.

3.6. SCHEDULING WITH PREEMPTIONS
AND PROCESSOR SHARING

If we introduce a preemption capability and remove the restriction that a task once begun must be executed to completion, we shall find in general that schedule times can be improved. A simple example is shown in Fig. 3.6-1, where a savings of 25 percent is achieved in an optimal schedule for three independent tasks with unit execution times. Of course, we have assumed in Fig. 3.6-1 that no appreciable cost is to be associated with the task preemption. In the computer application this will not generally be the case, for preemptions may imply the removal of tasks from main storage and a subsequent reloading of these tasks. However, in those cases when input/output opera-

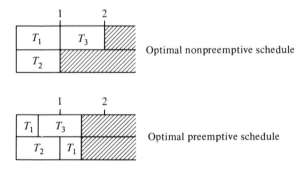

Fig. 3.6-1 Improvement with preemption.

tions cannot be overlapped sufficiently the time delays introduced will be so high that consideration of preemptions can frequently be ruled out a priori. In any event, with the models of preemptive scheduling for which theoretical results have been obtained it has been necessary to assume that preemption costs can be ignored.

For sets of independent tasks, results for optimal preemptive schedules have been known for some time [9].

Theorem 3.5

Let $\mathfrak{I} = \{T_1, T_2, \ldots, T_n\}$ be a set of independent tasks with the execution time for T_i ($1 \leq i \leq n$) given by τ_i. Let $t_{\min}$ be the length of an optimal preemptive schedule for $\mathfrak{I}$ on m processors. Then

$$(3.6.1) \qquad t_{\min} = \max \left\{ \max_{1 \leq i \leq n} \{\tau_i\}, \frac{1}{m} \sum_{i=1}^{n} \tau_i \right\}$$

Proof. It is clear that (3.6.1) must be a lower bound on $t_{\min}$ since no schedule can terminate in less time than it takes to execute that task with the largest execution time, and a schedule cannot be more efficient than to keep all the processors busy. To see that this bound is achieved we work out the following schedule for $\mathfrak{I}$ on m processors. (The construction is illustrated in Fig. 3.6-2.)

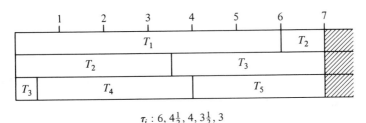

$$\tau_i : 6, 4\tfrac{1}{2}, 4, 3\tfrac{1}{2}, 3$$

Fig. 3.6-2   Example for 5 independent tasks.

First, let $t = (1/m) \sum_{i=1}^{n} \tau_i$ and assume that $t > \max_{1 \leq i \leq n} \{\tau_i\}$. We begin by assigning a sequence of tasks $T_1, T_2, \ldots, T_j$ ($j \geq 1$) to P_1, where j is the smallest integer such that $t < \sum_{i=1}^{j+1} \tau_i$. At this point we assign T_{j+1} to P_1 in the interval $(\sum_{i=1}^{j} \tau_i, t)$ and to P_2 in the interval $(0, t')$, where $t' = \sum_{i=1}^{j+1} \tau_i - t$; i.e., that part of T_{j+1} not executed on P_1 is executed on P_2. We know that this cannot cause T_{j+1} to be assigned to both P_1 and P_2 at any given time instant in $(0, t)$ because $t > \tau_{j+1}$. We now continue assigning to P_2 tasks $T_{j+2}, T_{j+3}, \ldots, T_{j+k}$ until once again a task assignment (for T_{j+k+1}) would exceed the interval $(0, t)$. At this point T_{j+k+1} is assigned to the remaining time on P_2 with the remainder of T_{j+k+1} assigned as an initial task for P_3. We proceed in this way until we have made the assignment for T_n. We know that T_n will be completed at time t on P_m since $t = (1/m) \sum_{i=1}^{n} \tau_i$ and since there is no idle time in $(0, t)$ on any processor. Also, from the fact that $\tau_i < t$ for all i $(1 \leq i \leq n)$ we know that at no time is there more than one processor assigned to any given task.

Finally, if we assume that $\tau_{max} = \max_{1 \leq i \leq n} \{\tau_i\} > t$, then one or more tasks will have to be assigned for their entire execution time on a single processor. From the construction above it is obvious that $\mathcal{S}$ can be assigned in the interval $(0, \tau_{max})$. ∎

A scheduling discipline closely related to preemptive scheduling is termed *processor sharing*. For this discipline the m processors are considered to comprise a certain amount of computing capability rather than being discrete units. It is assumed that this computing capability can be assigned to tasks in any amount between zero and the equivalent of one processor; as before a task can never execute at a rate that exceeds that achievable on a single processor. If we assign a fixed amount $\beta, 0 < \beta \leq 1$, of computing capability to a task, then we assume that the execution time of the task is increased by a factor of $1/\beta$. For example, if $\beta = \frac{1}{2}$ for a task T with execution time τ, then T will take 2τ units of time to complete. An example is shown in Fig. 3.6-3. The Gantt chart representation is extended in an obvious way for

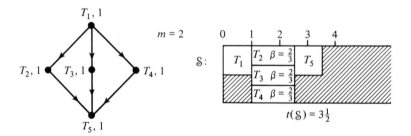

Fig. 3.6-3   Processor sharing.

processor-sharing schedules—we simply use a vertical subdivision to denote the assigned βs. Note that the best schedule without preemptions and processor sharing requires 4 time units, while the processor-sharing schedule requires only $3\frac{1}{2}$ time units. It is to be emphasized that according to our definition the fraction of computing capability assigned to a task does not change during the course of execution.

Although the physical implementation of processor sharing may be difficult to envision, the concept will be useful for two reasons. First, it will greatly simplify our statement of optimal preemptive scheduling algorithms, and, second, it will provide in Chapter 4 a useful and relatively simple model of time-sharing scheduling algorithms.

If we allow the amount of computing capability assigned to a task to change before the task is completed (we include the case where the task is not executed at all for some interval), then we call this the *general scheduling* discipline. It should be clear that in allowing the value of β for a given task to change before the completion of the task we have effectively introduced an explicit preemptive capability. It follows that every preemptive schedule is a general schedule. An example of an optimal general schedule is shown in Fig. 3.6-4. Note that both T_3 and T_5 are tasks for which the assigned computing capability does not remain constant throughout their execution.

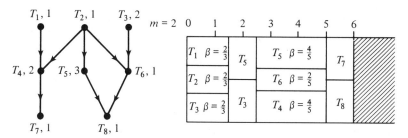

Fig. 3.6-4   General scheduling.

It is of immediate interest to ascertain the relative effectiveness of processor-sharing, preemptive, and general scheduling. For this purpose we shall introduce the following terminology. For a given number of processors we say that discipline D_1 is *more effective* than discipline D_2 if and only if 1) for every schedule for a given graph according to D_2 there is a schedule according to D_1 which is at most as long, and 2) there exists a graph for which the optimal schedule according to D_1 is shorter than any schedule according to D_2. D_1 and D_2 will be *equally effective* if for all graphs the optimal schedules according to both disciplines have the same length.

Figure 3.6-3 demonstrates that processor-sharing (and hence general) scheduling is more effective than nonpreemptive scheduling. Also, Fig. 3.6-1 shows that preemptive scheduling is more effective than nonpreemptive. The following result compares processor-sharing, preemptive, and general scheduling [10].

Theorem 3.6

1. The general and preemptive disciplines are equally effective.
2. The preemptive (and therefore the general) discipline is more effective than the processor-sharing discipline.

Proof. 1. It will be sufficient if we can show that any general schedule on m processors for a given graph G can be transformed into a valid preemptive schedule for G of equal length. Hence let $\math8{S}$ be a general schedule for G and let $t_1 < t_2 < \cdots < t_k$ be the sequence of times when task assignments change in S. For example, in Fig. 3.6-4 $k = 4$, $t_1 = 1\frac{1}{2}$, $t_2 = 2\frac{1}{2}$, $t_3 = 5$, and $t_4 = 6$. The intervals $(0, t_1) (t_1, t_2) \cdots (t_{k-1}, t_k)$ have the property that any two tasks which are assigned in the same interval must be independent, for if this is not true, then one of the tasks must complete in the interval, and this contradicts the definition of the sequence $t_1 \cdots t_k$.

Consider the interval (t_i, t_{i+1}) and let $T_{i_1}, T_{i_2}, \ldots, T_{i_s}$ be the tasks executed in this interval at rates $\alpha_{i_1}, \alpha_{i_2}, \ldots, \alpha_{i_s}$, respectively. Thus the task T_{i_j} $(1 \leq j \leq s)$ receives $\alpha_{i_j}(t_{i+1} - t_i)$ units of execution time in (t_i, t_{i+1}). Now, using the execution times $\alpha_{i_j}(t_{i+1} - t_i)$ we simply apply the construction in Theorem 3.5 to produce a preemptive schedule for this interval which is of equal length. Doing this for all intervals (t_i, t_{i+1}) the general schedule will be transformed into a preemptive schedule for G which has equal length and which does not violate any precedence constraints.

2. Since 1 above shows that processor sharing cannot be more effective than preemptive scheduling, it is sufficient to give an example for which the optimal preemptive schedule is shorter than the optimal processor-sharing schedule. Such an example is shown in Fig. 3.6-5 along with an optimal

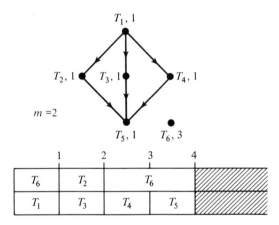

An optimal preemptive schedule

Fig. 3.6-5 Preemption vs. processor sharing.

preemptive schedule. It is not difficult to verify that the optimal processor-sharing schedule must have a length exceeding that of the optimal preemptive schedule. ∎

In our next result we shall bound the maximum improvement obtainable by preemptive (and hence general) scheduling as compared to nonpreemptive scheduling [3, 10]. First, however, we shall extend the definitions of path length and level as follows. Let $T_{i_1}, T_{i_2}, \ldots, T_{i_s}$ be the tasks in some given chain (or path). Then the path length of this chain is $\sum_{j=1}^{s} \tau_{i_j}$. As before, the level of a task T in G is the length of a longest path from T to a terminal task of G. Note that the present definition coincides with our original definition when we assume that $\tau_i = 1$ for all i.

Theorem 3.7

For an arbitrary graph G and $m \geq 1$ processors let t_N and t_P denote the lengths of optimal nonpreemptive and preemptive schedules, respectively. Then

(3.6.2)
$$\frac{t_N}{t_P} \leq 2 - \frac{1}{m}$$

Moreover, (3.6.2) represents a best possible bound; i.e., there is no smaller function of the single variable m which satisfies (3.6.2)†.

Proof. We proceed by comparing an upper bound for t_N with a lower bound for t_P.

Let $\mathcal{S}$ be any list schedule for G and let I denote the total idle time (on all processors) in $\mathcal{S}$. According to Lemma 3.3, there exists a chain of tasks in G such that whenever a processor is idle in $\mathcal{S}$ a task in this chain must be executing on another processor. Since this chain can have a length at most L, the maximum path length in G, we have

$$I \leq (m - 1)L$$

From the equality (for all scheduling disciplines)

$$t_N = \frac{I + \sum_{T_i \in G} \tau_i}{m}$$

We therefore have

(3.6.3)
$$t_N \leq \frac{\sum_{T_i \in G} \tau_i + (m - 1)L}{m}$$

Now for any of the scheduling disciplines discussed in this chapter the length of a schedule $\mathcal{S}$ can never be less than a longest path length nor can a schedule $\mathcal{S}$ be more efficient than to keep all processors busy all the time.

---

†However, (3.6.2) does *not* represent a best possible bound if we allow for nonpreemptive schedules in which processors can remain idle when tasks are available for execution. See Fig. 3.1-2 and Problems 3-16 and 3-17.

Thus

(3.6.4)
$$t_P \geq \max \left\{ L, \frac{\sum\limits_{T_i \in G} \tau_i}{m} \right\}$$

Combining (3.6.3) and (3.6.4) we have

$$\frac{t_N}{t_P} \leq \frac{\sum\limits_{T_i \in G} \tau_i + (m-1)L}{m \max \left\{ L, \frac{1}{m} \sum\limits_{T_i \in G} \tau_i \right\}}$$

Recognizing that this ratio is maximum when $(1/m) \sum_{T_i \in G} \tau_i = L$, after substitution we have the result in (3.6.2).

We can show that this is in fact a best possible bound by an example. In Fig. 3.6-6 is shown a graph for which the best nonpreemptive and preemptive schedules have lengths $2m - 1 + \epsilon$, and $m + 2\epsilon$, respectively. Therefore

$$\frac{t_N}{t_P} = \frac{2m - 1 + \epsilon}{m + 2\epsilon}$$

and the bound (3.6.2) can be approached arbitrarily closely by our selection of ϵ. ∎

It is interesting to note that, in view of Theorem 3.4, we may characterize the removal of preemptions from a preemptive schedule as producing an "anomaly" whose maximum effect is also governed by (3.5.1) (with $m' = m$).

Before presenting specific preemptive scheduling algorithms we shall extend the bounds on schedule lengths and the minimum number of processors mentioned in Section 3.3 for graphs having tasks with equal execution times. Basically, all we need is a generalization of level. Let $L'(T_i) = L(T_i) - \tau_i$ denote the length of a longest path from T_i to a terminal task diminished by the execution time of T_i. For $0 \leq y \leq \tau_i$ we say that T_i has $\tau_i - y$ units of processing at level greater than or equal to $L'(T_i) + y$. The total processing in G at level greater than or equal to x is denoted by W_x and defined as follows. Let

$$\Omega = \{T_j \,|\, T_j \in G \text{ and } L'(T_j) \leq x \leq L'(T_j) + \tau_j\}$$

and

$$\Lambda = \{T_r \,|\, T_r \in G \text{ and } L'(T_r) > x\}$$

Then

(3.6.5)
$$W_x = \sum_{T_r \in \Lambda} \tau_r + \sum_{T_j \in \Omega} [L(T_j) - x]$$

The same arguments that were used to establish (3.3.1) and (3.3.2) carry

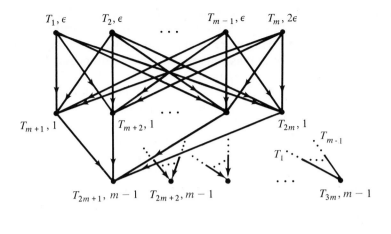

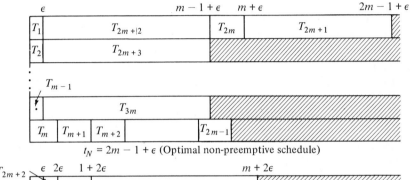

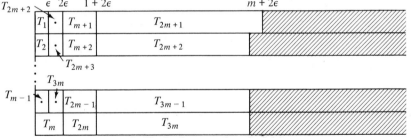

Fig. 3.6-6 Preemptive vs. nonpreemptive scheduling.

through when we use the generalized notion of level [11]. For example, a lower bound on the minimum number of processors required to execute a graph in $t \geq L$ time units, where L is the maximum path length in the given graph, is given by

$$(3.6.6) \qquad m_{\min} \geq \max_{0 \leq x \leq L} \left\{ \frac{W_x}{t - x} \right\}, \quad t \geq L$$

where x is a continuous variable in the interval $0 \leq x \leq L$. The lower bound on computation time given a fixed number of processors can be similarly generalized. These new bounds are valid for any of the scheduling disciplines discussed so far and for graphs whose tasks have arbitrary execution times. These bounds are clearly better than (3.3.1) and (3.3.2) for the preemptive and general scheduling disciplines. For the case of tasks with equal execution time it is not difficult to verify that the new bounds give the same results as the discrete versions.

We shall now introduce algorithms for optimal preemptive scheduling subject to the conditions of Sections 3.2 and 3.3, except that tasks may have arbitrary execution times. That is, we consider arbitrary graphs and two processors and tree structures with an arbitrary number of processors. The preemptive algorithms will be developed informally as limits of Algorithms A and B, i.e., the algorithms generating A-schedules and B-schedules. We begin with Algorithm A; based on the limiting operation to be described we shall see that the resulting algorithm also applies to tree structures and $m \geq 2$ processors.

Suppose that we have an arbitrary graph G whose tasks have execution times $\tau_1, \tau_2, \ldots, \tau_n$, respectively. We assume that the τ_is are arbitrary subject to the constraint that they be *mutually commensurable;* i.e., there exists a positive real number w such that each task execution time can be expressed as an integral multiple of w. (Hereafter, w will be taken as the largest such number). Note that the assumption of commensurability is not important from a practical point of view, for any set of τ_is can be approximated arbitrarily closely by mutually commensurable ones.

In terms of w we define a graph G_w which is obtained from G by replacing each task T_i by a chain of n_i subtasks $T_{i1}, \ldots, T_{in_i}$ having execution times of w time units where $\tau_i = n_i w$. For example, in Fig. 3.6-7(a) we choose $w = 1$ and obtain the graph G_1 in Fig. 3.6-7(b). Assuming that we have a system in which preemptions are allowed only at times $w, 2w, 3w, \ldots$, an optimal nonpreemptive schedule for G_w (as obtained by Algorithm A, for example, when $m = 2$) can be viewed as an optimal preemptive schedule for G. In Fig. 3.6-7 we have also shown optimal schedules for G which indicate the improvement by a factor of $\frac{7}{6}$ made possible by allowing preemptions at the end of each unit interval.

Now consider the sequencing produced by Algorithm A for the graph $G_{w/n}$ as $n \rightarrow \infty$, assuming an arbitrary number $m \geq 2$ of processors. Recall that Algorithm A at each decision point always sequences the highest-level available tasks first. Since a given task in G can only retain its scheduling priority in $G_{w/n}$ over a time interval w/n, we note that the ordering of task labels produced by the labeling algorithm *at a given level* has less importance as w/n becomes small. Thus, because of the highest-level-first property, it is apparent that in the limit Algorithm A converges to an algorithm which at each point in time gives highest priority to those tasks in G requiring process-

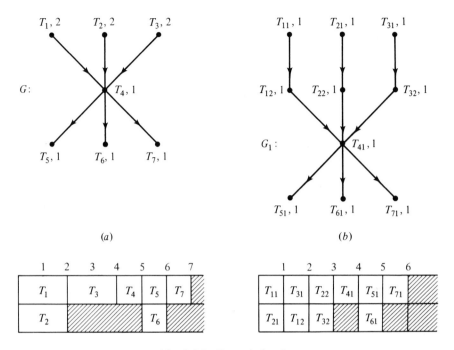

Fig. 3.6-7 Example for G_w.

ing at the highest level in the graph remaining to be executed. Since $w/n \rightarrow 0$, we also see that if there is more than one highest-level task, then these tasks effectively share the m processors in the processor-sharing mode described earlier. Specifically, we have in the limit the following *general* scheduling algorithm.

Algorithm C

Assign one processor each to the tasks at the highest level. If there is a tie among b tasks (because they are at the same level) for the last a ($a < b$) processors, then assign a/b of a processor to each of these b tasks. Whenever either of the two events described below occurs, reassign the processors to the unexecuted portion of the graph G according to the above rule. These are

Event 1: A task is completed.

Event 2: We reach a point where, if we were to continue the present assignment, we would be executing some tasks at a lower level at a faster rate than other tasks at a higher level.

An example is shown in Fig. 3.6-8 along with the equivalent preemptive schedule obtained according to the procedure described in Theorem 3.5. From the figure we observe that at $t = 1$ we have an occurrence of event 2 (this is the only such occurrence). For scheduling purposes it is natural to

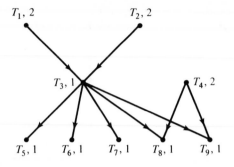

Schedule from Algorithm C

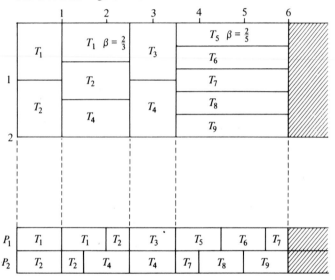

An optimal preemptive schedule

Fig. 3.6-8 Example for Algorithm C.

refer to paths of maximal length in a graph as *critical paths*, and in this sense Algorithm C can be called a critical path algorithm. (See also Problem 3-8).

It is easily verified with reference to Section 3.3 that Algorithm B applied to trees $G_{w/n}$ also converges to Algorithm C (applied to G) when $n \rightarrow \infty$. Accordingly, we have demonstrated informally that the significance of Algorithm C is contained in the following result.

Theorem 3.8

Algorithm C produces minimal length schedules when either $m = 2$ or the graph is a tree.

A detailed proof of this theorem is quite long [10, 12]; we shall therefore not go beyond the arguments provided by the limiting operation we have described. An example showing that the schedules provided by Algorithm C for arbitrary graphs and $m \geq 2$ processors are not necessarily optimal is given in Fig. 3.6-9. According to Algorithm C, $s_1, \ldots, s_m$ and $r_1, \ldots, r_{m-1}$

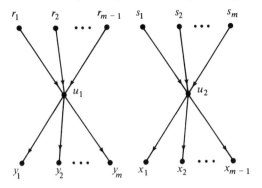

Unit execution times, m processors

Fig. 3.6-9   Counterexample: Algorithm C.

would all be executed in parallel. Then would come the concurrent execution of u_1 and u_2 followed by the parallel execution of $x_1, \ldots, x_{m-1}$ and $y_1, \ldots,$ y_m. This would give a schedule length of $5 - 2/m$, whereas the optimal schedule is easily seen to have length 4.

One question that we have not yet addressed is the following. For each $n \geq 1$ can we find a graph G such that for some $k \geq 1$ the optimal nonpreemptive schedule for $G_{w/(n+k)}$ is shorter than the optimal nonpreemptive schedule for $G_{w/n}$? For the two-processor case the answer is known to be no. In particular, it is known that an optimal nonpreemptive schedule for $G_{w/2}$ is exactly the same length as the optimal preemptive schedule for G (see Figs. 3.6-7 and 3.6-8 for illustrations of this fact). Thus for two processors we have alternative but equivalent methods of computing the optimal preemptive schedule for an arbitrary graph: Either Algorithm A can be applied to $G_{w/2}$ or Algorithm C can be applied to G. As an extension to $m > 2$ processors it has been conjectured [11] that an optimal preemptive schedule for G has the same length as an optimal nonpreemptive schedule for $G_{w/m!}$.

3.7.   SYSTEMS OF DIFFERENT PROCESSORS

There are a number of important applications in which tasks must be executed on a number of different processors, each with different capabilities. One obvious example is a system comprising central processing units (CPUs) and input/output processors. We shall consider task systems containing at most m independent tasks which require a distinct processor. The corresponding problem of finding minimal length schedules, assuming that all task execution times are known in advance, is usually referred to as the job-shop problem because of its many industrial applications. Nonenumerative procedures for solving this general problem even for the simplest nontrivial case of $m = 2$ are not known. As with other combinatorial problems of similar importance, however, heuristic, branch-and-bound, and various programming approaches have been applied effectively. A comprehensive treatment can be found in [2].

An important special case of the job-shop problem occurs when we assume that processors are linearly ordered and that the tasks of a given task system must be executed in the sequence determined by this linear ordering. Thus, for example, it may be necessary to assume that an input task first executes on an input processor, a CPU task executes next, and finally a task is executed on an output processor. This specialization of the job-shop problem is well known as the flow-shop problem. The most general, efficient solution [13] known for this problem is restricted to $m = 2$. After presenting this classic result we shall mention two specialized extensions that have also been amenable to this type of solution and have meaning in the computer application.

For the two-processor flow-shop problem let C_i $(1 \leq i \leq n)$ be a set of chains consisting of two tasks each; A_i and B_i denote the execution times of the first and second tasks of C_i. The first task of C_i is to be executed on processor P_1 and the second on processor P_2. An example schedule is shown in Fig. 3.7-1, where we have used α_i and β_i to denote the execution times of the

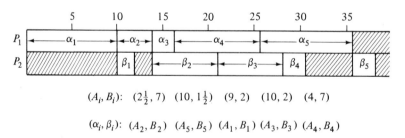

$$(A_i, B_i): \quad (2\tfrac{1}{2}, 7) \quad (10, 1\tfrac{1}{2}) \quad (9, 2) \quad (10, 2) \quad (4, 7)$$

$$(\alpha_i, \beta_i): \quad (A_2, B_2) \quad (A_5, B_5) \quad (A_1, B_1) \quad (A_3, B_3) \quad (A_4, B_4)$$

Fig. 3.7-1 An example schedule.

ith tasks scheduled on processors 1 and 2, respectively. (Thus the sequences of αs and βs are simply permutations of $A_1, A_2, \ldots, A_n$ and $B_1, B_2, \ldots B_n$, respectively.) We shall begin by restricting considerably the class of schedules that needs to be examined for the two-processor case.

Lemma 3.4

From every two-processor flow-shop schedule we can construct a schedule at most as long and with the following properties:

1. Neither processor is ever idle when a task is available for it to execute (idle time never needs to be introduced).
2. The sequences of task systems represented on the two processors are identical (i.e., the ith tasks on the first and second processor belong to the same task system).

Proof. We shall prove 2 and leave the proof of 1 to the reader.
Suppose that we have a schedule $\mathcal{S}$ as shown in Fig. 3.7-2(a) where (the

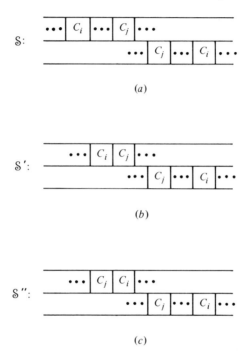

(a)

(b)

(c)

Fig. 3.7-2 Establishing the same sequence on P_1 and P_2.

first task of) C_i precedes (the first task of) C_j on P_1 but follows C_j on P_2. Clearly, without violating precedence constraints we can resequence the tasks on P_1 so as to transform $\mathcal{S}$ into the schedule $\mathcal{S}'$ of Fig. 3.7-2(b); i.e., the tasks between those for C_i and C_j are moved to the left so that the latter tasks are adjacent. Finally, $\mathcal{S}'$ can obviously be transformed into the schedule of Fig. 3.7-2(c). Inductively, we can therefore construct a schedule having the same sequence of task systems on both processors. ∎

As a result of the first property we see that the only schedules we need to consider are those in which the assignment on P_1 is compact and left-justified, as in Fig. 3.7-1. As a result of the second property we can (and shall) speak of one sequence for a two-processor problem, with the understanding that this sequence applies to both P_1 and P_2. The first property in Lemma 3.4 is easily generalized for an arbitrary number of processors. The second property can be slightly generalized by a symmetric application to processors P_{m-1} and P_m. That is, for an m-processor flow-shop problem the task sequences on P_1 and P_2 can be made the same and the sequences on P_{m-1} and P_m can be made the same. Note the implication that in the three-processor case (as in the two-processor case) we need only consider schedules having the same task-system sequence on all processors. Problem 3-15 shows an example for $m = 4$ which proves that this "order-preserving" property does not extend to all processors when $m > 3$. We shall now present the main result.

Theorem 3.9

Let $\mathcal{S}$ be a schedule for a two-processor flow-shop problem and suppose that $\mathcal{S}$ has the properties stated in Lemma 3.4. $\mathcal{S}$ will be of minimal length if for all i and j, C_i precedes C_j whenever $\min(A_i, B_j) < \min(A_j, B_i)$.

Proof. $\mathcal{S}$ will be shown to have minimal length by showing that the (internal) idle time on P_2 is minimal. Accordingly, we shall first develop an expression for this idle time in terms of the α_is and β_is.

Define X_i to be the idle time on P_2 while the ith task is executing on P_1. From the example in Fig. 3.7-1 we have $X_1 = 10$, $X_2 = 2\frac{1}{2}$, $X_3 = 0$, $X_4 = 0$, and $X_5 = 5\frac{1}{2}$. We observe immediately that $X_i > 0$ if and only if

$$(3.7.1) \qquad \sum_{j=1}^{i-1} X_j + \sum_{j=1}^{i-1} \beta_j < \sum_{j=1}^{i} \alpha_j$$

Thus we have

$$(3.7.2) \qquad X_i = \max\left\{0, \sum_{j=1}^{i} \alpha_j - \sum_{j=1}^{i-1} \beta_j - \sum_{j=1}^{i-1} X_j\right\}$$

To solve (3.7.2), we first add

$$(3.7.3) \qquad R_{i-1} = \sum_{j=1}^{i-1} X_j$$

to both sides and obtain

$$(3.7.4) \qquad R_i = \max\{R_{i-1}, Y_i\}, \quad i > 1$$

where $R_1 = Y_1 = \alpha_1$ and

$$(3.7.5) \qquad Y_i = \sum_{j=1}^{i} \alpha_j - \sum_{j=1}^{i-1} \beta_j, \quad i > 1$$

However, (3.7.4) is easily recognized as a recursive form of the function

$$(3.7.6) \qquad R_i = \max\{Y_1, Y_2, \ldots, Y_i\}$$

Thus the length of $\mathcal{S}$ will be minimal if R_n, the maximum of the Y_is ($1 \leq i \leq n$), is minimized. We shall now show that this follows from the hypothesis of the theorem. For simplicity we shall begin by assuming that $\min(A_i, B_j) \neq \min(A_j, B_i)$ for all i and j.

Suppose that we have already assigned $k - 1$ task systems on P_1 and P_2 and C_i and C_j are to be considered for the kth and $(k + 1)$st positions in the schedule. If we suppose that C_i occupies the kth position and C_j the $(k + 1)$st, then from (3.7.5)

$$(3.7.7) \qquad Y_k = A_i - \beta_{k-1} + Y_{k-1}; \qquad Y_{k+1} = A_j - B_i + Y_k$$

Reversing the order of C_j and C_i gives for the new sequence

$$(3.7\ 8) \qquad Y'_k = A_j - \beta_{k-1} + Y_{k-1}; \qquad Y'_{k+1} = A_i - B_j + Y'_k$$

From (3.7.7) and (3.7.8) we shall have

$$\max(Y_k, Y_{k+1}) < \max(Y'_k, Y'_{k+1})$$

if

$$\min(-Y'_k, -Y'_{k+1}) < \min(-Y_k, -Y_{k+1})$$

or

$$\min(-Y'_k, B_j - A_i - Y'_k) < \min(-Y_k, B_i - A_j - Y_k)$$

Adding $A_j + Y_k$ to all terms the inequality becomes

$$\min(Y_k - Y'_k + A_j, Y_k - Y'_k - (A_i - A_j) + B_j) < \min(A_j, B_i)$$

Substituting from (3.7.7) and (3.7.8) the relation $Y_k - Y'_k = A_i - A_j$, we get

$$(3.7.9) \qquad\qquad \min(A_i, B_j) < \min(A_j, B_i)$$

Thus, if (3.7.9) holds, then the larger of the above two values of Y_i is less when we put C_i before C_j. It follows that in any schedule $\max\{Y_1, \ldots, Y_n\}$ can only decrease by reversing the positions of consecutive tasks for which (3.7.9) is violated. If we now demonstrate that the relation in (3.7.9) constitutes a linear ordering of the task systems, then we are done, for in this case a schedule satisfying the statement of the theorem must always exist and be unique. However, the relation will clearly be a linear ordering if it can be shown to be transitive. A simple case analysis suffices for this purpose, but the details are left to the reader.

In those cases where $\min(A_i, B_j) = \min(A_j, B_i)$ for some i and j it is easy to verify that $\max\{Y_1, \ldots, Y_n\}$ is unaffected by the relative ordering chosen for C_i and C_j. Hence, in general, there may be more than one minimal length schedule. ■

It is clearly desirable in the computer application to extend our results to cover modes of job operation in which disjoint input, execute, and output phases are executed in sequence. This extension is possible to a limited extent. In particular, consider the case $m = 3$ and let A_i, B_i, and D_i be defined as the execution times on P_1, P_2, and P_3, respectively. We assume that task systems must execute on processors P_1, P_2, and P_3 in that order. Using techniques similar to those of the preceding theorem it is possible to show that if either $\min\{A_i\} \geq \max\{B_i\}$ or $\min\{D_i\} \geq \max\{B_i\}$, then minimal lengths are obtained by putting C_i before C_j whenever

$$(3.7.10) \qquad \min(A_i + B_i, B_j + D_j) < \min(A_j + B_j, B_i + D_i)$$

Thus for this special case we have a scheduling algorithm identical to the one implied by Theorem 3.9 except that A_i is replaced by $A_i + B_i$ and B_i is replaced by $B_i + D_i$. Note that the conditions of this special case require that the execution times on P_2 be completely dominated by the execution times on either P_1 or P_3. If the B_i represent CPU activities while the A_i or D_i apply to input/output processing, then in several important applications involving I/O-bound systems these conditions might very well be met. It is also worth pointing out that experimental studies [2] have shown (3.7.10) to be an excellent "first-cut" scheduling criterion even when the B_i are not dominated by either the A_i or D_i.

Finally, Jackson [14] has examined a model in which the first and third tasks execute on the same processor, but the second task of each task system is executed on a processor that is different for each task. With the A_i, B_i, and D_i defined as before it has been shown that the criterion in (3.7.10) again leads to minimal length schedules.

In the above computer application it is perhaps best to interpret the second task as a CPU task. It must be assumed that the CPU capacity of the system (i.e., the number of CPUs) is sufficient to ensure an execution time for each task which is the same for all sequences of task systems on the first (input/output) processor. The implication of this assumption is once again an I/O-bound system.

3.8. SCHEDULING TO MINIMIZE MEAN FLOW TIME

In addition to total schedule length, a principal schedule measure of interest is the mean *flow time* (or time in system). More precisely, let t_i denote the completion time of task T_i in a schedule for a task system C containing n

tasks. Then the mean flow time is defined to be

(3.8.1)
$$\bar{t} = \frac{1}{n} \sum_{i=1}^{n} t_i$$

A major reason for the importance of this measure lies in its connection with the mean number $\bar{n}$ of incomplete tasks over the schedule-length, $t_{max} = \max\{t_i\}$. (Although $\bar{t}$, t_{max}, and $\bar{n}$ vary with different schedules, this dependence will be suppressed from the notation in this section, as long as ambiguities do not arise.) For the application being studied, the number of incomplete tasks as a function of time is a discrete process. In particular, it changes by at most n discrete jumps from n at $t = 0$ to zero at $t = t_{max}$. Now, for a given schedule, let us order the tasks according to the sequence in which they complete; if any two or more tasks complete at the same time, then their relative positions in the ordering are immaterial. Let $t(1) \leq t(2) \leq \cdots \leq t(n)$ denote the task completion times according to this ordering. If we define $t(0) = 0$, then we have

(3.8.2)
$$\bar{n} = \frac{1}{t_{max}} \sum_{i=0}^{n-1} (n - i)[t(i + 1) - t(i)]$$

An example illustrating these definitions is given in Fig. 3.8-1.

Expanding (3.8.2) into two sums we can write

$$\bar{n} = \frac{1}{t_{max}} \left\{ \sum_{i=1}^{n} (n - i + 1)t(i) - \sum_{i=1}^{n} (n - i)t(i) \right\} = \frac{1}{t_{max}} \sum_{i=1}^{n} t(i)$$

However,

$$\sum_{i=1}^{n} t(i) = \sum_{i=1}^{n} t_i = n\bar{t}$$

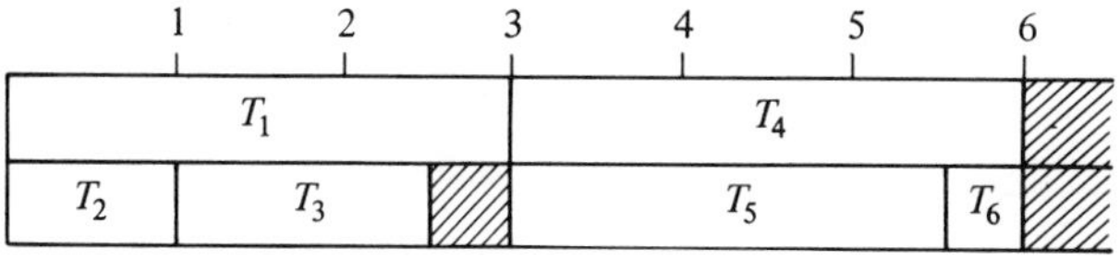

$$t(i): \quad 1, 2\tfrac{1}{2}, 3, 5\tfrac{1}{2}, 6, 6$$

$$t_i: \quad 3, 1, 2\tfrac{1}{2}, 6, 5\tfrac{1}{2}, 6$$

$$\bar{t} = \frac{1 + 2\tfrac{1}{2} + 3 + 5\tfrac{1}{2} + 6 + 6}{6} = 4$$

$$\bar{n} = \tfrac{1}{6} \left\{ 6 \times 1 + 5 \times 1\tfrac{1}{2} + 4 \times \tfrac{1}{2} + 3 \times 2\tfrac{1}{2} + 2 \times \tfrac{1}{2} \right\} = 4$$

Fig. 3.8-1 Example for $\bar{t}$ and $\bar{n}$.

and hence

(3.8.3)
$$\frac{\bar{n}}{n} = \frac{\bar{t}}{t_{max}}$$

Thus the mean number of incomplete tasks is in the same ratio to the maximum number of tasks as the mean flow time is to the maximum flow time (schedule length). For a given set of tasks and schedule length, (3.8.3) also indicates that mean flow times are directly proportional to the mean number of incomplete tasks.

This important relation extends also to dynamic systems in which we remove the assumptions that all tasks are present for scheduling at the same time. In particular, under the general equilibrium assumption that the long-run, mean numbers of completing tasks and arriving tasks are equal, the linear relationship between $\bar{t}$ and $\bar{n}$ will hold. The generality of this result should be emphasized. Effectively, the system, including processors and sequencing algorithms, may be regarded as a black box. Subject to the assumption of the steady state, the internal structure of the black box and the nature of the tasks (and the characteristics assumed known about them) will not affect the validity of the result. In Chapter 4, this relationship between $\bar{t}$ and $\bar{n}$ will be used to great advantage in simplifying the analysis of certain probability models.

In a single-processor scheduling problem, it is never beneficial to introduce idle time. Thus t_{max} in (3.8.3) is a constant (the sum of task execution times) and any procedure which minimizes (maximizes) mean flow time will minimize (maximize) the mean number in system, and conversely. In the following, we shall solve the equivalent problems of minimizing mean flow time and the mean number in the system for special cases with a single processor. This section will conclude with a few remarks on similar results for the multiprocessor models of previous sections.

For the purposes of minimizing $\bar{t}$ and t_{max}, it is not difficult to show that preemptions of tasks need never be considered when we are limited to one processor. Since it is also never beneficial to introduce idle time, we need only concern ourselves with the class of *permutation* schedules. A permutation schedule is fully defined by a permutation of the tasks to be executed; it is assumed that the tasks are individually executed to completion in a left-justified sequence determined by the given permutation. The following algorithm incorporates a precedence structure for which sequences leading to minimal mean flow time are efficiently determined [2]. [See Problem 3-21 for a generalization.]

Let C denote a task system consisting of r independent chains

(3.8.4)
$$C_i = T_{i1} T_{i2} \cdots T_{ip_i} \quad (1 \le i \le r)$$

That is, for each i, $T_{i1} \ll T_{i2} \ll \cdots \ll T_{ip_i}$. The execution time of T_{ij} is denoted τ_{ij} and we let

$$n = \sum_{i=1}^{r} p_i$$

Algorithm D

1. For each task compute

$$\bar{n}_{ij} = \frac{1}{j} \sum_{h=1}^{j} \tau_{ih}$$

and then for each chain compute

$$z_i(h_i) = \min[\bar{n}_{i1}, \ldots, \bar{n}_{ip_i}]$$

where h_i indexes the minimum value $(\bar{n}_{ih_i})$.

2. Select a chain C_k for which

$$z_k(h_k) \leq z_i(h_i) \quad (1 \leq i \leq r)$$

and begin (or extend) the sequence with the subchain

$$T_{k1} T_{k2} \cdots T_{kh_k}$$

3. Removing from C_k the tasks assigned in step 2, recompute $z_k(h_k)$ for the new chain C_k.

4. Steps 2 and 3 are iterated until all tasks have been added to the sequence.

For the proof that the algorithm produces a sequence with minimal mean flow time, the following lemma is useful.

Lemma 3.5

Let $\tau_1, \tau_2, \ldots, \tau_n$ be a collection of positive integers with the property that

$$(3.8.5) \qquad \frac{1}{k} \sum_{i=1}^{k} \tau_i > \frac{1}{n} \sum_{i=1}^{n} \tau_i \quad (1 \leq k < n)$$

and let $w_1, w_2, \ldots, w_n$ be nonnegative numbers satisfying $w_1 \leq w_2 \leq \cdots \leq w_n$ and $\sum_{i=1}^{n} w_i = 1$. Then

$$(3.8.6) \qquad \frac{1}{n} \sum_{i=1}^{n} \tau_i \geq \sum_{i=1}^{n} w_i \tau_i$$

That is, the sum on the right of (3.8.6) is maximized by the choice $w_i = 1/n$ $(1 \leq i \leq n)$.

Proof. Suppose that $w_1, w_2, \ldots, w_n$ is an arbitrary collection of weights satisfying the conditions of the lemma. Define $k \leq n - 1$ as the least integer such that $w_{k+1} = w_{k+2} = \cdots = w_n$. Assuming that $k > 0$ it is clear that there must exist a maximum $\epsilon > 0$ such that we can increase $w_1, \ldots, w_k$ by ϵ and decrease $w_{k+1}, \ldots, w_n$ by $k\epsilon/(n - k)$ and still preserve $0 \leq w_1 \leq w_2 \leq \cdots \leq w_n$ and $\sum_{i=1}^n w_i = 1$. On performing these operations the change produced in $\sum_{i=1}^n w_i \tau_i$ is given by

$$\Delta = \left[\sum_{i=1}^k (w_i + \epsilon)\tau_i + \sum_{i=k+1}^n \left(w_i - \frac{k}{n-k}\epsilon \right)\tau_i \right] - \sum_{i=1}^n w_i\tau_i$$

or

$$(3.8.7) \qquad \Delta = \epsilon \left[\sum_{i=1}^k \tau_i - \frac{k}{n-k} \sum_{i=k+1}^n \tau_i \right] = \epsilon \left[\sum_{i=1}^n \tau_i - \frac{n}{n-k} \sum_{i=k+1}^n \tau_i \right]$$

To show that $\Delta \geq 0$ we need only observe that

$$\sum_{i=k+1}^n \tau_i = \sum_{i=1}^n \tau_i - \sum_{i=1}^k \tau_i = n\left[\frac{1}{n} \sum_{i=1}^n \tau_i \right] - k\left[\frac{1}{k} \sum_{i=1}^k \tau_i \right]$$

and that, therefore, on using (3.8.5) we have

$$(3.8.8) \qquad\qquad \sum_{i=k+1}^n \tau_i \leq \frac{n-k}{n} \sum_{i=1}^n \tau_i$$

The inequality $\Delta \geq 0$ follows directly from (3.8.8). Iterating this transformation clearly shows that $\sum_{i=1}^n w_i\tau_i$ is maximized when $w_i = w_{i+1}$ ($1 \leq i \leq n - 1$), and hence $w_i = 1/n$ ($1 \leq i \leq n$). $\blacksquare$

Theorem 3.10

We consider the task system defined in Algorithm D and let $\mathcal{P}_0$ denote the sequence produced by this algorithm. Then the mean flow time $\bar{t}$ for $\mathcal{P}_0$ is minimal.

Proof. We shall proceed by showing that any optimal sequence for the task system C can be transformed into a valid sequence produced by Algorithm D which does not increase the mean flow time.

Let $\mathcal{P} = T(1)T(2) \cdots T(n)$ denote an optimal sequence in which the first subchain produced by Algorithm D does not occupy the initial positions. Let $b = T_1^* T_2^* \cdots T_p^*$ denote this subchain and let $\{\tau_i^*\}$ denote the respective execution times. With respect to $\mathcal{P}$ define X_i ($2 \leq i \leq p$) as the possibly zero-length interval in which tasks not in b execute between the tasks T_{i-1}^* and T_i^* of b. X_1 is the interval extending from 0 to the starting time of T_1^* and X_{p+1} is the interval extending from the finishing time of T_p^* to the end of $\mathcal{P}$. Figure 3.8-2 shows an example for $p = 3$.

Let us now shift the subchain b to the left so that b begins the transformed sequence $\mathcal{P}'$. The intervals X_i are moved to the right accordingly, but without changing their relative order. This simple transformation is illustrated in Fig. 3.8-2. We want to show that the mean flow time $\bar{t} = (1/n) \sum_{i=1}^{n} t_i$ for $\mathcal{P}$ is at least as large as the mean flow time $\bar{t}' = (1/n) \sum_{i=1}^{n} t_i'$ for $\mathcal{P}'$.

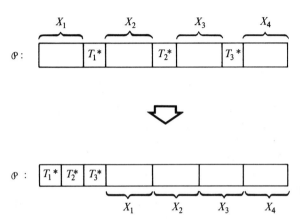

Fig. 3.8-2   Example for Theorem 3.10 ($p = 3$).

First, we represent $\bar{t}'$ in terms of the t_i in $\mathcal{P}$. To do this we note that the completion times of tasks in X_i have increased from t_i in $\mathcal{P}$ to $t_i + \sum_{j=i}^{p} \tau_j^*$ in $\mathcal{P}'$. With reference to Fig. 3.8-2 we therefore have

$$(3.8.9) \quad \sum_{i=1}^{n} t_i' = \sum_{i=1}^{p} (p - i + 1)\tau_i^* + \sum_{t_j \in X_1}\left[t_j + \sum_{i=1}^{p} \tau_i^* \right]$$
$$+ \sum_{t_j \in X_2}\left[t_j + \sum_{i=2}^{p} \tau_i^* \right] + \cdots + \sum_{t_j \in X_p} [t_j + \tau_p^*] + \sum_{t_j \in X_{p+1}} t_j$$

Letting n_i denote the number of tasks executed in X_i and letting

$$Y_j = \bigcup_{i=1}^{j} X_i$$

we may write (3.8.9) as

$$(3.8.10) \quad n\bar{t}' = \sum_{i=1}^{p} (p - i + 1)\tau_i^* + \sum_{t_j \in Y_{p+1}} t_j + \sum_{j=1}^{p} n_j \sum_{i=j}^{p} \tau_i^*$$

As before let $\tau(j)$ denote the execution time of the jth task executed in $\mathcal{P}$. Then by treating the tasks in the intervals X_i separately from those in b, we can write

$$(3.8.11) \quad n\bar{t} = \sum_{tj \in Y_{p+1}} t_j + [\tau_1^* + \sum_{tj \in Y_1} \tau(j)] + [\tau_1^* + \tau_2^* + \sum_{tj \in Y_2} \tau(j)]$$
$$+ \cdots + [\tau_1^* + \cdots + \tau_p^* + \sum_{tj \in Y_p} \tau(j)]$$

Computing $\Delta = n(\bar{t} - \bar{t}')$ we have

$$(3.8.12) \quad \Delta = \sum_{i=1}^{p} (p - i + 1) \sum_{tj \in X_i} \tau(j) - \sum_{i=1}^{p} n_i \sum_{j=i}^{p} \tau_j^*$$

Our object now is to show that $\Delta \geq 0$. We begin by observing that the sum in (3.8.12) is performed over a set B of (maximal length) subchains each of which spans some subset of the intervals $X_1, \ldots, X_p$ and which collectively exhaust the terms $\tau(j)$. In other words, we can partition (3.8.12) into sums over the subchains of B. If, for an arbitrary subchain in B, the function in (3.8.12) [i.e., the sum in (3.8.12) restricted to an arbitrary subchain] is non-negative, then Δ will be a (nonnegative) sum of nonnegative terms. We shall now show that (3.8.12) restricted to an arbitrary subchain in B is indeed nonnegative.

Suppose that the subchain

$$(3.8.13) \quad T_{i1} T_{i2} \cdots T_{ik_1} \cdots T_{ik_2} \cdots T_{ik_p}, \quad 0 \leq k_1 \leq k_2 \leq \cdots \leq k_p$$

of the ith chain is one of the subchains in B, where $T_{ik_j} \cdots T_{i(k_{j+1})}$ is that part of the ith chain executing in X_{j+1} ($0 \leq i \leq p - 1$) and $k_0 \equiv 0$. If $k_{j+1} = k_j$, then no part of the ith chain executes in X_{j+1} ($k_1 = k_2 = \cdots = k_j = 0$, $j \geq 1$, implies that the subchain commences execution in X_{j+1}). In specializing (3.8.12) to the terms contributed by the tasks in (3.8.13) we replace n_i by $k_i - k_{i-1}$. Doing this and reorganizing the sums restricted to the tasks of (3.8.13) we have

$$(3.8.14) \quad \Delta_i = \sum_{j=1}^{k_p} \tau_{ij} + \sum_{j=1}^{k_{p-1}} \tau_{ij} + \cdots + \sum_{j=1}^{k_1} \tau_{ij} - k_1 \tau_1^* - k_2 \tau_2^*$$
$$- \cdots - k_p \tau_p^*$$

From the statement of Algorithm D we know that

$$\frac{1}{k_h} \sum_{j=1}^{k_h} \tau_{ij} > \frac{1}{p} \sum_{i=1}^{p} \tau_i^* \quad (1 \leq h \leq p)$$

or

$$(3.8.15) \quad \sum_{j=1}^{k_h} \tau_{ij} > \frac{k_h}{p} \sum_{i=1}^{p} \tau_i^* \quad (1 \leq h \leq p)$$

Substituting the right-hand side of (3.8.15) for each sum in (3.8.14) we can state that $\Delta_i \geq 0$ if $\Delta_i' \geq 0$, where

$$\Delta_i' = \sum_{i=1}^{P} k_i \frac{\sum_{i=1}^{P} \tau_i^*}{p} - \sum_{i=1}^{P} k_i \tau_i^*$$

Clearly, $\Delta_i' \geq 0$ if

(3.8.16) $$\frac{1}{p} \sum_{i=1}^{P} \tau_i^* \geq \sum_{i=1}^{P} w_i \tau_i^*$$

where $w_i = k_i / \sum_{i=1}^{P} k_i$. However, the w_i are nondecreasing, they sum to 1, and (3.8.5) in Lemma 3.5 is assured by the statement of Algorithm D. Hence the inequality in (3.8.16), $\Delta_i' \geq 0$, and $\Delta_i \geq 0$ all hold.

It remains to observe that the transformation of $\mathcal{P}$ can be repeated on $\mathcal{P}'$ with respect to the second subchain selected by Algorithm D. Using an induction argument it is readily verified that after iterating this transformation until we have produced $\mathcal{P}_0$, we succeed in obtaining a sequence $(\mathcal{P}_0)$ whose mean flow time cannot exceed that of $\mathcal{P}$. ∎

Algorithm D becomes quite simple for the special case in which C contains a set of independent tasks. In particular, we have

Corollary 3.1

For sets of independent tasks and a single processor, if $\mathcal{P}_0$ is ordered so that the corresponding execution times form a nondecreasing sequence, then the mean flow time is minimal. The mechanism producing this ordering will be called the *shortest-processing-time* (SPT) rule.

A separate proof of Corollary 3.1 is provided by the well-known result that weighted sums, such as

$$n\bar{t} = \sum_{i=1}^{n} (n - i + 1)\tau(i)$$

in which the weights $(n - i + 1)$ form a decreasing sequence, are minimized by choosing $\tau(1) \leq \tau(2) \leq \cdots \leq \tau(n)$.

In general, it may not be possible to assume that task chains can be preempted after any task. However, for a more general case in which some or all preemptions are disallowed for one or more chains, Algorithm D can be revised in step 1 so as to compute only those $\bar{n}_{ij}$ which are allowable in the given situation. We have the following important special case.

Corollary 3.2

Suppose that preemptions are not allowed between any two tasks of the same chain. (That is, $\mathcal{P}$ is simply a permutation of the chains.) If the mean flow time of $\mathcal{P}$ is to be minimized, then for all i and j, C_i must precede C_j in $\mathcal{P}$ if

$$\frac{1}{p_i} \sum_{k=1}^{pi} \tau_{ik} < \frac{1}{p_j} \sum_{k=1}^{pi} \tau_{jk}$$

SPT sequencing extends readily to the multiprocessor model when we assume that all tasks are independent. For this special case the rule is as follows: Whenever a processor becomes free, assign that task of those remaining which has the least execution time. Note especially that this rule is antithetical to the largest-processing-time (LPT) scheduling rule discussed in Section 3.4. Although for all $m \geq 1$ LPT sequencing produces "reasonable" if not minimal length schedules, it is the worst possible discipline for minimizing mean flow time. For the latter purpose, SPT is best, but intuitively one would prefer LPT for minimizing schedule lengths, especially for large variations in execution times.

PROBLEMS

3-1. Let $L(T)$ denote the level of T in a graph G. Suppose that G is labeled by the algorithm in Section 3.2. Prove that if $L(T) > L(T')$ for any two tasks T and T' in G, then $\alpha(T) > \alpha(T')$.

3-2. Consider the two-processor problem of Section 3.2. Suppose that we have a different labeling algorithm with the following property. Let T and T' be any two tasks in a labeled graph G. Then $|S(T)| > |S(T')|$ implies that $\alpha(T) > \alpha(T')$. Find a graph which shows that the given labeling algorithm cannot be optimal.

3-3. In Problem 3-2 suppose that the new labeling algorithm had instead the following property. Let $D(T)$ denote the set of *all* successors (descendants) of T. Then $|D(T)| > |D(T')|$ for any pair of tasks T and T' in a labeled graph G implies that $\alpha(T) > \alpha(T')$. Show that the graph in Fig. P3-3 provides a counterexample to the optimality of such a labeling algorithm.

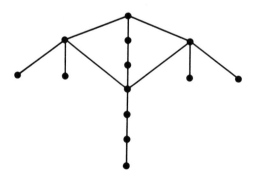

Fig. P3-3

3-4. Consider the following simpler algorithm for the two-processor problem of Section 3.2. Whenever a processor becomes available the next task assigned is that one of the unexecuted tasks which is

1. At the highest level, and
2. Such that its set of successors is not properly contained in the set of successors of any other unexecuted task.

An arbitrary rule may be assumed for resolving ties. Verify that the graph in Fig. P3-4 shows that the above algorithm does not always produce minimal length schedules.

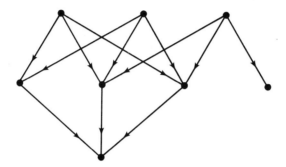

Fig. P3-4

3-5. Consider the execution of the two-processor labeling algorithm on a given graph. Show that if the labeling of tasks in $S(T)$ is completed before the labeling of tasks in $S(T')$, then $\alpha(T) < \alpha(T')$. This property enables the following simplification of the algorithm. Let U denote the set of unlabeled tasks available for labeling at some point in time; i.e., for all $T \in U$ every task in $S(T)$ is labeled. The tasks in U can be (partially) ordered and then labeled according to the sequences $N(T)$, $T \in U$. No predecessor of any task in U need be examined before all tasks in U have been labeled. After all tasks in U have been labeled a new set U' can be defined and the process repeated until all tasks have been labeled.

3-6. Choose an appropriate graph representation and exhibit a detailed version of the two-processor labeling algorithm whose execution time is proportional to the square of the number (n) of tasks. Note that this algorithm exhibits least complexity for the two-processor scheduling problem in the sense that (from Problem 2-9) it requires up to $n^2/4$ arcs to specify a partial order.

3-7. Consider an arbitrary precedence graph G and $m \geq 1$ processors and let S be a schedule for G. Define S^R as the *reverse* of S; i.e., the completion time of S is the origin of S^R and the task sequence in S^R is formed by reading S from right to left. Let G^R denote the graph formed from G by reversing all precedence constraints (arc direction); i.e., $T_i < T_j$ in the partial ordering for G becomes $T_j < T_i$ in the partial ordering for G^R. Show that S is a minimal length schedule for G if and only if S^R is of minimal length for G^R.

3-8. Design an algorithm that labels each task of an arbitrary task system with its level. (Use the more general definition of level given in Section 3.6.)

This algorithm is closely related to so-called *critical route analysis* [15] which concerns scheduling task systems when the number of processors is unlimited. Let us say that a task is critical if increasing its execution time by a given amount causes the minimal execution time of the task system to increase by an equal amount. With an unlimited number of processors every maximal length path is a critical route; every task in these paths is critical and the length of these paths defines the minimum achievable schedule length. Augment the labeling algorithm requested above and come up with an algorithm for finding all critical routes in a given graph.

3-9. The problem is to find a graph and a corresponding task list from which we can remove a task (and all precedence relations involving this task) so that the list schedule for the new graph and list is *longer* than for the original graph and list. (Note the relation between this anomaly and the anomaly produced by reducing execution times.)

3-10. In this problem the proof that (3.5.1) is a best possible bound is completed. (Figure 3.5-6 showed that a change in priority list can produce a change in schedule length by a factor $2 - 1/m$.)

a. Use Fig. 3.6-6 to demonstrate that a decrease in execution times can produce a change in schedule length by a factor arbitrarily close to $2 - 1/m$. Use as the *changed* values, $\{\tau_i'\}$, those given in Fig. 3.6-6 and use as the original values $\tau_i = 2\epsilon$ $(1 \leq i < m)$ and $\tau_i = \tau_i'$ $(m \leq i \leq 3m)$.

b. Consider the task system $C = (\mathcal{J}, <)$, where $\mathcal{J} = \{T_1, T_2, \ldots, T_{m(m-1)+2}\}$, $< = \{(T_1, T_2), (T_1, T_3), \ldots, (T_1, T_{m(m-1)+1})\}$, and

$$
\tau_i = \begin{cases}
\epsilon, & i = 1 \\
1, & 2 \leq i \leq m(m-1)+1 \\
m, & i = m(m-1)+2
\end{cases}
$$

Using the list $L = (T_1, T_2, \ldots, T_{m(m-1)+2})$ show that if all precedence relations in $<$ are removed, the list schedule increases in length by a factor that can be made arbitrary close to $2 - 1/m$.

c. For the graph shown in Fig. P3-10 let $n = mm' - m' + m + 2$, where

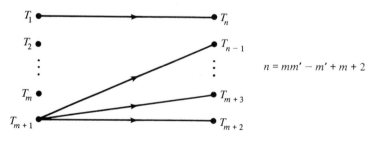

$$n = mm' - m' + m + 2$$

Fig. P3-10

$m' > m > 1$. Suppose that the execution times are given by

$$\tau_i = \begin{cases} \epsilon, & 1 \leq i \leq m + 1 \\ 1, & m + 2 \leq i \leq mm' - m' + m + 1 \\ m', & i = mm' - m' + m + 2 \end{cases}$$

Show that the ratio of schedule lengths arising when the number of processors is increased from m to m' can be made arbitrarily close to (3.5.1).

3-11. (Sequencing according to due date [2]). Consider a set of n independent tasks $\{T_i\}_{i=1}^n$ to be scheduled on a single processor with execution times $\{\tau_i\}_{i=1}^n$. Let d_i ($1 \leq i \leq n$) be a positive number that specifies the *due date* of T_i to be interpreted as the time at which T_i *should* finish (if possible). If for any given schedule t_i denotes the completion time of T_i, then $t_i - d_i$ is called the *lateness* of T_i and max$\{t_i - d_i, 0\}$ is called the *tardiness*. Show that the maximum task lateness and maximum task tardiness are minimized by sequencing tasks in order of nondecreasing due dates. That is, if $d[i]$ denotes the due date of the ith task scheduled, then

$$d[1] \leq d[2] \leq \cdots \leq d[n]$$

ensures the lateness and tardiness properties just stated. (Use an "interchange" argument as illustrated in the proof of Theorem 3.9.) Verify that SPT sequencing minimizes mean lateness.

3-12. Consider a single processor and the definitions given in Problem 3-11. At any point t in a schedule $\S$ the *slack time* for T_i is defined as $d_i - \tau_i - t$. Intuitively, at any given decision point it would seem most urgent for the purpose of meeting due dates to schedule next the unexecuted task with the minimum slack time. Since t does not affect relative slack times, applying the minimum slack-time criterion over the entire schedule would imply a sequence having the property that

$$d[1] - \tau[1] \leq d[2] - \tau[2] \leq \cdots \leq d[n] - \tau[n]$$

Prove the (somewhat unexpected) result that such a sequence maximizes the minimum task lateness and the minimum task tardiness. (A proof paralleling that of Problem 3-11 is easily constructed.)

3-13. Consider the example of four tasks for which the due dates and execution times are

$$d_i: \quad 1 \quad 2 \quad 4 \quad 6$$
$$\tau_i: \quad 2 \quad 4 \quad 3 \quad 1$$

Give the single-processor schedule which provides minimum *mean* tardiness and verify that it corresponds to neither SPT, due-date, nor slack-time sequencing.

3-14. To distinguish tasks not only on the basis of execution time but also on some independent priority basis we may wish to schedule n tasks so that we minimize a mean *weighted* flow time

$$\bar{t} = \frac{1}{n} \sum_{i=1}^{n} a_i t_i$$

where the t_i are completion times and the weights a_i are specified as indicators of relative importance. Show that a schedule for which

$$\frac{\tau[1]}{a[1]} \le \frac{\tau[2]}{a[2]} \le \cdots \le \frac{\tau[n]}{a[n]}$$

minimizes the mean weighted flow time. Verify that the mean weighted lateness is also minimized.

3-15. Define the following two four-task chains:

	τ_{i1}	τ_{i2}	τ_{i3}	τ_{i4}
C_1	4	1	1	4
C_2	1	4	4	1

Suppose that we have a four-processor flow-shop system as described in Section 3.7; i.e., T_{ij} must be executed on processor j and it cannot commence execution until $T_{i(j-1)}$ is complete. Use the two chains given above to provide a counterexample to the statement that the set of optimal flow-shop schedules always contains an order-preserving schedule; i.e., a schedule in which the chain sequences on all processors are the same (cf. Lemma 3.4).

3-16. The improvement bound of preemptive over nonpreemptive scheduling given in (3.6.2) is not a best bound if we allow for nonpreemptive schedules .in which processors are allowed to be idle when tasks are ready to execute. (Clearly, we need not consider cases in which all processors are idle at any time.) Note that a nonpreemptive schedule considerably better than that of Fig. 3.6-6 can be found under these less restrictive circumstances. For this more general case we want to prove that for any task system [16]

(P1) $$\frac{t_N}{t_P} \le \frac{4}{3}$$

where t_N and t_P denote the lengths of the optimal nonpreemptive and preemptive schedules, respectively, and where $m = 2$. We begin by looking at the relative magnitudes of t_N and $t_E = \sum_{i=1}^{n} \tau_i$, the total execution time required by the n-task system. Clearly, if $t_E \ge \frac{3}{2} t_N$, then, since $t_P \ge t_E/2$, we have the result in (P1). It remains to show that (P1) holds also when $t_E < \frac{3}{2} t_N$. Since $t_N = \frac{1}{2}(t_E + I_N)$, where I_N is the total idle time, we see that $t_E < \frac{3}{2} t_N$ implies that $I_N > t_N/2$.

Next, we proceed as follows:

a. For a given nonpreemptive schedule let the concurrency of a chain C in . a given graph G be defined as the total time during which one processor is working on a task in C and the other processor is busy. Show that the maximal concurrency of any chain C, over all nonpreemptive schedules for G, is not greater than $t_N/2$.

b. Use Lemma 3.3 and show as a result of (a) that

$$I_P \geq I_N - \frac{t_N}{2}$$

where I_P is the idle time in an optimal preemptive for G. It remains to show (by some simple algebra) that (P1) follows from the this inequality. (Fig. 3.6-1 shows that this bound is the best possible.)

3-17. Using Lemma 3.3 and the general approach in Problem 3-16 show that for an arbitrary number of processors we have

$$\frac{t_N}{t_P} \leq \frac{2m}{m+1}$$

3-18. We generalize Johnson's two-processor flow-shop problem in Section 3.7 and suppose that we have more than one processor of each of the two types. Specifically, assume that there are m_1 identical A processors on which the first execution phases must be performed and m_2 identical B processors on which the second phases must be performed. Each task system consists of a chain of exactly two tasks corresponding to the two execution phases. A task system C_i is thus identifiable by a pair (A_i, B_i) denoting the execution times of the two tasks, the A task and B task, respectively.

Shen and Chen [17] have indicated that the following simple scheduling algorithm is rather efficient. Impose a precedence relation (partial order) $\prec$ on the set $\{C_i\}$ of task systems so that $C_i \prec C_j$ if and only if $A_i + B_i \geq A_j + B_j$ and $A_i \leq A_j$. (An arbitrary tie-breaking rule may be assumed.) The set $\{C_i\}$ is then scheduled according to any sequence satisfying $\prec$. As usual, processors are kept busy as long as there is a task of the appropriate type to execute. Show that the set $\{(1, 2), (1, 2), (2, 1), (2, 1), (2, 1)\}$ is a counterexample to the claim that the given algorithm is optimal when $m_1 = m_2 = 2$. (Note that $\prec$ *linearly* orders the C_i in this example.)

Suppose that the relation $\prec$ linearly orders the set $\{C_i\}$ to be scheduled. Let t_L be the total execution time achieved by the above rule and let $t_{\min}$ denote the minimum execution time achievable. Using the methods of Section 3.4 show that if there is no internal idle time on the B processors, then

$$\frac{t_L}{t_{\min}} \leq \frac{3}{2} - \frac{1}{2m_2}$$

Show also that if the last B task to terminate begins execution immediately after its corresponding A task terminates, then

$$\frac{t_L}{t_{\min}} \leq \frac{3}{2} - \frac{1}{2m_1}$$

(The latter case supposes congestion on the A processors while the former supposes congestion on the B processors.)

3-19. Investigate simple techniques whereby preemptions can be included with list scheduling in such a way as to eliminate the anomalies whereby schedule lengths can increase with decreases in execution times [11]. Note that preemptions may be included dynamically or statically. In the latter case, for example, all tasks could be decomposed beforehand into series of small equal-size subtasks, which are executed nonpreemptively. It can be shown that static preemptions of this sort are not sufficient to remove the above anomalies.

3-20. For a given set of independent tasks let t_{SPT} and t_{LPT} denote the lengths of SPT and LPT schedules on m processors. Show that

$$1 \leq \frac{t_{\text{SPT}}}{t_{\text{LPT}}} \leq 2 - \frac{1}{m}$$

and that these are best possible bounds. (Use Theorem 3.4.)

3-21. Consider a collection of trees (as defined in Section 3.3). Extend Algorithm D in the natural way so as to consider the normalized sum of execution times of the nodes in subtrees rather than subchains. After specifying the new algorithm in detail show that the sequence it produces for collections of trees gives minimal mean flow time [18].

REFERENCES

1. CLARK, W., *The Gantt Chart* (3rd ed.). Sir Isaac Pitman & Sons Ltd., London (1952).

2. CONWAY, R. W., W. L. MAXWELL, and L. W. MILLER, *Theory of Scheduling*. Addison-Wesley, Reading, Mass. (1967).

3. COFFMAN, E. G., JR., and R. L. GRAHAM, "Optimal scheduling for two-processor systems." *Acta Informatica 1*, 3 (1972), 200–213.

4. HU, T. C., "Parallel sequencing and assembly line problems." *Opns. Res. 9*, 6 (Nov. 1961), 841–848.

5. KRONE, M., "Heuristic programming applied to scheduling models," in *Proc. 5th Annual Conf. Inform. Sci. Sys.* Dept. of Electrical Engineering, Princeton Univ., Princeton, N. J. (1971), 193–196. See also, KRONE M., *"Heuristic programming applied to scheduling problems."* Ph. D. thesis, Dept. of Electrical Engineering, Princeton Univ., Princeton, N. J. (Sept. 1970).

6. GRAHAM, R. L., "Bounds on multiprocessing timing anomalies." *SIAM J. Appl. Math. 17*, 2, (Mar. 1969), 416–429.

7. GRAHAM, R. L., "Bounds for certain multiprocessing anomalies." *Bell Sys. Tech. J.* (Nov. 1966), 1563–1581.

8. MANACHER, G. K., "Production and stabilization of real-time task schedules." *J. ACM 14*, 3 (July 1967), 439–465.

9. McNAUGHTON, R., "Scheduling with deadlines and loss functions." *Manag. Sci. 12*, 1 (Oct. 1959). See also, ROTHKOPF, M. H., "Scheduling independent tasks on parallel processors." *Manag. Sci. 12*, 5 (Jan. 1966).

10. MUNTZ, R. R., and E. G. COFFMAN, JR., "Preemptive scheduling of real-time tasks on multiprocessor systems." *J. ACM 17*, 2 (Apr. 1970), 324–338.

11. MUNTZ, R. R., "Scheduling of computations on multiprocessor systems: The preemptive assignment discipline." Ph. D. thesis, Dept. of Electrical Engineering, Princeton Univ., Princeton, N. J. (Mar. 1969).

12. MUNTZ, R. R., and E. G. COFFMAN, JR., "Optimal preemptive scheduling on two-processor systems." *IEEE Trans. Comp. C-18*, 11 (Nov. 1969), 1014–1020.

13. JOHNSON, S. M., "Optimal two- and three-stage production schedules with set-up times included." *Nav. Res. Log. Quart. 1*, 1 (Mar. 1954).

14. JACKSON, J. R., "An extension of Johnson's results on job-lot scheduling." *Nav. Res. Log. Quart. 3*, 3 (Sept. 1956).

15. MODER, J. J., and C. R. PHILLIPS, *Project Management with CPM and PERT*. Van Nostrand Reinhold, New York (1964).

16. LIU, C. L., "Optimal scheduling on multiprocessor computing systems." *Proc. 13th Switching Automata Theory Symp. IEEE.* (1972), 155–160.

17. SHEN, V. Y., and Y. E. CHEN, "A scheduling strategy for the flow-stop problem in a system with two classes of processors," in *Proc. 6th Annual Conf. Inform. Sys. Sci.*, Dept. of Electrical Engineering, Princeton Univ., Princeton, N.J. (Mar. 1972).

18. SIDNEY, J. B., "One machine sequencing with precedence relations and deferral costs," Working Paper #125, Faculty of Commerce and Business Administration, University of British Columbia (1972) (to appear, *Journal of Operations Research Society of America*).

19. ULLMAN, J. D., "Polynomial completeness of the equal execution time scheduling problem." Princeton Univ., Dept. of Elec. Engrg., Computer Science Report TR-115 (Dec. 1972).

20. KARP, R. M., "Reducibility among combinatorial problems." Dept. Computer Science, Univ. Calif. at Berkeley, TR-3 (Apr. 1972).

4 PROBABILITY MODELS OF COMPUTER SEQUENCING PROBLEMS

4.1. INTRODUCTION

4.1.1. Basic Definitions

The analysis of probability models of computer operation constitutes a useful technique for preliminary studies of operating systems. As a mathematical approach probability models are generally more realistic than deterministic models, because they can represent the irregular and unpredictable demands made by computer users. These demands are reflected in the complex of queues that are developed and controlled by the operating system for the use of auxiliary and main storage units, processors, input/output devices, and system routines. Thus when probability models are formulated to study the properties of dynamic scheduling techniques they take the form of queueing systems.

In this chapter we shall concentrate our attention on the scheduling of processor queues and take the macroscopic view that the remaining queueing activities are subsumed in a general execution requirement. (In Chapter 5 we shall examine input/output queueing problems.) Our specific object will be the study of time-sharing algorithms and certain batch-processing algorithms that improve system performance by making use of information assumed known about execution requirements. Such studies can help provide insight into the properties of new sequencing algorithms even though idealizations or simplifying assumptions have to be made in order to keep the models mathematically tractable. These mathematical models may also be formulated to help validate simulation studies, and in certain cases they can be used to obtain direct measures or predictions of actual system performance—this again in spite of simplifications found necessary in the modeling process. The remainder of this section will be devoted to a characterization of mathematical queueing systems with the appropriate specializations pertinent to our modeling of processor scheduling. Our treatment of queueing theory will be introductory and can be found in the frequently cited references [1–8].

As pictured in Fig. 4.1-1, the principal components of a queueing system

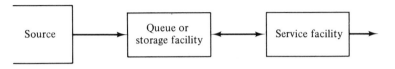

Fig. 4.1-1   A queueing system.

are a *server*, a *queue* consisting of a waiting or storage area to accommodate customers that must be delayed, and a *source*, which is a collection of system users or customers. In the computer application the server will normally consist of one or more processors; the waiting facilities may be input/output devices, auxiliary storage, or even main storage; and the customers will be jobs batched on magnetic tape, for example, or service requests of various types made by users connected on-line to the computer system. Throughout this chapter the terms server/processor, service/execution/operation, and jobs/arrivals will be used interchangeably in order to minimize unpleasant repetition of words. The terms user and (service) request will occasionally be employed when appropriate in our discussion of time-sharing systems.

Mathematical descriptions of probability models for queueing systems require specifications of the probability distribution functions describing the times between successive arrivals (to be called interarrival times) and the running or service times of jobs, along with a specification of the queueing discipline. By queueing or service discipline we mean simply a rule or procedure embodied in an operating system which determines the sequence in which jobs are executed and how much execution time a job is allocated each time it is selected for service.

We shall consistently assume that interarrival and service times are statistically independent. Moreover, with the exception of Section 4.3 both the successive interarrival times and the service times of successive arrivals will be assumed independent. We let T and S be the random variables corresponding to interarrival and service times, respectively. We adopt the notation $A(x) = \Pr[T \leq x]$ and $B(x) = \Pr[S \leq x]$ for the interarrival and service time distribution functions. The random variables T and S will be either discrete or continuous. In the latter case we shall use lowercase symbols to denote the corresponding density functions (when these exist); e.g. $f(x) = dF(x)/dx$ denotes the density function corresponding to the distribution function $F(x)$.

In general, although the existence of density functions will almost always be assumed in this chapter, the ith moment of a nonnegative random variable X with distribution function $F(x)$ will normally be expressed by the Stieltjes integral

$$E(X^i) = \int_0^\infty x^i \, dF(x), \quad i = 1, 2, \ldots$$

rather than

$$E(X^i) = \int_0^\infty x^i f(x) \, dx$$

In so doing, the advantages, apart from the applicability to more general distributions, are an economy of notation and the limiting of descriptions of random variables to their distribution functions.

4.1.2. The Arrival Process

For all the models we analyze we shall assume that $A(x)$ is a (negative) exponential distribution given by

$$(4.1.1) \qquad A(x) = 1 - e^{-\lambda x}, \quad x \geq 0$$

The corresponding density function is

$$(4.1.2) \qquad a(x) = \lambda e^{-\lambda x}, \quad x \geq 0$$

Working out the first two moments we have

$$(4.1.3) \qquad E(T) = \frac{1}{\lambda}$$

$$(4.1.4) \qquad E(T^2) = \frac{2}{\lambda^2}$$

from which the variance is found to be

$$(4.1.5) \qquad \text{Var}(T) = \frac{1}{\lambda^2}$$

Later on we shall consider arrival processes in which the parameter of the exponential distribution is a function of the state of the system. For the present, however, we shall assume that λ is independent of the system state. The assumption of independent and exponentially distributed interarrival times is perhaps the single most characteristic assumption of queueing theory. Consequently, we shall take time to study its properties in more detail.

First, let us investigate the so-called *memoryless* or *Markov* property of the exponential distribution, which accounts for the central importance of this assumption. Suppose that at the time we begin waiting for an event the distribution of our waiting time is known to be exponential with parameter λ, as in (4.1.1). After having waited t time units we inquire as to the distribution function $R_t(x)$ governing the remaining (residual) time we must wait for the event. With T denoting the random variable whose value is the total waiting time we have

$$R_t(x) = \Pr[T \le x + t \mid T > t] = \frac{\Pr[t < T \le t + x]}{\Pr[T > t]}$$

Using (4.1.1)

$$R_t(x) = \frac{\int_t^{t+x} \lambda e^{-\lambda y}\, dy}{\int_t^\infty \lambda e^{-\lambda y}\, dy} = \frac{e^{-\lambda t}[1 - e^{-\lambda x}]}{e^{-\lambda t}}$$

from which

(4.1.6) $$R_t(x) = 1 - e^{-\lambda x}$$

Thus $R_t(x)$ is independent of t and identical to the original waiting time distribution.† Clearly, the system does not "age" with the passage of time.

The memoryless property is also exhibited in the following problem, stated in terms of arrival processes. Let arrivals occur according to a process in which interarrival times are independent and have the common distribution function (4.1.1). For an arbitrary but fixed $t > 0$, what is the distribution of the time until the next arrival? Again, this distribution is independent of t and given by (4.1.1). This result will be verified later when we calculate the corresponding result under the assumption that the times between events have a general distribution. In summary, the assumption of exponential interarrival times means that the time we must wait for a new arrival is statistically independent of how long we have already spent waiting for it.

The discrete analog of the exponential distribution is the geometric distribution. For example, consider a sequence of independent coin tossings (Bernoulli trials) where the probability of a head is p and the probability of a tail is $1 - p$. Starting with any given coin toss the distribution of the number, N, of consecutive heads required before a tail appears is geometric

$$\Pr[N = n] = (1 - p)p^n, \quad n = 0, 1, \ldots$$

independent of when the last tail occurred. This follows from the property

---

†It can also be shown without much difficulty that the exponential distribution is the only continuous distribution having this memoryless property [1].

that the probability of a tail occurring on any given toss is $1 - p$, independent of the results of previous coin tossings. Thus we have the memoryless property in discrete time events (arrivals) whose interarrival times are independently and geometrically distributed. Such arrivals constitute so-called Bernoulli arrival processes.

The arrival process we have defined in continuous time is the well-known Poisson process in which λ is simply called the arrival rate. We shall now give another definition of the Poisson process and show that it leads to the exponential distribution for interarrival times. Let $o(\Delta t)$ denote any quantity having an order of magnitude smaller than Δt. Suppose that there exists a constant λ such that for any small element of time Δt, the probability of no arrivals in $(t, t + \Delta t)$ is $1 - \lambda \Delta t + o(\Delta t)$ and the probability of one arrival is $\lambda \Delta t + o(\Delta t)$, where the events in the interval $(t, t + \Delta t)$ are statistically independent of t and of the events in any other nonoverlapping interval. A process satisfying the above properties is a Poisson process and the corresponding interarrival time distribution can be computed as follows. For an arbitrary time t_0 let $A_c(t)$ denote the probability that the time x of the next arrival exceeds $t_0 + t$; i.e., $A_c(t)$ is the probability that there were no arrivals in $(t_0, t_0 + t)$. Letting $z = x - t_0$ we have

$$A_c(t + \Delta t) = \Pr[z > t + \Delta t]$$

or

(4.1.7)
$$A_c(t + \Delta t) = \Pr[z > t]\Pr[\text{no arrivals in } \Delta t]$$
$$= A_c(t)[1 - \lambda \Delta t + o(\Delta t)]$$

where we have used the assumption of independent events in disjoint intervals. Rearranging (4.1.7), dividing by Δt, and neglecting terms of order $o(\Delta t)$

$$\lim_{\Delta t \to 0} \frac{A_c(t + \Delta t) - A_c(t)}{\Delta t} = -\lambda A_c(t)$$

Thus,

(4.1.8)
$$A_c'(t) = -\lambda A_c(t)$$

Subject to the boundary condition $A_c(0) = 1$ we find the following solution to (4.1.8):

$$A_c(t) = e^{-\lambda t}, \quad t \geq 0$$

This is obviously independent of t_0 and we have

$$A(t) = 1 - A_c(t) = 1 - e^{-\lambda t}, \quad t \geq 0$$

which demonstrates that the exponential distribution for interarrival times is implied by the properties defining the Poisson process.

Finally, let us indicate briefly a method of determining the discrete probability mass function (pmf) $f_i(t)$ ($i = 0, 1, 2, \ldots$) that specifies the probability of i Poisson arrivals in a time interval t. We immediately make use of the fact that this probability is independent of where the interval begins. We set $t = m \, \Delta t$, use the statistical independence of disjoint intervals, and compute the probability of one arrival in i of the m intervals of length Δt and no arrival in each of the remaining $m - i$ intervals. We find $f_i(t)$ by taking the limit of the binomial probability as shown below:

$$f_i(t) = \lim_{\Delta t \to 0} \binom{m}{i} [\lambda \, \Delta t + o(\Delta t)]^i [1 - \lambda \, \Delta t + o(\Delta t)]^{m-i}, \quad m = \frac{t}{\Delta t}$$

This can be reduced to

$$f_i(t) = \frac{(\lambda t)^i}{i!} \lim_{m \to \infty} \frac{m(m-1) \cdots (m-i+1)}{m^i} \lim_{m \to \infty} \left[1 - \frac{\lambda t}{m}\right]^m$$

from which we obtain

(4.1.9) $$f_i(t) = \frac{(\lambda t)^i}{i!} e^{-\lambda t}$$

Equation (4.1.9) defines the *Poisson distribution*. Note that the interarrival time distribution is given by $A(t) = 1 - f_0(t)$. It is easily verified from (4.1.9) that

(4.1.10) $$f_i(\Delta t) = \begin{cases} 1 - \lambda \, \Delta t + o(\Delta t), & i = 0 \\ \lambda \, \Delta t + o(\Delta t), & i = 1 \\ o(\Delta t), & i > 1 \end{cases}$$

thus showing the consistency of the definitions we have given for the Poisson process. The mean value of (4.1.9) is easily computed to be λt. In other words, the mean number of arrivals in a time interval t is the (mean) arrival rate λ times the length of the interval. The second moment of the Poisson distribution is given by $\lambda t(1 + \lambda t)$ from which we observe that the variance is λt, the same as the mean. For reasons based on the properties we have exhibited, Poisson arrivals are often called *random* arrivals.

Two important properties of parallel Poisson arrival processes will be of subsequent use. In Fig. 4.1-2(a) we have shown the confluence or sum of k independent Poisson "streams" with parameters λ_i, $i = 1, 2, \ldots, k$. The resulting process is also Poisson with rate $\lambda' = \lambda_1 + \lambda_2 + \cdots + \lambda_k$. This result is easily motivated by observing that the probability of an arrival in the sum process in a small time interval Δt is $\lambda' \, \Delta t + o(\Delta t)$ and the probability of no arrival is $1 - \lambda' \, \Delta t + o(\Delta t)$.

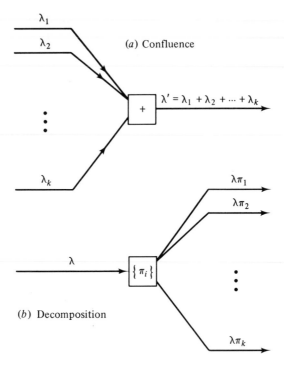

λ_1

λ_2 (a) Confluence

$\lambda' = \lambda_1 + \lambda_2 + \cdots + \lambda_k$

λ_k

$\lambda\pi_1$

$\lambda\pi_2$

λ

$\{\pi_i\}$

(b) Decomposition

$\lambda\pi_k$

Fig. 4.1-2   Combination of Poisson processes.

The decomposition of a Poisson process according to a stationary probability distribution $\{\pi_i\}_{i=1}^{k}$ is shown in Fig. 4.1-2(b). Each time an arrival occurs from the source process it is assigned to one of the branch processes. The probability that the ith branch is assigned the arrival is π_i ($1 \leq i \leq k$). The proof that the branch processes are independent and Poisson with the respective rates $\lambda\pi_i$ ($1 \leq i \leq k$) is straightforward and left as an exercise.

4.1.3. The Service Mechanism

Although most of the models we shall analyze assume an arbitrary service time distribution, the exponential distribution will again play a special role in a couple of important models. In particular, with the latter models we shall have need of the memoryless property of the exponential distribution. This property will enable us to say that no matter how much service any given job has received at the time we choose to observe the system, the distribution function governing the service still required will be identical to the original exponential distribution.

The third component of a queueing system that we must define is the service discipline. First, we shall distinguish *preemptive* from *nonpreemptive* disciplines. According to nonpreemptive disciplines, jobs, once they commence execution, must be run to completion. With preemptive disciplines we shall assume that jobs once begun can be interrupted at any point and removed from the processor. Preempted jobs are returned to a queueing or storage facility and subsequently reallocated to the processor when their turn for service comes up again. No limits will be placed on the number of preemptions.

The amount of information used by a service discipline can vary widely and depends, of course, on what information can be assumed available. In the computer application the information used takes the form of prior knowledge of execution time, execution time already received, time of arrival, storage and input/output requirements, and priorities reflecting the importance or urgency of jobs. The scope of this book will be restricted to service disciplines using information concerning

1. *Time of arrival*. For example, the common first-in-first-out (FIFO) rule simply executes the jobs in the order in which they arrive.

2. *Job execution times*. As an example, we have the shortest-processing-time (SPT) rule according to which the next job executed is the one having the shortest execution time of those jobs currently waiting.

3. *Simple priorities*. The basic priority model that we analyze assumes that each job in the system is assigned to a priority class at (or by) the time it arrives. The set of priority classes is assumed countable. Such priorities can be used to discriminate between jobs on the basis of storage requirements, etc.; however, we shall not concern ourselves with the mechanism of priority assignment, primarily because it depends so strongly on the objectives and limitations of specific installations.

The above disciplines, along with several others, will be defined more fully in the remaining sections of this chapter. We shall conclude this section with a brief discussion of the performance measures generally sought in the analysis of queueing models of computer systems.

4.1.4. Performance Measures

Usually, the first and most basic measure of performance (or congestion) to be calculated is the distribution of the number in the system (server and queue) as a function of time. For most systems of interest the complexity of this calculation is extreme and the form of the results such as to make them difficult to interpret. Thus one usually settles for the long-run or steady-state behavior in terms of stationary probability distributions. The latter results are much simpler in general and are further justified by the fact that the transient behavior of systems is sufficiently short-lived in many cases to be of little interest.

Perhaps the most important performance measure from the point of view of the user is the distribution of the time he must spend in the system. This distribution will normally be conditioned on the amount of service he requires in those systems which discriminate between jobs on the basis of some known measure of execution times. (Hereafter, conditional waiting times will refer to waiting times conditioned specifically on the execution time required.) The distribution of waiting times in queue is also of interest in those systems where this distribution is essentially different from the previous one. In the models examined in the subsequent sections our main interest will be in finding the mean values of conditional waiting time distributions.

A third measure of congestion that is commonly studied is the distribution of the length of *busy periods*. In a single-server system a busy period begins when a job arrives to find an empty system and ends at the instant the system again becomes empty. For several of the models that we shall analyze the busy-period distributions are the same. We shall develop a functional equation for the transform of this equilibrium busy-period distribution. Calculation of the first two moments is given in the Problems.

In the next section we shall be presenting only the most basic results in applied queueing theory. Our primary purpose is to provide the reader lacking experience in this area with enough background to study basic applications to probability models of computer scheduling problems (Sections 3.4-3.8). These results will also provide a useful background to many of the techniques employed in Chapters 5 and 6 on other resource allocation problems.

Especially in the calculation of waiting times, queueing theory deals frequently with sums of independent random variables. This is one of the principal reasons why the use of Laplace transforms will be extremely convenient in certain of the following sections. We shall also make heavy use of generating functions (z-transforms) in dealing with discrete probability distributions, particularly in solving the difference equations describing stochastic processes. Because of their importance we have provided in Appendix A the definitions and basic properties of generating functions and Laplace transforms relevant to probability theory.

4.2. BASIC QUEUEING RESULTS

4.2.1. The M/M/1 Queueing System

We shall consider a single-processor queue with Poisson arrivals and service times exponentially distributed according to

$$(4.2.1) \qquad\qquad B(x) = 1 - e^{-\mu x}, \quad x \geq 0$$

with the first and second moments $E(S) = 1/\mu$ and $E(S^2) = 2/\mu^2$. Our main objective is the probability distribution describing the number in the system during statistical equilibrium. The results obtained will be valid for any service discipline that does not use any information concerning known execution times in determining the sequence of job executions. Examples of such disciplines include FIFO, LIFO (last-in-first-out), and random sequencing, as well as priority disciplines in which priority assignments are independent of job execution times.

In queueing parlance the systems defined above are members of the class of M/M/1 queueing systems (also called Poisson queues because of the exponential assumptions). In this notation the first element denotes the interarrival time distribution, the second element denotes the service time distribution, and the third element denotes the number of servers. M stands for the (Markov) exponential distribution, G for a general distribution, and D for the (deterministic) assumption of constant interarrival or service times.

Now suppose that the system commences operation at time $t = 0$. Let $X(t)$, $t \geq 0$, denote the number of jobs (in service and waiting) in the system at time t. The transitions $X(t) \longrightarrow X(t')$, $t' > t$, are clearly determined by the chance effects introduced by our assumption of random arrivals and service times that are subject to the distribution $B(x)$. Accordingly, $X(t)$ is called a *stochastic* or *random process*. Since the system state represented by $X(t)$ is the number of jobs in the system we can associate a state space with $X(t)$ which consists simply of the nonnegative integers. In general, $X(t)$ will be defined when we specify an initial value $X(0)$ and the probability distributions governing the transitions $X(t) \longrightarrow X(t')$ for all t and $t' > t \geq 0$. These transitions will be completely determined by our assumptions regarding arrivals, service times, and the service discipline.† As stated in the last section our interest will be in characterizing $X(t)$ by computing the probability distribution

$$(4.2.2) \qquad p_n(t) = \Pr[X(t) = n], \quad t > 0, n = 0, 1, 2, \ldots$$

assuming that we are given $X(0)$ and hence

$$(4.2.3) \qquad\qquad p_n(0) = 1, \quad X(0) = n$$
$$= 0, \quad \text{otherwise}$$

We calculate the $p_n(t)$ as follows. Let us suppose that the system is in state $X(t) \geq 1$. We want to evaluate the possible transitions $X(t) \longrightarrow X(t + \Delta t)$ for a small time interval Δt. According to our assumptions, the probability of an arrival in Δt is $\lambda \Delta t + o(\Delta t)$ and the probability of no arrivals is $1 - \lambda \Delta t + o(\Delta t)$, all other arrival events occurring with probability $o(\Delta t)$. Simi-

---

†For the present purposes the service discipline will have no effect, since we have assumed that sequencing is independent of execution times. (Also, it is understood that we shall be concerned only with disciplines that keep the processor occupied whenever there is one or more jobs in the system.)

larly, since $X(t) \geq 1$, the probabilities of one departure and no departures are $\mu \Delta t + o(\Delta t)$ and $1 - \mu \Delta t + o(\Delta t)$, respectively, with all other departure events having probability $o(\Delta t)$. Thus, using the independence of interarrival and service times and considering only events whose occurrence has probability on the order of magnitude of Δt, we can write (for $X(t) \geq 1$)

$$\Pr[X(t + \Delta t) = X(t) + 1] = \Pr[\text{one arrival and no departures}].$$
$$= [\lambda \Delta t + o(\Delta t)][1 - \mu \Delta t + o(\Delta t)]$$
$$= \lambda \Delta t + o(\Delta t)$$
$$\Pr[X(t + \Delta t) = X(t)] = \Pr[\text{no arrivals and no departures}].$$
$$= [1 - \lambda \Delta t + o(\Delta t)][1 - \mu \Delta t + o(\Delta t)]$$
$$= 1 - (\lambda + \mu) \Delta t + o(\Delta t)$$
$$\Pr[X(t + \Delta t) = X(t) - 1] = \Pr[\text{no arrivals and one departure}]$$
$$= [\mu \Delta t + o(\Delta t)][1 - \lambda \Delta t + o(\Delta t)]$$
$$= \mu \Delta t + o(\Delta t)$$

Relative to $X(t)$ all other possibilities for $X(t + \Delta t)$ have probabilities $o(\Delta t)$. Consequently, in terms of our notation we can accumulate the above equations into

$$p_n(t + \Delta t) = p_n(t)[1 - (\lambda + \mu) \Delta t + o(\Delta t)] + p_{n+1}(t)[\mu \Delta t + o(\Delta t)]$$
$$+ p_{n-1}(t)[\lambda \Delta t + o(\Delta t)]$$

Neglecting terms whose order of magnitude is less than Δt we find on regrouping terms and dividing by Δt

$$\lim_{\Delta t \to 0} \frac{p_n(t + \Delta t) - p_n(t)}{\Delta t} = \mu p_{n+1}(t) - (\lambda + \mu)p_n(t) + \lambda p_{n-1}(t)$$

Thus,

(4.2.4) $$p_n'(t) = \mu p_{n+1}(t) - (\lambda + \mu)p_n(t) + \lambda p_{n-1}(t)$$

Now suppose that $X(t) = 0$. In this case we can ignore the possibility of departures and write

$$p_0(t + \Delta t) = (1 - \lambda \Delta t)p_0(t) + \mu \Delta t p_1(t)$$

from which we obtain

(4.2.5) $$p_0'(t) = \mu p_1(t) - \lambda p_0(t)$$

The solution to (4.2.4) and (4.2.5) with the given initial condition in (4.2.3) and the constraint $\sum_{n=0}^{\infty} p_n(t) = 1$ describes the time-dependent behavior of the system and can be found in standard texts on queueing theory.† The solution even for this simple queue is rather complex and superficially difficult to interpret. For this reason and for the more fundamental reason that such solutions have not been found for most of the other models we shall consider, we shall not dwell any further on the transient or time-dependent behavior described by these solutions. Instead, we shall restrict our interest to the limiting behavior of the probabilities $p_n(t)$ for large t.

If in fact the probabilities $p_n(t)$ approach a limit we say that these limiting probabilities describe the behavior of the system during *statistical equilibrium* (or the *steady state*). Also, the probabilities $p_n = \lim_{t \to \infty} p_n(t)$ constitute the *stationary probability distribution*. Intuitively, one might expect the existence of a stationary distribution under the simple condition that the arrival rate λ of jobs is less than the rate μ at which jobs can be executed. This can indeed be proved along with the fact that this distribution is independent of the initial condition $X(0)$. However, we shall proceed on the assumption that a stationary distribution exists and then show that these probabilities are well defined only if $\lambda < \mu$. We shall proceed in a similar way with the other models analyzed.

To calculate the stationary probabilities p_n we use the fact that in the steady state $\lim_{t \to \infty} p'_n(t) = 0$. Simplifying (4.2.4) and (4.2.5) we have

(4.2.6) $$\mu p_{n+1} - (\lambda + \mu)p_n + \lambda p_{n-1} = 0, \quad n \geq 1$$

(4.2.7) $$\mu p_1 - \lambda p_0 = 0$$

Note that (4.2.6) and (4.2.7) have the characteristic feature of steady-state *balance* equations in which the rate of transitions or flow $(\mu p_{n+1} + \lambda p_{n-1})$ into a given state $n \geq 1$ is balanced by the flow $(\lambda p_n + \mu p_n)$ out of that state. Defining $\rho = \lambda/\mu$ and solving (4.2.6) and (4.2.7) systematically, we find

$$p_n = \rho^n p_0, \quad n = 0, 1, 2, \ldots$$

Imposing the constraints $\rho < 1$ and $\sum_{n=0}^{\infty} p_n = 1$ gives $p_0 = 1 - \rho$ and hence

(4.2.8) $$p_n = (1 - \rho)\rho^n, \quad n = 0, 1, 2, \ldots$$

Note that $\rho = 1 - p_0$ is the equilibrium probability that the system is busy. As can be seen, (4.2.8) denotes a geometric distribution with parameter ρ, and $\rho < 1$ is the condition for the existence of this distribution. Clearly, $\rho < 1$

---

†Because of their application to population models, (4.2.4) and (4.2.5) are frequently called *birth-and-death equations* and the corresponding process $X(t)$ is called a birth-and-death process [1].

implies that $\lambda < \mu$ and hence an arrival rate that is less than the maximum departure rate. Because of its significance, the parameter ρ is frequently referred to as the *utilization factor* or *traffic intensity*. We shall use the former term.

Let us now derive (4.2.8) using the method of generating functions. Let $P(z) = \sum_{n=0}^{\infty} p_n z^n$ denote the (probability) generating function for the p_n. Multiplying (4.2.6) by z^n, summing over all $n \geq 1$, and then adding (4.2.7) we have

$$\sum_{n=0}^{\infty} p_{n+1} z^n + \rho \sum_{n=1}^{\infty} p_{n-1} z^n = (1 + \rho) \sum_{n=0}^{\infty} p_n z^n - p_0$$

Introducing $P(z)$ we find

$$\frac{1}{z}[P(z) - p_0] + \rho z P(z) = (1 + \rho)P(z) - p_0$$

from which we obtain

$$P(z) = \frac{p_0}{1 - \rho z}$$

Using $\lim_{z \to 1} P(z) = 1$ gives $p_0 = 1 - \rho$. Expressing $P(z)$ as a power series in z we find

$$P(z) = (1 - \rho) + (1 - \rho)\rho z + \cdots + (1 - \rho)\rho^n z^n + \cdots$$

which gives us (4.2.8) as the coefficient of the nth term.

We have gone through this exercise in computing $P(z)$ because in many similar problems we can obtain $P(z)$ but we cannot conveniently solve for the p_n directly. Having $P(z)$ enables us to compute the first two moments in a routine fashion (see Appendix A), and this will normally account for most of what we want to know about system congestion. Also, we can easily find $p_0 = \lim_{z \to 0} P(z)$ and hence the probability $1 - p_0$ of a busy system.

From (4.2.8) the mean and variance of the number in the system during statistical equilibrium are given by

(4.2.9)
$$\bar{n} = \frac{\rho}{1 - \rho}$$

(4.2.10)
$$\text{Var}(n) = \frac{\rho}{(1 - \rho)^2}$$

As a final remark we emphasize the applicability of the previous results to all service disciplines that do not base job sequencing on execution time information assumed known a priori about arriving jobs. We shall next examine the more general M/G/1 system after which waiting time distributions will be derived for FIFO systems.

4.2.2. The M/G/1 Queueing System

Under the assumption of independent exponential interarrival and service times the process $X(t)$ has the following extremely important property: At any given time t_0 the future behavior of $X(t)$ depends only on the current state $X(t_0)$ and not on the past prior to t_0. Informally, this memoryless or Markov property defines *Markov processes*, and it introduces a substantial simplification into the analysis. Although this property will be retained in the arrival processes of subsequent queueing models, we shall be interested in carrying out the analysis of $X(t)$ assuming general service time distributions. With this assumption if at some point t_0 a job is in execution, then the behavior of $X(t)$, $t > t_0$, will depend not only on $X(t_0)$ but on the amount of service already received by the executing job. Thus $X(t)$ is no longer a Markov process. An extension to the previous approach which is suggested by the above property can be sketched as follows.

We can redefine $X(t)$ so that its state space includes the values of a supplementary variable x that specifies the amount of service already received by the job (if any) in execution at time t. Specifically, the value of the new process $X'(t)$ is a pair (n, x), where n is the number in the system at time t and x is defined as above. The new process now has the Markov property and the analysis can proceed on that basis. We shall avoid the difficult analysis of this approach and consider an alternative which is far simpler for our limited purposes.

The technique to be described is motivated by recognition of the fact that although $X(t)$ does not have the Markov property at every point in time, there exist many embedded sequences of time points at which $X(t)$ does have the Markov property. Suppose, for example, that we define the time instants (or epochs) $t_1, t_2, \ldots$ so that t_i is the instant immediately after the ith job execution in an M/G/1 system with service distribution $B(x)$.

Since the service and interarrival intervals are mutually independent, $X(t)$ at the epochs t_i has the Markov property. As a result the t_i are also called *regeneration points*. The discrete time process $X(t_i)$, $i = 1, 2, \ldots$, constitutes a Markov chain which is said to be an *embedded* Markov chain with respect to $X(t)$. For ease of notation we shall let $X_i \equiv X(t_i)$ and denote the Markov chain $\{X_i\}$.

The Markov chain $\{X_i\}$ is *homogeneous* in the sense that the *one-step transition probabilities*

$$(4.2.11) \qquad \pi_{ij} = \Pr\{X_{k+1} = j \,|\, X_k = i\}, \quad k = 1, 2, \ldots$$

are not functions of the time parameter k. The stationary distribution for $\{X_i\}$

is defined as the solution to the system of *equilibrium equations*†

(4.2.12) $$\pi_j = \sum_{i=0}^{\infty} \pi_{ij}\pi_i, \qquad j = 0, 1, 2, \ldots$$

subject to the normalization $\sum_{j=0}^{\infty} \pi_j = 1$. We shall now compute the generating function for the probabilities in (4.2.12) under the assumptions of Poisson arrivals and a general service time distribution. In Problem 4-10 we shall indicate a more direct technique for finding moments of the stationary distribution.

We begin by multiplying (4.2.12) by z^j and summing over all $j \geq 0$. On changing the order of summation we have the following generating function:

(4.2.13) $$P(z) = \sum_{j=0}^{\infty} \pi_j z^j = \sum_{j=0}^{\infty} z^j \sum_{i=0}^{\infty} \pi_i \pi_{ij} = \sum_{i=0}^{\infty} \pi_i \sum_{j=0}^{\infty} \pi_{ij} z^j$$

Next, we shall compute the transition probabilities π_{ij}.

Suppose that $X_k = n > 0$; i.e., there is at least one job in the system and (t_k, t_{k+1}) corresponds to a service period. Since the job executing in (t_k, t_{k+1}) is the only job to depart, we must have $X_{k+1} \geq n - 1$. It follows that $\pi_{ij} = 0$ for $j < i - 1$ and that $X_{k+1} - X_k + 1$ represents the number of arrivals occurring in (t_k, t_{k+1}). Thus, if we let q_m, $m = 0, 1, 2, \ldots$, denote the probability of m arrivals in a service period, we have $\pi_{ij} = q_{j-i+1}$ for $i > 0$ and $j \geq i - 1$.

Now suppose that $X_k = 0$; i.e., t_k commences an idle period. Regardless of the length of this idle period the probability that $X_{k+1} = j$ is simply the probability that there are j arrivals during the execution of the job whose arrival terminated the idle period. Thus $\pi_{0j} = \pi_{1j} = q_j$ for $j \geq 0$. Let us now substitute for π_{ij} in (4.2.13). On separating out the first term of the summation, we have

(4.2.14) $$P(z) = \pi_0 \sum_{j=0}^{\infty} q_j z^j + \sum_{i=1}^{\infty} \pi_i \sum_{j=i-1}^{\infty} q_{j-i+1} z^j$$

Letting $A(z) = \sum_{m=0}^{\infty} q_m z^m$ denote the generating function for the distribution of the number of arrivals in a service period, we can simplify (4.2.14) to

(4.2.15) $$P(z) = \pi_0 A(z) + \frac{A(z)}{z}[P(z) - \pi_0]$$

Solving for $P(z)$ we get

(4.2.16) $$P(z) = \pi_0 \frac{(1 - z)A(z)}{A(z) - z}$$

---

†The general conditions under which a stationary distribution exists for $\{X_i\}$ are given in Appendix A. These conditions will always hold for the applications discussed in this book.

To proceed further we need to examine $A(z)$. Now $f_m(t)$ as given by (4.1.9) specifies the probability of m Poisson arrivals in time t. Hence averaging this probability over the service time distribution we have

$$q_m = \int_0^\infty f_m(t)\, dB(t), \quad m = 0, 1, 2, \ldots$$

Substituting (4.1.9) and computing the generating function we have

$$A(z) = \sum_{m=0}^\infty z^m \int_0^\infty \frac{(\lambda t)^m}{m!} e^{-\lambda t}\, dB(t)$$

Reversing the order of summation and integration we obtain

(4.2.17)
$$A(z) = \int_0^\infty e^{-\lambda t(1-z)}\, dB(t)$$

Using the Laplace transform $B^*(s) = \mathrm{E}[e^{-sS}]$ of service times we get

(4.2.18)
$$A(z) = B^*(\lambda - \lambda z)$$

Using (4.2.17) we can return to (4.2.16) and compute π_0 and the moments of the distribution $\{\pi_i\}$. Making use of $\lim_{z \to 1} P(z) = 1$ and noting that both the numerator and denominator of (4.2.16) vanish at $z = 1$, we find on applying l'Hospital's rule

$$\frac{-\pi_0 A(1)}{A'(1) - 1} = 1$$

Now $A(1) = 1$ from (4.2.17). Differentiating (4.2.17) we find $A'(1) = \rho$ and hence

(4.2.19)
$$\pi_0 = 1 - \rho$$

where $\rho = \lambda \mathrm{E}(S)$ is the utilization factor. (Clearly, $0 \le \rho < 1$ is necessary for statistical equilibrium.) Thus the stationary distribution is defined by the generating function

(4.2.20)
$$P(z) = \frac{(1 - \rho)(1 - z)B^*(\lambda - \lambda z)}{B^*(\lambda - \lambda z) - z}$$

We find for the first moment, again using l'Hospital's rule,

$$\bar{n} = \lim_{z \to 1} \frac{dP(z)}{dz} = \rho + \frac{A''(1)}{2(1 - \rho)}$$

From (4.2.17) we obtain $A''(1) = \lambda^2 E(S^2)$ and hence

$$(4.2.21) \qquad \bar{n} = \rho + \frac{\lambda^2 E(S^2)}{2(1 - \rho)}$$

Introducing the *coefficient of variation* $C(S)$ defined by

$$(4.2.22) \qquad C^2(S) = \frac{\text{Var}(S)}{E^2(S)} = \frac{E(S^2)}{E^2(S)} - 1$$

we can put (4.2.21) into the more common form

$$(4.2.23) \qquad \bar{n} = \rho + \frac{\rho^2[1 + C^2(S)]}{2(1 - \rho)}$$

Higher moments of the distribution $\{\pi_j\}$ can be computed in a similar fashion.

According to the definition of $\{X_i\}$, the expression (4.2.23) represents the mean number of jobs that are left in the system by departing jobs. In general, since the state of the system is being oberved only at the instants just following departures, one might reasonably expect the distribution $\{\pi_j\}_{j=0}^{\infty}$ to differ from the stationary distribution for the continuous time-parameter process, $X(t)$; i.e., one's evaluation of a system is generally dependent on (biased by) the times at which he has chosen to observe it. But in fact these two distributions turn out to be precisely the same. In general, this property applies to any queueing system in which the only state-changes possible at any instant of time are $+1$ (arrival) and -1 (departure). Consistent with this property we find on substituting $E(S^2) = 2/\mu^2$ into (4.2.21) the result of (4.2.9) for the exponential service time distribution.

Note particularly that $\bar{n}$ is determined not only by the mean interarrival and service times but also by the second moment of the service time distribution. As shown by (4.2.21) $\bar{n}$ increases linearly with the variance of service times. Considering constant service times, for example, the variation in service times is zero and we have

$$(4.2.24) \qquad \bar{n} = \rho + \frac{\rho^2}{2(1 - \rho)} = \frac{\rho(1 - \rho/2)}{(1 - \rho)}$$

which is to be compared with the expression $\rho/(1 - \rho)$ for exponential service times (whose coefficient of variation is 1). For small ρ the difference in the means is small, but as ρ approaches 1 (the *saturation* condition), the two differ by almost a factor of 2.

Interpreting the probability $1 - \pi_0 = \rho$ of a busy system as the average number of jobs in the processor one would expect that the second term in (4.2.23) is the mean number $\bar{n}_q$ waiting in queue. As a direct calculation would show, it is indeed true that

(4.2.25)
$$\bar{n}_q = \frac{\rho^2[1 + C^2(S)]}{2(1 - \rho)}$$

Again, the above results for general service times are applicable to any nonpreemptive queue selection rule which does not use information about job execution times.

4.2.3. Waiting Times

4.2.3.1. Residual Waiting Times.   Before computing waiting times for the FIFO system we shall deal with a simpler problem whose solution will be used later in deriving expected waiting times for nonpreemptive disciplines.

Consider a random arrival to an M/G/1 system in statistical equilibrium. Let $R(x)$ denote the (conditional) probability distribution governing the remaining execution time of the job in progress, given that the system is busy at the time of arrival. Our problem is to find the expected value R of the remaining execution time. In renewal theory R is referred to as the mean forward recurrence time and in the reliability context as the mean residual lifetime. We shall give below a brief, informal derivation of R; a full analysis leading to $R(x)$ is given in Appendix B. (See also Problem 4-12.)

One's first inclination might be to say that R is simply $E(S)/2$. That this is a mistake for general service time distributions is explained by the statement that our random arrival is more likely to occur during the execution of a long job than a short one. We shall exploit this observation in the following argument. Let $b(x)$ be the service time density and $b'(x)$ the density function for the length of the service period in which a random arrival occurs. Since we may interpret $b(x) \, dx$ as the relative frequency of service periods of length x, the density $b'(x)$ should be proportional to x and $b(x)$. Letting K be the constant of proportionality we find that in order for $Kxb(x)$ to be a probability density we must have $K = 1/E(S)$. Whence

(4.2.26)
$$b'(x) = \frac{xb(x)}{E(S)}$$

Now given a random arrival during a service period of length x, the conditional expectation of the remaining execution time is simply $x/2$. Hence

(4.2.27)
$$R = \int_0^\infty \left(\frac{x}{2}\right) \frac{xb(x)}{E(S)} \, dx = \frac{E(S^2)}{2E(S)}$$

Very shortly, we shall have occasion to verify this result by means of an independent argument. Note that R increases linearly with the variation in service times and is equal to the minimum of $E(S)/2$ only when service times are constant. Also, for exponential service times we see that (4.2.27) reduces to $E(S)$, consistent with the memoryless property.

Let us now remove the conditioning on the existence of a busy system at arrival time. In other words, suppose that we ask for the mean time following the time of arrival which elapses before the processor becomes free for allocation to the next job selected from the queue. This quantity is denoted $E(S_r)$. Since an arrival finds the processor available immediately when the system† is empty and since p is the probability of a busy system, we have in statistical equilibrium

$$E(S_r) = pR$$

Substituting for R and $p = \lambda E(S)$ we have

(4.2.28)
$$E(S_r) = \frac{\lambda E(S^2)}{2}$$

This result is extended easily to systems in which the arriving jobs can be grouped into classes each having a distinct service time distribution. In particular, if we let λ_p and $B_p(x)$ $(p = 1, 2, \ldots)$ denote the arrival rate and service time distribution, respectively, for jobs of class p, we have by applying the same arguments

(4.2.29)
$$E(S_r) = \frac{1}{2} \sum_{p \geq 1} \lambda_p E(S_p^2)$$

under the assumption of statistical equilibrium. In Section 4.5 we shall make use of (4.2.29) in an analysis of priority queues.

4.2.3.2. FIFO Waiting Time Distributions. For the FIFO system the Laplace transform of the equilibrium waiting time distribution $W(x)$ is easily obtained from the generating function $P(z)$ of the number in system. Recall that $\{\pi_i\}$ gives the probability mass function for the number of jobs left behind by a departing job. However, the jobs left behind are precisely those which arrived during the departing job's stay in system. Now by (4.2.18), $A(z) = B^*(\lambda - \lambda z)$ describes the number of arrivals during service periods; by analogy, therefore, the number of arrivals during waiting times in the system is described by

(4.2.30)
$$P(z) = W^*(\lambda - \lambda z)$$

†We are making, and will continue to make, implicit use of an important property of queues *with Poisson arrivals*. Specifically, it can be shown that the equilibrium queue-length distribution is identical to the distribution encountered by arrivals during statistical equilibrium. Intuitively, the result follows from the "randomness" of Poisson arrivals. (For purposes of distinction the former distribution is also called the "external observer" distribution.)

Introducing the change of variable $s = \lambda - \lambda z$ into (4.2.30) we obtain from (4.2.20)

$$(4.2.31) \qquad W^*(s) = \frac{(1 - \rho)sB^*(s)}{s - \lambda + \lambda B^*(s)}$$

The waiting time in the system is the sum of a queueing time (waiting time in queue) and a service period. Hence the Laplace transform of the queueing time distribution $V(x)$ can be found from $W^*(s) = B^*(s)V^*(s)$. Thus

$$(4.2.32) \qquad V^*(s) = \frac{(1 - \rho)s}{s - \lambda + \lambda B^*(s)}$$

Denoting first moments by W and V we obtain by differentiation of (4.2.31) and (4.2.32)

$$(4.2.33) \qquad W = E(S)\left[1 + \frac{\rho[1 + C^2(S)]}{2(1 - \rho)}\right]$$

and

$$(4.2.34) \qquad V = E(S)\frac{\rho[1 + C^2(S)]}{2(1 - \rho)}$$

Equation (4.2.33) or (4.2.34) is frequently called the Pollaczek-Khintchine formula.

We may verify (4.2.31) for the M/M/1 system by the following independent argument. Let $W_n(x)$ denote the equilibrium distribution of waiting times, conditioned on the number n in the system at arrival time. Because of the memoryless property, the remaining execution time for the job in progress at arrival has the same exponential distribution as for the jobs in queue. Consequently, with the FIFO rule $W_n(x)$ is distributed as the sum of $n + 1$ identical and independent exponentials. This corresponds to the gamma-type (or special Erlangian) density described in Appendix A. Letting μ be the parameter of the service time distribution we thus have

$$(4.2.35) \qquad W_n^*(s) = \left(\frac{\mu}{\mu + s}\right)^{n+1}$$

From the geometric stationary distribution in (4.2.8), for the unconditional distribution we find

$$(4.2.36) \qquad W^*(s) = \sum_{n=0}^{\infty} p_n W_n^*(s) = (1 - \rho) \sum_{n=0}^{\infty} \rho^n \left(\frac{\mu}{\mu + s}\right)^{n+1}$$

or

$$(4.2.37) \qquad W^*(s) = \frac{(1 - \rho)\mu}{(1 - \rho)\mu + s}$$

This is seen to be the transform of the following exponential distribution, also obtainable from (4.2.31):

$$(4.2.38) \qquad W(x) = 1 - e^{-(1-\rho)\mu x}, \quad x \geq 0$$

with mean value

$$(4.2.39) \qquad W = \frac{1/\mu}{1 - \rho}$$

Thus the waiting time in the system also has the Markov property. It is worth noting the fact illustrated in (4.2.38) that a geometrically distributed sum of independent random variables each with an identical exponential distribution is itself exponentially distributed. In the discrete case the resulting distribution would be geometric if the individual distributions were geometric.

The conditional queueing time distribution $V_n(x)$ given $n \geq 1$ in the system at arrival time is clearly $W_{n-1}(x)$. Since no waiting time in queue is experienced by an arrival to an empty system, we have

$$V(x) = p_0 + \sum_{n=1}^{\infty} p_n W_{n-1}(x)$$

Using transforms we readily obtain from (4.2.8)

$$(4.2.40) \qquad V(x) = 1 - \rho e^{-(1-\rho)\mu x}$$

which is consistent with (4.2.32). Note that $V(x)$ is a mixed distribution with a probability mass $(1 - \rho)$ concentrated at $x = 0$.

The mean value expressions in (4.2.33) and (4.2.34) can also be arrived at directly. For example, V can be expressed as the sum of the expected time for the processor to become available for the next job plus the mean number $\bar{n}_q$ waiting in queue times the expected service time. Specifically,

$$(4.2.41) \qquad V = \bar{n}_q E(S) + E(S_r)$$

Substituting (4.2.25) and (4.2.28) we obtain (4.2.34).†

4.2.3.3. Little's Result.   On differentiating (4.2.30) and taking the limit $z \rightarrow 1$ we obtain *Little's result*

$$(4.2.42) \qquad \bar{n} = \lambda W$$

---

†Note that by substituting (4.2.34) for V and (4.2.25) for $\bar{n}_q$ into (4.2.41) we verify independently the expression obtained for $E(S_r)$ in (4.2.28).

which states that the equilibrium mean number in the system is equal to the product of the arrival rate and the mean time in the system. Also, this result implies a conservation principle whereby the mean number ($\bar{n}$) in the system encountered by a new arrival is equal to the mean number (λW) it leaves behind on departure. The validity of (4.2.42) extends far beyond the contexts discussed so far and essentially depends only on the existence of a steady state in which the long-run rate of arrival is equal to the long-run rate of departure. Specifically, this result does not depend on the scheduling rule or on any particular properties of the arrival process. (See also Section 3.8, where Little's result is adapted to deterministic sequencing problems.) A detailed proof of these properties has been given by Little [9].

Little's result restricted to the number in queue leads to

$$(4.2.43) \qquad\qquad \bar{n}_q = \lambda V$$

It is interesting to observe that on substituting (4.2.43) for $\bar{n}_q$ in (4.2.41) we could have solved for V without having known $\bar{n}_q$ [or $P(z)$] beforehand. Finally, in our study of priority queues we shall have occasion to apply Little's result to individual priority classes. Thus, for example,

$$(4.2.44) \qquad\qquad \bar{n}_k = \lambda_k W_k, \quad k = 1, 2, \ldots$$

states that for each k the mean number of priority k jobs is equal to their arrival rate times their mean waiting time.

4.2.4. The Busy-Period Distribution

Let D be the random variable denoting the length of busy periods in an $M/G/1$ queue during statistical equilibrium. We seek the busy-period distribution $H(y) = \Pr[D \leq y]$. Suppose that a job J_0 initiating a busy period requires x time units and that during its execution there are n arriving jobs $J_1, J_2, \ldots, J_n$. Now the distribution $H(y)$ is insensitive to the sequence in which $J_1, J_2, \ldots, J_n$ and subsequent arrivals are executed, and so let us adopt the following discipline. After J_0 completes we execute J_1 and the subsequently arriving jobs until $J_2, \ldots, J_n$ are the only remaining jobs in the system. At this point we proceed in a similar manner executing J_2 and subsequent arrivals until $J_3, \ldots, J_n$ are the only jobs remaining. This process is repeated so that finally J_n is executed along with subsequent arrivals until the system again becomes empty and the busy period terminates.

Let D_i denote the time elapsing between the beginning of J_i's execution and the beginning of J_{i+1}'s execution, $i < n$, and let D_n be the time interval beginning with J_n's execution and ending with the termination of the busy period. Let X and N be the random variables denoting, respectively, J_0's execution time and the number of arrivals during its execution time. A little reflection leads to the key observation that the D_i $(1 \leq i \leq n)$ are independent random variables, each having the same distribution $H(y)$ of a busy period. Thus the conditional distribution of a busy period given that J_0 requires x time units and n arrivals occur during these x time units has the following Laplace transform:

$$E(e^{-sD} \mid X = x, N = n) = e^{-sx}E(e^{-s\sum_{i=1}^{n} D_i})$$
$$= e^{-sx}[H^*(s)]^n$$

Removing the conditioning on n, the number of Poisson arrivals during x, and the service time x of J_0, we obtain

$$E(e^{-sD}) = \int_0^\infty e^{-sx} \sum_{n=0}^\infty \frac{(\lambda x)^n}{n!}[H^*(s)]^n e^{-\lambda x} \, dB(x)$$

or

(4.2.45) $$H^*(s) = \int_0^\infty e^{-sx}e^{-\lambda x[1-H^*(s)]} \, dB(x)$$

Finally, we get

(4.2.46) $$H^*(s) = B^*(s + \lambda - \lambda H^*(s))$$

Although this functional equation cannot usually be solved to give explicit solutions for $H^*(s)$, moments are readily derived. (See Problem 4-1.) The above analysis will also be exploited in Problem 4-13 to obtain waiting time distributions for the LIFO discipline.

4.3. STATE-DEPENDENT ARRIVAL AND SERVICE TIMES IN POISSON QUEUES

The equilibrium equations of (4.2.6) and (4.2.7) can easily be generalized to apply to a variety of interesting and useful variations of the basic Poisson queue in which the service discipline is not influenced by service times. In particular, let us assume that the arrival rate and (maximum) service rates are functions of the system state (i.e., number in the system). Let λ_n and μ_n denote these arrival and service rates when the system contains n jobs, waiting and in execution. Reworking (4.2.4) and (4.2.5) we obtain

(4.3.1) $p_n'(t) = \mu_{n+1}p_{n+1}(t) - (\lambda_n + \mu_n)p_n(t) + \lambda_{n-1}p_{n-1}(t), \quad n \geq 1$

(4.3.2) $p_0'(t) = \mu_1 p_1(t) - \lambda_0 p_0(t)$

The corresponding equilibrium equations become

$$(4.3.3) \qquad \mu_{n+1}p_{n+1} - (\lambda_n + \mu_n)p_n + \lambda_{n-1}p_{n-1} = 0$$

$$(4.3.4) \qquad \mu_1 p_1 - \lambda_0 p_0 = 0$$

Solving (4.3.3) and (4.3.4) systematically we find

$$p_1 = \frac{\lambda_0}{\mu_1}p_0, \qquad p_2 = \frac{\lambda_1 \lambda_0}{\mu_2 \mu_1}p_0, \qquad p_3 = \frac{\lambda_2 \lambda_1 \lambda_0}{\mu_3 \mu_2 \mu_1}p_0, \qquad \ldots$$

or

$$(4.3.5) \qquad p_n = p_0 \prod_{i=1}^{n} \frac{\lambda_{i-1}}{\mu_i}, \quad n = 1, 2, \ldots$$

We obtain p_0 by equating the sum of the probabilities to 1. Thus

$$(4.3.6) \qquad p_0 = \left\{ 1 + \sum_{n=1}^{\infty} \prod_{i=1}^{n} \frac{\lambda_{i-1}}{\mu_i} \right\}^{-1}$$

We shall now work out some examples having meaning in the computer application.

In many queueing processes arising in computer operation the assumption of a waiting or storage facility of unlimited size is quite untenable. To model such systems under exponential assumptions suppose that a maximum of L jobs (including the one on the processor) can be accommodated in a single-server system. Assume that jobs arriving to find the system full ($n = L$) leave without returning. We may use the results in (4.3.5) and (4.3.6) by assigning

$$(4.3.7) \qquad \lambda_n = \lambda, \quad n < L$$
$$= 0, \quad n \geq L$$
$$\mu_n = \mu, \quad n = 1, 2, \ldots, L$$

Substituting into (4.3.5) and (4.3.6) and using $\rho = \lambda/\mu$ we find

$$(4.3.8) \qquad p_n = \frac{\rho^n(1 - \rho)}{1 - \rho^{L+1}}, \qquad n = 0, 1, \ldots, L$$

from which the moments and waiting times can be found in the usual ways. Note that (4.3.8) is valid for all $\rho \geq 0$. [When $\rho = 1$ (4.3.8) becomes the uniform distribution $p_n = 1/(L + 1)$.] No matter what the relative values of λ and μ are, the number in the system is bounded by L, and p_n is nonzero for all n, $0 \leq n \leq L$, and $0 < \rho < \infty$.

Another important constraint to many computer models is that represented by the *finite-source* assumption. In time-sharing applications especially, the number of users (e.g., consoles) may be so few as to make the infinite-source assumption inherent in the basic Poisson arrival mechanism a poor representation of the actual arrival process.

Suppose that we have N terminals (in a remote job entry system, say) and suppose that the time elapsing from the completion of one job entered at a terminal to the time the next job is entered is exponentially distributed with parameter λ. Assuming exponentially distributed service times as before we may use the results of (4.3.5) and (4.3.6) as follows. When there are n jobs in the system there are $N - n$ terminals available for entering new jobs. Thus

$$(4.3.9) \qquad \begin{aligned} \lambda_n &= (N - n)\lambda, \quad n \le N \\ &= 0, \qquad\qquad n > N \\ \mu_n &= \mu, \qquad\qquad n \ge 1 \end{aligned}$$

Substituting into (4.3.5) and (4.3.6) and using $\rho = \lambda/\mu$ yields

$$(4.3.10) \qquad p_0 = \left\{ \sum_{i=0}^{N} \frac{N!}{(N - i)!} \rho^i \right\}^{-1}$$

$$(4.3.11) \qquad p_n = \frac{\rho^n[N!/(N - n)!]}{\sum_{i=0}^{N} [N!/(N - i)!\rho^i]}, \qquad n = 0, 1, \ldots, N$$

In the next section we shall return to this model and discuss its use in a study of time-sharing systems. The original motivation for models of the type analyzed here arose from the study of machine servicing problems in which the machines were the customers and the repairman was the server.

As a final example we shall consider the multiserver (M/M/m) Poisson queue. Suppose that there are m processors and a service discipline that assigns jobs to these processors as they become available. Clearly, if there are $n \le m$ jobs in the system, the queue will be empty and n of the processors busy. To apply our results we make

$$(4.3.12) \qquad \begin{aligned} \lambda_n &= \lambda, \qquad n = 0, 1, 2, \ldots \\ \mu_n &= n\mu, \qquad 1 \le n \le m \\ &= m\mu, \qquad n \ge m \end{aligned}$$

Working out the results of (4.3.5) and (4.3.6) and defining a new utilization factor for m processors, $\rho = \lambda/m\mu$, we obtain

$$(4.3.13) \qquad p_n = \begin{cases} \dfrac{(m\rho)^n}{n!} p_0, & n < m \\[2ex] \dfrac{m^m}{m!} \rho^n p_0, & n \ge m \end{cases}$$

where

(4.3.14)
$$p_0 = \left\{ \frac{(m\rho)^m}{m!(1-\rho)} + \sum_{i=0}^{m-1} \frac{(m\rho)^i}{i!} \right\}^{-1}$$

The moments are found directly but no simple forms result.

4.4. THE ROUND-ROBIN SERVICE DISCIPLINE

The round-robin (RR) service discipline was one of the first to be used in time-sharing systems, primarily because of its simplicity and because it has the property of providing shorter waiting times for shorter jobs. After defining the RR discipline we shall set about the task of quantifying its waiting time property.

An RR system is pictured in Fig. 4.4-1. Poisson arrivals are assumed at an

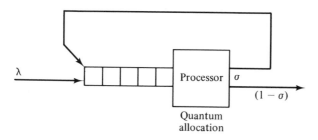

Fig. 4.4-1   The round-robin system.

average rate λ. Assuming an arbitrary service time distribution, job sequencing proceeds as follows. Each time a job is selected for operation it is selected from the head of the ordered queue and allocated a fixed amount of execution time called a *quantum* or *time slice*. We let the given quantum size be Q time units. If the job completes prior to the expiration of the quantum, then it simply departs from the system. If after Q time units the job requires additional execution time, it is returned (fed back) to the end of the queue to await its next turn at the processor. In this way a job makes as many passes through the queue as it requires quanta of service. New arrivals simply join the end of the queue at the time of arrival.

To simplify the analysis without altering the basic structure of the conditional waiting time distribution we shall assume that service times are integral multiples of the quantum size. We shall continue to make this assumption in our discussion of other disciplines according to which service is allocated a quantum at a time. With respect to the time interval Q the specific (discrete) service time distribution to be assumed is the geometric distribution

(4.4.1)
$$g_i = \sigma^{i-1}(1-\sigma), \quad i = 1, 2, \ldots$$

where $0 < \sigma < 1$. That is, the probability that a given job requires i quanta (i.e., iQ time units) is given by g_i. The first and second moments of the service time distribution are given by

(4.4.2)
$$E(S) = \sum_{i=1}^{\infty} (iQ)g_i = \frac{Q}{1 - \sigma}$$

(4.4.3)
$$E(S^2) = \sum_{i=1}^{\infty} (iQ)^2 g_i = \frac{1 + \sigma}{(1 - \sigma)^2} Q^2$$

Because of the memoryless property, the assumption of the geometric distribution (or the exponential distribution for continuous service times) is essential to the analysis of the RR system, for this property enables us to say that, regardless of the number of quanta already received by a job, the probability that it requires one more is always the same and given by the parameter σ.

Consider a random arrival to the system in statistical equilibrium and suppose that it finds j in the system and requires k quanta of service. Let $W_k(j)$ denote the conditional expectation of the time spent by the arrival in the system given j in the system at arrival time. Thus the conditional waiting time in the system of such a job is defined as

(4.4.4)
$$W_k = \sum_{j=0}^{\infty} p_j W_k(j)$$

where $\{p_j\}_{j=0}^{\infty}$ is the stationary probability distribution for the number in the RR system.[†] Our objective now is to develop an expression for W_k in terms of the parameters $\lambda, \sigma,$ and Q. First, however, we shall calculate $W_k(j)$. In effect, our approach is to "tag" the arrival whose waiting time we seek and to follow it through the system.

A job requiring k quanta of service must make k passes through the queue; i.e., such jobs are fed back to the end of the queue $k - 1$ times. The length of a pass is measured from the instant the job joins the queue to the instant it next rejoins the queue (or departs if the job's next quantum is its last). According to this definition, each pass except the first requires an integral number of quanta.

Let $U_i(j)$, $i = 1, 2, \ldots, k$, be the random variable denoting the time required on the ith pass, assuming j in the system at arrival. Clearly,

(4.4.5)
$$W_k(j) = \sum_{i=1}^{k} E(U_i(j))$$

Now if $U_i(j) = x$, $i \geq 2$, then $(x/Q) - 1$ denotes the number of jobs ahead of the tagged job on the ith pass. On the average $\sigma[(x/Q) - 1]$ of these will return for a quantum on the $(i + 1)$st pass (this is where we invoke the memoryless property of the geometric distribution). Therefore, since λx is the mean number of arrivals during the ith pass, for the $(i + 1)$st pass we have

$$E[U_{i+1}(j) \mid U_i(j) = x] = \sigma Q\left(\frac{x}{Q} - 1\right) + \lambda x Q + Q$$

from which

(4.4.6) $\qquad E[U_{i+1}(j)] = (\lambda Q + \sigma)E[U_i(j)] + Q(1 - \sigma), \quad i = 2, 3, \ldots$

Since j jobs are given to be ahead of the tagged job on the first pass, we have

(4.4.7) $\qquad E[U_2(j)] = \lambda Q E[U_1(j)] + Q(\sigma j + 1)$

By a simple induction argument we can establish the following explicit expression for $E[U_i(j)]$ $(2 \leq i \leq k)$:

(4.4.8) $\qquad E[U_i(j)] = (\lambda Q + \sigma)^{i-2} E[U_2(j)] + Q(1 - \sigma)\dfrac{1 - (\lambda Q + \sigma)^{i-2}}{1 - \lambda Q - \sigma}$

Substituting into (4.4.5) and carrying out the summation we find

(4.4.9) $\qquad W_k(j) = E[U_1(j)] + \dfrac{(k - 1)Q}{1 - \rho}$

$$+ Q\left[\lambda E[U_1(j)] + \sigma j - \frac{\rho}{1 - \rho}\right]\frac{1 - \alpha^{k-1}}{1 - \alpha}$$

where

(4.4.10) $\qquad \alpha = \lambda Q + \sigma$

and where ρ is the utilization factor for the system:

(4.4.11) $\qquad \rho = \dfrac{\lambda Q}{1 - \sigma}$

Substituting into (4.4.4) and noting that

$$W_1 = \sum_{j=0}^{\infty} p_j E[U_1(j)]$$

we have

(4.4.12) $\qquad W_k = W_1 + \dfrac{(k - 1)Q}{1 - \rho} + Q\left[\lambda W_1 + \sigma \bar{n} - \frac{\rho}{1 - \rho}\right]\frac{1 - \alpha^{k-1}}{1 - \alpha},$

$$k \geq 1$$

where $\bar{n}$ is the mean of the stationary distribution $\{p_j\}$. However, this distribution is precisely the same as the one applying to an M/M/1 system, as can be seen, for example, from the fact that the interdeparture intervals during busy periods in both systems have a geometric distribution with parameter σ. Hence, using (4.4.3) for $E(S^2)$ in (4.2.21), we have

$$(4.4.13) \qquad \bar{n} = \rho + \frac{(1 + \sigma)\rho^2}{2(1 - \rho)}$$

Finally, for the expected time to make the first pass,

$$(4.4.14) \qquad W_1 = E(Q_r) + \bar{n}_q Q + Q$$

where $E(Q_r)$ is the mean time to finish the quantum (if any) in progress at arrival time. Since quanta are of fixed length, from (4.2.28) we have $E(Q_r) = \rho Q/2$. Using $\bar{n}_q = \bar{n} - \rho$ we have

$$(4.4.15) \qquad W_1 = \frac{1 - \rho}{2}Q + \bar{n}Q$$

With (4.4.13) and (4.4.15) W_k is completely determined in (4.4.12).

It is readily seen from (4.4.12) that for fixed parameter values the dependence of W_k on k is dominated by the linear term $(k - 1)Q/(1 - \rho)$ when k is large. We shall now show that this linear dependence is precise when, for fixed mean service time $Q/(1 - \sigma)$, we consider the limit of (4.4.12) as Q approaches zero.

Note first that as Q becomes very small with $Q/(1 - \sigma)$ fixed, jobs are cycled a large number of times, receiving on each cycle a very small amount of service. Clearly, the relative position of the jobs in queue has less effect as Q is made smaller. Thus in the limit $Q \to 0$ the geometrically distributed service times become exponentially distributed with the same mean and the resulting system corresponds to one in which the processor sharing of Chapter 3 is implemented in a dynamic scheduling discipline. More specifically, if at some point there are n jobs in the processor-sharing (PS) system, each of them is receiving service at $(1/n)$th the rate that is received by a job in sole possession of the processor.

To find a corresponding expression for conditional waiting times from (4.4.12) we denote the service requirement $t = kQ$ and the associated mean waiting time $W(t)$. Informally, we substitute t/Q for k in (4.4.12) and take the limit as Q approaches zero with $\rho = \lambda Q/(1 - \sigma)$ held fixed. It is not difficult to verify that the second term in (4.4.12) is the only term not to vanish in the limit. Hence we find

$$(4.4.16) \qquad W(t) = \frac{t}{1 - \rho}$$

Thus the mean time spent in the PS system under exponential assumptions is directly proportional to the service required. Note especially that $W(t)$ is not affected by the variance of service times. Intuitively, this arises from the sharing property that prevents longer jobs from blocking the shorter jobs as in the FIFO system. Since the mean $(\bar{n})$ in the PS and FIFO system is the same under the assumption of exponential interarrival and service time distributions, then by Little's result we see that the mean (unconditional) waiting times for both systems are the same and given by

$$(4.4.17) \qquad\qquad W = \frac{E(S)}{1 - \rho}$$

where $E(S)$ is the mean of the service time distribution and $\rho = \lambda E(S)$ is the utilization factor. It has been shown [10] that the mean time spent in the PS system is also given by (4.4.17) for *any* service time distribution with mean $E(S)$.

As stated in the previous section it is more realistic to assume a finite source in those time-sharing systems having a relatively small number of user terminals. Under a processor-sharing discipline a finite-source system can be studied using the model of Section 4.3. The results in (4.3.10) and (4.3.11) carry over for the present purpose since the processor-sharing discipline does not alter the (exponential) distribution of interdeparture intervals during busy periods. In view of the systems being represented by finite-source time-sharing models the mean time in system is frequently called the *mean response time,* while the time taken to produce a new request after the previous request has been serviced is called *think time.*

The mean response time W is easily calculated using the following argument. Since the mean think time is $1/\lambda$ for each terminal, the (mean) fraction of the time spent in the system by a user is given by $W/(W + 1/\lambda)$. Thus the mean number $\bar{n}$ of users being processed by the system can be written as

$$(4.4.18) \qquad\qquad \bar{n} = N \frac{W}{W + 1/\lambda}$$

Equating (4.4.18) to the mean calculated from the distribution in (4.3.10) we have

$$N \frac{W}{W + 1/\lambda} = \sum_{n=0}^{N} n p_n = p_0 \sum_{n=1}^{N} \frac{N!}{(N - n)!} n \rho^n$$

where

$$(4.4.19) \qquad\qquad p_0 = \left\{ \sum_{n=0}^{N} \frac{N!}{(N - n)!} \rho^n \right\}^{-1}$$

Solving for W we obtain, after some routine algebra,

(4.4.20)
$$W = \frac{N(1/\mu)}{1 - p_0} - \frac{1}{\lambda}$$

The principal shortcoming of the time-sharing analysis so far has been the failure to take into account the costs (time delays) generally occasioned by the switching mechanism that removes one job from the processor and loads or prepares the next job to be executed. Such costs would be negligible only in a system where there is sufficient main memory to store all executing programs or at least to assure a high degree of overlapping of input/output and execution. One common but approximate technique for including these delays is to assume that a quantum always consists of a fixed, initial time interval devoted to these so-called program *swapping* time delays. One source of the approximation in this technique is the fact that while there is only one job in the system we cannot assume that this job is transferred in and out of main memory during its execution. Clearly, the extent of this approximation becomes less as the demand on the system (as measured by p) increases. With this method of accounting for swapping costs, experiments with a general purpose time-sharing system have shown remarkably good agreement between observed measures and those we have calculated here for a mathematical model [11].

Another source of approximation rests with the assumption that swapping times are fixed. However, a constant swap time should be a usable approximation for those systems having drum or disk auxiliary memories in which the time to swap a process is dominated by a single near-constant seek or latency delay. Further details on these systems are provided in Chapter 5.

A precise modeling of swap time, removing both of the approximations above, necessarily leads to a queueing process not having the Markov property. Similar to the analysis in Section 4.2 the approaches to the general model have consisted of applications of the theory of Markov chains. A Markov chain is defined at the epochs just following the service received during each quantum, including the swap times incurred. Note that one has a finite Markov chain in the case of the finite-source model. Thus stationary probability distributions can always be found by inverting (possibly large) matrices formulated from the one-step transition probabilities. In general, such Markov chain approaches to finite-source models lead to cumbersome waiting time results that cannot be interpreted directly. On the other hand, efficient computational methods have been developed, and, of course, the numerical studies have led to more realistic descriptions of system behavior.

Conditional waiting times for the infinite-source RR system were first obtained by Kleinrock [12] using a discrete time model (i.e., geometric interarrival and service times). The analysis in this section parallels more closely the treatments provided for the RR model in continuous time [13, 14]. Processor-sharing results were obtained as limits of the RR results [13, 14, 15]. It is worth noting that for the RR system [16] and the processor-sharing system [17] the complete distribution (in fact its Laplace transform) has been determined for conditional waiting times. Conditional waiting times for the finite-source RR models (including a swap time parameter) were first obtained by Coffman [18] and Krishnamoorthi and Wood [19]. Since the appearance of the above work a substantial literature has evolved on the RR system and certain variations of it. For further references the interested reader can consult the survey by McKinney [20].

4.5. NONPREEMPTIVE PRIORITY QUEUES

In this section we shall consider systems in which the jobs are given preferential treatment based on priorities associated with the jobs. We assume that the priority of a job is an integer fixed at arrival time; thus we shall speak of the kth priority class as being the class of jobs with priority k ($k = 1, 2, \ldots$). Since it is conventional in the literature, we shall say that one job has higher priority than another if it belongs to a priority class with lower index.

The priority queueing system to be studied is pictured in Fig. 4.5-1, where

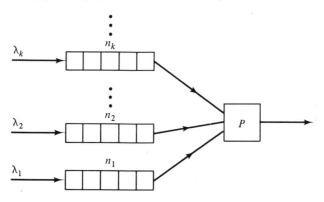

Fig. 4.5-1   Nonpreemptive priority queue.

the different queue levels correspond to the different priority classes. For the service discipline we assume that whenever a job is completed the processor is next assigned to that job at the head of the highest priority (lowest level) nonempty queue. Once a job is begun on a processor it is allowed to run to completion; i.e., the service discipline is nonpreemptive. Independent Poisson arrivals are assumed for the different priority classes with the arrival rate for the kth class denoted by λ_k ($k = 1, 2, \ldots$). Arbitrary, possibly different service time distributions exist for the priority classes. We denote the ith moment of the distribution for the kth class by $E(S_k^i)$. [As usual, we let $E(S_k) = E(S_k^1)$.]

Let us now consider the mean waiting time W_k of random arrivals to the kth queue during statistical equilibrium. It follows from the definition of the service discipline that

(4.5.1)
$$W_k = V_k + E(S_k)$$

where V_k is the mean waiting time in queue for the priority k jobs. Thus we proceed to find an expression for V_k.

Let n_i ($i = 1, 2, \ldots$) be the number of jobs encountered in the ith queue at the time of arrival of a priority k job (to be called the tagged job as before). Clearly, the tagged job cannot commence processing until all jobs of equal or higher priority at queue levels 1 through k have been completed. Moreover, the tagged job must wait for the completion of all jobs of priority 1 through $k - 1$ which arrive during its waiting time. For the purpose of computing V_k let us assume that all the $n_1 + n_2 + \cdots + n_k$ jobs of priorities 1 through k in the system at the time of arrival are executed first. Let us call the expected value of this time interval V_k'. Let V_k'' denote the expected value of the following interval during which the processor executes all jobs of higher priority arriving while the tagged job is waiting in queue. For V_k we can write

(4.5.2)
$$V_k = E(S_r) + V_k' + V_k''$$

where $E(S_r)$ is the mean execution time that remains for the job on the processor at the time of arrival and is given by (4.2.29) as

(4.5.3)
$$E(S_r) = \frac{1}{2} \sum_{k=1}^{\infty} \lambda_k E(S_k^2)$$

Although (4.5.2) is based on a resequencing of the processing times for which the tagged job must wait, its validity is justified by the fact that the arrival process is Poisson and independent of the service mechanism and the state of the system. According to our definition,

(4.5.4)
$$V_k' = \sum_{i=1}^{k} E(n_i)E(S_i)$$

Letting $\rho_i = \lambda_i E(S_i)$ and applying Little's result to each of the first k queues we get

(4.5.5)
$$V_k' = \sum_{i=1}^{k} \lambda_i V_i E(S_i) = \sum_{i=1}^{k} \rho_i V_i$$

Now the mean number of ith priority arrivals during the time the tagged job spends in queue is $\lambda_i V_k$. Hence

(4.5.6) $$V_k'' = \sum_{i=1}^{k-1} \lambda_i V_k E(S_i) = \sum_{i=1}^{k-1} \rho_i V_k$$

Substituting (4.5.5) and (4.5.6) into (4.5.2) gives

$$V_k = E(S_r) + \sum_{i=1}^{k} \rho_i V_i + \sum_{i=1}^{k-1} \rho_i V_k$$

or

(4.5.7) $$V_k = \frac{E(S_r) + \sum_{i=1}^{k} \rho_i V_i}{1 - \sum_{i=1}^{k-1} \rho_i}$$

Using (4.5.3) for $E(S_r)$ it is readily shown by induction that the solution to (4.5.7) is given by

(4.5.8) $$V_k = \frac{\sum_{i=1}^{\infty} \lambda_i E(S_i^2)}{2(1 - \beta_k)(1 - \beta_{k-1})}$$

where

(4.5.9) $$\beta_j = \sum_{i=1}^{j} \rho_i$$

This result was first derived by Cobham [21]. Laplace transforms of the waiting-time distributions for the nonpreemptive priority queue were first calculated by Kesten and Runnenberg [22].

Using these results for the nonpreemptive priority queue we can obtain rather simply the analogous results for a so-called *shortest-processing-time* (SPT) discipline. For this discipline we assume that the execution time of a job is known at the time of arrival. Whenever the processor completes the execution of a job the next job executed by the SPT discipline is that one of those waiting with the least execution time.

To obtain mean waiting times we can simplify matters with the assumption of discrete service times. Let g_i, $i = 1, 2, \ldots$, denote the probability that a job requires iQ units of execution time, and let $E(S^i)$, $i = 1, 2, \ldots$, denote the moments of the service time distribution as before. If λ denotes the total arrival rate of jobs to the system, then λg_k denotes the arrival rate of jobs requiring k quanta. Since the decomposition of a Poisson process according to a stationary probability distribution gives rise to independent Poisson processes (see Section 4.2), the SPT system is representable as in Fig. 4.5-1 with $\lambda_k = \lambda g_k$. Substituting λg_k for λ_k and $iQ\lambda g_i$ for ρ_i (4.5.8) yields the following expression for the mean waiting time in queue for a job requiring

k quanta:

(4.5.10)
$$V_k = \frac{\lambda E(S^2)}{2(1 - \lambda H_k(S))(1 - \lambda H_{k-1}(S))}$$

where

(4.5.11)
$$H_j(S) = \sum_{i=1}^{j} (iQ)g_i$$

Informally, the result for a continuous service time distribution $B(x)$ is found by letting Q be a differential element of time and g_i be the probability mass function corresponding to $B(x)$ (in the sense that the geometric distribution is a discretization of the exponential distribution). Taking the limit $Q \to 0$ of (4.5.10) as we did in the previous section to obtain the processor-sharing result, we find Phipps' result [23] for the conditional waiting time in queue of a job whose service requirement is t:

(4.5.12)
$$V(t) = \frac{\lambda E(S^2)}{2\left[1 - \lambda \int_0^t x\, dB(x)\right]^2}$$

4.6. THE SHORTEST-ELAPSED-TIME DISCIPLINE

We now return to our investigation of time-sharing algorithms under the assumption that job running times are not known in advance. Besides the RR discipline of Section 4.4, the discrete versions of the so-called *shortest-elapsed-time* (SET) discipline have been investigated as a further means of providing favored service for jobs that have short execution times.

A system using a discrete SET discipline is shown in Fig. 4.6-1. Because of the structure of Fig. 4.6-1 and because of the definition below, the discrete SET disciplines have also been called multiple-level, feedback queueing disciplines. For the particular system we have chosen to analyze, the jobs arrive in a Poisson stream at rate λ and are assumed to have service times taken from a discrete but otherwise general probability distribution. As before g_i $(i = 1, 2, \ldots)$ will represent the probability that a job requires iQ units of execution time, and $G(k) = \sum_{i=1}^{k} g_i$ will denote the cumulative distribution function.

A general statement of the service discipline is as follows. After the processor has completed the quantum allocated to a given job the next job to be allocated a quantum of execution time is the one having received the fewest quanta of all those jobs currently waiting. If there is a tie among several jobs having received the least service, then the job selected is the one with the earliest arrival time. This discipline can be put in terms of priority queues, as shown in Fig. 4.6-1, by simply associating the kth $(k = 1, 2, \ldots)$

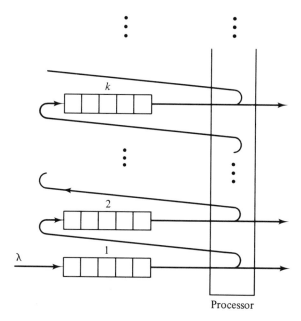

Fig. 4.6-1 The discrete SET system.

queue level (priority) with the set of jobs having already received $k - 1$ quanta and waiting for their kth quantum. At the time a job at the kth level begins a quantum the first $k - 1$ queues must be empty. After such a job completes its kth quantum the job either leaves the system because it is complete or it joins the end of the $(k + 1)$st queue level to await its $(k + 1)$st quantum.

A superficial comparison of the RR and SET disciplines leads one to expect that the SET discipline favors short jobs more than the RR discipline but at the expense of longer waiting times for long jobs. We shall now develop waiting time results for the SET discipline with which a more specific comparison can be made. For the mean waiting time of a random arrival requiring k quanta we have

$$(4.6.1) \qquad\qquad W_k = V_k + kQ$$

To compute V_k we first partition it into

$$(4.6.2) \qquad\qquad V_k = V_k' + V_k''$$

where V_k' and V_k'' are defined as follows. V_k' consists of the mean time to complete the quantum in progress and to complete the allocation of up to k quanta to the jobs in the system at the time of arrival. In other words V_k' is the mean time to finish the job in progress plus the mean time to service the jobs in the first k queue levels at the time of arrival.

Now, according to our priority discipline, every job that arrives while the new arrival (the tagged job) is waiting in queue and receiving its first $k - 1$ quanta must be allocated up to a maximum of $k - 1$ quanta of execution time. That is, each such job must be allowed to ascend to the kth queue level if it requires in excess of $(k - 1)Q$ units of execution time. The total execution time required by these new arrivals has a mean value which we define as V_k''.

Let $E_k(S)$ denote the mean amount of execution time used by a job to which kQ time units have been allocated. We have

(4.6.3) $$E_k(S) = \sum_{i=1}^{k} (iQ)g_i + kQ[1 - G(k)]$$

For later use we also define the second moment

$$E_k(S^2) = \sum_{i=1}^{k} (iQ)^2 g_i + (kQ)^2[1 - G(k)]$$

It follows immediately from our definition of V_k'' that

(4.6.4) $$V_k'' = \lambda[V_k + (k - 1)Q]E_{k-1}(S)$$

To compute V_k' we simplify matters as follows. Suppose that we consider a modified SET system in which the jobs served at the first queue level are allocated kQ units of execution time and those served at each higher level are allocated one quantum of service. The new system is pictured in Fig. 4.6-2. Observe that, from the point of view of a job requiring k quanta, the mean time spent in the first queue of the new system is precisely V_k', the mean time spent waiting for jobs in the original system at the time of arrival to receive their maximum of k quanta. Thus by examining the new system we find

(4.6.5) $$V_k' = E'(S_r) + N_1' E_k(S)$$

where $E'(S_r)$ is the mean time to complete the job in progress and N_1' is the mean number encountered in the first queue level at the time of arrival in the *new* system. Using Little's result we have

(4.6.6) $$V_k' = E'(S_r) + \lambda V_k' E_k(S)$$

or

(4.6.7) $$V_k' = \frac{E'(S_r)}{1 - \lambda E_k(S)}$$

To compute $E'(S_r)$ we must take into account the fact that in the new system

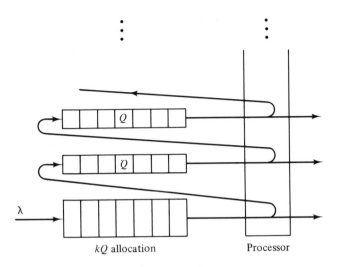

Fig. 4.6-2 Modified SET system.

we have two classes of executing jobs: those receiving an allocation of kQ units of execution time, having just waited through the first queue, and those receiving but one quantum, having just waited through a higher-level queue. The arrival rate to the first queue level in the new system is simply λ. The arrival rate λ'_i to the ith ($i = 2, 3, \ldots$) queue level is determined by that fraction of the arrivals which require greater than or equal to $(k + i - 1)Q$ units of execution time. Thus

$$(4.6.8) \qquad \lambda'_i = \lambda \sum_{j=k+i-1}^{\infty} g_j = \lambda[1 - G(k + i - 2)], \quad i = 2, 3, \ldots$$

Now the arrival process for the first queue is Poisson, but the arrivals to the higher-level queues do not constitute Poisson processes. (Note that arrivals to the higher-level queues occur only within processor busy periods.) However, the tagged job is assumed to be a random (i.e., Poisson) arrival and as a result the arguments leading to (4.2.29) still apply.† Consequently,

$$(4.6.9) \qquad E'(S_r) = \frac{\lambda}{2}\left[E_k(S^2) + Q^2 \sum_{i=0}^{\infty} [1 - G(k + i)] \right]$$

Substituting (4.6.7) and (4.6.4) into (4.6.2) we have

$$(4.6.10) \qquad V_k = \lambda E_{k-1}(S)V_k + \frac{E'(S_r)}{1 - \lambda E_k(S)} + \lambda E_{k-1}(S)(k - 1)Q$$

---

†We shall be making a similar observation in the next section in the discussion of the shortest-remaining-processing-time discipline. A rigorous justification of this observation can be found in [8].

Solving for V_k and using (4.6.9) we obtain the final result:

$$(4.6.11) \qquad V_k = \frac{\lambda \left[E_k(S^2) + Q^2 \sum_{i=k}^{\infty} [1 - G(i)] \right]}{2[1 - \lambda E_{k-1}(S)][1 - \lambda E_k(S)]} + \frac{\lambda E_{k-1}(S)}{1 - \lambda E_{k-1}(S)} (k - 1)Q$$

Using (4.6.1) we have

$$(4.6.12) \qquad W_k = \frac{\lambda \left[E_k(S^2) + Q^2 \sum_{i=k}^{\infty} [1 - G(i)] \right]}{2[1 - \lambda E_{k-1}(S)][1 - \lambda E_k(S)]} + \frac{(k - 1)Q}{1 - \lambda E_{k-1}(S)} + Q$$

The corresponding result for the basic SET discipline and a continuous service time distribution $B(x)$ is easily obtained from (4.6.12) by taking the limit $Q \rightarrow 0$ with $t = kQ$ held fixed. Specifically, the mean time in system for a job requiring t time units of service is given by

$$(4.6.13) \qquad W(t) = \frac{(\lambda/2) \int_0^{\infty} x^2 \, dB(x)}{\left[1 - \lambda \int_0^t x \, dB(x) - \lambda t [1 - B(t)] \right]^2}$$
$$+ \frac{t}{1 - \lambda \int_0^t x \, dB(x) - \lambda t [1 - B(t)]}$$

The results in (4.6.11) and (4.6.12) were obtained by Schrage [24] along with the Laplace transform of the waiting time distributions assuming arbitrary quantum sizes at each level.

As stated earlier the SET discipline always allocates the processor to the job having received the least execution time. In the event of ties the SET rule requires that the set of jobs having received the least execution time must share the processor in the processor-sharing mode discussed in Section 4.4. Also, a new arrival always preempts the job currently sharing the processor. This new arrival retains the processor until it departs, until the next arrival appears, or until it obtains an amount of service equal to that received by the jobs preempted on arrival, whichever occurs first. In the last case it must then share the processor with the jobs preempted at the time of arrival. As a result of the processor sharing produced by the SET discipline the waiting time in queue clearly does not have the same significance that it does in systems without processor sharing.

4.7. THE SHORTEST-REMAINING-PROCESSING-TIME DISCIPLINE

When processing times are known in advance and preemptive disciplines can be employed there are two basic preemptive versions of the SPT rule to consider. The most direct one simply sequences jobs, preempting when necessary, so that the job being executed at each point in time is the one of those currently in the system whose *original* service requirement was least. In the interest of reducing the steady-state mean number in the system we can use a second preemptive version of the SPT rule, viz., the shortest-remaining-processing-time (SRPT) rule. The SRPT discipline sequences jobs so that at each point in time the job on the processor is always the one with the least remaining processing time of all those jobs currently in the system. It is known [25] that the mean number in the system resulting from SRPT sequencing is in fact minimal over all possible service disciplines. Because of this important property, the remainder of this section will be devoted to an analysis of the SRPT discipline.

As before we shall first treat a discrete version of the SRPT discipline in which we assume that jobs require service times that are integral numbers of quanta. However, in the present case it will simplify matters somewhat if we assume that quanta are preemptible; i.e., an arriving job immediately preempts the job on the processor if the former has a service requirement which is less than that remaining for the latter. As before g_i will represent the general probability mass function for the number of quanta required by jobs, and $G(k) = \sum_{i=1}^{k} g_i$ will denote the cumulative distribution function.

A schematic of the discrete SRPT discipline is shown in Fig. 4.7-1, where the Poisson arrival mechanism is decomposed into separate Poisson arrivals to each of the queue levels $1, 2, \ldots, k, \ldots$ with λ_k denoting the arrival rate to the kth queue level. The queue level into which an arrival is placed is determined by the service it requires, jobs requiring k quanta being placed into the kth queue level. Hence $\lambda_k = \lambda g_k, k = 1, 2, \ldots$. A job at the service point of the kth queue level does not commence service until the first $k - 1$

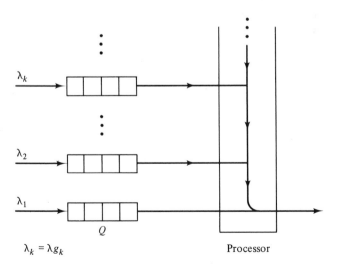

Fig. 4.7-1 The SRPT system.

queue levels are empty. On completing its quantum at the kth level a job immediately begins its next quantum at the $(k-1)$st level. As stated earlier a job is immediately preempted (and put back at the head of the queue determined by its *remaining* processing time) whenever a job arrives at a lower queue level.

We shall now compute the mean time in the system of a random arrival during statistical equilibrium which requires kQ units of execution time. This mean waiting time is decomposed into

$$(4.7.1) \qquad\qquad W_k = W'_k + W''_k$$

where W'_k is the mean time elapsing from the moment of arrival until the tagged job enters service for the first time and W''_k is the mean of the remaining time spent in the system. W''_k is also called the mean *residence* time.

To calculate W'_k we adopt a stratagem which is similar to that used in the analysis of the SET discipline. Specifically, we consider the modified system shown in Fig. 4.7-2 where the queue levels of Fig. 4.7-1 have been organized into a conventional priority system. The arrivals to a queue level $i \leq k$ require i quanta, but the arrivals to queues above the kth are all assumed to require only k quanta of service. Thus the priority sequencing in the first k queues amounts to SPT sequencing.

On examining this new system we are led to the observation that the mean waiting time *in queue* for an arrival requiring k quanta is precisely W'_k, the mean waiting time of the tagged job up to the point when it begins its

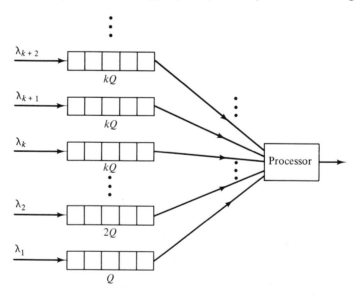

Fig. 4.7-2 A priority system for computing W'_k.

first quantum of service in the original system. In effect, we are observing from the preemption rule that lower-priority arrivals affect the tagged job during its initial wait in queue as though they arrived with a service requirement of only k quanta. The observation is also based on the fact that the jobs originally requiring k or fewer quanta affect (interfere with) the tagged job during its initial wait in queue in precisely the same way that they would affect the tagged job in the analogous, discrete SPT system during the time spent in queue. Thus an analysis of the new system for W'_k follows precisely the lines in Section 4.5 and results in

$$(4.7.2) \qquad W'_k = \frac{E'(S_r)}{[1 - \lambda H_k(S)][1 - \lambda H_{k-1}(S)]}$$

where

$$(4.7.3) \qquad H_k(S) = \sum_{i=1}^{k} (iQ)g_i$$

and $E'(S_r)$ is the mean time to finish the job (if any) in progress at the time of arrival. In computing $E'(S_r)$ we must consider two classes of executing jobs: those originally requiring $i \leq k$ quanta and those from the queues beyond the kth which originally required in excess of k quanta in the SRPT system. On the arrival of the tagged job the job in progress would be allocated i quanta and k quanta, respectively. The arrival process for the jobs whose service requirement has been reduced to k quanta in the original system is not Poisson, but as before only the arrival rates need be known. Thus, making use of (4.2.29) applied to the new system, we obtain

$$(4.7.4) \qquad E'(S_r) = \frac{\lambda}{2}\left[\sum_{i=1}^{k} (iQ)^2 g_i + (kQ)^2[1 - G(k)]\right] = \frac{\lambda E_k(S^2)}{2}$$

Having determined W'_k we now calculate the mean residence time W''_k. The tagged job must receive a quantum at each level from 1 to k, and so we can write

$$(4.7.5) \qquad W''_k = \sum_{j=1}^{k} (Q + Y_j)$$

where Y_j is the mean time the tagged job has to wait in the jth queue from the moment it begins to the moment it completes its $(k - j + 1)$st quantum. Clearly, the waiting time Y_j is occasioned by the arrival of higher-priority jobs (at levels lower than the jth) which preempt the tagged job. To compute Y_j we take into account separately the arrivals preempting the tagged job during its Q time units of execution and the remaining arrivals occurring during Y_j. Thus

$$(4.7.6) \qquad Y_j = \sum_{i=1}^{j-1} (\lambda_i Q)iQ + \sum_{i=1}^{j-1} (\lambda_i Y_j)(iQ)$$

Substituting λg_i for λ_i we have

(4.7.7)
$$Y_j = \lambda H_{j-1}(S)Q + \lambda H_{j-1}(S)Y_j$$

where $H_{j-1}(S)$ is given by (4.7.3). Solving (4.7.7) for Y_j yields

(4.7.8)
$$Y_j = \frac{\lambda H_{j-1}(S)}{1 - \lambda H_{j-1}(S)}Q$$

whereupon substitution into (4.7.5) gives

(4.7.9)
$$W_k'' = \sum_{j=1}^{k} \frac{Q}{1 - \lambda H_{j-1}(S)}$$

Adding (4.7.2) and (4.7.9) we obtain as our final result

(4.7.10)
$$W_k = \frac{\lambda E_k(S^2)}{2[1 - \lambda H_k(S)][1 - \lambda H_{k-1}(S)]} + \sum_{j=1}^{k} \frac{Q}{1 - \lambda H_{j-1}(S)}$$

For a continuous service time distribution $B(x)$ we can take the limit $Q \rightarrow 0$ of (4.7.10) and obtain the following general result for the SRPT discipline:

(4.7.11)
$$W(t) = \frac{\lambda \int_0^t x^2\, dB(x) + \lambda t^2[1 - B(t)]}{2[1 - \lambda \int_0^t x\, dB(x)]^2} + \int_0^t \frac{dx}{1 - \lambda \int_0^x y\, dB(y)}$$

with $V(t) = W(t) - t$. The results of this section can be found in Miller and Schrage [25].

4.8. A COMPARISON OF PROCESSING TIME PRIORITY DISCIPLINES [8, 26]

In the preceding sections we dwelt on the analytical techniques that have been applied to the study of probability models of computer operation. We focused on service disciplines according to which priority decisions are based on the processing times of jobs. In this section our purpose is to describe the relative merits of these disciplines and to identify those system performance criteria for which they are best suited.

We shall restrict our discussion primarily to the disciplines arising as limiting cases when the basic time interval or quantum is made to approach zero. The general properties of the latter disciplines will resemble those of the nonzero quantum systems for suitably small quantum sizes, i.e., for quantum sizes small compared to processing times. As will be seen it is much easier to characterize these disciplines.

First, let us consider the shortest-remaining-processing-time (SRPT) discipline just analyzed in the previous section. Since the SRPT rule assumes complete information on processing times, it is intuitively apparent that SRPT sequencing represents the best one can do in minimizing interdeparture intervals. It would follow, again intuitively, that the SRPT discipline incorporates that rule giving minimum mean waiting times in system. This has in fact been shown for general arrival and service time distributions, even when all arrival times are known in advance. Using Little's result it is observed as a consequence that the mean number in the system is also minimized. In general, this will tend to minimize the storage requirements for jobs; however, an exact statement regarding storage requirements must take into account the correlation, if any, between the size of a job and its execution time.

A limitation of the SRPT rule results from the potentially high cost of preemptions, particularly when this involves transferring jobs between a CPU and auxiliary storage devices. Variations of the SRPT rule which decrease the rate of preemptions, at the expense of a certain increase in mean waiting time, have also been studied [14]. If we must limit ourselves completely to nonpreemptive disciplines, then the SPT rule of Section 4.4 occupies the role for this class of disciplines that the SRPT rule occupies for the class of all disciplines. (Recall that SPT sequencing was also shown to provide for minimum mean time in the system for the deterministic models discussed in Section 3.8.)

The SRPT and SPT disciplines have also been analyzed [8] when processing time information is assumed to be imperfect; i.e., only estimates of processing times are assumed known. The fact that the mean waiting time is significantly reduced with even crude estimates of processing times greatly extends the class of systems to which these rules are applicable. For an interesting quantitative study of the effects of processing-time-dependent disciplines on mean flow time, see Conway et al. [8].

The objectives accomplished by the PS and SET rule are somewhat more subtle to describe. Unlike the SRPT and SPT disciplines the PS and SET disciplines assume that processing times are not known in advance, an assumption that is commonly necessary in modeling computer systems.

To characterize the SET rule we observe first that, without prior knowledge of processing times, the expected job processing time is a nondecreasing function of the elapsed processing time. Thus we see that the SET discipline favors shorter jobs in the sense that it schedules next that job or jobs whose expected total processing time (based on elapsed time) is least among those jobs currently in the system. In the PS system no job characteristics (fixed or time-varying) are explicitly used in making scheduling decisions. Thus no favoritism whatever is shown by the PS rule; all jobs are given an equal share of the processor capacity regardless of their relative characteristics. However, it is true that compared to the usual standard of reference, the FIFO rule, the PS discipline does get the shorter jobs through faster on the average. On the other hand, the FIFO rule schedules those jobs with the longest waiting times in queue; as a result the shorter jobs experience more interference from the longer jobs than in the PS system where no discrimination at all is shown. Finally, to clarify the distinction between the PS and SET disciplines we can state that the jobs in the PS system at any instant will complete in the order of least *remaining* processing time, whereas the jobs in the SET system at any instant will depart in the order of least *total* processing time.

It is important to realize that the service time distribution has an effect on the performance of the above disciplines. When the service time distribution is exponential any discipline that does not use processing time information yields the same mean time in system. For this case, then, the SET and PS rules do not change the system mean waiting time (although the higher-order moments of the waiting time are affected). For more general service times the mean time in system is affected by the variation in service times. It is intuitively clear that the PS and SET disciplines perform poorly with very small variations in service times. As an extreme case, with no variation (all service times are equal) we note that with the SET rule no job completes until the end of a busy period, while with FIFO all but one job completes earlier. On the other hand, if we have only very short jobs (say 1 second) and very long jobs (say 1 hour), which corresponds to a very large variation, it is clear that the PS and SET disciplines will complete the short jobs quickly, while with FIFO they may be delayed considerably by the longer jobs.

We can make the above remarks more precise for the PS rule by comparing the mean waiting time given in (4.4.17) for the PS system

$$W_{\text{PS}} = \frac{E(S)}{1 - \rho}$$

with the corresponding FIFO result in (4.2.33)

$$W_{\text{FIFO}} = E(S) + \rho \frac{[1 + C^2(S)]}{2(1 - \rho)} E(S)$$

Thus we have

$$W_{\text{FIFO}} - W_{\text{PS}} = \frac{\rho[C^2(S) - 1]}{2(1 - \rho)} E(S)$$

from which we see the dependence of relative performance on the coefficient of variation C. For the exponential distribution $C(S) = 1$ and $W_{\text{FIFO}} = W_{\text{PS}}$, as stated earlier. For larger variations in service times ($C(S) > 1$) the PS rule gives smaller mean times in the system, whereas the opposite is true for smaller variations in service times. A similar result for the SET discipline is not available but by considering the "extreme-case" service distributions again it seems likely that

$$W_{\text{SET}} < W_{\text{PS}}, \quad C > 1$$
$$W_{\text{SET}} > W_{\text{PS}}, \quad C < 1$$

In summary, we see that while the PS and SET disciplines have advantages in expediting the service of the shorter jobs they can degrade the response time for a large class of service time distributions. Numerical studies of these disciplines can be found in Coffman and Kleinrock [13] and Schrage [14].

PROBLEMS

4-1. Let a cycle of the process $X(t)$ be defined as the time interval composed of an idle period and the subsequent busy period. In statistical equilibrium we observe that the average number of arrivals in a cycle of the M/G/1 system is equal to the average number served in a busy period. Using this observation verify the following expression for the mean length $E(D)$ of a busy period in equilibrium:

$$E(D) = \frac{E(S)}{1 - \lambda E(S)}$$

Verify this result by computing the first moment from (4.2.46). Also, compute

$$E(D^2) = \frac{E(S^2)}{[1 - \lambda E(S)]^3}$$

4-2. Suppose that arrivals occur in groups but that interarrival times are still exponential with parameter λ. (This is the so-called *bulk arrival* mechanism.) The probability that an arriving group has size k is stationary and given by g_k. Let $G(z) = \sum_{k=1}^{\infty} g_k z^k$ be the corresponding generating function. Using the notation of Section 4.2 show that

$$A(z) = B^*(\lambda - \lambda G(z))$$

Substitution into the expression for $P(z)$ in (4.2.16) gives the solution for $\{\pi_i\}$ in the bulk arrival queue with general service times.

4-3. Using the *preemptive resume* rule the priority discipline of Section 4.5 is modified as follows. Whenever a higher-priority job arrives when a lower-priority job is on the processor, the latter is immediately removed from the processor and replaced at the head of the queue from which it originally came. The higher-priority job begins service immediately, and when the preempted job eventually returns to the processor it commences execution from the point at which it was interrupted by the preemption; i.e., no service time is lost because of preemptions. Using the definitions and notation of Section 4.5 show that the mean time in the system is given by

$$W_k = \frac{E(S_k)}{1 - \beta_{k-1}} + \frac{\sum_{i=1}^{k} \lambda_i E(S_i^2)}{2(1 - \beta_{k-1})(1 - \beta_k)}$$

(Use the methods illustrated in Sections 4.5–4.7.)

4-4. Define a service discipline such that at each point in time the processor is executing the job (or jobs in a processor-sharing mode) with the least *expected* remaining processing time, where the expectation is computed based only on the amount of time the job has already received on the processor [26]. The FIFO rule is used to break ties. Let $B(x)$ be the service time distribution and assume Poisson arrivals.

Under what condition on $B(x)$ will the above discipline reduce to the FIFO discipline? Under what condition will it reduce to the SET discipline? Give illustrative distributions satisfying these conditions. Exhibit a distribution for which the given discipline behaves as neither the FIFO nor the SET discipline.

4-5. Suppose that we want to model the fact that new arrivals are discouraged by long queues. For this purpose we define a Poisson queue governed by (4.3.5) and (4.3.6) in which $\lambda_n = \lambda/(n + 1)$. If μ is the parameter of the exponential service time distribution, show that the stationary distribution of the number in the system is the Poisson distribution with parameter λ/μ.

4-6. As another illustration of the methods in Section 4.2 we shall study the following two-level priority queue with a Poisson input at rate λ to the high-priority queue. The low-priority queue is assumed saturated with jobs having exponentially distributed service times of mean value $1/\mu$. The jobs of the high-priority queue have the general distribution function $B(x)$ with the first two moments $E(S)$ and $E(S^2)$. (See Fig. P4-6 for a schematic of the system.)

Whenever a high-priority job arrives when the high-priority queue is empty, the low-priority job that must be executing (because of the saturation assumption) is allowed $d \geq 0$ more time units of service; if the job completes within the d time units, the high-priority queue begins service without a preemption taking place. If the executing job requires more than d more time units, it is preempted after receiving the additional d time units and the processor is given over to the high-priority queue. Thus, if $d = \infty$, we have

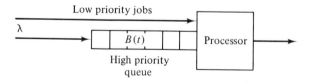

Fig. P4-6   Two-level preemption delay system.

a nonpreemptive, head-of-the-line priority queue, and if $d = 0$, we have a preemptive resume priority queue.

Let $\{X_i\}$ denote the Markov chain whose state is the number of jobs in the high-priority queue and whose epochs are the instants just following departures of high-priority jobs. Let $F(t)$ denote the distribution of the time spent in the system for a high-priority job arriving when the high-priority queue is empty. (This is the distribution of the service time plus delay.) The mean of $F(t)$ is denoted $E(S')$.

Determine the condition for the existence of the stationary distribution for $\{X_i\}$ and show that the generating function for this distribution is given by†

$$P(z) = \pi_0 \frac{zF^*(\lambda - \lambda z) - B^*(\lambda - \lambda z)}{z - B^*(\lambda - \lambda z)}$$

where

$$\pi_0 = \frac{1 - \lambda E(S)}{1 + \lambda E(S') - \lambda E(S)}$$

Compute the mean flow time from Little's result:

$$W = \frac{1}{\lambda} \lim_{z \to 1} P'(z)$$

4-7. We shall investigate a two-level (discrete) SPT discipline as follows. Let all jobs requiring less than or equal to L time units of service be called class 1 jobs, the remaining jobs being called class 2 jobs. We implement a conventional (nonpreemptive) priority queue (Section 4.5) of two levels, in which the high-priority level consists of class 1 jobs and the low-priority level consists of class 2 jobs. The composite arrival mechanism is Poisson with rate λ. Let $B(x)$ denote the service time distribution function with $E(S)$ and $E(S^2)$ denoting the first two moments.

Show that the overall mean time in the system

$$W = W_1 B(L) + W_2[1 - B(L)]$$

is given by

$$W = \frac{\lambda E(S^2)}{2(1 - \rho)} \left[\frac{1 - \rho B(L)}{1 - \rho_1} \right]$$

where $\rho = \lambda E(S)$ and $\rho_1 = \lambda_1 E(S_1)$ with λ_1 and $E(S_1)$ the mean arrival rate and mean service time of class 1 jobs.

Suppose that $B(x)$ is the uniform distribution on $(0, d)$. Show that the value of L minimizing the mean time in system W is given by

$$L = \frac{2}{\lambda} \left[1 - \sqrt{1 - \frac{\lambda d}{2}} \right]$$

†More generally, note that $P(z)$ is the solution for an important special class of M/G/1 queueing systems [27] in which the first job execution of a busy period has a distribution, $F(x)$, distinct from $B(x)$.

Let $B(x)$ be the exponential distribution with parameter μ. Show that the value of L minimizing W satisfies

$$\frac{\mu}{\lambda} - \frac{e^{-\mu L}}{\mu L - 1} = 1$$

4-8. In Fig. P4-8 is shown a system of *tandem queues*, or queues in series. After having received service at the first processor P_1, a job immediately joins the second queue to await a second "stage" of service on P_2. Queues in series are commonly used models in the study of computer systems (see Section 5.4 for a more general discussion).

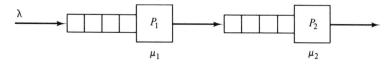

Fig. P4-8

Suppose that service times are exponential with parameters μ_1 and μ_2 on P_1 and P_2, respectively. The input is Poisson at rate λ. Let p_{ij} denote the equilibrium probability of i waiting and being served in the first queue and j waiting and being served in the second queue. Using the methods of Section 4.2 write out the balance equations for the p_{ij} and show that their solution yields

$$p_{ij} = [(1 - \rho_1)\rho_1^i][(1 - \rho_2)\rho_2^j], \quad i = 0, 1, \ldots$$

where $\rho_i = \lambda/\mu_i$ $(i = 1, 2)$. We conclude that the (marginal) queue-length distributions are independent and geometric with parameters ρ_1 and ρ_2 for the first and second queues, respectively. This statement generalizes in the obvious way to k exponential queues in series with Poisson input to the first queue.

Note that the above result suggests that the behavior of the second queue is the same as if it had a Poisson input at rate λ. It is indeed the case that the output of the first queue is Poisson at rate λ (see Problem 4-11). Note also that the last observation enables us to carry out an analysis with a general service time distribution for P_2 (or for P_k in the more general case of a series of k queues) using the results for the M/G/1 queue in Section 4.2.

4-9. Consider the SRPT system and let $B(x)$ be the service time distribution. Suppose that a job requiring p time units of service has just been given to the processor. Let $W_p(x)$ denote the probability that it suffers a preemption before $x \leq p$ time units has elapsed. Develop the differential equation

$$W_p'(x) + \lambda B(p - x)W_p(x) = \lambda B(p - x), \quad 0 \leq x \leq p$$

and show that the distribution of the number of preemptions experienced by a job requiring p time units is given by the Poisson distribution with parameter

$$\alpha = \lambda \int_0^p B(t)\, dt$$

4-10. From the discussion of the Markov chain $\{X_i\}$ described in Section 4.2 we may write

(P4-10.1) $X_{n+1} = X_n + a_n - \delta_n$

where a_n is the number of arrivals in (t_n, t_{n+1}) and

$$\delta_n = \begin{cases} 0, & X_n = 0 \\ 1, & X_n > 0 \end{cases}$$

The probability distribution for a_n is given by $\{q_i\}$ with the generating function in (4.2.17). Take the expected value of (P1) and show that

$$\lim_{n \to \infty} \Pr[X_n > 0] = \rho$$

where $\rho = \lambda E(S)$. Square both sides of (P4 − 10.1), take expected values, and show that in the limit $\bar{n} = \lim_{n \to \infty} E(X_n)$ as given by (4.2.21) is obtained from the resulting equation.

4-11. Show that the interdeparture intervals of a queue with exponential interarrival and service times is also exponential with the same parameter as the interarrival time distribution. Note that if t is an instant just following a departure epoch, then the time until the next departure will be a service period with probability $1 - p_0 = \Pr\{X(t) > 0\}$ and will be the sum of an idle period and service period with probability p_0.

The above result also extends to multiserver Poisson queues. In fact, the output of one or more parallel exponential servers with Poisson input is also Poisson. However, to show this, it is necessary to demonstrate that successive interdeparture intervals are independent as well as exponential with the same parameter. (See Takacs [5], for example.)

4-12. Equation (4.2.26) gives the density function for the execution time of a job in progress at the time of a random arrival. Now the conditional density of the remaining execution time given that the job in progress requires y time units is simply the uniform density dx/y, $0 \le x \le y$. Hence show that the Laplace transform $R^*(s)$ (see Section 4.2.3) is given by

$$R^*(s) = \frac{1 - B^*(s)}{sE(S)}$$

4-13. To find the Laplace transform of the equilibrium queueing time in the LIFO M/G/1 system observe that a job arriving to a busy system must wait for a busy period initiated by the remaining execution time of the job in progress at arrival time. The Laplace transform of this busy period is obtainable from

(4.2.46) by replacing $B(x)$ with $R(x)$. Using the result of Problem 4-12 show that in the LIFO system

$$V^*(s) = (1 - p) + \frac{\lambda(1 - H^*(s))}{s + \lambda - \lambda H^*(s)}$$

where $H^*(s)$ is the Laplace transform of the M/G/1 busy-period distribution. Compute and compare the second moments of the FIFO and LIFO queueing times.

4-14. There are several instances in computer systems where several distinct service facilities (sets of memories, I/O channels, etc.) must share a common, bounded queueing facility. Consider the simple such system shown in Fig. P4-14(a) in which the units that must execute on P_1 and those that must

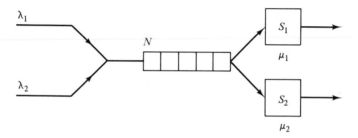

Fig. P4-14(a)

execute on P_2 arrive in Poisson streams with rates λ_1 and λ_2, respectively. Assume a shared queue of N places and exponential service times with parameters μ_1 and μ_2 for P_1 and P_2, respectively. Analyze this system, coming up with measures of throughput and the mutual interference between the two classes of units waiting in queue. (Assume that units arriving to find a full queue are turned away and "lost.")

Compare the performance of the above system with two separate queues each having $N/2$ places, assuming that N is even. That is, compare the above system with the system shown in Fig. P4-14(b).

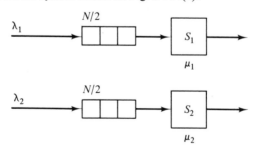

Fig. P4-14(b)

4-15. The theory of Poisson ($M/M/r$) queues can be extended, using the *method of stages*, so as to apply to many systems with nonexponential service or inter-arrival times. This and the following problem deal with this extension. Suppose a system with Poisson input at rate λ has a service time distribution that can be modeled by a series of k independent exponential "stages" each with parameter μ. Denote the sum-distribution by $B_k(x)$ and observe that it must have the Laplace transform $B_k^*(s) = \mu^k/(\mu + s)^k$. Verify that the coefficient of variation is given by

$$C_k(S) = \frac{1}{\sqrt{k}}$$

and hence that $B_k(x)$ can be considered for modeling distributions with smaller coefficients of variation than the exponential. (Note that when k becomes infinite $B_k(x)$ models constant service times.)

To apply the theory of Poisson queues the state of the system for a single server is now represented by the number of *stages* currently in the system. Letting p_i denote the equilibrium probabilities show that

$$\lambda p_0 = \mu p_1$$
$$(\lambda + \mu)p_r = \mu p_{r+1} + \lambda p_{r-k}$$

where p_j is defined to be zero when $j < 0$. Work out the generating function for the p_i (note the relation of this problem to Problem 4-2). Note that the probability of *n jobs* in the system is computable from

$$\sum_{r=(n-1)k+1}^{nk} p_r$$

Consider the application of the above method of stages to multiple-server queues. Also observe that we can generalize immediately to service times that are sums of independent but not necessarily identical exponentials. To proceed with an analysis of this case we augment the state variable to include an identification of the stage in service.

4-16. We may apply a method of stages-in-parallel when it is necessary to model distributions with coefficients of variation greater than unity. In particular, suppose that with probability σ_i ($\sum_{i=1}^{k} \sigma_i = 1$) a job has an exponential service time with parameter μ_i. Verify that the Laplace transform is now

$$B_k^*(s) = \sum_{i=1}^{k} \frac{\sigma_i \mu_i}{\mu_i + s}$$

and show that the coefficient of variation can be made arbitrarily large by suitable choices of parameters. Work out the single-server equilibrium equations of balance assuming a state variable (n, i) where n is the number of jobs in the system and i is the identity of the stage in service. Consider generalizations to multiple-server queues and to systems with nonexponential interarrival times. Finally, verify that we may extend our method by using combinations of exponentials in series and in parallel. (In fact, it is possible to show that with such distributions we can represent any distribution of a positive random variable whose Laplace transform is the ratio of two polynomials. These distributions constitute the family of general Erlangian distributions.)

As a practical matter, one cannot expect a general modeling to produce a system of equations admitting of a closed form solution. Thus, the approach to obtaining results will normally involve reducing the system of equations to a finite set (setting to zero the probabilities beyond a certain point), and solving numerically, iterating the process to the extent necessary. Clearly, the structural parameters involved in the modeling must be kept as small as possible in order to keep computation times acceptable.

REFERENCES

1. FELLER, W., *An Introduction to Probability Theory and Its Applications* (Vol. I). Wiley, New York (1950).

2. COX, D. R., and W. L. SMITH, *Queues*. Methuen, London (1961).

3. MORSE, P. M., *Queues, Inventories, and Maintenance*. Wiley, New York (1958).

4. SAATY, T. L., *Elements of Queueing Theory*. McGraw-Hill, New York (1961).

5. TAKACS, L., *Introduction to the Theory of Queues*. Oxford University Press, Inc., New York (1962).

6. RIORDAN, J., *Stochastic Service Systems*. Wiley, New York (1962).

7. PRABHU, N. U., *Queues and Inventories*. Wiley, New York (1965).

8. CONWAY, R. W., W. L. MAXWELL, and L. W. MILLER, *Theory of Scheduling*. Addison-Wesley, Reading, Mass. (1967).

9. LITTLE, J. D. C., "A proof for the queueing formula $L = \lambda W$." *Opns. Res.* 9, 3 (May 1961), 383–387.

10. SAKATA, M., S. NOGUCHI, and J. OIZUMI, "Analysis of a processor-shared queueing model for time-sharing systems," in *Proc. 2nd Hawaii Int'l Conf. Sys. Sci.*, Univ. of Hawaii, Honolulu (1969), 625–627.

11. SCHERR, A. L., "An Analysis of Time-shared Computer Systems." Ph.D. thesis, Dept. of Electrical Engineering, M. I. T., Cambridge, Mass. (June 1965).

12. KLEINROCK, L., "Analysis of a time-shared processor." *Nav. Res. Log. Quart.* 11, 10 (Mar. 1964), 59–73.

13. COFFMAN, E. G., JR., and L. KLEINROCK, "Feedback queueing models for time-shared systems." *J. ACM 15*, 4 (Oct. 1968), 549–576.

14. SCHRAGE, L. E., "Some queueing models for a time-shared facility." Ph.D. thesis, Cornell University (Feb. 1966).

15. KLEINROCK, L., "Time-shared systems: A theoretical treatment." *J. ACM 14*, 2 (Apr. 1967), 242–261.

16. MUNTZ, R. R., "Waiting time distribution for round-robin queueing systems," in *Proc. Symp. Comp.-Commun., Networks, Teletraffic.* Microwave Research Institute, Polytechnic Institute of Brooklyn (Apr. 1972).

17. COFFMAN, E. G., JR., R. R. MUNTZ, and H. TROTTER, "Waiting time distributions for processor-sharing systems. *J. ACM 17*, 1 (Jan. 1970), 123–130.

18. COFFMAN, E. G., JR., "Stochastic models of multiple and time-shared computer operations." Ph.D. thesis, Univ. of California at Los Angeles (June 1966).

19. KRISHNAMOORTHI, B., and R. C. WOOD, "Time-shared computer operation with both interarrival and service time exponential." *J. ACM 13*, 3 (July 1966), 317–338.

20. McKINNEY, J. M., "A survey of analytical time-sharing models." *Computing Surveys 1*, 2 (1969), 105–116.

21. COBHAM, A., "Priority assignment in waiting-line problems." *Opns. Res. 2* (Feb. 1954), 70–76.

22. KESTEN, H., and J. TH. RUNNENBERG, "Priority in waiting-line problems." *Proc. Akad. Wet. Amst., Ser. A*, 60, 3 (1957), 312–324 (Pt I), 325–336 (Pt II).

23. PHIPPS, T. E., "Machine repair as a priority waiting-line problem." *Opns. Res. 9* (Sept.–Oct. 1961), 732–742.

24. SCHRAGE, L. E., "The queue M/G/1 with feedback to lower priority queues. *Manag. Sci. 13* (1967), 466–474.

25. MILLER, L. W., and L. E. SCHRAGE, "The queue M/G/1 with the shortest remaining processing time discipline." *Opns. Res. 14* (1966), 670–683.

26. COFFMAN, E. G., and R. R. MUNTZ, "Models of resource allocation using pure-time-sharing disciplines." *Proc. 24th ACM Natl Conf.* (1969), 217–228.

27. WELCH, P. D., "On a generalized M/G/1 queueing process in which the first customer of each busy period receives exceptional service," *Opns. Res. 12* (Sept.–Oct. 1964), 736–752.

5 AUXILIARY AND BUFFER STORAGE MODELS

5.1. INTRODUCTION

Frequently, the major factor determining overall performance in multi-programming systems is the rate at which information can be transferred between main and auxiliary storage. This transfer rate is a function not only of physical device characteristics but also of the procedures by which requests for information are sequenced. A major purpose of this chapter will be to consider techniques for analyzing these subsystems and examine procedures for maximizing their performance. Our interest will be concentrated on drum- or disklike storage devices since these systems occupy the role of auxiliary storage in most current systems. The reader is assumed to be familiar with the basic organization of these devices (cf. Chapter 1). Knowledge of design details, especially those not common to all disk or drum systems, will not generally be required in order to follow our treatment.

The dynamics of these rotating-storage devices determines the optimization techniques that can be applied to their use. Drums are intrinsically the simpler of the two devices, since only one state variable is necessary to describe the state of the device; the angular position of the drum as a function of time completely describes the physical configuration of the device. With disk devices, on the other hand, two state variables are required to describe the physical configuration: The angular position of the disk constitutes one state variable and the position of the heads constitutes the other. Evidently, the properties of drum operation are a subset of those for disk operation. Thus, as we shall see, procedures for optimizing drum utilization may also be applied to disk systems.

As implied earlier, individual drum and especially disk systems frequently have rather specialized features and restrictions not common to the class of these devices that can have a dominating effect on their performance. Examples include the existence of recording gaps, certain aspects of head-switching times, and special organizations of information on disk. Since our goal is a general treatment with broadly applicable analytical approaches, we shall avoid the "special cases," as usual, by formulating an abstract model of these devices. The general techniques involved with the study of the abstract model can usually be applied with appropriate specializations and idealizations to actual systems.

Exclusive of queueing delays, there are three principal components of the time to complete a transfer between auxiliary and main storage: 1) seek time (arm positioning delay), 2) rotational latency, and 3) transfer time. The transfer time is not generally subject to manipulation by the operating-system designer, and it occurs immediately following the end of the latency delay. Thus our model, as shown in Fig. 5.1-1, will represent two service phases: a seek (SK) phase and a latency-and-transfer (LT) phase. In general, multiple

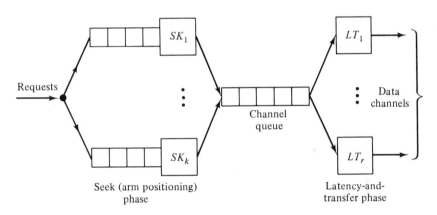

Fig. 5.1-1 The general model.

disk or drum units and multiple, independent arm positioners may be under centralized control and capable of parallel operation. Coupled with this parallelism, multiple data channels allow for parallelism in the LT phase. However, one must assume normally that once a disk arm has been selected and positioned for a given request, it is not available for use by a subsequent request until the LT phase corresponding to the given request has been performed. Thus the LT phase sees a finite source of k seek mechanisms. References [1–6] describe the varieties of parallelism inherent in the design of most current disk systems.

For purposes of analysis, the parallel queues in Fig. 5.1-1 are generally assumed to be independent, if not because they are in reality, then because it is the only way to keep the analysis tractable. In any case, the assumption of independence frequently allows us to obtain total performance measures by concentrating on a single queue. Given this independence assumption an analysis of the general model of Fig. 5.1-1 is still faced with considerable difficulty, especially with the more efficient (and mathematically complex) sequencing rules to be analyzed in subsequent sections. For an approximate analysis of the model of Fig. 5.1-1 with a single data channel, exponential assumptions, and FIFO sequencing, see [4].

To deal more simply with the tandem queues (queues in series) that can arise in the generalized disk system of Fig. 5.1-1, a common simplification is the assumption that the output of the seek phase is Poisson. (See Problem 4-11.) Fife and Smith [1] and Abate et al. [3] discuss and motivate this approximation. A different simplification results when the SK queues are assumed to be saturated, in which case the assumption of exponential distributions for the SK and LT phases gives us the finite-source, Poisson queue analyzed in Sections 4.3 and 4.4. Approximations of the above type will not always be necessary, for not all queues shown in Fig. 5.1-1 need exist in a specific system. In particular, a request may have to be processed clear through the two service phases before the following request commences service in the first phase.

Observe that we may view Fig. 5.1-1 as a model of drum systems simply by eliminating the seek phase. In the next two sections we shall study the SK and LT phases separately. Our specific object will be the characterization of existing and proposed sequencing procedures designed to maximize performance by reducing disk-head motion and latency delays. The reduction of latency delays applied to both drums and disks will be considered first. Although the analytical results provide insight into the various sequencing algorithms, a realistic system evaluation must take in far more detail. For numerical and simulation studies see the references, especially the work of Teorey and Pinkerton [6].

In Section 5.4 a broader view of auxiliary storage and input/output systems is taken. A general queueing network model representative of multiprocessor systems of almost arbitrary structure is analyzed under exponential assumptions. Illustrations drawn from systems of input/output processors are investigated as well.

In Section 5.5 we shall conclude this chapter with an analysis of buffer design problems. Knuth [7] provides a detailed treatment of queue storage techniques under FIFO, LIFO, and combinations of these disciplines. In Section 5.5 our emphasis will be on probability models of storage utilization and the real-time, low data-rate buffering problems arising in time-sharing and other applications.

5.2. MINIMIZATION OF ROTATIONAL LATENCY EFFECTS

We shall consider a single one of the LT phases in Fig. 5.1-1; i.e., $r = 1$ is assumed. The simplest scheme for servicing this queue is a FCFS (first-come-first-served) discipline. Let N denote the number of words stored around the circumference of the drum.† Let the sequence of requests arriving at the queue be described by the sequences $a_1, \ldots, a_i, \ldots$ and $\tau_1, \ldots, \tau_i, \ldots$, where a_i denotes the angular position of the starting address and $\tau_i \geq 1$ the time to transfer the ith request. A basic model results from the following assumptions:

1. Poisson arrivals are at rate λ.
2. The sequences $\{a_i\}$ and $\{\tau_i\}$ are independent and each is a sequence of independent random variables.
3. For each i, a_i is equally likely to be any of the starting addresses in $\{1, 2, \ldots, N\}$.

With this model and a moderately large value of N the expected service time of the ith request is approximately $T/2 + \tau_i$, where T is the (constant) time for one drum revolution. Now let the distribution for the τ_i have first and second moments $E(\tau)$ and $E(\tau^2)$. For the mean queue length we may use (4.2.21) with $\rho = \lambda[E(\tau) + T/2]$ and $E(S^2) = E[(\tau_i + \theta)^2]$, where θ is the random variable denoting the delay until the drum rotates to the starting address. For moderately large N, $E(S^2)$ is approximated very closely by $E(\tau^2) + TE(\tau) + T^2/3$, which corresponds to a continuous distribution of starting addresses over the drum circumference. Hence

$$\bar{n} \approx \lambda\left[E(\tau) + \frac{T}{2}\right] + \frac{\lambda^2[E(\tau^2) + TE(\tau) + T^2/3]}{2(1 - \lambda[E(\tau) + T/2])}$$

For the mean waiting time we may use Little's result.

Clearly, the capacity (maximum transfer rate) for the FCFS drum is given by $1/[E(\tau) + T/2]$. We can do much better than this if we avoid the mean, initial wait of half a drum revolution. To do this we simply modify the service discipline so that, at each decision point, the next request served is that one of those waiting whose starting address is nearest to the current angular position of the drum [2]. A general analysis of this shortest-access-time-first (SATF) system is very difficult [8]; however, in the important context of paging systems results are rather easily obtained through a Markov chain analysis [9].

---

†For convenience we shall use the terminology of drum systems, although the results will carry over to the latency problem with disks.

In the following, such a model will be analyzed and compared with FCFS sequencing.

We assume that the requests arriving at the system are for single pages and that precisely N pages (or page frames) exist on the circumference of the drum. From a cross-sectional view a page occupies a drum *sector*.

The mathematical model of the SATF paging drum is shown in Fig. 5.2-1. Each incoming request is placed at the end of the sector queue corresponding to the sector it addresses. Note that we have taken a complementary but equivalent view of the drum system by regarding the drum as stationary and the read/write heads as rotating at constant speed around the drum, once every T seconds. According to the operation of the drum, each time the read/write heads pass a sector with a nonempty queue the request at the head of the line is serviced (a page read or written) and ejected from the system.

We shall assume that arriving page requests are distributed to the N sector queues according to a stationary probability distribution $\{\lambda_k/\lambda_0\}_{k=1}^N$, where λ_0 is the average (total) arrival rate to the system and λ_k $(k = 1, 2, \ldots, N)$ is the rate of arrivals to the kth sector queue. Evidently, then,

$$(5.2.1) \qquad \lambda_0 = \sum_{k=1}^N \lambda_k$$

We assume that page requests arrive in a Poisson stream at rate λ_0. Consequently, as shown in Section 4.2, the arrivals at sector queues are also independently Poisson with rate λ_k for the kth queue. We denote the exponential interarrival time distribution for the kth sector by

$$(5.2.2) \qquad A_k(t) = 1 - e^{-\lambda_k t}, \quad t \geq 0$$

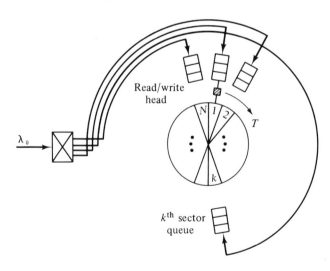

Fig. 5.2-1   The mathematical model.

Note particularly that although we may treat the sector queues as independent they are not individually subject to interpretation as constant service-time, single-server $(M/D/1)$ queues. It is true that arrivals to a nonempty queue see essentially a constant service time system with the service time equal to the drum rotation time, T, but arrivals to an empty queue clearly do not have a constant service time.

Our general objective in the analysis is the joint distribution function of the number in each of the N sector queues under the assumption that the system is operating in statistical equilibrium. Because of the statistical independence of the sector queues, this will be a product distribution; hence the result we need to obtain is the probability mass function (pmf) for the number in a single queue. Our approach is first to define a sequence of time instants equally spaced in time and then to calculate the desired pmf for the resulting process in discrete time. Later, we shall determine from this pmf a result valid for the continuous time process in statistical equilibrium. The process in discrete time will have the Markov property as a result of the arrival mechanism we have assumed.

Let the sequence of time instants $\{t_n\}_{n=1}^{\infty}$ be defined such that successive t_n correspond to those successive points in time just after the read/write heads pass the end of sector k. We wish to find the stationary pmf $\{\pi_i^{(k)}\}_{i=0}^{\infty}$ for the queue length of an arbitrary one of the N queues (viz., the kth), where $\pi_i^{(k)}$ is specifically the equilibrium probability that the number in the kth queue is i just after the read/write heads pass the end of sector k. For the purposes of the following analysis we shall simplify our notation by suppressing the dependence on k and letting $\lambda = \lambda_k$ and $\pi_i = \pi_i^{(k)}$. Now we shall proceed to calculate the following generating function for the probabilities π_i:

$$(5.2.3) \qquad \pi(z) = \sum_{i=0}^{\infty} \pi_i z^i$$

As verified later but intuitively clear from the model, the condition for statistical equilibrium at the kth queue is simply that the arrival rate λ does not exceed the maximum departure rate $1/T$. Now by definition of statistical equilibrium we have

$$(5.2.4) \qquad \pi_j = \sum_{i=0}^{\infty} \pi_{ij} \pi_i, \quad j = 0, 1, 2, \ldots$$

where the π_{ij} are the one-step transition probabilities defined for the sequence $\{t_n\}$; i.e.,

$$(5.2.5) \qquad \pi_{ij} = \Pr[k\text{th queue length at } t_{n+1} \text{ is } j, \text{ conditioned on its}$$
$$\text{being } i \text{ at } t_n]$$

To find the π_{ij}, first observe that $\pi_{ij} = 0$ for all $j < i - 1$, since there is a maximum of one departure for each period $t_{n+1} - t_n = T$. Similarly, it is clear from our definitions that if $i > 0$, then

(5.2.6) $\pi_{ij} = \Pr[j - i + 1 \text{ arrivals in } t_{n+1} - t_n = T], \quad 0 \le i - 1 \le j$

In calculating the π_{ij} for $i = 0$ one must distinguish between arrivals occurring in the interval $[1 - 1/N]T$ during which the read/write heads rotate from the end of sector k back to the beginning of sector k and those arriving in the interval of length T/N during which the read/write heads rotate across the kth sector, for it is clear that if there is at least one arrival in the former interval, then the first such arrival will have been serviced by the time the read/write heads again pass the end of the kth sector. Thus

(5.2.7) $\pi_{0j} = \sum_{r=1}^{j+1} \Pr\left[r \text{ arrivals in } \left(\dfrac{N-1}{N}\right)T \text{ and } j - r + 1 \text{ arrivals in} \right.$

$\left. T/N \right] + \Pr\left[0 \text{ arrivals in } \left(\dfrac{N-1}{N}\right)T \text{ and } j \text{ arrivals in } T/N \right]$

Now according to the Poisson pmf developed in Chapter 4 we have

(5.2.8) $$f_j(t) = \frac{(\lambda t)^j}{j!} e^{-\lambda t}$$

Thus the right-hand side of (5.2.6) is given by $f_{j-i+1}(t)$ and (5.2.7) becomes

(5.2.9) $\pi_{0j} = \sum_{r=1}^{j+1} f_r\left(\dfrac{N-1}{N}T\right) f_{j-r+1}\left(\dfrac{T}{N}\right) + f_0\left(\dfrac{N-1}{N}T\right) f_j\left(\dfrac{T}{N}\right)$

which simplifies to

(5.2.10) $\pi_{0j} = f_{j+1}(T) - f_0\left(\dfrac{N-1}{N}T\right)\left(f_{j+1}\left(\dfrac{T}{N}\right) - f_j\left(\dfrac{T}{N}\right)\right)$

Next, multiplying both sides of (5.2.4) by z^j and summing over $j \ge 0$ we obtain, after interchanging the order of summations and using (5.2.3),

(5.2.11) $$\pi(z) = \sum_{i=0}^{\infty} \pi_i \sum_{j=0}^{\infty} \pi_{ij} z^j$$

After some simplification substitution of the π_{ij} now yields

(5.2.12) $\pi(z) = \dfrac{\pi_0}{z}\left[A_T(z) - f_0\left(\dfrac{N-1}{N}T\right) A_{T/N}(z) \right.$

$\left. + z f_0\left(\dfrac{N-1}{N}T\right) A_{T/N}(z) \right] + \dfrac{A_T(z)}{z}[\pi(z) - \pi_0]$

where

(5.2.13)
$$A_t(z) = \sum_{j=0}^{\infty} f_j(t) z^j = e^{-\lambda t(1-z)}$$

is the generating function for the Poisson distribution. Solving for $\pi(z)$ in (5.2.12) now gives

(5.2.14)
$$\pi(z) = \pi_0 \frac{(z-1)e^{-\lambda T(1-z)/N}}{z - e^{-\lambda T(1-z)}} e^{-\lambda[(N-1)/N]T}$$

To find π_0 we use $\lim_{z \to 1} \pi(z) = 1$ and obtain

(5.2.15)
$$\pi_0 = (1 - \lambda T)e^{\lambda[(N-1)/N]T}$$

Next we observe that based only on the π_i we may calculate the pmf defined at any point on the drum. To verify this we refer to Fig. 5.2-1 and suppose that it is desired to find the pmf defined at a point displaced by τ seconds from the point just following the end of sector k. For any τ such that $0 \leq \tau < T$ the number in the kth queue *can only increase* while the read/write head rotates τ seconds from the end of sector k. Thus the desired pmf is given by

(5.2.16)
$$p_j(\tau) = \sum_{i=0}^{j} \pi_i f_{j-i}(\tau)$$

This means that for an observation of the state of the kth queue in equilibrium, if we are given τ, we know the corresponding pmf from (5.2.16). Therefore, to obtain the queue-length probabilities p_j for the process in continuous time, we simply remove the conditioning on τ in the interval $[0, T)$. That is, we obtain

(5.2.17)
$$p_j = \int_0^T p_j(x)\, dF(x)$$

where $F(x)$ denotes the distribution function for τ. Clearly, τ will be uniformly distributed in the interval $[0, T)$ so that

(5.2.18)
$$dF(x) = \frac{dx}{T}, \quad 0 \leq x < T$$

Working as before with generating functions, we find on computing the generating function for the $p_j(\tau)$

(5.2.19)
$$P(z, \tau) = \pi(z)A_\tau(z)$$

where we have made use of the fact that (5.2.16) represents a convolution. Transforming (5.2.17) and substituting (5.2.18) we obtain

$$(5.2.20) \qquad P(z) = \sum_{j=0}^{\infty} p_j z^j = \pi(z) \int_0^T A_x(z)\, dF(x)$$

Substitution of (5.2.13)–(5.2.15) and carrying out the integration gives

$$(5.2.21) \qquad P(z) = (1 - \lambda T)\frac{(z-1)e^{-\lambda T(1-z)/N}}{z - e^{-\lambda T(1-z)}}\left[\frac{1 - e^{-\lambda T(1-z)}}{\lambda T(1-z)}\right]$$

Equation (5.2.21) is the basic result we have been seeking; from (5.2.21) the probabilities p_j, the mean queue length $\bar{n}$, and higher moments may be found by differentiation. In particular, for the mean queue length we have

$$(5.2.22) \qquad \bar{n} = \lim_{z \to 1} P'(z) = \rho\left(\frac{N+2}{2N}\right) + \frac{\rho^2}{2(1-\rho)}$$

where ρ is the utilization factor (for the kth queue) and is given by

$$(5.2.23) \qquad \rho = \lambda T$$

A measure of the mean waiting times for the system is provided by an application of Little's result (see Section 4.2). Thus for the waiting time in the system we simply calculate $W = \bar{n}/\lambda$.

From (5.2.22) for the mean queue length we can observe the dependence on the number (N) of sectors. The cases of most interest in practical systems include the assumptions of $\lambda \equiv \lambda_k = \lambda_0/N$. Most paging drums use values of N sufficiently large that $(N+2)/2N$ is close enough to $\frac{1}{2}$ that system performance depends essentially on the loading factor $\rho = \lambda T = \lambda_0 T/N$. For a given drum speed $(1/T)$ and page size the number N is a measure of drum size (circumference). For fixed drum size and speed, N is a measure of the page size. In either case the capacity (saturation point) of the system is directly proportional to the value of N.

As implied earlier, the analysis we have provided for the paging drum may be approximated by assuming each sector queue to be a constant service, single-server system. Using the result derived in Section 4.2 [see (4.2.24)], for the mean number in the kth queue we obtain

$$(5.2.24) \qquad \bar{n} = \rho + \frac{\rho^2}{2(1-\rho)}$$

which is to be compared with (5.2.22). Note that for $N = 2$ (5.2.22) and (5.2.24) become identical and that (5.2.24) is conservative for all N except $N = 1$. For the degenerate case $N = 1$ one may observe that an arrival to an empty queue in the actual system waits an average of $3T/2$ seconds until service completion, while the above approximation implies a wait of only T seconds. Finally, it can be observed that the percentage difference between (5.2.22) and (5.2.24) becomes very small with large p. That is, the term $p^2/2(1 - p)$ dominates the value of $\bar{n}$ for both systems.

Under the assumption of Poisson arrivals of single-page requests, the above results for the paging drum may be viewed as performance bounds in the sense that existing systems unable to meet the timing and control demands of complete SATF scheduling will be characterized by poorer performance and lower capacity. A lower bound is provided by a system with FCFS scheduling in which no advantage is taken of knowing which sectors are addressed by page requests awaiting service.

To obtain a reasonable approximation for the FCFS paging drum, assuming $\lambda_k = \lambda_0/N$ for all k, we simply use the M/G/1 result of (4.2.21) and assume a service time consisting of a constant T/N plus an access time taking on any of the values mT/N, $m = 0, 1, 2, \ldots, N - 1$ with equal probability $(1/N)$. This gives

$$(5.2.25) \qquad \bar{n}_0 = p_0 + \frac{\lambda_0 E(S^2)}{2(1 - p_0)}, \qquad p_0 = \frac{\lambda_0}{\mu}$$

where $E(S^2)$ is the second moment of the service time distribution

$$E(S^2) = \left[2(N + 1)\frac{2N + 1}{3} \right]\left(\frac{T}{2N} \right)^2$$

and $1/\mu$ is the mean

$$(5.2.26) \qquad \frac{1}{\mu} = (N + 1)\frac{T}{2N}$$

A closer look at the FCFS system will reveal that the above result would be exact if it were not for a difference in the service time distribution of arrivals at an empty queue. This difference decreases with increases in either N or loading, since in the first case T/N becomes negligible and in the second case the probability of an empty queue approaches zero. We really need only compare the capacities of the SATF and FCFS disciplines to get an idea of the large disparity between them. From (5.2.22) and (5.2.25) it is easily seen that for a given N the shortest-access-time system has a capacity $(N + 1)/2$ times greater than that of the FCFS system.

One way to implement SATF scheduling when hardware delays or delays in processing prevent the servicing of consecutive sectors is to service on each revolution only every Mth sector for some suitable integer M such that $1 < M < N$. The *precessing drum scheme* has these characteristics [10]; furthermore, the results derived earlier apply to this scheme with only a trivial modification.

For the precessing drum scheme M is an arbitrary integer such that M and N are relatively prime and $1 < M < N$. (It is relatively simple to effectively adjust the scheme in case the former requirement is not met.) To explain the operation of this scheme take the simple example where M divides $N - 1$ (e.g., $M = 5$ and $N = 26$). There will exist a revolution of the drum in which every Mth sector beginning with sector M is serviced. After servicing sector $N - 1$, the next sector to be serviced (after skipping $M - 1$ sectors) will be sector $M - 1$. Thus the sectors serviced on the subsequent revolution are displaced by one from the sectors serviced on the previous revolution. This sort of precessing continues until M revolutions are made, at which time the drum begins anew with sector M. In this way every sector is serviced exactly once every M revolutions, and exactly $M - 1$ sectors are skipped between every pair of consecutively serviced queues. These last two statements are true for any M satisfying the above conditions, although the actual displacement sequence will depend on M.

Now if we assume that new arrivals require at least $(M - 1)T/N$ seconds before they can be serviced, then our previous analysis carries over directly by simply replacing T by MT in all the results derived earlier. This is most easily seen by considering an equivalent drum having M times the circumference of the original drum but the same circumferential velocity past the read/write heads. A sector of the equivalent drum consists of M of the sectors on the original drum, but only one of these actually contains information. If the sectors of the equivalent drum are defined so that it is the last subsector that contains the information, then with T replaced by MT the previous analysis leading to $P(z)$ follows through without change.

Burge and Konheim [11] have analyzed the SATF paging drum under the assumption that the total number of requests, including the one in service, remains fixed at a given queue size L. That is, when and only when a request departs a new request enters and joins the kth queue with probability $1/N$, $1 \leq k \leq N$. Although a detailed Markov chain analysis of this system has been developed, the principal engineering results are obtainable through an application of Little's result.

Let w be the random variable representing the time a request admitted to the kth sector spends in the system. By symmetry this will be the same for all k. We may write for a given request, to be called the tagged request,

$$\Pr[w \leq x] = \Pr[w' + w'' + w''' \leq x]$$

where w' is the time elapsing from the moment of admission to the moment the head has rotated to the beginning of sector k, w'' is the subsequent time interval required to service all sector-k requests in the system at the time of arrival, and $w''' = T/N$ is simply the time to process the tagged request. Taking expected values we have

$$W \equiv E(w) = E(w') + E(w'') + \frac{T}{N}$$

Now since the tagged request is admitted just after a departure and since this departure is equally likely to be from any sector, $E(w') = [(N-1)/2](T/N)$. Next, we write $E(w'') = \bar{n}_k T$, where $\bar{n}_k$ is the expected number of sector-k requests ahead of the tagged request. Because of symmetry and because the tagged request must see a total of precisely $L-1$ requests in the system at the time of arrival, we have $\bar{n}_k = (L-1)/N$. Thus

$$W = \frac{N-1}{2}\frac{T}{N} + (L-1)\frac{T}{N} + \frac{T}{N}$$

or

(5.2.27)
$$W = \frac{2L+N-1}{2}\frac{T}{N}$$

is the mean time spent in system. From Little's result

(5.2.28)
$$L = \lambda W$$

where λ is the rate at which requests are admitted to the system. Thus the mean number of requests serviced per drum revolution is given by

$$\rho_L = \lambda T = \frac{LT}{W} = \frac{2NL}{2L+N-1}$$

As expected, $\lim_{L\to\infty} \rho_L = N$, which is the saturation result for the SATF paging drum analyzed earlier, and $\rho_1 = 2N/(N+1)$ is equal to μT, the saturation result for the FCFS system according to (5.2.26).

5.3. MINIMIZATION OF SEEK-TIME EFFECTS

We shall now turn to the first service phase occurring in disk systems in which heads must be moved from track to track. In general, the head positioning and latency problems may be studied separately, since in most cases of interest there appears to be no advantage in attempting a joint optimization of the two service phases [6]. As implied earlier the SATF scheme analyzed for drum systems may be applied equally well to minimize the latency effects in disk rotation. It is worth noting, however, that in many disk systems the seek time is so large that minimizing latency has very little effect on overall performance. Of course, this increases the importance of the techniques presented and analyzed below for reducing head motion in disk systems, particularly when disk input/output is a controlling factor in total system performance.

Our concern will be restricted in the remainder of this section to head (arm) positioning operations in the seek phase. Moreover, we shall not be concerned with any differences that might exist in disk reading and writing operations, although head-switching times will generally have to be considered in a detailed analysis of a specific system [2]. We shall focus our attention in a comparative study of mathematical models of the various techniques for scheduling the seeks required by a queue of requests. To simplify our initial discussion we shall adopt the simple model pictured in Fig. 5.3-1, in which a single head and a single disk with N tracks are shown.

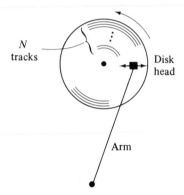

N tracks

Disk head

Arm

Fig. 5.3-1   A single disk.

As usual, the first discipline to consider is FIFO sequencing. Specifically, we shall assume that requests for information to be read or written on disk are stored in a FIFO queue; at each decision point the request at the head of the queue is selected and the disk head moved (if necessary) to the appropriate cylinder. A queueing analysis of this system amounts to a routine application of the results in Chapter 4 and is left to the reader.

At this point we should note the expected delay incurred by head positioning in the FIFO discipline. Suppose that there are N tracks and that the track addresses of successive requests are chosen independently and at random from the set $\{1, 2, \ldots, N\}$. It is easily shown that the mean number of tracks over which the head must move in servicing a request is asymptotically $N/3$. As in the drum-scheduling case, by making use of the track addresses assumed known for the waiting requests we can reduce this initial delay substantially.

As an extension to SATF sequencing, a possible method for improving service is the so-called shortest-seek-time-first (SSTF) procedure [2]. At each decision point with SSTF sequencing the next request selected for service is the one having a track address closest to the current position of the head. A little reflection reveals an apparent drawback of the SSTF rule: The (high- and low-numbered) tracks at the inside and outside extremities of the disk can expect poor service relative to internal tracks. However, relative to FIFO sequencing the above discrimination (at low loading) may very well be a small price to pay for the significant increase in system capacity.

Two methods can be used to reduce the discrimination at the "extremity" tracks while retaining the system capacity of the SSTF rule (under our continuing assumption that we have a uniform usage of all tracks). The first rule is called the SCAN rule [2] and simply applies the SSTF criterion in one direction only: The head scans across the tracks in a given direction, servicing requests as they are encountered, until one of two events occurs:

1. The last track in the given direction has been processed, or
2. There are no further requests ahead of the head position in the given direction.

In both cases, the head motion is reversed and scanning is carried out in the reverse direction (assuming a nonempty queue) until one of the above events again occurs.

The second method is a FIFO scanning rule that we shall term FSCAN [5]. At each decision point FSCAN takes the entire queue and services the requests in a scan whose direction is determined by the minimum distance the current head position is from the outermost and innermost track addresses of the requests to be serviced. Thus the scan is preceded by a move of the disk head to the nearer of the extreme track addresses (i.e., the nearer of the least and the maximum addresses). Arrivals during a given scan are placed in a queue and not serviced until the next scan; this is the principal difference between the SCAN and FSCAN rules. Clearly, during periods of moderate to heavy loading the head will be moving back and forth across the disk with both the SCAN and FSCAN rules. After servicing several requests by the FSCAN rule the head is likely to be at a high address, assuming a left-to-right scan and assuming that addresses increase from left to right. Thus assuming several requests are likely to arrive during this scan, the maximum address represented by the waiting requests will probably be the one closest to the current head position, thus causing a subsequent right-to-left scan.

We turn now to characterizing the structural similarities and differences between SCAN and FSCAN sequencing. We shall see that the response with SCAN is uniformly better (over all track addresses) than with FSCAN but that SCAN still involves a certain amount of discrimination against the innermost and outermost tracks.

The mathematical model is described as follows. The set of discrete track addresses is replaced by the interval $[0, d]$, i.e., the set of real numbers in $[0, d]$. For simplicity, but without loss of generality, we shall assume that $d = 1$ and that the speed at which the head can move across the interval is a. We assume a Poisson input of requests at rate λ and we assume that the "tracks" addressed are uniformly distributed across $[0, 1]$. Formally, the probability that a given arrival falls in the interval $(x, x + \Delta x)$ is given by $\Delta x/d = \Delta x$. Note that this assumption is consistent with the simplification of at most one request per track existing at any given time. Informally, since the probability of more than one arrival in a small interval Δx is of order $(\Delta x)^2$, we may regard the intervals Δx as corresponding to tracks. Clearly, this approximation improves as the actual number N of tracks becomes large.

We shall assume that the time required to service any request is a constant T. A more general assumption can be made here, but it is not essential to the type of comparisons that we intend to make. Clearly, we are lumping not only latency delays and transfer times in T but also delays incurred by starting and stopping the head motion and head switching times. Finally, we shall assume that *the head is always scanning when it is not servicing a request* and that *the direction of the scan is reversed only when the head reaches a boundary*† at 0 or 1. Our assumptions in the analysis of the SCAN rule are

1. If in one crossing of the head n requests are served, then the crossing time is given by $nT + a$.
2. The pmf for the number (n) of arrivals in time t in the interval (b, b'), $0 \leq b < b' \leq 1$, is given by the Poisson distribution

(5.3.1)
$$f_n(b, b') = \frac{[\lambda(b' - b)t]^n}{n!} e^{-\lambda(b'-b)t}$$

with mean value

(5.3.2)
$$\bar{f}(b, b') = \lambda(b' - b)t$$

Relaxation of certain of the above assumptions will be considered later and in the Problems.

We begin with an analysis of the SCAN rule. Our objectives are, first, an expression for the mean time for the head to move from 0 to x in the limit of statistical equilibrium, and, second, a measure of mean waiting or response time.

For convenience we shall assume that the odd-numbered crossings of the disk head are left to right. Let $y_{2n+1}(x)$ $(n \geq 0)$ denote the random variable whose value is the time taken by the head on the $(n + 1)$st left-to-right crossing to move a distance x from position 0, servicing the requests that it encounters enroute. Similarly, for the $(2n)$th crossing $y_{2n}(x)$ denotes the random variable corresponding to a right-to-left move of distance x from position 1.

From our description of the SCAN rule (see Fig. 5.3-2) we know that the last time prior to the $(2n + 1)$st crossing that the interval $(x, x + \Delta x)$ received service was while the head was moving right to left through this interval on the $(2n)$th crossing. Thus, given $y_{2n+1}(x)$, $y_{2n}(1 - x)$, and $y_{2n}(1)$, we have from (5.3.2) that the mean number of requests serviced in $(x, x + \Delta x)$ on the $(2n + 1)$st crossing is $\lambda \Delta x[y_{2n+1}(x) + y_{2n}(1) - y_{2n}(1 - x)]$, plus a term of order $(\Delta x)^2$, which we shall be able to ignore. Since each such request requires

---

†This simplification of the general model appears essential to an analysis of the SCAN rule, although not to the FSCAN rule.

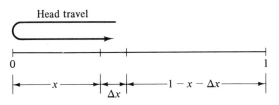

Fig. 5.3-2 Determining $y(x)$.

T time units and since the head requires $a\,\Delta x$ time units to cross the interval, we have

(5.3.3) $E[y_{2n+1}(x + \Delta x)\,|\,y_{2n+1}(x),\,y_{2n}(1),\,y_{2n}(1 - x)]$

$$= y_{2n+1}(x) + a\,\Delta x + \lambda T\,\Delta x[y_{2n+1}(x) + y_{2n}(1) - y_{2n}(1 - x)]$$

Define $E[y_i(x)] \equiv \bar{y}_i(x)$ and remove the conditioning in (5.3.3) to obtain

(5.3.4) $\bar{y}_{2n+1}(x + \Delta x) = \bar{y}_{2n+1}(x) + a\,\Delta x + \lambda T\,\Delta x[\bar{y}_{2n+1}(x)$

$$+ \bar{y}_{2n}(1) - \bar{y}_{2n}(1 - x)]$$

Now consider the limit $\bar{y}(x) \equiv \lim_{n \to \infty} \bar{y}_{2n+1}(x)$. Under the assumptions of our problem the existence of this limit is assured by the condition $\lambda < 1/T$. In other words, the existence of statistical equilibrium requires that the maximum service rate $1/T$ be greater than the arrival rate λ. Moreover, from the symmetry of our problem it is easily seen that $\lim_{n \to \infty} \bar{y}_{2n}(x) = \bar{y}(x)$. Thus, taking limits in (5.3.4), we have

$$\bar{y}(x + \Delta x) = \bar{y}(x) + a\,\Delta x + \lambda T\,\Delta x[\bar{y}(x) + \bar{y}(1) - \bar{y}(1 - x)]$$

Dividing by Δx and taking the limit $\Delta x \to 0$ we obtain

(5.3.5) $$\frac{d\bar{y}(x)}{dx} = a + \lambda T[\bar{y}(x) + \bar{y}(1) - \bar{y}(1 - x)]$$

To solve (5.3.5) we observe that

$$\frac{d\bar{y}(x)}{dx} + \frac{d\bar{y}(1 - x)}{dx} = 2\,\frac{d\bar{y}(x)}{dx}\bigg|_{x=\frac{1}{2}}$$

Using this relation in the derivative of (5.3.5) we obtain

(5.3.6) $$\frac{d^2\bar{y}(x)}{dx^2} = 2\lambda T\,\frac{d\bar{y}(x)}{dx}\bigg|_{x=\frac{1}{2}} = \text{constant}$$

from which we see that $\bar{y}(x)$ must be a quadratic in x.

Using the boundary conditions $\bar{y}(0) = 0$ and $d\bar{y}(x)/dx|_{x=0} = a$ along with (5.3.5) we obtain

(5.3.7)
$$\bar{y}(x) = \frac{1 - \lambda T(1 - x)}{1 - \lambda T} ax, \quad 0 \leq x \leq 1$$

Note that $\bar{y}(1)$, the mean crossing time, is given by

(5.3.8)
$$\bar{y}(1) = \frac{a}{1 - \lambda T}$$

Equation (5.3.8) can be verified by the following independent argument. We observe that the mean crossing time can be written as

(5.3.9)
$$\bar{y}(1) = \bar{n}_c T + a$$

where $\bar{n}_c$ is the (equilibrium) mean number serviced in a crossing. But the mean number served in $\bar{y}(1)$ must be the mean number arriving in $\bar{y}(1)$, and hence

(5.3.10)
$$\bar{n}_c = \lambda \bar{y}(1)$$

Upon substitution into (5.3.9) we get (5.3.8) as required.

Now suppose that we observe the system during statistical equilibrium at a time when the head is at position v and moving right. Let $w_r(x \mid v)$ denote the expected value of the time required for the head to move from the current position v to position x. We have

(5.3.11)
$$w_r(x \mid v) = \begin{cases} \bar{y}(x) - \bar{y}(v), & 0 \leq v \leq x \leq 1 \\ \bar{y}(1) - \bar{y}(v) + \bar{y}(1 - x), & 0 \leq x < v \leq 1 \end{cases}$$

To compute

(5.3.12)
$$\bar{w}_r(x) = \int_0^1 w_r(x \mid v) \, dP_r(v)$$

we need the stationary probability distribution $P_r(v)$ that the disk head is in the interval $(0, v)$ given that it is moving right. We identify $P_r(v)$ with the expected fraction of the time spent moving right that the head spends in the interval $(0, v)$ in statistical equilibrium. Now the time taken by a large number, M, of left-to-right crossings is approximately $M\bar{y}(1)$. Of this time the head spends approximately $\bar{y}(x)M$ time units within the interval $(0, x)$. Asymptotically, we have†

†This is a commonly used argument for determining the probability distribution of some given event in statistical equilibrium, and we shall have occasion to use it later. In general, however, care must be taken to ensure that the stochastic process being dealt with is such that the argument gives valid and meaningful results. A detailed treatment of this type of problem and of general questions of ergodicity is beyond the scope of our presentation; we refer the reader to [12, 13].

(5.3.13)
$$P_r(v) = \frac{\bar{y}(v)}{\bar{y}(1)}$$

with the corresponding density function

(5.3.14)
$$p_r(v) = \frac{d\bar{y}(v)/dv}{\bar{y}(1)}$$

Substituting into (5.3.12) the expressions in (5.3.11) we have

$$\bar{w}_r(x) = \int_0^x [\bar{y}(x) - \bar{y}(v)]p_r(v)\, dv + \int_x^1 [\bar{y}(1) - \bar{y}(v) + \bar{y}(1 - x)]p_r(v)\, dv$$

whereupon substitution of (5.3.14) and carrying out the integration yields

(5.3.15) $$\bar{w}_r(x) = \frac{a/2}{1 - \lambda T}[1 + 2(1 - x)(1 + \lambda Tx)(1 - 2x)]$$

We have assumed a left-to-right crossing of the disk head in calculating $\bar{w}_r(x)$. However, if we had assumed the head to be moving left, then $\bar{w}_l(x) = \bar{w}_r(1 - x)$ would be the mean time for the head to move to position x. The probability that a random observation finds the head moving right is equal to the probability ($\frac{1}{2}$) that it finds the head moving left. (Note, however, that the probabilities of rightward and leftward motion of the head are not equal when conditioned on the position of the head being at $z \neq \frac{1}{2}$.) Thus, removing the conditioning on the direction of head motion, for the overall response time we have

$$\bar{w}(x) = \frac{1}{2}(\bar{w}_r(x) + \bar{w}_l(x))$$

which on substitution becomes

(5.3.16)
$$\bar{w}(x) = \frac{a}{2}\frac{1 + (1 - 2x)^2}{1 - \lambda T}$$

This is the result we have been seeking. It shows explicitly the discrimination against tracks at the outer and inner extremities. As can be seen $\bar{w}(x)$ is minimized by $x = \frac{1}{2}$ and maximized at $x = 0$ and $x = 1$.

We shall now compute a comparable response time for the idealized FSCAN rule in which we assume that the head always scans the entire disk before reversing direction. Suppose that we observe the FSCAN system at a random point in equilibrium, but conditioned on the fact that the crossing in process is servicing n requests. Let $\bar{w}_n(x)$ denote the mean time we must wait for the head to move to position x after servicing all requests arriving in the current crossing which address tracks to be served before track x. (Such tracks will be in $[0, x)$ if the head is currently moving left, and in $(x, 1]$ if the head is currently moving right.) That is, $\bar{w}_n(x)$ will be the sum of the mean time to complete the present crossing plus the mean time to process (in the next crossing) all arrivals in the present crossing which will be serviced before position x is reached. Since the direction of head motion is equally probably left and right and since the present crossing must be precisely of length $t_n = nT + a$, we have

$$\bar{w}_n(x) = \frac{t_n}{2} + \frac{1}{2}[\lambda T t_n x + ax] + \frac{1}{2}[\lambda T t_n(1 - x) + a(1 - x)]$$

or

(5.3.17)
$$\bar{w}_n(x) = \frac{t_n}{2}[1 + \lambda T] + \frac{a}{2}$$

which we note is independent of x. Our object is now the calculation of the mean response time

(5.3.18)
$$\bar{w}(x) = \sum_{n=0}^{\infty} p_n \bar{w}_n(x)$$

where p_n is the stationary probability that a random observation finds the system executing a crossing that services n requests. To compute p_n we first analyze the stationary behavior of the Markov chain $\{X_k\}$, where X_k is the number of requests serviced in the kth crossing. Let $\{q_j\}$ denote the stationary probability distribution and let

$$q_{ij} = \Pr[X_{k+1} = j | X_k = i]$$

denote the one-step transition probabilities. It is easily verified that $\{X_k\}$ is homogeneous and that the q_{ij} are independent of the time parameter k. Moreover, for all $i \geq 0$ and $j \geq 0$, q_{ij} is simply the probability of j Poisson arrivals in $t_i = iT + a$. Thus

(5.3.19)
$$q_{ij} = \frac{(\lambda t_i)^j}{j!} e^{-\lambda t_i}$$

From the equation defining the stationary distribution

(5.3.20)
$$q_j = \sum_{i=0}^{\infty} q_{ij} q_i, \quad j = 0, 1, 2, \ldots$$

and the generating function

(5.3.21)
$$Q(z) = \sum_{j=0}^{\infty} q_j z^j$$

we obtain

$$Q(z) = \sum_{i=0}^{\infty} q_i \sum_{j=0}^{\infty} q_{ij} z^j$$

Substituting (5.3.19) and simplifying we get

$$Q(z) = \sum_{i=0}^{\infty} q_i e^{-\lambda t_i (1-z)}$$

Substituting $t_i = iT + a$ we arrive at

(5.3.22) $$Q(z) = e^{-\lambda a (1-z)} Q(e^{-\lambda T (1-z)})$$

From (5.3.22) we can find the moments by differentiation. Specifically, we have for the first two moments

(5.3.23) $$\bar{n}_c = \frac{\lambda a}{1 - \lambda T}$$

(5.3.24) $$\bar{n}_c^2 = \frac{(\lambda a)^2 + 2\lambda^2 a T \bar{n}_c + \bar{n}_c}{1 - (\lambda T)^2}$$

Note that (5.3.23) corresponds to (5.3.10); this we should expect on the basis of the same arguments given in support of the value found for $\bar{y}(1)$ in (5.3.8). By means of the arguments used to justify (5.3.13) we can establish the following relation between p_n and q_n:

(5.3.25) $$p_n = \frac{nT + a}{\bar{n}_c T + a} q_n$$

In particular, in a large number of crossings, q_n is approximately that fraction which services n requests. Since each such crossing requires exactly t_n time units, we arrive at $t_n q_n / \sum_{n=0}^{\infty} t_n q_n$ as the fraction of time spent in crossings servicing n requests. On substituting for t_n we get (5.3.25) directly.

Substituting (5.3.25) into (5.3.18) we get

$$\bar{w}(x) = \frac{a}{2} + \frac{1 + \lambda T}{2(\bar{n}_c T + a)} \sum_{n=0}^{\infty} t_n^2 q_n$$

$$= \frac{a}{2} + \frac{1 + \lambda T}{2(\bar{n}_c T + a)} \sum_{n=0}^{\infty} [T^2 n^2 q_n + 2aTnq_n + a^2 q_n]$$

Using the moments given in (5.3.23) and (5.3.24) we find on substitution and simplification

(5.3.26) $$\bar{w}(x) = \frac{a + \lambda T^2/2}{1 - \lambda T}$$

This is the expression to compare with (5.3.16) for the SCAN system. The major point to make is that, for all x ($0 \leq x \leq 1$), $\bar{w}(x)$ is greater in the FSCAN system than in the SCAN system.

5.4. MODELS OF INTERACTING INPUT/OUTPUT AND CPU QUEUES

A completely general study of operating-system processes must be concerned with networks of interacting queues. Such queues will exist for jobs waiting for processors, input/output units, data base access, etc. Effective models of such systems of queues are difficult to analyze except under restrictive assumptions, the principal one being exponential service times. In this section we shall briefly examine closed and cyclic systems of queues particularly suited to the study of CPU and input/output interaction, subject to the assumption of exponential service.

We shall call a system closed if the population of (say, N) jobs contained in the system remains fixed. Such systems are frequently subject to an analysis using finite Markov chains whose states represent the configuration of jobs in the various queues. Unfortunately, the number of states (configurations) can easily make the analysis for even moderate values of N quite costly. An interesting computer-based system has been described by Wallace et al. [14, 15] which facilitates and to some extent automates the formulation and solution of finite Markov chains, especially those arising in the applications of this and the preceding chapters.

Let us first examine the simple *cyclic queue* model [16] in Fig. 5.4-1, where single CPU and I/O processors are shown. Jobs enter the system by joining the CPU queue, but only at the instants when jobs depart from the system; thus the number in system stays constant at N. After receiving service at the CPU a job leaves the system with stationary probability α (whereupon a new job immediately joins the CPU queue) and joins the I/O queue with probability $1 - \alpha$. The I/O queue is a conventional FIFO queue whose departures immediately join the CPU queue. The distribution for each CPU service is

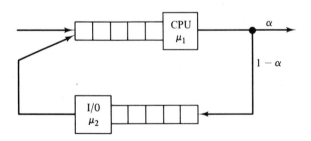

Fig. 5.4-1 Cyclic queue model.

exponential with parameter μ_1, while that for each I/O service is exponential with parameter μ_2. Note that the *total* CPU execution requirement of a job must also be exponential because it is a geometrically distributed sum of exponential service times. Since the mean number of times a job waits through the CPU queue is $1/\alpha = \sum_{i=1}^{\infty} i(1 - \alpha)^{i-1}\alpha$, it follows that the parameter of the distribution of total CPU execution time is $\alpha\mu_1$. A similar argument shows that the total I/O service required has an exponential distribution with parameter $\alpha\mu_2/(1 - \alpha)$.

Let $X(t)$ denote the number in the CPU queue, waiting and being served, at time t. It is readily seen that $X(t)$ is a homogeneous Markov process. Moreover, the stationary distribution $\{p_i\}_{i=0}^{N} = 0$ exists for $0 < \mu_1 < \infty$, $0 < \mu_2 < \infty$, and $0 \le \alpha < 1$. Using the methods of Section 4.2 the following balance equations are easily developed:

$$(5.4.1) \qquad (1 - \alpha)\mu_1 p_i = \mu_2 p_{i-1}, \quad i = 1, 2, \ldots, N$$

The solution of (5.4.1) satisfying $\sum_{i=0}^{N} p_i = 1$ is given by

$$(5.4.2) \qquad p_i = \frac{1 - \rho}{1 - \rho^{N+1}} \rho^i$$

where

$$(5.4.3) \qquad \rho = \frac{\mu_2}{(1 - \alpha)\mu_1}$$

To obtain a measure of the mean time in the system let us first consider the expected value $\bar{d}$ of the time between successive departures in statistical equilibrium. The rate of departures from a nonempty CPU queue is clearly $\alpha\mu_1$, since $1/\alpha\mu_1$ is the expected value of the total service requirement. Since $1 - p_0$ is the stationary probability of a nonempty CPU queue, as the average departure rate we have

$$\frac{1}{\bar{d}} = \alpha\mu_1(1 - p_0)$$

Using (5.4.2) and solving for $\bar{d}$ we obtain

$$(5.4.4) \qquad \bar{d} = \frac{1}{\alpha\mu_1} \frac{1 - \rho^{N+1}}{\rho - \rho^{N+1}}$$

Now $1/\bar{d}$ is also the average arrival rate. Hence, applying Little's result, we have

$$(5.4.5) \qquad W = \bar{d}N$$

as the mean time in the system.

The foregoing results can be generalized to encompass any closed network of queues having exponential service times [17]. Note that we can "close" the system of Fig. 5.4-1 by simply stipulating that previously "departing" jobs are actually fed back to the end of the CPU queue. The new, closed system is equivalent to the original system in the sense that the distribution $\{p_i\}_{i=0}^N$ remains the same, a property that follows from the Poisson assumptions.

The general system comprises a set of M *stages*, indexed $1, 2, \ldots, M$. The ith stage is assumed to be an $M/M/r_i$ queue with service rate μ_i (see Section 4.3). Jobs completing service at the ith stage immediately join the queue of the jth stage with a fixed probability q_{ij}, independent of the state of the system and the job having just completed service. Denote the interstage transition matrix $\mathbf{Q} = ((q_{ij}))$ and let N denote the fixed number of jobs in the system. The states of the system will be denoted by M-tuples $(n_1, n_2, \ldots, n_M)$, where n_i is the number waiting and being served in the ith stage and where

$$(5.4.6) \qquad \sum_{i=1}^{M} n_i = N$$

We shall make the usual assumption that by a finite sequence of transitions, each having nonzero probability, the system can move from any given state to any other state. The corresponding Markov process $X(t)$ is therefore irreducible and will have a unique stationary probability distribution. A formal method for computing this distribution is considered in the following discussion. We shall present only the main steps of the analysis and leave the routine (but at times elaborate) algebra to the interested reader.

Let $p(n_1, n_2, \ldots, n_M)$ denote the equilibrium probability of the state $(n_1, n_2, \ldots, n_M)$. Using the methods of Section 4.2 we obtain the balance equations (cf. Fig. 5.4-2)

$$(5.4.7) \qquad \left[\sum_{k=1}^{M} \delta(n_k)\alpha_k(n_k)\mu_k \right] p(n_1, \ldots, n_M)$$

$$= \sum_{j=1}^{M} \sum_{k=1}^{M} \delta(n_k)\alpha_j(n_j + 1)\mu_j q_{jk} p(n_1, \ldots, n_j + 1,$$

$$\ldots, n_k - 1, \ldots, n_M)$$

where

$$\delta(n_j) = \begin{cases} 0, & n_j = 0 \\ 1, & n_j > 0 \end{cases}$$

and

$$(5.4.8) \qquad \alpha_k(n_k) = \begin{cases} n_k, & n_k \leq r_k \\ r_k, & n_k \geq r_k \end{cases}$$

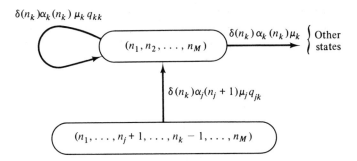

Fig. 5.4-2 Adjacent states in general queueing network.

The purpose of the "filter" $\delta(n_i)$ is to eliminate those terms which would correspond to departures from an empty queue ($n_i = 0$). The function $\alpha_k(n_k)$ simply gives the number of jobs being served at the kth stage when the total number at that stage is n_k. As usual, (5.4.7) may be interpreted as balancing the flow out of a state with the flow into that state. Specifically, the left-hand side of (5.4.7) gives the rate of transitions out of state $(n_1, n_2, \ldots, n_M)$ and the right-hand side gives the rate into state $(n_1, n_2, \ldots, n_M)$.

An attempt to find a solution to (5.4.7) in which there is a separation of variables will succeed in the following way. First, define the numbers

$$(5.4.9) \qquad \beta_i(n) = \begin{cases} n!, & n \leq r_i \\ r_i^{n-r_i} r_i!, & n \geq r_i \end{cases}$$

Next, consider the trial solution

$$(5.4.10) \qquad p(n_1, \ldots, n_M) = \frac{1}{G(N)} \prod_{i=1}^{M} \frac{x_i^{n_i}}{\beta_i(n_i)}$$

where $G(N)$ is a normalization parameter and the parameters x_i are to be determined. Substituting (5.4.10) into (5.4.7) one finds after noting that $\beta_i(n + 1) = \alpha_i(n + 1)\beta_i(n)$ and performing a certain amount of algebra, that (5.4.10) is a probability distribution satisfying (5.4.7) if and only if $\mathbf{x}' = (\mu_1 x_1, \mu_2 x_2, \ldots, \mu_M x_M)$ satisfies the linear system of equations

$$(5.4.11) \qquad \mathbf{x}' = \mathbf{x}'\mathbf{Q}$$

under the normalization condition

$$(5.4.12) \qquad G(N) = \sum_{N} \left\{ \prod_{i=1}^{M} \frac{x_i^{n_i}}{\beta_i(n_i)} \right\}$$

where $\sum_N$ denotes the sum over all states $(n_1, n_2, \ldots, n_M)$ such that $n_1 + \cdots + n_M = N$. The existence and uniqueness of the solution is assured by the irreducibility of the matrix Q, which in turn follows from our original assumption that the Markov process $X(t)$ is irreducible [17]. In summary, then, the probability distribution for any closed, exponential system can be computed by solving the system (5.4.11), i.e., by solving the eigenvector problem for the matrix Q.

Many interesting structures may be studied by means of these results. The so-called central-server network [18] is an illustration that we shall describe below. (See Problem 5-10 for another illustration.)

A central-server network is shown in Fig. 5.4-3, where stage 1 is a proces-

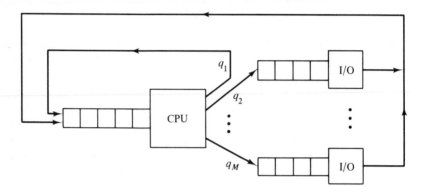

Fig. 5.4-3   Central-server model.

sor and stages 2 through M are to be regarded as input/output units. The matrix Q corresponding to the directions of flow in Fig. 5.4-3 is given by

(5.4.13)
$$Q = \begin{bmatrix} q_1 & q_2 & \cdots & q_M \\ 1 & 0 & \cdots & 0 \\ 1 & 0 & \cdots & 0 \\ \cdot & \cdot & & \cdot \\ \cdot & \cdot & & \cdot \\ \cdot & \cdot & & \cdot \\ 1 & 0 & \cdots & 0 \end{bmatrix}$$

where q_i is the probability that a job departing the processor proceeds next to the ith stage. Equation (5.4.11) represents an easily solved system of equations with Q given by (5.4.13). In particular, any vector of the form $(z, q_2 z, \ldots, q_M z)$ will satisfy (5.4.11). Since we are free to choose z, it is convenient to select $z = \mu_1$. Thus, making use of $x_1 = \mu_1/\mu_1 = 1$ and noting that $r_i = 1$ implies that $\beta_i(n) = 1$ for all n, we have from (5.4.10)

(5.4.14)
$$p(n_1, \ldots, n_M) = \frac{1}{G(N)} \prod_{i=2}^{M} \left(\frac{q_i \mu_1}{\mu_i} \right)^{n_i}$$

where

(5.4.15)
$$G(N) = \sum_N \prod_{i=2}^M \left(\frac{q_i \mu_1}{\mu_i}\right)^{n_i}$$

Note that n_1 does not appear in the summand of (5.4.15); hence we can also express the summation as

(5.4.16)
$$G(N) = \sum_{\mathbf{n} \in \Lambda(N)} \prod_{i=2}^M \left(\frac{q_i \mu_1}{\mu_i}\right)^{n_i}$$

where $\Lambda(N)$ is the set of states $\mathbf{n} = (n_1, n_2, \ldots, n_M)$ for which $\sum_{i=2}^M n_i \leq N$. The latter summation for $G(N)$ will be used again below. We shall conclude this section by developing expressions for the mean queue lengths in the central-server network.

Let $\bar{n}_j$ denote the steady-state mean number of jobs waiting and being served at the jth stage. We can write

(5.4.17)
$$\bar{n}_j = \sum_{k=1}^N \bar{P}_j(k)$$

where $\bar{P}_j(k) = \Pr[n_j \geq k]$ denotes the equilibrium probability that the jth queue length is greater than or equal to k. In calculating the $\bar{P}_j(k)$ it is convenient to let $p(\mathbf{n})$ denote the equilibrium probability of the state $\mathbf{n} = (n_1, n_2, \ldots, n_M)$ and to define the sets

(5.4.18)
$$\Lambda_j(k) = \left\{ \mathbf{n} \,\middle|\, \sum_{i=2}^M n_i \leq N \text{ and } n_j \geq k \right\}$$

Now for the processor stage we have

$$\bar{P}_1(k) = \sum_{\mathbf{n} \in \Lambda(N-k)} p(\mathbf{n}) = \sum_{\mathbf{n} \in \Lambda(N-k)} \frac{1}{G(N)} \prod_{i=2}^M \left(\frac{q_i \mu_1}{\mu_i}\right)^{n_i}$$

which on applying (5.4.16) yields

(5.4.19)
$$\bar{P}_1(k) = \frac{G(N-k)}{G(N)}$$

For $j = 2, 3, \ldots, M$ we have

$$\bar{P}_j(k) = \sum_{\mathbf{n} \in \Lambda_j(k)} p(\mathbf{n})$$

which can be put in the form

(5.4.20)
$$\bar{P}_j(k) = \frac{1}{G(N)} \left[\frac{q_j \mu_1}{\mu_j}\right]^k \sum_{\mathbf{n} \in \Lambda(N-k)} \prod_{i=2}^M \left(\frac{q_i \mu_1}{\mu_i}\right)^{n_i}$$

Thus, using (5.4.16) and (5.4.19) we get

$$(5.4.21) \qquad \bar{P}_j(k) = \left[\frac{q_j \mu_1}{\mu_j}\right]^k \bar{P}_1(k) = \left[\frac{q_j \mu_1}{\mu_j}\right]^k \frac{G(N-k)}{G(N)}$$

Finally, substitution into (5.4.17) leaves us with

$$(5.4.22) \qquad \bar{n}_1 = \sum_{k=1}^{N} \frac{G(N-k)}{G(N)}$$

$$(5.4.23) \qquad \bar{n}_j = \sum_{k=1}^{N} \left[\frac{q_j \mu_1}{\mu_j}\right]^k \frac{G(N-k)}{G(N)}, \quad j = 2, 3, \ldots, M$$

If we define the polynomial

$$(5.4.24) \qquad F(x) = \sum_{k=1}^{N} x^k \frac{G(N-k)}{G(N)}$$

we can reduce (5.4.22) and (5.4.23) to

$$\bar{n}_1 = F(1)$$

$$\bar{n}_j = F\left(\frac{q_j \mu_1}{\mu_j}\right), \quad j > 1$$

Thus one can compute the mean queue lengths by computing the numbers $G(0), G(1), \ldots, G(N)$ and evaluating (5.4.24).

The work of Lewis and Shedler [19] is related to the models of this section. They have devised a queueing model of a paging system (see Chapter 6) whose principal purpose is studying CPU utilization and system overhead costs. The model is not so dependent on exponential assumptions as those in this section, but the structure is limited to a cyclic queue. The analysis and results are rather elaborate and for this reason we have not included them here.

5.5. BUFFER STORAGE ALLOCATION PROBLEMS

Some very important problems in system design are concerned with the structure and parameter specification of buffer storage techniques. The need for buffer storage arises in at least three important contexts: 1) the storage of information prior to output and following input from auxiliary storage or input/output devices, 2) the storage of messages and data communicated between active tasks, and 3) the storage of messages arriving from or being transmitted to remote terminals such as in a time-sharing system.

The issues involved in buffer design problems can be illustrated by the buffer problem discussed in Section 2.6 on synchronization. In the simplest version we have a cyclic task generating output messages one at a time, a buffer of N cells in which these messages are placed, and a cyclic output task executing asynchronously with respect to message generation and transmitting from the buffer to some output device. One of the first questions that arises in the design of this system concerns the value of N to be used, assuming a fixed block of storage is to be allocated for the buffer. An obvious trade-off exists between storage utilization and throughput rate, an improvement in one creating degradation in the other.

To be more specific, suppose that the times required to generate successive messages are independently and exponentially distributed with parameter λ. Whenever an arriving message causes the buffer to become full it is assumed that the message source ceases to function until a buffer cell becomes available. Assume that the time required to output a message after it is removed from the buffer is an exponentially distributed random variable with mean $1/\mu$. Defining the system state as the number of messages waiting in the buffer and being output, we may use the model in Section 4.3. In particular, from (4.3.8) we obtain the mean number of messages

$$(5.5.1) \qquad \bar{B}_N = \sum_{n=0}^{N} \frac{n\rho^n(1-\rho)}{1-\rho^{N+1}} = \frac{\rho}{1-\rho} - \frac{(N+1)\rho^{N+1}}{1-\rho^{N+1}}$$

where

$$\rho = \frac{\lambda}{\mu}$$

The throughput rate of messages will be λ times the probability that the source is functioning:

$$(5.5.2) \qquad H_N = \lambda(1 - p_N)$$

where from (4.3.8)

$$p_N = \frac{(1-\rho)\rho^N}{1-\rho^{N+1}}$$

From these results one may study the trade-off between throughput H_N and the storage utilization $\bar{B}_N/N$.

As illustrated above, queueing theory lends itself naturally to the analysis of many buffer storage problems. However, the interests of realism and mathematical tractability are frequently conflicting. For example, assumptions leading to difficult models are *bulk* arrivals (see Problems 4-2 and 5-5) and bulk service. On the other hand, with the usual assumption of a finite buffer size we obtain a finite-state system. Thus we can frequently obtain the desired engineering results by the solution of finite systems of linear (equilibrium) equations arising in a Markov chain analysis.

Another important problem that arises when many variable-length messages must share the same storage area involves the decision between dynamic storage allocation and a fixed partitioning method. In particular, suppose that we have M input lines feeding into a given buffer storage area. In a fixed partition scheme a distinct and fixed-length block of the storage area is reserved for each input, and the block sizes may depend on the traffic produced by the message sources. In the event that overflows occur some mechanism must be assumed which provides either for additional storage or for temporarily blocking the source from further communication until sufficient buffer space becomes available. The principal disadvantage of this method of storage allocation lies in the potentially poor utilization of storage that results when space available in unsaturated blocks is not made available for blocks experiencing overflow. By comparison with other allocation procedures, however, the fixed partition method has the advantage of simplicity.

In the dynamic or linked-list method of storage allocation each message is conventionally stored as a chain of linked cells in the buffer storage area [7]. Whenever a message is removed from the buffer the space it has been occupying is returned to an available space list; whenever a new message arrives it is stored in the appropriate number of cells taken from the top of the available space list. In general, an overflow mechanism will again have to be assumed. Also, routine techniques must be assumed for queueing messages from the same source and providing head-of-queue pointers for each input line.

An obvious disadvantage of linked allocation is the space that must be reserved for links. In this respect a trade-off can be introduced by varying the number b of characters in each cell or block. In each cell we assume a fixed number c of characters reserved for the link so that $b - c$ characters are available for message storage. Now consider the storage of a message whose length m is reasonably large compared to the cell size b. As a first approximation the number of cells occupied by the message is $m/(b - c)$ and the space unused in the last cell is $(b - c)/2$. Thus the total space unusable for the storage of other messages that results from the storage of the given message is approximately

$$(5.5.3) \qquad w_m = \frac{b - c}{2} + \frac{mc}{b - c}$$

That value of b which minimizes w_m is found by differentiation to be

$$(5.5.4) \qquad b_{opt} = c + \sqrt{2mc}$$

If message length is a random variable, the value of m in the above expression can be taken to be the expected value. Although a more careful, less approximate analysis can be carried out for this problem [20], the functional dependence of b_{opt} remains essentially the same.

Without explicit consideration of the allocation policy we now specialize the above message buffering model so that it corresponds to a large class of low-data-rate systems in which teletypes, typewriters, etc., communicate directly to a central computer system [20]. Our goal will again be an analysis of buffer performance as a function of buffer size. As shown in Fig. 5.5-1 we assume M input lines and a transmission rate $1/\alpha$ on each. For convenience suppose that α gives the time in seconds required for loading one character. We begin by considering the statistical characterization of the activity on a single line.

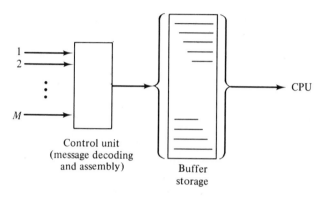

1
2
⋮
M

CPU

Control unit
(message decoding
and assembly)

Buffer
storage

Fig. 5.5-1   Model for input buffer.

The low-data-rate assumption means that the time to assemble a message, character by character, in the buffer is very much longer than the time required by a program to read the message from the buffer. In fact, we shall assume that on the time scale of the input rate, the process of reading a message from the buffer is effectively instantaneous. Thus, if we focus attention on the space occupied by messages from a single source, we have a process $Z(t)$ having sample functions like the one shown in Fig. 5.5-2. Although $Z(t)$ increases in discrete steps (one character at a time) in the intervals X_n, we have approximated the increase by a straight line. For purposes of analysis we assume that the message sizes Z_n and hence the transmission intervals X_n $(n = 1, 2, \ldots)$

Buffer occupancy $Z_n/X_n = \alpha^{-1}$ (characters/sec)

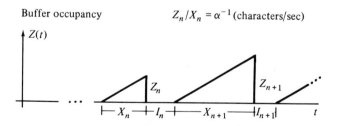

Fig. 5.5-2   Buffer occupancy process.

are statistically independent and that the stationary distribution for the X_n is denoted by

$$F(x) = \Pr[X_n \leq x], \quad n = 1, 2, \ldots$$

The ith $(i \geq 1)$ moment will be denoted $E(X^i)$. For simplicity we shall assume that $F(x)$ is continuous and that this is a reasonable first approximation. The results are easily revised to apply to an arbitrary distribution.

The idle intervals $I_1, I_2, \ldots$ constitute a sequence of independent, identically distributed random variables, each of which is statistically independent of the X_n $(n = 1, 2, \ldots)$. The ith $(i \geq 1)$ moment of the idle-period distribution will be denoted $E(I^i)$. We shall assume that the so-called alternating renewal process $Z(t)$ is initiated with an idle period I_0, whose length is governed by some appropriate probability distribution. Since our concern is with equilibrium behavior the initial condition will have no significance.

We shall now proceed to compute the long-run mean buffer occupancy:

$$(5.5.5) \qquad \bar{B} = \lim_{t \to \infty} E(Z(t))$$

We observe first that the distribution for $Z(t)$ must be of mixed type. Because of the existence of idle periods, there will be a discrete probability mass concentrated at $Z(t) = 0$. Consider an observation at a random point t; after separating out the discrete component corresponding to an empty buffer, we have

$$(5.5.6) \qquad \Pr[Z(t) = 0] = \Pr[t \text{ is contained in an idle period}]$$

and for $x > 0$

$$(5.5.7) \qquad \Pr[Z(t) \leq x] = \Pr[Z(t) = 0] + \Pr[t \text{ is in a transmission interval}$$
$$\text{whose elapsed time does not exceed } \alpha x]$$

Identifying the limiting value of (5.5.6) with the fraction of time spent in idle periods during statistical equilibrium we have (see the footnote on p. 214).

$$(5.5.8) \qquad \lim_{t \to \infty} \Pr[Z(t) = 0] = \frac{E(I)}{E(I) + E(X)}$$

Given that t falls in a transmission interval the distribution of the elapsed time of this interval prior to t is given by the distribution for backward recurrence times in the renewal process consisting of the sequence $X_1, X_2, \ldots$. (See Appendix B.) Thus the probability $P_e(\alpha x)$ that the elapsed time is less than or equal to αx is given by

$$(5.5.9) \qquad P_e(\alpha x) = \frac{1}{E(X)} \int_0^{\alpha x} [1 - F(u)]\, du$$

Multiplying by the limiting probability that t falls in a transmission interval yields

$$\lim_{t \to \infty} \Pr[Z(t) \leq x] = \frac{E(I)}{E(I) + E(X)} + \frac{E(X)}{E(I) + E(X)} P_e(\alpha x)$$

or

(5.5.10) $$\lim_{t \to \infty} \Pr[Z(t) \leq x] = \frac{1}{E(I) + E(X)} \left[E(I) + \int_0^{\alpha x} [1 - F(u)] \, du \right],$$

$$x > 0$$

The mean of the distribution in (5.5.8) and (5.5.10) gives the mean buffer occupancy of (5.5.5). Specifically, we obtain

(5.5.11) $$\bar{B} = \frac{E(X^2)}{2\alpha[E(I) + E(X)]}$$

Also from (5.5.8) and (5.5.10) we have

(5.5.12) $$R(N) = \frac{1}{E(I) + E(X)} \int_{\alpha N}^{\infty} [1 - F(u)] \, du$$

as the long-run probability of overflow in a buffer of size N. This also represents the expected fraction of time the process $Z(t)$ spends above the level N during statistical equilibrium. In addition to the expected time spent above a given level, the frequency of overflow events (upcrossings) is also important, especially when a significant overhead cost is incurred (as it usually is) each time extra storage has to be made available for buffering. To compute this performance measure we note that at most one upcrossing occurs in each idle period-transmission cycle and that the event occurs with probability $1 - F(\alpha N)$ in each cycle. Thus we have

(5.5.13) $$\bar{U} = \frac{1 - F(\alpha N)}{E(I) + E(X)}$$

as the average upcrossing rate.

Now consider an N-cell buffer shared by M statistically independent sources, each of which has the characteristics that were either given or derived above. Assume also that we have the dynamic storage allocation scheme in use. Let $Z_j(t)$ denote the buffer occupancy process for the jth source. Assuming that M is reasonably large, the distribution of the sum process

(5.5.14) $$Z_S(t) = \sum_{j=1}^{M} Z_j(t)$$

is subject to a central-limit-theorem effect and hence can be approximated by a normal distribution with the density function

$$(5.5.15) \qquad g(x) = \frac{1}{\sqrt{2\pi\sigma_S^2}} e^{-(x-m_S)^2/2\sigma_S^2}$$

The moments are supplied from the distribution in (5.5.8) and (5.5.11) summed over the M sources. If we let $E(X_j^i)$ denote the ith moment of the transmission times and $E(I_j)$ the mean idle times for the jth source, then

$$(5.5.16) \qquad m_S = \frac{1}{2\alpha} \sum_{j=1}^{M} \frac{E(X_j^2)}{E(I_j) + E(X_j)}$$

and

$$(5.5.17) \qquad \sigma_S^2 = \sum_{j=1}^{M} \left[\frac{E(X_j^3)}{3\alpha^2[E(I_j)+E(X_j)]} \right] - m_S^2$$

Thus the probability of overflow in the shared buffer is given by

$$(5.5.18) \qquad R_S(N) = \frac{1}{\sqrt{2\pi}} \int_{(N-m_S)/\sigma_S}^{\infty} e^{-u^2/2} \, du$$

The results for the dynamic case can be compared with those of a fixed partition system in more than one way, depending on specific implementations and the operational requirements of most interest. For example, one may ask for the equilibrium mean number of "overflow" characters in each method. In the fixed-partition case this would be M times the mean amount by which the block-size for each source is exceeded and can be found from the distribution given by (5.5.8) and (5.5.10). For dynamic storage allocation it is the mean amount by which the total buffer is exceeded by $Z(t)$ and is computable from (5.5.15).

To obtain a fair comparison it may be necessary to take into account a significant amount of storage taken up by special characters (e.g., link space) and the space wasted in the last block occupied by a message. A simple, approximate approach for this purpose consists of computing the distribution of the random variable in (5.5.3) from the known message-length distribution and then using this distribution in the above analysis.

As noted earlier, another important performance measure is the frequency at which the nominal buffer size is exceeded. Assuming $Z(t)$ to be a normal distribution, results of this type can be found from the classical theory of Gaussian processes. A useful illustration is given in the Problems. This illustration as well as the analysis of this section follow the results of Gaver and Lewis [20], whose work extends that of Delgavis and Davison [21].

PROBLEMS

5-1. Analyze a paging-drum system (Section 5.2) in which it is best to assume that at most one request per sector can be waiting for service (or currently be in service) at any given time. Assume that on the departure of a given request the time until the next request arrives for the same sector is exponentially distributed with parameter λ. Find the mean number of requests serviced per drum revolution and the mean time requests spend in the system.

5-2. Define an FSCAN system as discussed in Section 5.3 in which the number taken from the queue at the start of each scan is bounded by N, i.e., the number served in each scan is $\min\{i, N\}$, where i was the number waiting at the beginning of the scan. Call the new system NSCAN. You are to investigate the behavior of the NSCAN system when operating in saturation—specifically, under the assumption that the queue always contains at least N requests and that precisely N requests are served on each scan. Use the assumptions and notation of Section 5.3 except that you are not to make the simplifying assumption that the head always traverses all tracks in each scan. Thus the first and last tracks visited are determined as originally described for the FSCAN system. The expected time for a scan is given by $E(S) = NT + \bar{u} + \bar{v}$, where $\bar{u}$ is the expected distance the head must move to reach the first request and $\bar{v}$ is the expected distance the head must move from the first to the last request served. Assuming that track addresses are sampled at random from the unit interval, work out a detailed expression for $E(S)$ in terms of N, T, and a, the head-traversal rate.

5-3. We can define a generalization of the SCAN procedure in Section 5.2 which combines SCAN and FSCAN sequencing. In the mathematical model of Section 5.3 suppose that the unit interval is subdivided into N equal subintervals. Consider a combined discipline according to which the requests served in the ith subinterval in any given scan are just those requests with addresses in the ith subinterval that were in the system when the disk head first entered this interval (from the left or right). In other words, a request for a track address in the ith subinterval which arrives in advance of the current disk-head position must be served in the next scan if the disk head is currently in the ith subinterval.

Let y_i denote the mean time required for the disk head to travel through the first i subintervals in statistical equilibrium. Show that, with the mathematical model of Section 5.3, we have

$$y_i = \frac{ia}{N} \frac{[1 - (N - i - 1)\lambda T/N]}{(1 - \lambda T)(1 + \lambda T/N)}, \quad 1 \le i \le N$$

Verify that in the limit $N \longrightarrow \infty$ the above result becomes (5.3.7) and that for $N = 1$ we have (5.3.8).

5-4. Our purpose is to extend the results of Section 5.3 to include arbitrary distributions of request addresses across the disk [22]. Suppose that we are given a continuous density function $f(x)$ such that the probability that a given arrival has an address in $[x, x + \Delta x]$ is given by $f(x) \Delta x$ [plus a term of order $(\Delta x)^2$]. Using the model and methods of Section 5.3 show that when $\lambda T < 1$

$$\bar{y}_r(x + \Delta x) = \bar{y}_r(x) + a\,\Delta x + \lambda T f(x)\,\Delta x \bar{z}_r(x)$$

plus a term of order $(\Delta x)^2$, where $\bar{y}_r(x)$ is the equilibrium mean time for the head to move from position 0 to position x and $\bar{z}_r(x)$ is the mean time to move from x to 0 and back to x. Using Little's argument show that

$$\bar{z}_r(x) = \frac{2a\lambda T}{1 - \lambda T} F(x) + 2ax$$

where $F(x) = \int_0^x f(t)\,dt$. Proceed to show that

$$\bar{y}_r(x) = ax + \frac{a\lambda^2 T^2}{1 - \lambda T} F^2(x) + 2a\lambda T \int_0^x tf(t)\,dt$$

Defining $\bar{y}_l(x)$ as the average time to move from position 1 to position x in equilibrium, show similarly that when $\lambda T < 1$

$$\bar{y}_l(x) = ax + \frac{a\lambda^2 T^2}{1 - \lambda T}[1 - F(1 - x)]^2 + 2a\lambda T \int_0^x tf(1 - t)\,dt$$

Using the approach in the text prove that

$$\bar{w}(x) = \frac{2a}{1 - \lambda T}\left\{\left[\left(x - \frac{1}{2}\right)(1 - \lambda T) + \lambda T\left(F(x) - \frac{1}{2}\right)\right]^2 + \frac{1}{4}\right\}$$

and that this reduces to (5.3.16) when $f(x)$ is the uniform density.

5-5. Examine buffer storage models in which messages are to be regarded as bulk arrivals of characters, all characters of a message being stored in the buffer effectively simultaneously at the time of arrival (assuming sufficient buffer space). Begin by postulating a given, stationary message-length (bulk-size) distribution, a finite buffer of N characters, and exponential or geometric message interarrival times. Although closed-form results are generally difficult to obtain, the assumption of a bound on message lengths enables a finite Markov chain analysis for the equilibrium buffer occupancy.

In fully defining such a model note particularly that a decision has to be made as to what happens when a message of k characters arrives when the buffer has only $j < k$ empty cells. For example, one possibility is to discard the entire message along with all subsequent messages whose size exceeds available space; i.e., an arriving message is stored if and only if sufficient space exists at the time of arrival.

5-6. Consider the linked-list buffer model leading to (5.5.4) for the optimal number of characters per list cell. Let us refine the model by removing the approximation governing the mean number of characters in the last cell. Suppose that the message length m has a distribution function $F(x)$ with mean value $\bar{m}$. Let b and c be defined as in Section 5.5 and let $a = b - c$. Show that the expected overflow into the last cell is

$$E(V) = \bar{m} - a \sum_{k=1}^{\infty} [1 - F(ka)]$$

Verify that when we assume $F(x)$ to be exponential with mean $\bar{m}$ we have

$$E(V) = \frac{\bar{m}(e^{a/\bar{m}} - 1) - a}{e^{a/\bar{m}} - 1}$$

which in the limit $\bar{m} \longrightarrow \infty$ becomes $a/2$.

5-7. We want to analyze the motion of a Poisson, FIFO queue [23] in buffer storage under the constraint that messages must be stored sequentially as illustrated in Fig. P5-7. New messages are always placed at the end of the

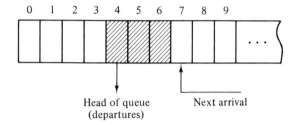

Fig. P5-7

queue. Messages removed from the queue clearly cause the head of the queue to move one position to the right; however, we shall assume that when the queue becomes empty the next message to arrive is placed in the first cell location, thus resetting the head of the queue. For simplicity assume the buffer size to be unbounded.

Let π_{ij} denote the stationary (joint) probability that the address (relative location) of the head of the queue is i and that the queue length is j; e.g., in Fig. P5-7 $i = 4$ and $j = 3$. Let λ, μ, and $\rho = \lambda/\mu$ denote the arrival rate, departure rate, and utilization factor, respectively. Verify the following equilibrium equations for the π_{ij}:

$$\pi_{0j} = \frac{\rho}{1 + \rho} \pi_{0(j-1)} \quad (j \geq 1), \qquad \pi_{00} = \frac{1}{\rho} \sum_{m=0}^{\infty} \pi_{m1}$$

$$\pi_{i1} = \frac{1}{1 + \rho} \pi_{(i-1)2} \quad (i \geq 1)$$

$$\pi_{ij} = \frac{1}{1 + \rho} \pi_{(i-1)(j+1)} + \frac{\rho}{1 + \rho} \pi_{i(j-1)} \quad (i > 0, j > 1)$$

Show that these equations are satisfied by

$$\pi_{ij} = \begin{cases} \pi_{00} \left(\dfrac{\rho}{1 + \rho} \right)^j, & i = 0 \\[2ex] \pi_{00} \left[\dfrac{\rho}{(1 + \rho)^2} \right]^i \left(\dfrac{\rho}{1 + \rho} \right)^j \dfrac{j}{2i + j} \binom{2i + j}{i}, & i > 0 \end{cases}$$

Define the bivariate generating function

$$M(z_1, z_2) = \sum_{i=0}^{\infty} \sum_{j=0}^{\infty} \pi_{ij} z_1^i z_2^j$$

and show that

$$M(z_1, z_2) = \frac{\rho(1 - \rho)z_2 + (1 - \rho)(z_2 - z_1) - z_1 z_2 M_1(z_1)}{(z_2 - z_1) + \rho(1 - z_2)z_2}$$

where

$$M_1(z_1) = \sum_{i=0}^{\infty} \pi_{i1} z_1^i$$

Work out the mean location of the head of the queue

$$\lim_{z_1 \to 1} \frac{dM(z_1, 1)}{dz_1} = \left(\frac{\rho}{1 - \rho}\right)^2$$

and the mean queue length

$$\lim_{z_2 \to 1} \frac{dM(1, z_2)}{dz_2} = \frac{\rho}{1 - \rho}$$

5-8. It is possible to generalize the model of Section 5.5 by allowing for a non-zero, buffer readout time β, thus removing the discontinuities in the sample functions $Z(t)$. An illustrative sample function is shown in Fig. P5-8, where $Z'(t)$ denotes the new buffer occupancy process. Show that

$$m = \lim_{t \to \infty} \mathrm{E}(Z'(t)) = \frac{1}{2\alpha} \frac{\mathrm{E}(X^2)(1 + \beta/\alpha)}{\mathrm{E}(X)(1 + \beta/\alpha) + \mathrm{E}(I)}$$

$$\lim_{t \to \infty} \mathrm{Var}(Z'(t)) = \frac{1}{3\alpha^2} \frac{\mathrm{E}(X^3)(1 + \beta/\alpha)}{\mathrm{E}(X)(1 + \beta/\alpha) + \mathrm{E}(I)} - m^2$$

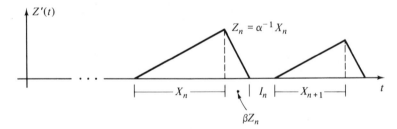

Fig. P5-8   Non-zero readout times.

5-9. A performance measure of interest in the buffer design problem is the mean number of times the nominal buffer size is exceeded. Let $Z'_S(t)$ denote the Gaussian process approximating the sum of M individual processes $Z'_i(t)$ ($1 \leq i \leq M$) and let each individual process be as defined in Problem 5-8.

In general, level-crossing statistics depend on the (stationary) covariance function $C(\tau) = E[Z'_S(t + \tau)Z'_S(t)] - E^2[Z'_S(t)]$ of the process $Z'_S(t)$. Specifically, let $\bar{U}(l, T)$ denote the long-run mean number of times that the process $Z'_S(t)$ crosses the level $l \geq 0$ from below in a time interval T. Since $Z'_S(t)$ is Gaussian, we may apply Rice's classical result [24]:

$$\bar{U}(l, T) = \frac{T}{2\pi\sigma} e^{-(l-m)^2/2\sigma^2} \left\{ -\frac{d^2C(\tau)}{d\tau^2} \bigg|_{\tau=0} \right\}^{1/2}$$

where m and σ^2 are the mean and variance of $Z'_S(t)$. [The continuity of the sample functions $Z'_i(t)$ is needed for the above result [24]; $Z_i(t)$ does not have this property.] To obtain the second derivative of $C(\tau)$ we can make use of the result [25] that it is equal to the covariance function of the derivative process $dZ'_S(t)/dt$. Using the arguments of Section 5.4 verify that

$$\lim_{t\to\infty} \Pr\left[\frac{dZ'_i(t)}{dt} = \alpha^{-1}\right] = \frac{E(X)}{E(X)(1 + \beta/\alpha) + E(I)}$$

$$\lim_{t\to\infty} \Pr\left[\frac{dZ'_i(t)}{dt} = -\beta^{-1}\right] = \frac{(\beta/\alpha)E(X)}{E(X)(1 + \beta/\alpha) + E(I)}$$

$$\lim_{t\to\infty} \Pr\left[\frac{dZ'_i(t)}{dt} = 0\right] = \frac{E(I)}{E(X)(1 + \beta/\alpha) + E(I)}$$

and hence that

$$-\frac{d^2C}{d\tau^2}\bigg|_{\tau=0} = \lim_{t\to\infty} \text{Var}\left(\frac{dZ'_S}{dt}\right)$$

$$= \frac{1 + \alpha/\beta}{\alpha^2} \frac{NE(X)}{E(X)(1 + \beta/\alpha) + E(I)}$$

5-10. Consider the queueing network shown in Fig. P5-10. Assume that the number in the system stays constant at N; i.e., as soon as a departure occurs from the IO_2 processor a new arrival immediately enters the IO_1 queue. Following a CPU service a job joins the IO_2 queue with probability α and the IO_3 queue with probability $1 - \alpha$. Exponential service times are to be assumed. Analyze this system using the methods of Section 5.4. (The I/O

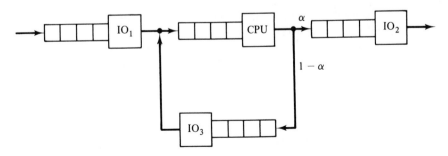

Fig. P5-10   Model of Problem 5-10.

queues shown as IO_1 and IO_2 are meant to model the initial loading and terminal unloading associated with job execution.)

5-11. (Kobayashi [26]). In this problem we shall generalize Problem 5-10 and the model of Section 5.4. In particular, consider the "open" system in Fig. P5-11, where λ is the rate of Poisson arrivals to the system, λ_i is the arrival rate to the ith processor, and $\mu_i(n_i)$ is the (state-dependent) parameter of the exponential service times at the ith processor, given as a function of the number n_i currently in and waiting for the ith processor. Observe that

$$\lambda_j = \lambda \delta_{j0} + \sum_{i=0}^{N} \lambda_i p_{ij}$$

where $\delta_{i0} = 1$ for $i = 0$ and is 0 otherwise and where p_{ij} is the stationary probability that an output of the ith processor proceeds to the jth processor. Let $p_i(n_i)$ be the equilibrium probability of n_i waiting and being served in the ith processor, and let $\mathbf{n} = (n_0, n_1, \ldots, n_N)$ denote the state variable of the system.

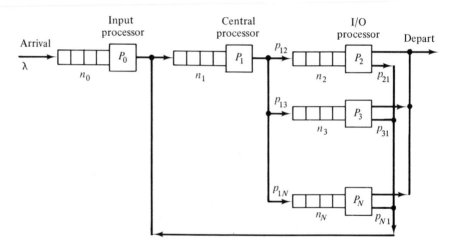

Fig. P5-11   Queueing network model.

Use the fact that the output of a Poisson queue is itself a Poisson process (Problems 4-8 and 4-11) to verify that the distribution $\{p_i(n_i)\}$ is determined by the result for an independent Poisson queue with arrival and service time parameters λ_i and $\mu_i(n_i)$. Hence from Section 4.3

$$p_i(n_i) = p_i(0) \prod_{n=1}^{n_i} \frac{\lambda_i}{\mu_i(n)}, \quad n_i = 0, 1, 2, \ldots$$

and

$$p(\mathbf{n}) = \prod_{i=0}^{N} p_i(n_i)$$

where $p(\mathbf{n}) = \Pr[\mathbf{n} = (n_0, \ldots, n_N)]$.

Assuming that $\mu_i(n_i) = \mu_i$ and letting $\rho_i = \lambda_i/\mu_i$ show that

$$p(\mathbf{n}) = \prod_{i=0}^{N} (1 - \rho_i) \prod_{i=0}^{N} \rho_i^{n_i}$$

The natural generalization of this model to arbitrary networks is treated by Jackson [27]. Note that, as in Section 4.3, the arrival rate may also be state-dependent, thus providing the means to study a number of variations in system operation. For example, one can rather easily show [26] that the closed-system results of Section 5.4 can be obtained in this way.

5-12. With reference to the model of Section 5.3, the so-called CSCAN rule differs from the SCAN rule in the following way. Scans in which requests are served occur in one (fixed) direction only; following a complete "service" scan the the head is returned to the starting position at rate a. Using the remaining assumptions and notation of Section 5.3 show that for CSCAN

$$w(x) = \frac{a}{1 - \lambda T}, \quad 0 \le x \le 1$$

Compare this result with those for SCAN and FSCAN.

5-13. For the paging drum of Section 2 you are to compute the generating function $H(z)$ of the pmf $\{h_i\}$ for the number of requests in a given sector queue as seen by departures (processed requests), and verify that $H(z)$ is identical to (5.2.21). To proceed, first verify that

$$g_n = g_0 f_n(T) + \sum_{i=1}^{n+1} g_i f_{n-i+1}(T) \qquad n = 1, 2, \ldots$$

defines the equilibrium probability that the read/write head encounters n $(n \ge 1)$ requests when it passes the beginning of a given sector. Next, show that

$$h_n = \sum_{i=1}^{n+1} \frac{g_i}{1 - g_0} f_{n-i+1}\left(\frac{T}{N}\right)$$

5-14. (Tasks waiting for console messages [28]). Consider a set of n independent, statistically identical tasks, each receiving messages from consoles concurrently. Assume that characters arrive from each console at exponential rate λ, and are deposited into the buffer assigned to the corresponding task. The time from the moment a task picks up a message from its buffer until next it requests to pick up a message is exponentially distributed with parameter μ. Each message consists of a string of symbols followed by an end-of-line (EOL) symbol; $\{q_j\}_{j\ge1}$ is the pmf for the EOL position j and $Q(z)$ is its generating function. If a task requests to pick up a message but no EOL symbol is in its buffer, the task is blocked until an EOL character arrives.

When there is at least one EOL symbol in the buffer, a task removes the entire contents of the buffer.

A. Suppose the random variable x denotes the number of symbols to accumulate in a buffer during the computing interval of a task. Show

$$\Pr[x = k] = (1 - \sigma)\sigma^k \qquad k = 0, 1, 2, \ldots, \qquad \sigma = \frac{\lambda}{\lambda + \mu}$$

B. To find $E(w)$, the mean blocked time, proceed as follows. Let j denote the position of the EOL symbol and x the number of symbols to have accumulated since the last pickup. Then

$$E(w \mid j, x) = \begin{cases} 0 & x \geq j \\ \dfrac{j - x}{\lambda} & x < j \end{cases}$$

Use this to show that $E(w) = 1/\lambda[m - \lambda/\mu(1 - Q(\lambda/(\lambda + \mu)))]$, where $m = E(j)$. Show that the probability a task blocks on arrival is $1 - Q(\lambda/(\lambda + \mu))$.

C. Suppose the position j of the EOL symbol is geometrically distributed with parameter q: $q_j = q(1 - q)^{j-1}$, $j \geq 1$, so that $E(j) = m = 1/q$. Show that the distribution function for waiting time is defined by

$$dF(w) = \frac{\alpha\mu}{\alpha + \mu} e^{-\alpha w} dw \qquad w > 0$$

$$F(0) = \frac{\alpha}{\alpha + \mu}$$

where $\alpha = q\lambda$.

D. Assuming there is sufficient buffer space to hold the messages for all the tasks, show that the

$$\Pr[k \text{ tasks are blocked}] = \binom{n}{k}(1 - \beta)^k \beta^{n-k} \qquad k = 0, 1, \ldots, n$$

where
$$\beta = \frac{1/\mu}{E(w) + 1/\mu}$$

is the fraction of time a task spends waiting.

REFERENCES

1. FIFE, D. W., and J. L. SMITH, "Transmission capacity of disk storage systems with concurrent arm positioning." *IEEE Trans. EC-14*, 4 (Aug. 1965), 575–582.

2. DENNING, P. J., "Effects of scheduling on file memory operations." *Proc. AFIPS Conf. 30* 1967 Spring Joint Computer Conference 9–21.

3. ABATE J., H. DUBNER, and S. B. WEINBERG, "Queueing analysis of the IBM 2314 disk storage facility." *J. ACM 15*, 4 (Oct. 1968), 577–589.

4. SEAMAN, P. H., R. A. LAIRD, and T. L. WILSON, "On teleprocessing system design. Pt IV: Analysis of auxiliary-storage activity." *IBM Sys. J. 5*, 3 (1966), 158–170.

5. FRANK, H., "Analysis and optimization of disk storage devices for time-sharing systems." *J. ACM 16*, 4 (Oct. 1969), 602–620.

6. TEOREY, T. J., and T. B. PINKERTON, "A comparative analysis of disk scheduling policies," in *Proc. 3rd Symp. Op. Sys. Princ.* (Oct. 1971), 114–121.

7. KNUTH, D. E., *The Art of Computer Programming* (Vol. I). Addison-Wesley, Reading, Mass. (1968).

8. ABATE, J., and H. DUBNER, "Optimizing the performance of a drum-like storage." *IEEE Trans. Comp. C-18*, 11 (Nov. 1969), 992–996.

9. COFFMAN, E. G., JR., "Analysis of a drum input/output queue under scheduled operation in a paged computer system." *J. ACM 16*, 1 (Jan. 1969), 73–90. [Erratum: *J. ACM 16*, 4 (Oct. 1969), 646.]

10. WEINGARTEN, A., "The Eschenbach drum scheme." *Comm. ACM 9*, 7 (July 1966), 509–512.

11. BURGE, W. H., and A. G. KONHEIM, "An accessing model." *J. ACM 18*, 3 (July 1971), 400–404.

12. FELLER, W., *An Introduction to Probability Theory and Its Applications* (Vol. II). Wiley, New York (1966).

13. COX, D. R., *Renewal Theory*. Methuen, London (1962).

14. WALLACE, V. L., and R. S. ROSENBERG, "Markovian models and numerical analysis of computer system behavior." *Proc. AFIPS SJCC 28* (1966), 141–148.

15. IRANI, K. B., and V. L. WALLACE, "On network linguistics and the conversational design of queueing networks." *J. ACM 18*, 4 (Oct. 1971), 616–629.

16. MITRANI, I., "Non-priority multiprogramming systems under heavy demand conditions from a customer's point of view." Technical report No. 11, *Computing Laboratory*, University of Newcastle upon Tyne, Newcastle upon Tyne, England (Aug. 1970).

17. GORDON, W. J., and G. F. NEWELL, "Closed queueing systems with exponential servers." *Opns. Res. 15*, 2 (Apr. 1967), 254–265.

18. BUZEN, J., *Queueing Network Models of Multiprogramming*. Ph.D. thesis, Division of Engineering and Applied Physics, Harvard Univ., Cambridge, Mass. (June 1971).

19. LEWIS, P. A. W., and G. S. SHEDLER, "A cyclic-queue model of system overhead in multiprogrammed computer systems." *J. ACM 18*, 2 (Apr. 1971), 199–220.

20. GAVER, D. P., JR., and P. A. W. LEWIS, "Probability models for buffer storage allocation problems." *J. ACM 18*, 2 (Apr. 1971), 186–198.

21. DELGAVIS, I., and G. DAVISON, "Storage requirements for a data exchange." *IBM Sys. J. 3*, 1 (1964), 2–31.

22. COFFMAN, E. G., JR., L. A. KLIMKO, and B. RYAN, "Analysis of scanning policies for reducing disk seek times." *SIAM J. Computing* (to appear).

23. COFFMAN, E. G., JR., and A. C. MCKELLER, "On the motion of an unbounded, Markov queue in random-access storage." *IEEE Trans. Comp. C-17*, 6 (June 1968), 600–603.

24. CRAMER, H., and M. R. LEADBETTER, *Stationary and Related Stochastic Processes*. Wiley, New York (1967).

25. YAGLOM, A. M., *An Introduction to the Theory of Stationary Random Functions*. Prentice-Hall, Englewood Cliffs, N.J. (1962).

26. KOBAYASHI, H., "Some Recent Progress in Analytic Studies of System Performance," *IBM Research Report*. T. J. Watson Research Center, Yorktown Heights, N.Y. (1972).

27. JACKSON, J., "Job shop-like queueing systems." *Manag. Sci. 10*, 1 (1963), 131–142.

28. DENNING, P. J., "A model for console behavior in multiuser computers." *Comm. ACM 11*, 9 (Sept. 1968), 605–612.

6 STORAGE ALLOCATION IN PAGING SYSTEMS

6.1. INTRODUCTION

The formalization of memory management (or storage allocation) problems has taken place quite recently, compared to that of scheduling problems. The topics studied include optimal demand paging algorithms [1], paging algorithms for efficient simulation design of memory hierarchies [2], Markov chain analyses of certain paging algorithms [3], and the prediction of performance of extended, paged memory systems [4]. This chapter will present a number of the more important results. However, we have chosen to restrict our coverage of storage allocation problems to paging systems, in which memory is allocated in blocks of equal size. There are few results from mathematical models of storage allocation in general systems, for even the simplest problems tend to be rather difficult. For a general discussion see Knuth [5]; more recent results bearing on Knuth's treatment can be found in [6, 7]. The problems of storage allocation peculiar to multiprogramming systems will be deferred to Chapter 7.

We shall confine our attention to a system consisting of two memory levels, main and auxiliary. We shall assume that a program's name space N is divided into pages each consisting of c contiguous addresses and that the system's main memory space M is divided into page frames each consisting of c contiguous location addresses. Throughout this chapter we shall be concerned only with the indices of the pages (or page frames) which are referenced but not with individual words within pages. Therefore we shall regard $N = \{1, 2, \ldots, n\}$ as a set of pages and $M = \{1, 2, \ldots, m\}$ as a set of page frames, and $1 \leq m \leq n$. No confusion will result from the ambiguity in this notation, since it will always be stated whether an integer denotes a page or page frame.

At each moment of time t there is a page map $f_t\colon N \longrightarrow M \cup \{0\}$ such that

$$f_t(x) = \begin{cases} y, & \text{if page } x \text{ resides in page frame } y \text{ at time } t \\ 0, & \text{if page } x \text{ is missing from } M \text{ at time } t \end{cases}$$

Physically, the page map is part of address-translation hardware interposed between the processor and the memory. When the processor generates an address α, this hardware computes a memory location address $\beta = f_t(x)c + w$ ($0 \leq w < c$), where x is determined from $\alpha = xc + w$. By making use of the (usual) property that c is a power of 2, the hardware is organized to make this computation very efficient. If $f_t(x) = 0$, the hardware generates a *page fault interrupt* that signals an appropriate system task to secure the missing page from auxiliary memory, place it in main memory, update the map f_t, and attempt the reference again.

The average time to access a word when the page containing it is in M is Δ_M, and the average time to transfer a page between auxiliary and main memory is Δ_A. An important system parameter is the speed ratio $\Delta = \Delta_A/\Delta_M$. Even though many existing systems are built on the assumption that $\Delta \geq 10^4$, it is important to realize that new memory organizations having a Δ on the order of 10 or 100 may not be uncommon; therefore one must try not to base any key assumptions in modeling on the magnitude of Δ.

A program's paging behavior for given input is described in machine-independent terms by its (page) *reference string*, which is a sequence

$$\omega = r_1 r_2 \ldots r_t \ldots, \qquad r_t \in N, t \geq 1$$

The discrete time parameter $t = 1, 2, 3, \ldots$ represents instants in "process" or "execution" time, and $r_t = i$ means that page i is referenced at the tth reference. We use the notation N^T for the set of all reference strings of length T. N^+ will denote the set of all finite-length strings over N, not including the empty string.

Corresponding to the references $r_1 r_2 \ldots r_t \ldots$ is a sequence of instants in real time $a_1 a_2 \ldots a_t \ldots$ such that a_t is the instant at which r_t is made. The real time elapsing between t and $t + 1$ in process time is approximately

$$(6.1.1) \qquad a_{t+1} - a_t = \begin{cases} \Delta_M, & \text{if } r_{t+1} \text{ is in memory} \\ \Delta_M + \Delta_A, & \text{otherwise} \end{cases}$$

Later we shall introduce a *fault rate*, $F(\omega)$, defined as the number of page faults encountered while processing the reference string ω, normalized by the length of ω. If page-waiting and execution intervals are disjoint, then the mean real time elapsing between t and $t + 1$ of process time is approximately

$$(6.1.2) \qquad E[a_{t+1} - a_t] = \Delta_M(1 - F(\omega)) + (\Delta_M + \Delta_A)F(\omega)$$
$$= \Delta_M(1 + \Delta F(\omega))$$

Thus we have a simple, although generally approximate, means of relating the results we obtain in process time to the observed real-time behavior of the program. This fact along with the desire for simplicity justifies our restriction to the problems of characterizing process time behavior of programs.

If the reference string ω of length T is to be regarded as a random sequence, we shall assume the existence of a probability mass function $p(\omega)$ over N^T such that $p(\omega)$ denotes the probability of ω's occurrence. The corresponding probability models will be most effective in assessing the performance of various paging algorithms.

6.2. PAGING ALGORITHMS

A paging algorithm implements three subpolicies. The *fetch policy* determines which page, and when, will be brought into main memory; the *placement policy* chooses an available page frame into which a fetched page is deposited; and the *replacement policy* chooses which page or pages will be removed from main memory in order to make space available for new pages.

Since we are assuming that page frames are logically equivalent, the placement policy can have no effect on a paging algorithm's behavior. (Typically, the placement policy would invoke the replacement policy k times to obtain k page frames and would assign them in the order they were obtained.) Thus a paging algorithm's behavior depends on only the fetch and replacement policies. Under *demand paging*, defined formally below, a demand fetch policy is used in which only the missing page is fetched and replacements occur only when the memory is full; thus a demand paging algorithm's behavior depends only on its replacement policy.

Unless stated otherwise, we shall assume that the page size c, memory size m, speed ratio Δ, and manner of distributing a program's words among its pages are fixed. Moreover, only one program—the one with the given page set N—will occupy main memory, and it will not be interrupted except for page faults. Under these assumptions, the only improvements we can effect on system behavior will be through the paging algorithm.

Before proceeding with a more formal description we shall introduce some notational conventions to be used throughout this chapter. Sets will always be denoted by uppercase (Italic) letters. Elements of sets will normally be denoted with lowercase letters. When the left-hand side of an equation denotes a set the operators $+$ (plus) and $-$ (minus) that appear on the right are to be interpreted as set addition and subtraction. Also, the equation $S = S' + x - y$ should be taken to mean $S = S' + \{x\} - \{y\}$. With these conventions the notation will be unambiguous except for the occasional appearance of a function $R(\cdot)$. $R(\cdot)$ denotes a *replacement page* (an element of N) so that equations such as $S = S' + x - R(\cdot)$, for example, should be taken to mean $S = S' + \{x\} - \{R(\cdot)\}$. No difficulties should arise since the above conventions are immediately suggested by the context of the equations appearing in this chapter.

In the abstract, a *paging algorithm* A is a mechanism for processing a reference string $\omega = r_1 r_2 \ldots r_t \ldots$ and generating in response a sequence of *memory states* $S_0 S_1 \ldots S_t \ldots$, where S_0 is a given initial memory state. Each memory state S_t is the set of pages from N which reside in M at time t; they satisfy the conditions

$$(6.2.1) \qquad S_t \subseteq N, \qquad |S_t| \leq m, \qquad r_t \in S_t \quad (t > 0)$$

where $|S|$ denotes the number of elements in set S. For convenience we shall take the initial memory state to be empty, i.e., $S_0 = \varnothing$, although this does not affect the generality of our treatment. Moreover, S_t and S_{t-1} are related by

$$(6.2.2) \qquad\qquad S_t = S_{t-1} + X_t - Y_t$$

where $X_t \subseteq N - S_{t-1}$ is the set of fetched pages and $Y_t \subseteq S_{t-1}$ is the set of replaced pages.

To determine X_t and Y_t at each time t, the paging algorithm A must maintain internal records. We shall represent these records by a set Q of *control states*, with an initial control state q_0. A *configuration* of the algorithm is any pair (S, q) in which $|S| \leq m$ and $q \in Q$. Associated with the algorithm is a *transition function* g_A such that

$$(6.2.3) \qquad\qquad g_A(S, q, x) = (S', q'), \quad x \in S'$$

where (S, q) is the current configuration, (S', q') the next configuration, and x the reference causing the transition. In particular, the memory state sequence $S_0 S_1 \ldots S_t \ldots$ is contained in the configuration sequence $(S_0, q_0)(S_1, q_1) \cdots (S_t, q_t) \ldots$ generated by

$$(6.2.4) \qquad\qquad (S_t, q_t) = g_A(S_{t-1}, q_{t-1}, r_t), \quad t \geq 1$$

In most of our discussions we shall not deal explicitly with the control states of A.

A paging algorithm A is a *demand paging algorithm* if for a given $m > 0$ the transition function has the property that $g_A(S, q, x) = (S', q')$ implies that

$$(6.2.5) \qquad S' = \begin{cases} S, & \text{if } x \in S \\ S + x, & \text{if } x \notin S, |S| < m \\ S + x - y \text{ for some } y \in S, & \text{if } x \notin S, |S| = m \end{cases}$$

Thus we have $0 \leq |Y_t| \leq |X_t| \leq 1$ under demand paging. The choice y of page to be replaced is, of course, the prerogative of algorithm A. We shall use

$R(S, q, x)$ to denote the page A replaces from S when in configuration (S, q). In (6.2.5), $y = R(S, q, x)$.

In a reference string $r_1 r_2 \ldots r_t \ldots$, the *forward distance* $d_t(x)$ at time t for page x is the distance to the first reference to x after time t:

$$(6.2.6) \qquad d_t(x) = \begin{cases} k, & \text{if } r_{t+k} \text{ is the first occurrence} \\ & \text{of } x \text{ in } r_{t+1}, r_{t+2}, \ldots \\ \infty, & \text{if } x \text{ does not appear in } r_{t+1}, r_{t+2} \ldots \end{cases}$$

Similarly, the *backward distance* $b_t(x)$ is the distance to the most recent reference to x:

$$(6.2.7) \qquad b_t(x) = \begin{cases} k, & \text{if } r_{t-k} \text{ is the last occurrence} \\ & \text{of } x \text{ in } r_1 r_2 \ldots r_t \\ \infty, & \text{if } x \text{ does not appear in } r_1 r_2 \ldots r_t \end{cases}$$

Examples

The following are examples of common demand paging algorithms, described using the formalism developed above. Let $S = S_t$ denote the current memory state, $x = r_{t+1}$ the next reference, and $S' = S_{t+1}$ the next memory state. Since we are stating replacement rules only, we shall suppose that $|S| = m$ and $x \notin S$. As above, $R(S, q, x)$ denotes the page in S that is replaced, so that

$$S' = S + x - R(S, q, x)$$

The following examples exhibit a similar structure in the sense that the replacement page is chosen in each case as the least or greatest element in a linear ordering of some subset of N. After a brief, prose description of the replacement rules this common structure will be demonstrated in a more formal description.

1. LRU (least recently used). The page in S that is replaced is the one with largest backward distance. Thus

$$R(S, q, x) = y \text{ if and only if } b_t(y) = \max_{z \in S}[b_t(z)]$$

2. B_0 (Belady's optimal algorithm [8]). The page replaced has the largest forward distance. The tie-breaking rule uses a lexicographic ordering. (Note that the tie-breaking rule can have no effect on fault-rate performance, since ties can only involve pages with infinite forward distance.) Thus

$$R(S, q, x) = y \text{ if and only if } y = \min_{z \in S^*}[z]$$

where $z \in S^*$ if and only if $d_t(z) = \max_{u \in S}[d_t(u)]$.

3. LFU (least frequently used). The page replaced is the one having received least use (number of references). The tie-breaking rule is LRU. More formally, let $f_t(x)$ denote the number of references to x in $r_1 \ldots r_t$. Then

$$R(S, q, x) = y \text{ if and only if } b_t(y) = \max_{z \in S^*}[b_t(z)]$$

where $z \in S^*$ if and only if $f_t(z) = \min_{u \in S}[f_t(u)]$.

4. FIFO (first-in-first-out). The page replaced is the one having been in memory for the longest time. Define $g_t(z) = i$ as the largest integer less than or equal to t such that $S_i - S_{i-1} = r_i = z$. Then

$$R(S, q, x) = y \text{ if and only if } g_t(y) = \min_{z \in S}[g_t(z)]$$

5. LIFO (last-in-first-out). The page replaced has been in memory for the least time. That is,

$$R(S, q, x) = y \text{ if and only if } g_t(y) = \max_{z \in S}[g_t(z)]$$

If $R(S, q, x)$ is independent of $r_{t+2}r_{t+3} \ldots$, we call A a nonlookahead algorithm. The algorithms LRU, LFU, LIFO, and FIFO are examples of nonlookahead algorithms, whereas B_0 is a lookahead algorithm. Nonlookahead algorithms are realizable in the sense that they operate without any prior knowledge of the reference string. Clearly, probability models in which page reference strings are modeled as random sequences constitute a natural approach to an analysis of their performance. (We shall return to the analysis of such models in Section 6.6.) Although the B_0 algorithm is unrealizable, it provides a useful benchmark against which to compare the performance of the realizable algorithms. The proof that B_0 minimizes the number of page faults for each reference string is given in the next section.

It is of some interest to observe that the basic model adopted in this chapter is not significantly different in structure from the model of Chapters 2 and 3. For execution sequences we have page reference strings and for system states we have configurations. Of course, a major difference is that we shall not be concerned with precedence structures related to page referencing.

6.3. OPTIMAL PAGING ALGORITHMS

6.3.1. Cost Function

From (6.2.2) the memory states S_t and S_{t-1} are related by $S_t = S_{t-1} + X_t - Y_t$, where $X_t \cap Y_t = \varnothing$. The *cost* generated by paging algorithm A, operating on reference string $\omega = r_1 r_2 \ldots r_T$ in a memory of size m, is denoted by $C(A, m, \omega)$. In general, cost is some function of the sequences $\{X_t\}$ and

$\{Y_t\}$ since these sequences represent transactions with the auxiliary memory. In practice, the component of cost due to $\{Y_t\}$ tends to be some fixed fraction of the component due to $\{X_t\}$, and so we can simplify the definition of $C(A, m, \omega)$ by ignoring $\{Y_t\}$. Now suppose that $h(k)$ represents the cost of a single auxiliary memory transaction involving a group of k pages. For simplicity we shall assume that a single page transfer incurs unit cost and that

$$(6.3.1) \qquad h(0) = 0, \qquad h(k) \geq h(1) = 1$$

We also note that in systems of practical interest $h(k)$ is monotonically nondecreasing in k. The rate at which $h(k)$ increases with k affects the optimality of demand paging algorithms, as we shall see shortly. We shall define cost to be

$$(6.3.2) \qquad C(A, m, \omega) = \sum_{t=1}^{T} h(|X_t|)$$

If A is a demand paging algorithm, then $|X_t| \leq 1$ for $1 \leq t \leq T$, and the cost is simply

$$(6.3.3) \qquad C(A, m, \omega) = \sum_{t=1}^{T} |X_t|$$

When a probability distribution is defined over N^+, we define the *expected cost* as

$$(6.3.4) \qquad C(A, m) = \sum_{\omega \in N^+} p(\omega)C(A, m, \omega)$$

A paging algorithm is optimal if it minimizes $C(A, m, \omega)$ for all m and ω. However, when we deal with nonlookahead algorithms we shall assume a given distribution $p(\omega)$ over N^+ and define A to be optimal with respect to $p(\omega)$ if it minimizes $C(A, m)$.

A one-page transfer takes time $T_w + T_t$, where T_w is a waiting time (e.g., queueing delays, latency delays in rotating-medium auxiliary stores) and T_t the page transmission time. A k-page transfer will take time $k(T_w + T_t)$ if the auxiliary memory uses electronic selection (e.g., core memory) or time $T'_w + kT'_t$ if the auxiliary memory uses rotational selection (e.g., disk or drum). Normally, $T'_w > T_w$. In the former case we would have $h(k) = k$, in the latter case $h(k) < k$; e.g., $h(k) = 1 + a(k - 1)$ for some $0 < a < 1$, where $k \geq 1$. Theorem 6.1, given shortly, shows that $h(k) \geq k$ implies that the class of optimal (cost-minimizing) algorithms must include a demand paging algorithm. Even though the case $h(k) < k$ occurs frequently in current practice (core-drum systems), there is no simple condition on h which determines when an optimal demand algorithm exists; the condition will in general depend on the probability assignment to reference strings and on the magnitude of $k - h(k)$.

The case $h(k) = k$ will become predominant as the use of semiconductor main memory and core-memory backing stores increases (i.e., the *cache* or *slave memory*). In this case, Theorem 6.1 demonstrates that the system designer may confine his attention to demand algorithms when looking for optimal or near-optimal ones. For this reason and because current results are largely confined to the many systems that are committed by their implementation to using demand paging [whether or not $h(k) < k$], we shall restrict our attention to demand paging algorithms following Theorem 6.1, and the term *algorithm* will refer to *demand paging algorithm*.

Theorem 6.1

Suppose that $h(k) \geq k$. For any given paging algorithm A there exists a demand paging algorithm A' such that

$$C(A', m, \omega) \leq C(A, m, \omega)$$

for all m and ω.

Proof. The proof is based on the idea of removing situations in which A (which may do some prepaging) may bring into memory a page which later is removed without having been referenced. The demand algorithm A' does this by remembering in its control states what decisions A would make but deferring them until a page fault occurs. Assume that A generates a memory state sequence $\{S_t\}$, which is equivalent to the sequence $\{(X_t, Y_t)\}$ according to the relation $S_t = S_{t-1} + X_t - Y_t$ in which $X_t \cap Y_t = \varnothing$. Similarly, A' generates $\{S'_t\}$. Algorithm A' simulates A, keeping track of placements made by A but not yet by A' in the sets P_t (deferred placements) and of replacements made by A but not yet by A' in the sets R_t (deferred replacements). The relation between S_t and S'_t is

$$S'_t = S_t + R_t - P_t$$

A page is a deferred placement at time t if it was so at time $t - 1$ or was fetched by A at time t but not if it is placed by A' by time t; therefore

$$P_t = (P_{t-1} + X_t - Y_t) - (S'_{t-1} + r_t)$$

The new memory state S'_t is defined as $S'_t = S'_{t-1} + X'_t - Y'_t$, where X'_t is empty if $r_t \in S'_{t-1}$ and is equal to r_t otherwise; and Y'_t is empty if X'_t is, or if $|S'_{t-1}| < m$, and $Y'_t = \{y\}$ for some $y \in R_{t-1} + Y_t$ otherwise. (Note that A' may not be unique since $R_{t-1} + Y_t$ may contain more than one page.) A page is a deferred replacement at time t if it was so at time $t - 1$ or was replaced by A at time t, and only if it is in memory at time t; therefore

$$R_t = (R_{t-1} + Y_t - X_t) \cap S_t'$$

By construction, every page placed by A' must also have been placed by A, implying that $\sum_t |X_t| \geq \sum_t |X_t'|$. Therefore

$$C(A, m, \omega) = \sum_t h(|X_t|) \geq \sum_t |X_t| \geq \sum_t |X_t'| = C(A', m, \omega)$$

where we have used $h(k) \geq k$ for the first inequality and (6.3.3) for the last equality. ∎

6.3.2. Optimal Replacement Policies

A replacement criterion that has been proposed for demand paging asserts that the "best" choice of a page to be replaced is the one with the longest expected time until its next reference, i.e., the one with the longest expected forward distance. The rationale is: By so doing, one maximizes the expected time between page faults due to returning pages, minimizing thereby the rate of page faults and therefore the cost. If the criterion can be implemented assuming advance knowledge of the full reference string, then we have the deterministic B_0 algorithm, proved to be optimal later in this section. However, if we can make only probability statements, then it is possible to construct probability assignments for which the replacement choices minimizing (6.3.4) do not have the maximum expected forward distance. This fact is illustrated by the following rather artificial example.

Let $N = \{1, 2, 3\}$, $m = 2$, and introduce the symbol $(k)^n$ to denote n consecutive occurrences of the integer k. Suppose that the only two reference strings possible are 1 2 3 3 $(2)^n$ 1 and 1 2 3 1 3 $(2)^n$ and that these occur with probabilities $1 - p$ and p, respectively. Let us examine the replacement decision when page 3 is first referenced and the state is $S = \{1, 2\}$. Without knowing whether $3(2)^n1$ or $1\ 3\ (2)^n$ constitutes the remaining reference string, the expected forward distances are

$$d(1) = p + (n + 2)(1 - p) = 1 + (n + 1)(1 - p)$$
$$d(2) = 3p + 2(1 - p) = 2 + p$$

Letting $R(x)$ be the minimum expected (total) number of replacements if page x is replaced at the third reference we have

$$R(1) = 3p + 2(1 - p) = 2 + p$$
$$R(2) = 2p + 2(1 - p) = 2$$

Clearly, for $p > 0$ page 1 should not be replaced. However, if $n > 2p/(1 - p)$, then $d(1) > d(2)$, and the expected-forward-distance criterion would advise us incorrectly to replace page 1.

The independent-reference model is a commonly studied probability structure within which the forward-distance criterion yields an optimal algorithm, as we shall prove in Section 6.6. Moreover, the criterion is known to provide a very good heuristic. Experimental evidence bearing on the last statement is summarized in Fig. 6.3-1, this evidence being extrapolated from data in [8, 10, 11]. It shows quantitively the fault rate

$$(6.3.5) \qquad\qquad F(A, m, \omega) = \frac{C(A, m, \omega)}{|\omega|}$$

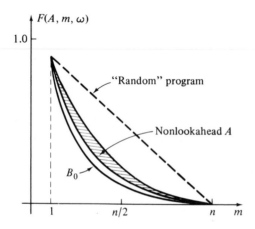

Fig. 6.3-1 Fault-rate performance.

versus memory size m for a typical (long) reference string ω taken from a set of such strings derived from the execution of a number of "typical" programs. The fault rate curves for nonlookahead algorithms tend to lie in the shaded region of the figure. Typically, there exists a range of values of memory size such that even the best algorithm (B_0) generates intolerably many faults per unit time, and typically the upper limit of this range will be around $n/2$.

If the paging algorithm is operated in the allowable range of memory sizes $m > n/2$, then $F(A, m, \omega)$ and $F(B_0, m, \omega)$ tend to differ by at most a few percent. This suggests that *program performance is much more sensitive to m than to A*, especially when page fault rates are kept at an acceptable level. This in turn suggests that the study of paging algorithms should be concerned more with techniques for finding and analyzing stable, easily implemented algorithms than with finding optimal ones.

Figure 6.3-1 also shows another important aspect of program behavior, this aspect being manifested as a tendency for the $F(A, m, \omega)$ curves to lie below the straight line marked "random program." A program is random if each page is referenced with probability $1/n$ at each reference. In this case we would have $(n - m)/n$ as the expected fault rate for all realizable algorithms. No such program has ever been observed, however. That $F(A, m, \omega)$ lies significantly below the line $(n - m)/n$ for those nonlookahead algorithms studied indicates that programs tend to concentrate their references heavily into subsets of their pages. This property, known as locality, will be studied and exploited in Chapter 7.

The FIFO algorithm is of interest not only because of the performance characteristics indicated in Fig. 6.3-1 but also because it is very easy to implement. However, it has the disadvantage of exhibiting an erratic and undesirable behavior under certain practical conditions [9]. Intuitively, one might expect that, for any A and ω, $C(A, m, \omega) > C(A, m + 1, \omega)$; i.e., allocating the program more memory space will reduce the rate of page faults. For FIFO, however, there exist ω and m such that $C(A, m, \omega) < C(A, m + 1, \omega)$ [9]. We shall see later that *stack algorithms* are not susceptible to this anomalous behavior and that LRU, B_0, LFU, and LIFO are examples of stack algorithms.

As an example of the FIFO anomaly let $N = \{1, 2, 3, 4, 5\}$ and consider the reference string 1 2 3 4 1 2 5 1 2 3 4 5. The sequence of memory states for $m = 3$ is shown below with the pages ordered top-down by the FIFO criterion:

$$
\begin{array}{cccccccccccc}
1 & 1 & 1 & 2 & 3 & 4 & 1 & 1^* & 1^* & 2 & 5 & 5^* \\
  & 2 & 2 & 3 & 4 & 1 & 2 & 2 & 2 & 5 & 3 & 3 \\
  &   & 3 & 4 & 1 & 2 & 5 & 5 & 5 & 3 & 4 & 4
\end{array}
$$

The states *not* produced by a page fault are starred. Now for $m = 4$ we have the sequence

$$
\begin{array}{cccccccccccc}
1 & 1 & 1 & 1 & 1^* & 1^* & 2 & 3 & 4 & 5 & 1 & 2 \\
  & 2 & 2 & 2 & 2 & 2 & 3 & 4 & 5 & 1 & 2 & 3 \\
  &   & 3 & 3 & 3 & 3 & 4 & 5 & 1 & 2 & 3 & 4 \\
  &   &   & 4 & 4 & 4 & 5 & 1 & 2 & 3 & 4 & 5
\end{array}
$$

from which we see that 10 page faults occur for $m = 4$, while only 9 occur for $m = 3$. Examples can also be given (see the Problems) which show that the anomaly can involve paging in larger memories that is up to twice that in smaller memories.

Next we shall prove the optimality of B_0. This result was first proved in [2], and a different proof has also been indicated in [12]. Our proof uses a dynamic programming approach which we shall find useful in later sections.

Theorem 6.2

The algorithm B_0 minimizes $C(A, m, \omega)$ for all m and ω.

Proof. Let $C_k(S, t)$ denote the minimum achievable cost under demand paging of processing references $r_{t+1} \ldots r_{t+k}$ given that $S_t = S$. If we define

$C_0(S, t) = 0$ and let $r_{t+1} = x$, then we can write

$$(6.3.6) \qquad C_k(S, t) = \begin{cases} C_{k-1}(S, t+1), & x \in S \\ 1 + \min_{y \in S}[C_{k-1}(S + x - y, t + 1)], & x \notin S \end{cases}$$

This relation may be recognized as the *principle of optimality* in a dynamic programming problem. The proof of the theorem now amounts to showing that paging according to B_0 is characterized by (6.3.6).

Let $<$ denote a linear ordering on the page set N at each time t such that $x < y$ means that x has greater forward distance then y at time t.† We shall let min[S] denote the least element of N contained in $S \subseteq N$. To show that B_0 is described by (6.3.6) we must show that if $s = \min[S]$, then

$$(6.3.7) \qquad C_k(S + x - s, t) = \min_{y \in S}[C_k(S + x - y, t)]$$

for all $k \geq 0$ and $t \geq 1$. To prove (6.3.7) it is sufficient to show that, for any S containing both y and z, then $y < z$ implies that

$$(6.3.8) \qquad \Delta C_k = C_k(S - z, t) - C_k(S - y, t) \geq 0$$

In fact, we shall prove that ΔC_k is 0 or 1. The proof is by induction on k. The result is trivially true for $k = 0$, and so suppose that it holds for all values less than an arbitrary, positive k. Applying (6.3.6) with $r_{t+1} = x$ we can distinguish three cases. Note that although $x = z$ is possible, $x = y$ is not, since we have assumed that y's forward distance is greater than z's (i.e., $y < z$).

Case 1. $x \in S - y - z$. We have from (6.3.6)

$$\Delta C_k = C_{k-1}(S - z, t + 1) - C_{k-1}(S - y, t + 1)$$

which from the induction hypothesis is either 0 or 1.

Case 2. $x = z$. From (6.3.6)

$$\Delta C_k = 1 + \min_{u \in S-z}[C_{k-1}(S - u, t + 1)] - C_{k-1}(S - y, t + 1)$$

Let u_0 denote that page in $S - z$ for which $C_{k-1}(S - u_0, t + 1)$ is minimal. Clearly, either $u_0 = y$ or $u_0 < y$ and hence by the induction hypothesis the contribution of the second two terms is either 0 or-1, and therefore ΔC_k is either 0 or 1.

---

†As before, if $d_t(x) = d_t(y) = \infty$, then $x < y$ if and only if x is lexicographically less than y.

Case 3. $x \notin S$. We have

(6.3.9)
$$\Delta C_k = \min_{u \in S-z} [C_{k-1}(S - z + x - u, t + 1)]$$
$$- \min_{v \in S-y} [C_{k-1}(S - y + x - v, t + 1)]$$

There are three possibilities for the replacement page $s = \min[S - z - y]$. If $s < y < z$, then (6.3.9) reduces to

$$\Delta C_k = C_{k-1}((S + x - s) - z, t + 1) - C_{k-1}((S + x - s) - y, t + 1)$$

which from the induction hypothesis is either 0 or 1. If $y < s < z$, then (6.3.9) reduces to

$$\Delta C_k = C_{k-1}(S - z + x - y, t + 1) - C_{k-1}(S - y + x - s, t + 1)$$

which again is either 0 or 1 by the induction hypothesis. Finally, if $y < z < s$, then we have

$$\Delta C_k = C_{k-1}(S - z + x - y, t + 1) - C_{k-1}(S - y + x - z, t + 1) = 0$$

Thus it follows that in all cases ΔC_k is either 0 or 1. ∎

The next two results are interesting because they shed additional light on the behavior of LRU and B_0. Let ω^R denote the reverse of ω. Then

(6.3.10) $C(\text{LRU}, m, \omega^R) = C(\text{LRU}, m, \omega)$

(6.3.11) $C(B_0, m, \omega^R) = C(B_0, m, \omega)$

To prove (6.3.10) let $t_1, t_2, \ldots, t_i, \ldots, t_r$ denote the sequence of time instants in ω at which references to a given page x occur. Define the *distance* $a_x(i)$ between t_i and t_{i+1} to be the number of distinct pages referenced between t_i and t_{i+1} (not including t_i and t_{i+1}). Now suppose that $a_x(i) = k$; then $r_{t_{i+1}}$ will be in the m-page memory if and only if $m > k$. Clearly, then, the number of page faults for page x in ω depends only on the sequence of distances $a_x(i)$ in ω, which is the reverse of that in ω^R. It follows that the number of faults to x is the same in ω as in ω^R.

To prove (6.3.11) suppose that $C(B_0, m, \omega^R) < C(B_0, m, \omega)$. Now, B_0 on ω^R has page faults at times $t_1, t_2, \ldots, t_p$. Define the algorithm A on ω such that, at times $t_p, \ldots, t_2, t_1$, A changes its memory states to match those of B_0 on ω^R; i.e., the memory state sequence for A on ω is the reverse of that of B_0 on ω^R. In general, A is a nondemand algorithm. By Theorem 6.1 there is a demand algorithm A' for which $C(A', m, \omega) \leq C(A, m, \omega)$. From Theorem 6.2 B_0 is optimal, and therefore

$$C(B_0, m, \omega) \leq C(A', m, \omega) \leq C(A, m, \omega) = C(B_0, m, \omega^R) < C(B_0, m, \omega)$$

which is a contradiction. Reversing the roles of ω and ω^R, we can also show that $C(B_0, m, \omega^R) > C(B_0, m, \omega)$ is impossible; hence (6.3.11) follows. Both (6.3.10) and (6.3.11) were proved in [2], where they were used to construct an algorithm that, on a forward-reverse scan of ω, could determine both $(C(\text{LRU}, m, \omega)$ and $C(B_0, m, \omega)$.

6.4. STACK ALGORITHMS [2]

6.4.1. Introduction

We shall introduce the notation $S(A, m, \omega)$ to stand for the memory state resulting after algorithm A has processed reference string ω in a memory of size m under demand paging, assuming that $S_0 = \varnothing$. That is, if $\omega = r_1 r_2 \ldots r_t$ generates $S_0 S_1 \ldots S_t$ under A, then $S(A, m, \omega) = S_t$. As before, if A is understood we write simply $S(m, \omega)$. The notation $R(S, q, x)$ stands for the page A replaces from S when in configuration (S, q) and the next reference is x. We define $R(S, q, x) = 0$ if $x \in S$ or if $|S| < m$.

An algorithm A is called a *stack algorithm* if its memory states satisfy the *inclusion property*:

$$(6.4.1) \qquad\qquad S(m, \omega) \subseteq S(m + 1, \omega)$$

for all m and ω. That is, the memory states form a collection of nested sets. The condition (6.4.1) is equivalent to the following condition: For each ω there exists a permutation of N, $\mathbf{s}(\omega) = [s_1(\omega), \ldots, s_n(\omega)]$, such that, for all m, $S(m, \omega) = \{s_1(\omega), \ldots, s_m(\omega)\}$. [The equivalence will follow by taking $S(0, \omega) = \varnothing$ and $\{s_i(\omega)\} = S(i, \omega) - S(i - 1, \omega)$.] The vector $\mathbf{s}(\omega)$ will be called the *stack vector*, or simply the *stack*. If $i < j$, $s_i(\omega)$ is said to be higher in the stack than $s_j(\omega)$, and $s_1(\omega)$ is the top of the stack. The initial stack is empty, and we define $\mathbf{s}(\omega) = [s_1(\omega), s_2(\omega), \ldots, s_k(\omega)]$ if ω contains only $k < n$ distinct pages. Thus for a given stack algorithm the inclusion property implies that for each reference string $r_1, \ldots, r_t$ a sequence of stacks $\mathbf{s}_1, \ldots, \mathbf{s}_t$ can be constructed so that the memory state sequence for each value of m can be determined by simply taking the highest m pages in the stack.

Examples

LRU is a stack algorithm since $S(\text{LRU}, m, \omega)$ always contains the m most recently referenced pages in ω and thus is a subset of $S(\text{LRU}, m + 1, \omega)$. Moreover, the LRU stack $\mathbf{s}(\omega)$ orders the pages according to increasing backward distance. FIFO is not a stack algorithm, as verified by Table 6.4-1. The columns under each reference in ω represent the memory contents (arranged in order of placement) for the given memory sizes. Evidently, the final memory states do not satisfy the inclusion property.

Table 6.4-1 FIFO EXAMPLE

				ω			
	1	2	3	4	1	2	5
$m = 3$	1	2	3	4	1	2	5
	—	1	2	3	4	1	2
	—	—	1	2	3	4	1
$m = 4$	1	2	3	4	4	4	5
	—	1	2	3	3	3	4
	—	—	1	2	2	2	3
	—	—	—	1	1	1	2

One of the principal advantages possessed by algorithms having the inclusion property is that in performance studies of such algorithms the page fault behavior of a given reference string can be computed effectively in parallel for all memory sizes $1 \leq m \leq n$ and in one scan of the reference string. In this way efficient simulation studies of memory hierarchies and paging algorithms can be conducted. The principal results of this section consist of efficient procedures for computing stack sequences and the corresponding cost functions, $C(A, m, \omega)$ [cf. (6.3.3)]. First, however, we shall describe certain properties of stack transitions required by the inclusion property, and we shall provide a somewhat more constructive definition of stack algorithms.

Define the *stack distance* $D_x(\omega)$ for page x to be the position of x in the stack $s(\omega)$. Thus if $s_k(\omega) = x$, then $D_x(\omega) = k$. If x does not appear in $s(\omega)$, we take $D_x(\omega) = \infty$. Observe that a page fault occurs for page x as the last reference in the string ωx if and only if $D_x(\omega) > m$, since the first m elements of $s(\omega)$ constitute the contents of memory.

Now, suppose that we consider the two stacks $s(\omega)$ and $s(\omega x)$ and study how the sequence of pages in $s(\omega)$ is altered to obtain $s(\omega x)$. Because the most recently referenced page must always be in memory, we know that $x \in S(1, \omega x)$, which implies that the most recently referenced page is the top of the stack:

(6.4.2) $$D_x(\omega x) = 1$$

This is suggested in Fig. 6.4-1.

The next important property is that an unreferenced page never moves up the stack:

(6.4.3) $$D_y(\omega) \leq D_y(\omega x), \quad y \neq x$$

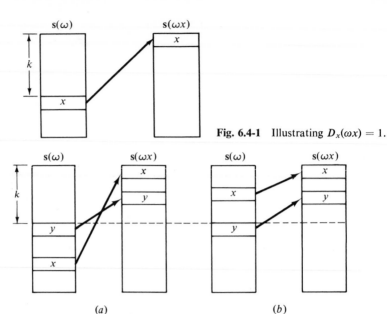

Fig. 6.4-1   Illustrating $D_x(\omega x) = 1$.

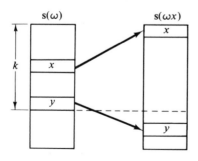

(a)   (b)

Fig. 6.4-2   Illustrating $D_y(\omega) \leq D_y(\omega x)$.

Figure 6.4.2 shows why this is true. In (a) and (b), page y is at position $k + 1$ in $s(\omega)$. Suppose that y moves to position k or higher in $s(\omega x)$. In Fig. 6.4-2(a) we see that this implies that two pages entered the k-page memory on the page fault to x, which is impossible under demand paging. In Fig. 6.4-2(b) we see that page y entered the k-page memory even though no page fault to x occurred. Since both Figs. 6.4-2(a) and (b) are impossible, we conclude that a page can move up the stack if and only if it is referenced.

Another property characteristic of stack transitions is that pages below the one referenced remain fixed in the stack:

(6.4.4) $s_k(\omega x) = s_k(\omega)$ if $D_x(\omega) < k$

Figure 6.4-3 shows why this must be true. From condition (6.4.3) the page y cannot move up, but assuming that y is at position k in $s(\omega)$ and at some

Fig. 6.4-3   Illustrating when $s_k(\omega x) = s_k(\omega)$.

lower position in $s(\omega x)$ would force us to conclude that page y was replaced from the k-page memory even though no page fault occurred to x, the page referenced.

Figure 6.4-4 shows in a single picture the effect of the change from $s(\omega)$ to $s(\omega x)$; arrows indicate a change in position of a page. Since page x is moved from position $D_x(\omega)$ to position 1, the pages in positions above x must be rearranged, consistent with (6.4.3). In the figure, let S denote the contents of

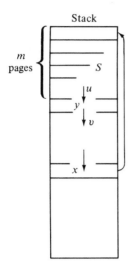

Fig. 6.4-4   Motion of pages in stack.

the m-page memory; i.e., S consists of the pages in the first m positions of the stack. Clearly, some page u is replaced from S as a result of the reference to x. Similarly, if page y was originally in position $m + 1$ of the stack, then some page v is replaced from $S + y$ resulting from the reference to x. Since v is either u or y, we have the important result that $R(S + y, q, x)$ is either $R(S, q, x)$ or y.

It is easily seen that this statement is in fact a characterization of Fig. 6.4-4; accordingly we have the following characterization of stack algorithms.

Proposition 6.1

An algorithm A is a stack algorithm if and only if

$$(6.4.5) \qquad R(S + y, q, x) = R(S, q, x) \quad \text{or} \quad y$$

whenever $R(S + y, q, x) \neq 0$; i.e., $x \notin S + y$.

6.4.2. Priority Algorithms

The examples of Section 6.2 were algorithms that used some form of priority ordering on the pages of N to make their replacement decisions. It was suggested earlier in this section that all these algorithms (except FIFO) are stack algorithms. To demonstrate this, we shall first describe a class of so-called priority algorithms and show that they are all stack algorithms by virtue of (6.4.5).

Paging algorithm A will be called a *priority algorithm* if there exists a mapping that associates with each reference string $\omega = r_1 \ldots r_T$ a sequence of linear orderings $\mathbf{p}_1 \cdots \mathbf{p}_{T-1}$ such that

1. $\mathbf{p}_t$ $(1 \leq t \leq T - 1)$ is an ordering of the distinct pages in $r_1 \cdots r_t$, and

2. For all $m \geq 1$, if $r_{t+1} \notin S(m, r_1 \ldots r_t)$ and $|S(m, r_1 \ldots r_t)| = m$ $(1 \leq t \leq T - 1)$, then the page A replaces in $S(m, r_1 \ldots r_t)$ is given by the least element of $\mathbf{p}_t$ contained in $S(m, r_1 \ldots r_t)$.

We shall let $\min_{\mathbf{p}_t}[S]$ denote the least element of $\mathbf{p}_t$ contained in S. The notation $\max_{\mathbf{p}_t}[S]$ will also be used, with the obvious meaning. Since $\mathbf{p}_t$ can normally be understood, it will frequently be omitted in this notation. Using our earlier notation in which m and A are understood we define, consistent with the above definition,

$$(6.4.6) \qquad R(S_t, q, r_{t+1}) = \min_{\mathbf{p}_t}[S_t], \quad |S_t| = m, \, r_{t+1} \notin S_t$$
$$= 0, \qquad |S_t| < m \text{ or } r_{t+1} \in S_t$$

The priority lists are represented and maintained as part of the control state q; as illustrated below there are important priority algorithms that can be formulated so that each state q is determined entirely by the corresponding priority list $\mathbf{p}_t$.

Examples

The LRU, B_0, LFU, and LIFO algorithms are priority algorithms whose priority lists order pages, respectively, by increasing backward distance, increasing forward distance (and then lexiographically), decreasing frequency of use (and then increasing backward distance), and increasing time of entry into main memory.

Note that the LRU priority lists are identical to the LRU stack and that the LRU and LIFO algorithms can be formulated so that the state set Q is finite. In particular, for the LRU algorithm, Q can be defined as the set of all permutations of m or fewer elements taken from N. Each state can be interpreted as the top m or fewer pages in an LRU stack. (In this way a configuration will be completely defined by the control state.) The corresponding transition function is easily constructed. The new state for each reference is formed by placing the page just referenced at the top of the stack (previous state) and pushing down those pages originally above the referenced page (see Fig. 6.4-7). Clearly, if the previous state had m pages, none of which was the referenced page, then the bottom page of this state will not appear in the new state. Detailed, finite-state formulations of the LRU and LIFO algorithms and their transition functions are left as an exercise. Finally, we note that although the LFU algorithm is realizable in the sense that it is nonlookahead, an infinite state set must be assumed in order to maintain a ranking by frequency of use.

When applied to (6.4.5), (6.4.6) shows immediately that a priority algorithm is a stack algorithm. Specifically, if $x = r_{t+1} \notin S + y$ and $|S + y| = m$, then

(6.4.7) $$R(S + y, q, x) = \min_{\mathbf{p}_t}[S + y] = \min_{\mathbf{p}_t}[\min_{\mathbf{p}_t}[S], y]$$

$$= \min_{\mathbf{p}_t}[R(S, q, x), y]$$

whence $R(S + y, q, x)$ is either $R(S, q, x)$ or y. The converse is also true; i.e., for each stack algorithm and reference string we can define a sequence of priority lists such that (6.4.7) is true. To verify this informally let $s_1, \ldots,$ $s_t, \ldots$ denote the sequence of stacks generated by the stack algorithm A for the string $r_1, \ldots, r_t, \ldots$. By defining a sequence of priority lists so that $\mathbf{p}_t = s_{t+1}$, $t = 1, 2, \ldots$, we see that A is a priority algorithm. This follows from the fact that if x causes a page fault in $S(m, \omega)$, then $s_{m+1}(\omega x)$ is the page in $S(m, \omega)$ that is replaced. In other words, $s(\omega x)$ gives the replacement ordering on the elements of $S(m, \omega)$ for each memory size $m < D_x(\omega)$ such that a replacement is necessary. Clearly, the ordering of elements at a distance greater than $D_x(\omega)$ is unimportant. See [2] for further discussion and [13] for a formal treatment of the equivalence of priority and stack algorithms.

We have seen that FIFO is not a stack algorithm, and yet we were able to express it in terms of a priority rule in Section 6.2. This is not a contradiction. In general, the priority lists used by FIFO are not independent of the memory size. (Recall that the priority lists must be functions only of the reference string.) In Table 6.4-1, which demonstrates that FIFO is not a stack algorithm, consider the memory state for $\omega = 123412$; arranged as vectors indicating their order of placement in memory, they are

$$S(3, \omega) = (2, 1, 4)$$

$$S(4, \omega) = (4, 3, 2, 1)$$

Observe that 2 precedes 4 in (2,1,4) but that 2 follows 4 in (4, 3, 2, 1). Because of this priority conflict, there does not exist a single priority list applicable to all memory sizes, so that FIFO is not equivalent to any priority algorithm.

Some replacement rules of interest involve random selection to some extent. For example the RANDOM paging algorithm selects the replacement page at random from S; i.e., each page is equally likely to be selected. We can also envision an LFU rule in which the tie-breaking mechanism is random selection rather than LRU. Since the effect of such rules on a given reference string is not deterministic, the corresponding algorithms cannot be described by the formalism developed in this chapter. However, for purposes of simulation we can define priority algorithms using a pseudorandom number generator which have statistical properties equivalent to those of random-selection algorithms like the two described above [2]. In particular, suppose that we want to simulate the RANDOM algorithm. Using a pseudorandom number generator we construct a procedure for generating random permutations (linear orderings) of the subsets of N. For a given initial state let $\mathbf{l}_i$ denote the ith ordering generated by the procedure. Then an appropriate priority algorithm will be defined by stipulating that $\mathbf{p}_i = \mathbf{l}_i$. In principle each $y \in S \subseteq N$ is equally likely to be $\min_{\mathbf{l}_i}[S]$; it follows that the priority algorithm has the appropriate statistical properties. (This statement, however, is subject as always to the limitiations of pseudorandom number generators.) We shall now describe a stack updating procedure after which a simpler realization of the RANDOM algorithm is presented.

Since the priority list and stack need not coincide in general, a paging algorithm simulator must maintain implicitly or explicitly both a stack vector and a priority vector. Thus we require a method for updating the stack vector from the priority list. We shall call this method the *stack updating procedure*. It results from applying the definition $R(S, q, x) = \min[S]$ to (6.4.5) and using the properties in (6.4.2)–(6.4.4).

Proposition 6.2 (Stack Updating Procedure)

Let $s(\omega)$ and $s(\omega x)$ be two successive stacks and suppose that $D_x(\omega) = m$. Then

$$(6.4.8) \qquad s_i(\omega x) = \begin{cases} x, & i = 1 \\ \max[s_i(\omega), \min[S(i - 1, \omega)]], & 1 < i < m \\ \min[S(m - 1, \omega)] & i = m \\ s_i(\omega), & i > m \end{cases}$$

where $S(k, \omega) = \{s_1(\omega), \ldots, s_k(\omega)\}$.

Line 1 follows from (6.4.2), and line 4 from (6.4.4). Line 2 follows from Fig. 6.4-4 by observing that the page remaining at stack position k must be the one that was not replaced; i.e., $\min[R(S, q, x), y]$ replaced implies that $\max[R(S, q, x), y]$ remains. Line 3 follows from Fig. 6.4-4 and because the position vacated by x must be filled with the page replaced from the set of $m - 1$ pages above x in the stack.

The result of (6.4.8) has a nice pictorial representation. Define the *priority operator* shown in Fig. 6.4-5; then Fig. 6.4-6 shows the updating procedure for $D_x(\omega) = m$. (In general, if n_ω is the number of distinct pages referenced in ω, the stack contains n_ω entries. If $D_x(\omega) = \infty$, then $s(\omega x)$ contains $n_\omega + 1$ entries, and only the updating steps for $1 \leq i \leq n_\omega + 1$ are performed.)

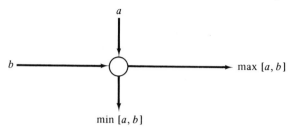

Fig. 6.4-5 Priority operator.

Example

Belady's algorithm B_0 produces the sequence of priority lists and stacks shown in Table 6.4-2 for the given reference string.

Table 6.4-2 B_0 STACK ALGORITHM

					ω					
	1	2	3	4	1	2	3	2	3	1
p	1	1	1	1	2	3	2	3	1	1
	—	2	2	2	3	2	3	1	2	2
	—	—	3	3	1	1	1	2	3	3
	—	—	—	4	4	4	4	4	4	4
s	1	2	3	4	1	2	3	2	3	1
	—	1	1	1	4	1	2	3	2	2
	—	—	2	2	2	4	1	1	1	3
	—	—	—	3	3	3	4	4	4	4

Example

As stated earlier, the RANDOM replacement algorithm depends on a priority list chosen at random among the permutations of a subset of N. A simulation of this algorithm can be considerably simplified in view of Fig. 6.4-6, since we need only insert random decisions into the priority operators. One property of the algorithm is that a given page is chosen from the m-page memory with probability $1/m$. Therefore a given page x enters the mth priority operator with probability $1/m$. If it is to leave that same operator with probability $1/(m + 1)$, the decision in that operator must be the following: Choose s_{m+1} with probability $1/(m + 1)$ and the incoming page x with probability $m/(m + 1)$.

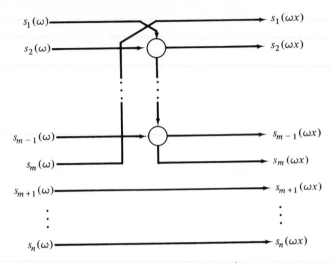

Fig. 6.4-6 Stack updating procedure.

We stated earlier that the LRU algorithm's stack is identical to its priority list, since $S(m, \omega)$ contains the m most recently referenced pages in ω, i.e., the m highest-priority pages. Proposition 6.2 provides the basis for proving the converse, viz., that a paging algorithm's stack and priority list are identical at each moment of time only if the algorithm is LRU. As the induction hypothesis, suppose that $s(\omega) = [s_1(\omega), \ldots, s_n(\omega)]$ is the LRU stack so that $i < j$ implies that page $s_i(\omega)$ was referenced more recently in ω than $s_j(\omega)$. It is sufficient to show that $s(\omega x)$ is ordered likewise; i.e., if $x = s_m(\omega)$, then

$$(6.4.9) \qquad s(\omega x) = [x, s_1(\omega), \ldots, s_{m-1}(\omega), s_{m+1}(\omega), \ldots, s_n(\omega)]$$

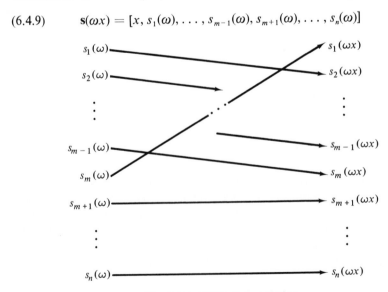

Fig. 6.4-7 LRU stack updating.

Applying Proposition 6.2 with $x = s_m(\omega)$, (6.4.9) is easily established. Thus we have

Corollary 6.1

A stack algorithm is LRU if and only if its stack and priority list coincide at each page reference.

Figure 6.4-7 shows the corresponding LRU stack updating procedure. As will be shown later, this result has some important implications with respect to multiprogramming.

6.4.3. Procedure for Determining the Cost Function

Stack algorithms are important not only because they model a number of practical paging algorithms but also because there exists an efficient method for measuring the cost function $C(A, m, \omega)$ for any stack algorithm A. To simplify notation, we shall assume that A is given and write $C(m, \omega)$ for the cost (number of page faults) generated by A in processing ω with a memory space of m pages.

The first important fact about the cost of a stack algorithm is that $C(m, \omega)$ is nonincreasing in m:

$$(6.4.10) \qquad C(m, \omega) \geq C(m + 1, \omega)$$

This follows directly from the inclusion property, since for a given reference string ω, a page fault in $S(m + k, \omega)$ $(k \geq 1)$ always implies a page fault in $S(m, \omega) \subseteq S(m + k, \omega)$. This property need not hold for nonstack algorithms as illustrated by the anomaly presented in Section 6.2 for the FIFO algorithm.

The notion of stack distance introduced earlier together with the stack updating procedure provide the basis for a procedure that computes $C(m, \omega)$ for given ω and for all m $(1 \leq m \leq n)$. Suppose that $\omega = r_1 r_2 \ldots r_t \ldots r_T$ is processed by A with the resulting sequence $s_1 s_2 \ldots s_t \ldots s_T$ of stack vectors. There is associated with ω a corresponding sequence $D_1 D_2 \ldots D_t \ldots D_T$ of stack distances, where D_t is the position of r_t in s_{t-1}. Since a page fault occurs at time t if and only if $D_t > m$, $C(m, \omega)$ can be defined as

$$(6.4.11) \qquad C(m, \omega) = |\{t \,|\, D_t > m, 1 \leq t \leq T\}|$$

If we define a_k as the number of times the page in stack position k was moved to the top of the stack, then

$$(6.4.12) \qquad a_k = |\{t \,|\, D_t = k, 1 \leq t \leq T\}|$$

and we can write

$$(6.4.13) \qquad C(m, \omega) = a_\infty + \sum_{k=m+1}^{n} a_k$$

where a_∞ is the number of times a reference was made to a page as yet unreferenced.

This expression suggests that we determine $C(m, \omega)$ as a function of m simply by maintaining a representation of the stack and monitoring the number of references made at each stack position. We initialize the procedure with a vector $\mathbf{a} = (a_1, \ldots, a_n, a_\infty) = (0, \ldots, 0, 0)$. When reference r_t ($1 \leq t \leq T$) is considered and is found at distance D_t in the stack, we add 1 to the component a_{D_t} of $\mathbf{a}$, update the stack, and repeat until all references in ω have been considered. When the procedure terminates, the curve $C(m, \omega)$ is calculated from the vector $\mathbf{a}$ according to (6.4.13).

Example

Table 6.4-3 shows for the LRU algorithm the calculation of $C(m, \omega)$ by two methods: enumeration of the memory state sequences for $m = 1, 2, 3, 4$, and using the procedure outlined above. For each m and reference in ω, the memory state is represented as a column vector with the pages ordered as in $\mathbf{s}$ (reading downward). A fault is indicated by the symbol $+$.

Table 6.4-3   COST COMPUTATION FOR LRU

								ω				
	1	2	3	4	1	2	3	2	3	1	C
$m = 1$	—	1+	2+	3+	4+	1+	2+	3+	2+	3+	1+	10
$m = 2$	—	1+	2+	3+	4+	1+	2+	3+	2	3	1+	8
	—	—	1	2	3	4	1	2	3	2	3	
$m = 3$	—	1+	2+	3+	4+	1+	2+	3+	2	3	1	
	—	—	1	2	3	4	1	2	3	2	3	7
	—	—	—	1	2	3	4	1	1	1	2	
$m = 4$	—	1+	2+	3+	4+	1	2	3	2	3	1	
	—	—	1	2	3	4	1	2	3	2	3	4
	—	—	—	1	2	3	4	1	1	1	2	
	—	—	—	—	1	2	3	4	4	4	4	
p, s	—	1	2	3	4	1	2	3	2	3	1	
	—	—	1	2	3	4	1	2	3	2	3	
	—	—	—	1	2	3	4	1	1	1	2	
	—	—	—	—	1	2	3	4	4	4	4	
D	—	∞	∞	∞	∞	4	4	4	2	2	3	
$\mathbf{a}$												
a_1	0	0	0	0	0	0	0	0	0	0	0	10
a_2	0	0	0	0	0	0	0	0	1	2	2	8
a_3	0	0	0	0	0	0	0	0	0	0	1	7
a_4	0	0	0	0	0	1	2	3	3	3	3	4
a_∞	0	1	2	3	4	4	4	4	4	4	4	—

6.5. THE EXTENSION PROBLEM [4]

Consider a demand paging algorithm which, in response to some reference string in a memory of size m, produces a fetch-replacement sequence

$$(6.5.1) \qquad [(x, y)]_m = (x_1, y_1)(x_2, y_2) \cdots (x_i, y_i) \cdots$$

where the pair (x_i, y_i), $i > m$, means that at the ith page fault x_i was *pulled* (placed) into memory and y_i was *pushed* (replaced) from memory. The sequence $[(x, y)]_m$ is called a *push-pull sequence*. The first m pairs must denote only pulls since the memory is initially empty. For this reason we define $y_i = 0$, $1 \leq i \leq m$.

The description of a paging algorithm's behavior in terms of its push-pull sequence is weaker than the description in terms of the memory state sequence $S_0 S_1 \ldots S_t \ldots$. Let $t_1 t_2 \ldots t_i \ldots$ denote the sequence of instants at which page faults occur, i.e., at which $S_{t_i} \neq S_{t_i-1}$. If we compute (x_i, y_i) so that

$$(6.5.2) \qquad S_{t_i} = \begin{cases} S_{t_i-1} + x_i, & i \leq m \\ S_{t_i-1} + x_i - y_i, & i > m \end{cases}$$

then we may clearly construct $[(x, y)]_m$ from $\{S_t\}$. However, it should be clear that, given $[(x, y)]_m$, the only states of S_t that we can construct are those contained in $\{S_{t_i}\}$. Informally, the *extension problem* is: Given a paging algorithm and state information (normally including $[(x, y)]_m$) *recorded only at page-faulting times*, can we determine $[(x, y)]_{m+k}$ for a memory extended by $k \geq 1$ pages? As we shall demonstrate, this problem is solvable for a stack algorithm because the inclusion property implies that the pull (x_i) sequence in $[(x, y)]_{m+k}$ is a subsequence of the pull sequence in $[(x, y)]_m$.

The extension problem is motivated by the physical problem of trying to ascertain, from information recorded at page-fault times, the extent of performance improvement which would result from an increase in memory size. It is of practical interest since recordings can be made at the time of page faults without significant additional system overhead. On the other hand, generating a complete record of the priority lists or stacks is prohibitively costly since the program would have to be interrupted after each reference.

To solve the extension problem for a general stack algorithm, we need to know the priority lists from which replacement pages are determined; i.e., these lists must be contained in the information recorded at page-fault times, along with the sequence $[(x, y)]_m$. The solution consists of maintaining a record of the stack segment between distances m and $m + k$; this stack segment is updated by using the updating procedure in (6.4.8). Although it might at first seem that we require knowledge of the priority list after each reference in order to be able to update the stack correctly, it is easy to see that the references between the fetched pages in (x_{i-1}, y_{i-1}) and (x_i, y_i) do not affect the stack positions $s_{m+1}, \ldots, s_n$. None of these intervening references cause a page fault; hence their stack distances do not exceed m and (6.4.8) shows that the stack positions at distances greater than m are unchanged.

The procedure for obtaining $[(x, y)]_{m+k}$ from $[(x, y)]_m$ operates as follows. For each push-pull (x_i, y_i)† there are two cases to consider: 1) If the stack distance of x_i exceeds $m + k$, x_i must cause a page fault and replacement of some y_i' in the $(m + k)$-page memory; in this case we replace (x_i, y_i) with (x_i, y_i') as described below. 2) If the stack distance of x_i lies in the range $m + 1$ to $m + k$, then no push-pull pair occurs in the $(m + k)$-page memory; in this case we delete (x_i, y_i) from $[(x, y)]_m$. After having transformed each (x_i, y_i) of $[(x, y)]_m$ in this way, $[(x, y)]_m$ will have been transformed into $[(x, y)]_{m+k}$.

The computation required to transform (x_i, y_i) to (x_i, y_i') in case 1 is shown in Fig. 6.5-1(a); this figure is the portion of Fig. 6.4-6 pertaining when the stack distance of x_i exceeds $m + k$. The computations require knowledge of the priority list just before each (x_i, y_i) in $[(x, y)]_m$ in order to perform the requisite updating of the stack segment $(s_{m+1}, \ldots, s_{m+k})$.‡ If only the sequence $[(x, y)]_m$ has been given, the class of algorithms for which the extension problem is solvable is considerably restricted; LIFO and LRU are examples of those algorithms whose priority lists can be deduced from $[(x, y)]_m$.

In the case of the LRU algorithm, the extension problem has a particularly simple solution since the stack and priority list are identical, in accordance with the diagram of Fig. 6.4-7. Suppose that $(s_{m+1}, \ldots, s_{m+k})$ is the current stack segment and that (x_i, y_i) is the push-pull pair of $[(x, y)]_m$ under consideration. The computation of one step in the extension problem for LRU is

$$j \leftarrow 1; \quad done \leftarrow 0$$

$$\textbf{while } (j \leq k) \textbf{ and } (done = 0) \textbf{ do}$$

$$\textbf{begin if } x_i = s_{m+j}, \textbf{ then } done \leftarrow 1;$$

$$\textbf{exchange } (s_{m+j}, y_i); \quad j \leftarrow j + 1 \textbf{ end}$$

$$\textbf{if } done = 0, \textbf{ then output } (x_i, y_i)$$

After the jth iteration of this procedure, y_i is the page replaced from the $(m + j)$-page memory. The iteration is terminated if $x_i = s_{m+j}$ for some j, and the pair (x_i, y_i) is output only if $x_i \neq s_{m+j}$ for all j.

With an appropriate formalization of the ideas presented here it is not difficult to show that an extension problem is solvable if and only if the given paging algorithm has the inclusion property. This result and discussions of

---

†Note that $[(x, y)]_m$ may be assumed given or it may be derived from a sequence of stacks.

‡Actually, we need to know only the relative priorities of the pages $y, s_{m+1}, \ldots, s_{m+k}$.

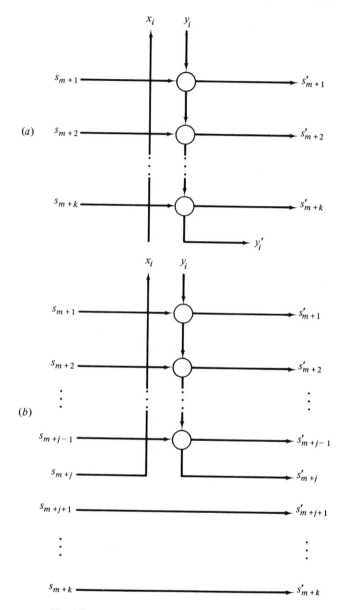

Fig. 6.5-1 Computation for the extension problem.

the various engineering aspects of the extension problem can be found in [4].
Note that the practical importance of the ability to predict performance with
increases in memory size strengthens the reason for using stack algorithms in
the design of paging systems.

6.6. THE INDEPENDENT REFERENCE MODEL

In this section we shall consider the problem of determining the performance of paging algorithms in terms of expected page-fault rates. For this purpose we shall introduce a simple probability model known as the independent reference model. There are good reasons to believe that this model is not a realistic representation of program behavior; however, the model is important for two reasons. First, it is a probability structure within which an optimal algorithm has been specified. (Another such structure will be discussed in Section 6.7.) Second, it demonstrates an analysis (and its complexity) of program behavior using classical methods.

According to the independent-reference assumption, the reference string $r_1 r_2 \cdots r_t \cdots$ is a sequence of independent random variables with the common, stationary distribution $\{\beta_1, \ldots, \beta_n\}$ such that $\Pr[r_t = i] = \beta_i$ for all $t \geq 1$. Let the random variable $d_t(x)$ denote the forward distance to x just after r_t; from our assumptions $d_t(x)$ has the stationary geometric distribution

$$(6.6.1) \qquad \Pr[d_t(x) = k] = \beta_x(1 - \beta_x)^{k-1}, \quad k = 1, 2, \ldots$$

with mean values $\overline{d(x)} = 1/\beta_x$.

Now let A_0 denote the algorithm in which the choice of page to replace is the one in memory whose expected forward distance is greatest, i.e., the one for which β_x is least. It is easily seen that A_0 is a stack algorithm. If we assume that pages have been numbered so that $\beta_1 \geq \beta_2 \geq \cdots \geq \beta_n$, the replacement rule of A_0 can be expressed simply as

$$(6.6.2) \qquad R(S, q, x) = \text{largest integer in } S$$

Note that A_0 resembles the LIFO algorithm, in the following sense. After a long period of time pages $1, 2, \ldots, m - 1$ can be expected to be in memory; once there they will never be replaced since $\beta_1, \ldots, \beta_{m-1}$ are larger than β_j for $j \geq m$. If the first $m - 1$ distinct references in a string are for pages $1, 2, \ldots, m - 1$, the LIFO algorithm will, after an appropriate period of time, also have pages $1, 2, \ldots, m - 1$ in memory and will never replace them.

Theorem 6.3

A_0 is optimal for the independent-reference assumption. That is, A_0 minimizes $C(A, m)$ for all $m \geq 1$ [see (6.3.4)].

To show this let $C_k(S)$ denote the minimum expected cost achievable under demand paging of processing $r_{t+1} \cdots r_{t+k}$ given that $S_t = S$; let $x = r_{t+1}$. Assume that $C_0(S) = 0$. Then we have the principle of optimality:

$$(6.6.3) \qquad C_k(S) = \sum_{x \in S} \beta_x C_{k-1}(S) + \sum_{x \in N-S} \beta_x \{1 + \min_{y \in S}[C_{k-1}(S + x - y)]\}$$

The proof of the theorem now consists of showing that A_0 is characterized by (6.6.3). The proof is very similar to that of Theorem 6.2 (see [1]) and so it is omitted here and left as an exercise.

Theorem 6.4

For the independent-reference model the limiting page-fault rate (cost per reference) assuming an initial state S_0 is defined as

$$(6.6.4) \qquad F_{S_0} = \lim_{k \to \infty} \frac{C_k(S_0)}{k}$$

Under A_0, F_{s_0} is independent of S_0 and given by

$$(6.6.5) \qquad F(A_0) = B - \sum_{i=m}^{n} \frac{\beta_i^2}{B}$$

where m is the memory size, $N = \{1, 2, \ldots, n\}$, $\beta_1 \geq \beta_2 \geq \cdots \geq \beta_n$, and

$$B = \sum_{i=m}^{n} \beta_i$$

Proof. The memory state sequence $S_1, \ldots, S_t, \ldots$ generated by A_0 is a sequence of random variables. In fact, with S_0 the initial state it is easily seen that $\{S_t\}$ is a Markov chain. Let $b_x(t) = \Pr[x \notin S_t]$ for $t \geq 0$ and $x \in N$. For a given initial state the expected cost can be expressed as

$$(6.6.6) \qquad C_k(S_0) = \sum_{t=1}^{k} \Pr[r_t \notin S_{t-1}] = \sum_{t=1}^{k} \sum_{x=1}^{n} \beta_x b_x(t-1)$$

We note that in the Markov chain $\{S_t\}$ states not containing $L_m = \{1, \ldots, m-1\}$ are transient states and all others are recurrent states. Let t_0 denote the earliest time at which $S_t \supseteq L_m$, assuming an arbitrary initial state S_0. Since the expected time between references to page x is $1/\beta_x$, we can bound the expected value of t_0 by

$$E(t_0) \leq \sum_{x \in N} \frac{1}{\beta_x}$$

Thus we can bound the number of page faults in $r_1, \ldots, r_{t_0}$ by $E(t_0)$. Since for some $S_0' \supseteq L_m$

$$\lim_{k \to \infty} \frac{C_k(S_0)}{k} \leq \lim_{k \to \infty} \left[\frac{E(t_0)}{k} + \frac{C_k(S_0')}{k} \right]$$

for an arbitrary initial state S_0 we can write

$$(6.6.7) \qquad F_{S_0} = \lim_{k \to \infty} \frac{C_k(S_0')}{k} \quad \text{for some } S_0' \supseteq L_m$$

Thus let us assume that $S_0 = L_m + z$ $(z \in N - L_m)$ and compute $b_x(t)$ under this condition. To determine $b_x(t)$ we write first

$$
b_x(t) = \begin{cases}
\Pr[x \notin S_{t-1} \text{ and } r_t \neq x] + \Pr[x \in S_{t-1} \text{ and } r_t \notin L_m + x], \\
\qquad\qquad\qquad\qquad\qquad\qquad\qquad\qquad t > 0,\ m \leq x \leq n \\
0, \qquad\qquad\qquad\qquad\qquad\qquad\qquad\quad t \geq 0,\ 1 \leq x \leq m - 1
\end{cases}
$$

Using the independence of successive references we have

$$b_x(t) = b_x(t-1)(1 - \beta_x) + [1 - b_x(t-1)](B - \beta_x)$$

or

(6.6.8) $b_x(t) = b_x(t-1)(1 - B) + (B - \beta_x), \quad t > 0,\ m \leq x \leq n$

where

$$B = \sum_{i=m}^{n} \beta_i$$

Solving (6.6.8) systematically we find that

$$b_x(t) = \left[b_x(0) - \left(1 - \frac{\beta_x}{B} \right) \right](1 - B)^t + \left(1 - \frac{\beta_x}{B} \right), \quad t > 0,\ m \leq x \leq n$$

where

$$b_x(0) = 1, \quad x \neq z$$
$$\qquad\ \ = 0, \quad \text{otherwise}$$

Substituting into (6.6.6) we obtain

(6.6.9) $C_k(S_0) = \sum_{x=1}^{n} \beta_x \left\{ \left[b_x(0) - \left(1 - \frac{\beta_x}{B} \right) \right] \sum_{t=0}^{k-1} (1 - B)^t + k \left(1 - \frac{\beta_x}{B} \right) \right\}$

Since the value of the summation within braces is bounded by $1/B$ and $b_x(t) = 0$ for $1 \leq x < m$,

(6.6.10) $\displaystyle \lim_{k \to \infty} \frac{C_k(S_0)}{k} = \sum_{x=m}^{n} \beta_x \left(1 - \frac{\beta_x}{B} \right)$

from which (6.6.5) follows directly.   ∎

Using the theory of finite Markov chains we shall now carry out an analysis of the LRU paging algorithm under the independent reference assumption. Subsequently, we shall show how to extend the analysis to the FIFO algorithm.

The Markov chain to be studied is denoted $\{s_i\}$, $i = 0, 1, 2, \ldots$, and corresponds to the sequence of stacks generated by the LRU algorithm for a reference string $r_1, \ldots, r_i, \ldots$ assuming a memory size of m and a set N of n pages. More precisely, the states of the Markov chain are the topmost m elements of the LRU stacks. Thus the set Q of states consists of the set of all permutations of m elements taken from N. The Markov property of $\{s_i\}$ is easily verified. We shall choose the initial state s_0 as an arbitrary permutation of m pages taken from N. This assumption is for convenience, since our purpose is the study of equilibrium page-fault rates. Because of the assumptions we make regarding the sequence $\{s_i\}$, the initial condition will have no effect.

The Markov chain is homogeneous in the sense that the one-step transition probabilities denoted

$$p(s, s') = \Pr[s_i = s' \,|\, s_{i-1} = s], \quad i \geq 1$$

are clearly independent of the time parameter i. The transition probabilities are easily found on the basis of the possible LRU stack transitions (see Fig. 6.4-7). In particular, if $s = [j_1, \ldots, j_m]$, $k \neq j_i$ ($1 \leq i \leq m$), and $s' = [k, j_1, \ldots, j_{m-1}]$, which results from a reference to page k, then $p(s, s') = \beta_k$. If $k = j_l$ and $s' = [k, j_1, \ldots, j_{l-1}, j_{l+1}, \ldots, j_m]$, then again we have $p(s, s') = \beta_k$. No other types of transitions are possible and hence $p(s, s') = 0$ for all s and s' not related as above.

It is not difficult to show that $\{s_i\}$ is irreducible; i.e., for each s and s' there exists a positive k such that the probability $p^{(k)}(s, s')$ of passing from state s to state s' in k transitions is nonzero. In particular, for an arbitrary pair of stacks $s = [j_1, \ldots, j_m]$ and $s' = [j'_1, \ldots, j'_m]$ it is clear that the sequence of references $j'_m, \ldots, j'_1$ will cause a transition from s to s' in m steps. Since this implies that $p^{(m)}(s, s') = \prod_{i=1}^{m} \beta_{j'_i} > 0$ for all s and s', the chain is irreducible. It follows that a stationary probability distribution exists which uniquely satisfies the equilibrium equation. If we let π denote the vector of equilibrium probabilities and P the matrix of transition probabilities $p(s, s')$, then the equilibrium equation is

(6.6.11) $\pi = \pi P$

Let π_s, $s = [j_1, \ldots, j_m]$, denote the equilibrium probability of state s, so that the normalization condition can be written as

(6.6.12) $\sum_{s \in Q} \pi_s = 1$

Let $p_f(s)$ denote the equilibrium probability that a page fault occurs, given that the current memory state is s. Interpreting π_s as the steady-state frequency of occurrence of state s, we have $p_f(s)\pi_s$ as the page-fault rate arising from state s and

$$(6.6.13) \qquad\qquad F(LRU) = \sum_{s \in Q} p_f(s)\pi_s$$

as the total page-fault rate in statistical equilibrium. We have the following result.

Theorem 6.5

For the independent reference model,

$$(6.6.14) \qquad\qquad F(LRU) = \sum_{s \in Q} D_1^2(s) \prod_{i=1}^{m} \frac{\beta_{j_i}}{D_i(s)}$$

where $s = [j_1, \ldots, j_m]$ and

$$(6.6.15) \qquad\qquad D_i(s) = 1 - \sum_{k=1}^{m-i+1} \beta_{j_k}$$

Proof. According to our definition of $D_i(s)$, it is immediately seen that $p_f(s) = D_1(s)$. Thus it remains to find expressions for the state probabilities satisfying (6.6.11). For the LRU system the solution to (6.6.11) satisfying (6.6.12) is given by

$$(6.6.16) \qquad\qquad \pi_s = \frac{\displaystyle\prod_{i=1}^{m} \beta_{j_i}}{\displaystyle\prod_{i=2}^{m} D_i(s)}$$

where $D_i(s)$ is given by (6.6.15).

To verify (6.6.16) we first show that it satisfies the equilibrium equation (6.6.11) According to our description of the LRU rule, (6.6.11) specialized to the state $s = [j_1, j_2, \ldots, j_m]$ gives

$$\pi_s = \beta_{j_1}\left[\sum_{j \neq j_i} \pi_{j_2,\ldots,j_m,j} + \sum_{1 \leq k \leq m} \pi_{j_2,\ldots,j_k,j_1,j_{k+1},\ldots,j_m} \right]$$

Substituting (6.6.16) we find that

$$(6.6.17) \qquad \pi_s = \beta_{j_1}\left[\sum_{j \neq j_i} \frac{\beta_j \displaystyle\prod_{i=2}^{m} \beta_{j_i}}{\displaystyle\prod_{i=2}^{m} D_i(q_j)} + \sum_{1 \leq k \leq m} \frac{\displaystyle\prod_{i=1}^{m} \beta_{j_i}}{\displaystyle\prod_{i=2}^{m} D_i(r_k)} \right]$$

where $q_j = [j_2, j_3, \ldots, j_m, j]$ and $r_k = [j_2, \ldots, j_k, j_1, j_{k+1}, \ldots, j_m]$. Now

$$(6.6.18) \qquad D_i(q_j) = 1 - \sum_{k=2}^{m-i+2} \beta_{j_k} = D_{i-1}(s) + \beta_{j_1}, \quad i > 1$$

Also, we can write

$$(6.6.19) \qquad D_i(\mathbf{r}_k) = \begin{cases} D_i(\mathbf{s}), & i \leq m - k + 1 \\ D_{i-1}(\mathbf{s}) + \beta_{j_1}, & i > m - k + 1 \end{cases}$$

Using (6.6.18) and (6.6.19) in (6.6.17) we obtain

(6.6.20)

$$\pi_{\mathbf{s}} = \prod_{i=1}^{m} \beta_{j_i} \left[\sum_{j \neq j_i} \frac{\beta_j}{\prod_{i=1}^{m} [D_i(\mathbf{s}) + \beta_{j_1}]} + \sum_{1 \leq k \leq m} \frac{\beta_{j_1}}{\prod_{i=2}^{k} D_i(\mathbf{s}) \prod_{i=k}^{m} [D_i(\mathbf{s}) + \beta_{j_1}]} \right]$$

Factoring and using $\sum_{j \neq j_i} \beta_j = D_1(\mathbf{s})$ we can put (6.6.20) into the form

$$(6.6.21) \qquad \pi_{\mathbf{s}} = \frac{\prod_{i=1}^{m} \beta_{j_i}}{\prod_{i=2}^{m} D_i(\mathbf{s})} \left[\frac{\prod_{i=1}^{m} D_i(\mathbf{s}) + \beta_{j_1} \sum_{1 \leq k \leq m} \prod_{i=k+1}^{m} D_i(\mathbf{s}) \prod_{i=1}^{k-1} [D_i(\mathbf{s}) + \beta_{j_1}]}{\prod_{i=1}^{m} [D_i(\mathbf{s}) + \beta_{j_1}]} \right]$$

By using the easily established identity

$$\prod_{i=1}^{m} x_i = \prod_{i=1}^{m} (x_i + \lambda) - \lambda \sum_{1 \leq k \leq m} \prod_{i=1}^{k-1} (x_i + \lambda) \prod_{i=k+1}^{m} x_i$$

the bracketed factor in (6.6.21) reduces to unity and (6.6.16) is obtained.

The normalization condition in (6.6.12) can be shown by induction on m. The details are left as a problem at the end of the chapter. Finally, substituting $p_f(\mathbf{s}) = D_1(\mathbf{s})$ and (6.6.16) into (6.6.13), we obtain the desired result. ∎

We shall now proceed to apply the previous analysis to the FIFO algorithm. With the FIFO algorithm the states of the Markov chain correspond to m-element FIFO lists (queues) instead of the topmost m elements of LRU stacks. Let the state $\mathbf{s} = [j_1, \ldots, j_m]$ denote a FIFO queue with j_1 the head of the queue; i.e., j_1 has been in memory for the longest time. Then the possible transitions produced by reference r_i are

$$[j_1, \ldots, j_m] \longrightarrow [j_1, \ldots, j_m], \qquad r_i = j_l \ (1 \leq l \leq m)$$
$$[j_1, \ldots, j_m] \longrightarrow [j_2, \ldots, j_m, k], \qquad r_i = k \neq j_l \ (1 \leq l \leq m)$$

Once again it is not difficult to show that $\{\mathbf{s}_i\}$ is irreducible by exhibiting an appropriate sequence of transitions from any given state to any other state. (See Problem 6-6.) For the same reasons as before we assume an initial state that is an arbitrary permutation of m pages.

To compute $F(\text{FIFO})$ we proceed as before to solve a system analogous to (6.6.11) and then substitute into the expression analogous to (6.6.13).

Theorem 6.6

For the independent-reference model,

$$(6.6.22) \qquad F(\text{FIFO}) = G^{-1} \sum_{s \in Q} D_1(s) \prod_{i=1}^{m} \beta_{j_i}$$

where

$$(6.6.23) \qquad G = \sum_{s \in Q} \prod_{i=1}^{m} \beta_{j_i}$$

and $s = [j_1, \ldots, j_m]$.

Proof. According to the transitions described earlier the equilibrium equation for $s = [j_1, \ldots, j_m]$ is given by

$$(6.6.24) \qquad \pi_s = \pi_s \sum_{i=1}^{m} \beta_{j_i} + \sum_{j \neq j_i} \beta_{j_m} \pi_{j, j_1, \ldots, j_{m-1}}$$

Into (6.6.24) we now substitute the proposed solution

$$(6.6.25) \qquad \pi_s = G^{-1} \prod_{i=1}^{m} \beta_{j_i}$$

where G is given by (6.6.23). We obtain

$$\pi_s = \pi_s[1 - D_1(s)] + \sum_{j \neq j_i} \beta_{j_m} \frac{\beta_j \prod_{i=1}^{m-1} \beta_{j_i}}{G}$$

$$= \pi_s[1 - D_1(s)] + \pi_s \sum_{j \neq j_i} \beta_j = \pi_s$$

From (6.6.25) the normalization condition (6.6.12) follows trivially; hence (6.6.25) is the desired solution of (6.6.11) for the FIFO algorithm. Finally, we substitute (6.6.25) into

$$F(\text{FIFO}) = \sum_{s \in Q} D_1(s)\pi_s$$

to obtain (6.6.22) directly. ∎

Although results have been given here only for the A_0, LRU, and FIFO algorithms with the independent-reference model, King [3] formalizes the structure of a class of paging algorithms for which the above techniques are appropriate. Also, it is not difficult to generalize the basic paging-behavior model to include the assumption that the page-reference probabilities for r_t are dependent on (and only on) the state after r_{t-1}. In particular, we do not lose the Markov property of the state sequences being analyzed. For results concerning bounds on fault rates for the independent-reference model see Problems 6-11 through 6-14.

6.7. THE LRU-STACK MODEL

In this section we shall study the *LRU-stack model*, which is known to be capable of generating reference strings whose statistical properties are very close to those of practical reference strings [14]. This model has been studied in some detail by various authors [15, 16], and its rudiments were first proposed by Shemer, et al. [17, 18].

In Section 6.4 we showed how to associate a sequence of LRU stacks $s_0 s_1 \cdots s_t \cdots$ with a reference string $r_1 r_2 \cdots r_t \cdots$. The LRU stack associated with $\omega = r_1 r_2 \cdots r_t$ is a vector $s(\omega) = [s_1(\omega), \ldots, s_n(\omega)]$ in which $s_i(\omega)$ is the ith most recently referenced page; i.e., $s(\omega)$ orders pages according to increasing backward distance. Letting $D_x(\omega)$ denote the position, or distance, of page x in stack $s(\omega)$, we were able to associate a *distance string* $D_1 D_2 \cdots D_t \cdots$ with the reference string, wherein D_t is the distance of r_t in the stack s_{t-1}. Alternatively, D_t is the number of distinct pages referenced since the most recent reference to page r_t.

According to the LRU-stack model for reference string generation, the string of LRU-stack distances is considered to be a sequence of independent random variables governed by a stationary probability mass function $\{a_i\}$

(6.7.1) $$\Pr[D_t = i] = a_i, \quad i = 1, 2, \ldots, n; t \geq 1$$

whose cumulative distribution function is given by

(6.7.2) $$A_i = \sum_{j=1}^{i} a_j$$

More precisely, suppose that we have an initial stack s_0 which, for convenience, we may take to be $s_0 = [1, 2, \ldots, n]$. Let $i = i_1 i_2 \cdots i_t \cdots$ be a sequence of sample values for the random variables D_t, $t = 1, 2, \ldots$, and let $s_0 s_1 \cdots s_t \cdots$ be the corresponding LRU-stack sequence with s_0 the initial stack. Using the notation $s_t = [s_t(1), \ldots, s_t(n)]$ the string generated by i is defined as $\omega = r_1 r_2 \cdots r_t \cdots$, where

(6.7.3) $$r_t = s_t(1), \quad t \geq 1$$

With the initial stack understood, and for a given pmf $\{a_i\}$, the class of strings definable in this manner will be called the class of *LRU reference strings*. It is meaningful, in the sense of Section 6.3, to consider optimal paging algorithms for the class of LRU reference strings defined by a given pmf $\{a_i\}$.

Before providing a solution to this problem we shall discuss some of the properties of this model.

The interest of the model derives from its ability to produce reference string patterns with correlations among references not unlike those encountered in practice. For example, if the distance distribution is chosen to be $a_k = 1$ and $a_i = 0$ for $i \neq k$, the reference string will consist of the loop

$$\omega = k, k - 1, \ldots, 2, 1, k, k - 1, \ldots, 2, 1, k, k - 1, \ldots$$

As another example, if the distance distribution is chosen to be biased toward short distances (e.g., $a_1 \geq a_2 \geq \cdots \geq a_n$), then the reference string will exhibit a tendency to cluster references to the pages near the top of the stack, modeling thereby one of the important properties of locality. (More will be said about locality in Chapter 7.) Conversely, if the distance distribution is biased toward long distances, the reference string will tend to exhibit random scattering of references across many pages.

It may be observed that, apart from our specification of s_0, our definitions amount to a probabilistic description of reference strings which is independent of the identities of specific pages. (This is in obvious contrast to the independent reference model of the previous section.) Thus it may reasonably be expected that the equilibrium probability that a given reference r_t in an LRU reference string is for page i is given by $1/n$ for all i. Problem 6-15 shows that this is in fact the case, assuming that $a_i > 0$ for all i.

Theorem 6.7

The LRU paging algorithm is optimal for a class of LRU reference strings and for all $m \geq 1$ whenever the distance distribution satisfies

$$a_1 \geq a_2 \geq \cdots \geq a_n$$

Proof. Let $r_1 r_2 \cdots r_t \cdots$ be an LRU reference string and let $C_k(S, \mathbf{s})$ denote the minimum expected number of page faults while processing $r_{t+1} \cdots r_{t+k}$, given an arbitrary memory contents $S = S_t$ ($|S| = m$) and stack $\mathbf{s} = \mathbf{s}_t$. Let $\mathbf{s} \cdot x$ denote the new stack resulting after referencing page x and updating $\mathbf{s}$ accordingly. We have the principle of optimality

(6.7.4) $C_0(S, \mathbf{s}) = 0$

$$C_{k+1}(S, \mathbf{s}) = \sum_{x \in S} b_x(\mathbf{s}) C_k(S, \mathbf{s} \cdot x)$$

$$+ \sum_{x \notin S} b_x(\mathbf{s})[1 + \min_{z \in S} C_k(S + x - z, \mathbf{s} \cdot x)]$$

where, if x is at position i in $\mathbf{s}$, $b_x(\mathbf{s}) = a_i$. Following the method of Theorem

6.2, it is sufficient to show that

$$(6.7.5) \qquad C_k(S + w', \mathbf{s}) - C_k(S + w, \mathbf{s}) \geq 0$$

where w' has greatest distance, according to $\mathbf{s}$, among the pages in $S + w + w'$. (Note that we are proving a result somewhat stronger than the theorem, for S and $\mathbf{s}$ are allowed to be arbitrary and not necessarily those values resulting from the LRU processing of $r_1 \cdots r_t$.) We proceed by induction.

Relation (6.7.5) clearly holds for $k = 0$. Suppose that it holds for an arbitrary $k \geq 0$; we shall show that it holds for $k + 1$. Applying (6.7.4) to $C_{k+1}(S + w', \mathbf{s}) - C_{k+1}(S + w, \mathbf{s})$ we get

$$
\begin{aligned}
& C_{k+1}(S + w', \mathbf{s}) - C_{k+1}(S + w, \mathbf{s}) \\
&= \sum_{x \in S} b_x(\mathbf{s})[C_k(S + w', \mathbf{s} \cdot x) - C_k(S + w, \mathbf{s} \cdot x)] + [b_w(\mathbf{s}) - b_{w'}(\mathbf{s})] \\
&\quad + b_w(\mathbf{s})[\min_{z \in S+w'} C_k(S + w' + w - z, \mathbf{s} \cdot w) - C_k(S + w, \mathbf{s} \cdot w)] \\
&\quad + b_{w'}(\mathbf{s})[C_k(S + w', \mathbf{s} \cdot w') - \min_{z \in S+w} C_k(S + w + w' - z, \mathbf{s} \cdot w')] \\
&\quad + \sum_{x \notin S+w+w'} b_x(\mathbf{s})[\min_{z \in S+w} C_k(S + w' + x - z, \mathbf{s} \cdot x) \\
&\qquad\qquad\qquad - \min_{z \in S+w} C_k(S + w + x - z, \mathbf{s} \cdot x)]
\end{aligned}
$$

By the induction hypothesis the first term is nonnegative. By assumption the second term is nonnegative. Since w' has greatest distance according to $\mathbf{s} \cdot w$, the induction hypothesis implies that $z = w'$ is optimal in the third term, in which case the third term vanishes. The (not necessarily optimal) choice $z = w$ causes the fourth term to vanish, whence a minimal cost z would make the fourth term nonnegative. Finally, the arguments showing that the third and fourth terms are nonnegative are easily applied to show that the fifth term is nonnegative. ∎

If we consider a *fixed* m, then the proof of Theorem 6.7 can be carried through under the weaker condition $\min\{a_1, \ldots, a_m\} \geq \max\{a_{m+1}, \ldots, a_n\}$. Also, if $\{m_i\}$ is a sequence of memory sizes, one can apply Theorem 6.7 separately to each interval during which memory size is constant and conclude that LRU is optimal under variations in memory size. This has obvious implications with respect to multiprogramming, which will be explored in Chapter 7.

As a final note, we observe that for the class of LRU reference strings with distance distribution $\{a_i\}$ we have

$$(6.7.6) \qquad F(\text{LRU}) = 1 - A_m$$

It is readily verified (following the methods of Theorem 6.4) that this result is independent of the initial stack s_0. Also, it follows from (6.7.6) that the equilibrium distribution of times between faults is geometric with parameter A_m.

PROBLEMS

6-1. Suppose that we want to consider *demand prepaging* algorithms that work as follows. When and only when a page is referenced which is not in memory we are allowed to bring in as many pages (necessarily including the one referenced) as we like.
    a.   Formalize this type of demand prepaging algorithm.
    b.   Work out an optimal algorithm (extending B_0) for deciding which additional pages to load and which to replace, assuming advance knowledge of the reference string.
    c.   Propose realizable prepaging algorithms of the above type and give arguments supporting their consideration.

6-2. Using the Markov chain method applied to the LRU and FIFO algorithms in this chapter verify the result for $F(A_0)$ given in (6.6.5). Note that a Markov chain can be defined for the A_0 algorithm whose state (say the ith) is given by the single page $\{z\} = S_i - L_m$, where $L_m = \{1, \ldots, m - 1\}$.

6-3. Work out the proof, by induction on m, that π_s as given by (6.6.16) satisfies (6.6.12).

6-4. Suppose that the extension problem is to be solved for the LFU algorithm. Define a minimum amount of information (state variable) that must be recorded at page-fault times in order to compute the push-pull sequences for larger memory sizes. Provide the corresponding algorithm.

6-5. Give the complete proof that A_0 is optimal (see Theorem 6.2).

6-6. Show that the Markov chain $\{s_j\}$ defined for the analysis of the FIFO algorithm is irreducible. Specifically, show that in a finite number of steps (transitions), each with nonzero probability, any given state $[j_1, \ldots, j_m]$ can be transformed into any other state $[j'_1, \ldots, j'_m]$.

6-7. Consider a set of n pages and two memory sizes m and m' satisfying $m < m' < 2m - 1$ and $n \geq [m' + m/2]$. Let $K_m[\omega]$ denote the number of page faults produced by the FIFO algorithm for the reference string ω in a memory of size m (the memory is initially empty). Define the two reference strings

$$\omega_1 = m, m + 1, \ldots, m' - 1, m', 1, 2, \ldots, m - 1$$

and

$$\omega_2 = m, 1, m + 1, 2, m + 2, 3, \ldots n, n - m + 1, 1, n - m$$
$$+ 2, \ldots, m - 1, n$$

Verify that for sufficiently large k

$$\frac{K_{m'}[\omega_1(\omega_2)^k]}{K_m[\omega_1(\omega_2)^k]}$$

can be made arbitrarily close to 2. Show that this anomalous behavior requires the above conditions on m, m', and n. A starting point is provided by study of the example $m = 4$, $m' = 6$, and $n = 8$ with

$$\omega_1 = 4, 5, 6, 1, 2, 3$$
$$\omega_2 = 4, 1, 5, 2, 6, 3, 7, 4, 8, 5, 1, 6, 2, 7, 3, 8$$

6-8. This and the next two problems investigate some of the effects of page size on the rate of page faults [19]. Let $\omega = \{r_i\}$ be a sequence of word addresses. For page size 2^a, $a \geq 0$, define $\omega(a) = \{r_i^a\}$ by deleting the a low-order bits from each member of ω. Thus $\omega(a)$ is a reference string over pages half as large as those referenced in $\omega(a + 1)$, and each page referenced in $\omega(a)$ is one half of the corresponding page in $\omega(a + 1)$. If pages i' and i'' are the halves of full page i, i' and i'' are called *buddies*.

For a given memory size m let $F_a(A, \omega)$ denote the page-entry rate of algorithm A operating on ω, i.e., with page size 2^a. Assume that m is a multiple of 2^a. Exhibit strings ω and ω' such that $F_a(A, \omega) < F_{a+1}(A, \omega)$ but $F_a(A, \omega') > F_{a+1}(A, \omega')$; i.e., halving the page size can decrease or increase the page-entry rate depending on the reference string.

Let the cost of obtaining one page from the auxiliary memory be $b + c2^a$, so that the expected cost of paging is measured by $C_a = (b + c2^a)F_a$. The parameter b signifies an initial seek or latency delay and c denotes a (word) transfer rate. Discuss the circumstances under which $C_a \leq C_{a+1}$, i.e., when halving the page size is advantageous.

6-9. We shall illustrate below that the intuitively plausible relation $F_a(A, \omega) \leq 2F_{a+1}(A, \omega)$ does not hold.

a. Consider the reference string for page size 2^a,

$$\omega(a) = \alpha_k = (1'2' \cdots n'n'' \cdots 2''1'')^k, \quad k \geq 1$$

The corresponding reference string for page size 2^{a+1} is

$$\omega(a + 1) = \beta_k = (12 \cdots nn \cdots 21)^k$$

Let $m = 2^{a+1}(n - 1)$ words. Show that

$$\lim_{k \to \infty} \frac{F_a(\text{LRU}, \alpha_k)}{F_{a+1}(\text{LRU}, \beta_k)} = n$$

(Assume an initially empty memory.)

b. Let $\omega_1 = 12 \cdots n$ and $\omega_2 = 21 \, n \cdots 3$ (where ω_2 is a permutation of ω_1). For $i = 1, 2$ define ω_i' and ω_i'' to be similar to ω_i but over pages $1', \cdots, n'$ and $1'', \cdots, n''$ respectively. Define

$$\omega(a) = \alpha_k = \omega_1''(\omega_2'\omega_2'')^k$$
$$\omega(a+1) = \beta_k = \omega_1(\omega_2\omega_2)^k$$

and let $m = 2^{a+1}(n-1)$ words. Show that

$$\lim_{k \to \infty} \frac{F_a(\text{FIFO}, \alpha_k)}{F_{a+1}(\text{FIFO}, \beta_k)} = n - 1$$

(Assume an initially empty memory.)

6-10. Suppose that A is a given stack algorithm, and consider the following algorithm A'. When a page is referenced and is not in memory, A' fetches both that page and its buddy; it replaces the pair of buddies corresponding to the page A replaces. Clearly, the same information is in memory for both A and A'. Note that $2F_{a+1}(A, \omega) = F_a(A', \omega)$ and that A' is not a demand paging algorithm. By Theorem 6.1 there exists a demand paging algorithm A'' such that $F_a(A'', \omega) \le F_a(A', \omega)$. Specify the operation of A'' and show that A'' need not be a stack algorithm even if A is.

Use the optimality of B_0 to conclude that

$$2F_{a+1}(B_0, \omega) = F_a(B_0', \omega) \ge F_a(B_0'', \omega) \ge F_a(B_0, \omega)$$

where B_0' and B_0'' are B_0 subject to the constraints of A' and A'', respectively. That is, the optimal algorithm has the property that halving the page size increases the page-entry rate by no more than a factor of 2.

6-11. In this and the following three problems, we shall consider bounds on the page-fault rates of demand paging algorithms relative to the minimum rates achievable. We shall assume the independent-reference model of Section 6.6 with page-request probabilities $\beta_1, \beta_2, \ldots, \beta_n$. Let $F(\text{MIN})$ denote the minimum paging rate over all replacement rules. We have, assuming that $\beta_1 \ge \beta_2 \ge \cdots \ge \beta_n$,

$$F(\text{MIN}) = B' = \sum_{i=m+1}^{n} \beta_i$$

where m is the number of pages in the main memory. Clearly, $F(\text{MIN})$ is achievable only when $\beta_i = 0$ for $i > m$. Show that [20]

$$1 \le \frac{F(A_0)}{F(\text{MIN})} \le 1 + \frac{(1 - B')}{1 + (m-1)B'} \le 2$$

6-12. We may write

$$F(\text{LRU}) = \sum_{i=1}^{n} \beta_i p_i \le B' + \sum_{i=1}^{m} \beta_i p_i$$

where p_i is the stationary probability that the ith page is not in main memory. Two conditions necessary for page i to be absent from main memory are that

1. A page $j(j > m)$ must have been referenced since the last reference to page i, and
2. Page i has not been referenced for $m - 1$ references. Verify from this observation that [20]

$$p_i \leq \left(1 - \frac{\beta_i}{\beta_i + B'}\right)(1 - \beta_i)^{m-1}$$

and hence that

$$\frac{F(\text{LRU})}{F(\text{MIN})} \leq 1 + \frac{m(1 - B')}{1 + (m - 1)B'}$$

For the last inequality it is convenient to use the fact that $\sum_{i=1}^{m} f(\beta_i)$ is maximized by taking $\beta_1 = \beta_2 = \cdots = \beta_m$ when $f(\beta_i)$ is convex:

$$2f\left(\frac{\beta_1 + \beta_2}{2}\right) \geq f(\beta_1) + f(\beta_2)$$

6-13. Our purpose now is to develop a bound on the amount of main memory required to guarantee a given performance using the LRU algorithm. Suppose that we have an $(m + k)$-page main memory. Verify that a necessary condition for page i $(1 \leq i \leq m)$ to be absent from main memory is that at least $k + 1$ pages in $\{m + 1, \ldots, m + k\}$ have been requested since the last request for page i. Show that the probability p_i of this condition is such that

$$p_i \leq \left(\frac{B'}{\beta_i + B'}\right)^{k+1} = g(\beta_i)$$

Verify that

$$\max_{\substack{0 \leq \beta_i \leq 1 \\ k \geq 1}} \beta_i g(\beta_i) = \frac{B'}{k}\left(1 - \frac{1}{k + 1}\right)^{k+1}$$

and hence that [20]

$$\frac{F_{m+k}(\text{LRU})}{F_m(\text{MIN})} \leq 1 + \frac{\sum_{i=1}^{m} \beta_i p_i}{B'} \leq 1 + \frac{m}{k}\left(1 - \frac{1}{k + 1}\right)^{k+1}$$

where the subscript in the notation $F_j(\cdot)$ makes explicit the main memory size to which the fault rate corresponds. Note that the above can be approximated for large k by $1 + m/ke$.

6-14. Show that for each $\epsilon > 0$, there exists a probability distribution $\{\beta_1, \ldots, \beta_n\}$ for the FIFO algorithm such that

$$\frac{F_{m+k}(\text{FIFO})}{F_m(\text{MIN})} \geq 1 + \frac{m}{k + 1} - \epsilon$$

[Use the FIFO result in Section 6.6 and suppose that $\beta_i = (1 - B')/m$ $(1 \leq i \leq m)$ and $\beta_i = B'/(n - m)\,(i > m)$.] Compare and interpret this result relative to the result in Problem 6-13.

6-15. Consider the LRU-stack model for reference-string generation (Section 6.7).
   a. Show that the reference string $r_1 r_2 \cdots r_t \cdots$ generated by this model is not a sequence of independent random variables.
   b. Define the Markov chain $\{X_i(j)\}$ so that $X_i(j)$ is the position of page j in the LRU stack just following the ith reference. Let $X_0(j) = j$ and note that $X_i(j) \in \{1, \ldots, n\}$ for all i. Let $\{\pi_k\}$ denote the steady-state distribution for the position of page j in the stack, and assume that $a_k > 0$ for all k. Show that the transition matrix for the chain $\{X_i(j)\}$ is doubly stochastic (its rows and columns sum to 1) and therefore that $\pi_k = 1/n$ for all k. The significance of this is, in the long run, that each page is equally likely to be referenced and that therefore the model is useful for treating the clustering effect of locality but not the nonuniform page referencing.

6-16. Using the techniques described in Section 6.6 show that for the independent-reference model [21]

$$F(\text{RAND}) = F(\text{FIFO})$$

where RAND denotes the page replacement rule that selects at random from current memory contents for the replacement page. [Specifically, each page in (full) memory has probabilty $1/m$ of being selected for replacement.]

6-17. Let $C_k(S, s)$ denote the minimal demand paging cost of processing $r_{t+1} \cdots r_{t+k}$ given that the memory state is $S_t = S$ and the reference string $r_{t+1} \cdots r_{t+k}$ is generated by the LRU-stack model with initial stack $s = s_t$.

Let S denote the topmost m elements of stack s and let S' be any set of m pages appearing in s. Show that

$$0 \leq C_k(S', s) - C_k(S, s) \leq |S - S'|$$

Use this to show that the page-fault probability of LRU on LRU reference strings is asymptotically $1 - A_m$ [see (6.7.6)]; that is,

$$F(\text{LRU}) = \lim_{k \to \infty} \frac{C_k(S', s)}{k} = 1 - A_m$$

REFERENCES

1. AHO, A. V., P. J. DENNING, and J. D. ULLMAN, "Principles of optimal page replacement." *J. ACM 18*, 1 (Jan. 1971), 80–93.

2. MATTSON, R. L., J. GECSEI, D. R. SLUTZ, and I. L. TRAIGER, "Evaluation techniques for storage hierarchies." *IBM Sys. J. 9*, 2 (1970), 78–117.

3. KING, W. F., III, "Analysis of paging algorithms." *IFIP Conf. Proc.* Ljubljana, Yugoslavia (Aug. 1971).

4. COFFMAN, E. G., JR., and B. RANDELL, "Performance predictions for extended paged memories." *Acta Informatica 1*, 1 (1971), 1–13.

5. KNUTH, D. E., *The Art of Computer Programming* (Vol. 1). Addison-Wesley, Reading, Mass. (1968), 435–455.

6. PURDOM, P. W., JR., and S. M. STIGLER, "Statistical properties of the buddy system." *J. ACM 17*, 4 (Oct. 1970), 683–697.

7. ROBSON, J. M., "An estimate of the store size necessary for dynamic storage allocation." *J. ACM 18*, 3 (July 1971), 416–423.

8. BELADY, L. A. "A study of replacement algorithms for virtual storage computers." *IBM Sys. J. 5*, 2 (1966), 78–101.

9. BELADY, L. A., R. A. NELSON, and G. S. SHEDLER, "An anomaly in the space-time characteristics of certain programs running in paging machines." *Comm. ACM 12*, 6 (June 1969), 349–353.

10. COFFMAN, E. G., JR., and L. C. VARIAN, "Further experimental data on the behavior of programs in a paging environment." *Comm. ACM 11*, 7 (July 1968), 471–474.

11. KUCK, D. J., and D. H. LAWRIE, "The use and performance of memory hierarchies—A survey," in *Software Engineering* Vol. I (J. T. Tou, ed.). Academic Press, New York (1970), 45–78.

12. POMERANZ, J. E., "Paging with fewest expected replacements." *Proc. IFIPS Congress* (Aug. 1971), 160–162.

13. COFFMAN, E. G., JR., and N. D. JONES, "Priority paging algorithms and the extension problem." *Proc. 11th Switching and Automata Theory Symp.* (Oct. 1971).

14. DENNING, P. J., J. E. SAVAGE, and J. R. SPIRN, "Models for locality in program behavior." Department of Electrical Engineering, Princeton Univ., Princeton, N. J., Computer Science report TR-107 (Apr. 1972).

15. ODEN, P. H., and G. S. SHEDLER, "A model of memory contention in a paging machine." IBM T. J. Watson Research Center report RC-3053, Yorktown Heights, N.Y. (Sept. 1970).

16. SHEDLER, G. S., and C. TUNG., "Locality in page reference strings." *SIAM J. Comput. 1*, 3 (Sept. 1972), 218–241.

17. SHEMER, J. E., and S. C. GUPTA, On the design of Bayesian storage allocation algorithms for paging and segmentation." *IEEE Trans. Comp. C-18*, 7 (July 1969), 644–651.

18. SHEMER, J. E., and B. SHIPPEY, "Statistical analysis of paged and segmented computer systems." *IEEE Trans. Comp. EC-15*, 6 (Dec. 1966), 855–863.

19. HATFIELD, D. J., "Experiments on page size, program access patterns, and virtual memory performance." *IBM J. Res. Develop. 16*, 1 (1972), 58–66.

20. FRANASZEK, P. A., and T. J. WAGNER., "Some distribution-free aspects of paging algorithm performance." Technical report, IBM Research Center, Yorktown Heights, N.Y. (Apr. 1972). To appear in *J. ACM*.

21. GELENBE, E. "Random partially pre-loaded page replacement algorithms." Technical report, Electrical and Computer Engineering Dept., Uni. of Michigan. Ann Arbor (Nov. 1971).

7 MULTIPROGRAMMED MEMORY MANAGEMENT

7.1. INTRODUCTION

Our results in Chapter 6 were concerned exclusively with the behavior of paging algorithms in fixed-size memory spaces. Except for the independent-reference model, all the results were with respect to a specific, but arbitrary, reference string. Inasmuch as practical multiprogramming situations often do not guarantee a program a fixed amount of space in which to operate and do not have prior knowledge of program reference strings, it is necessary to remove these two restrictions.

As noted in Chapter 1, the basic problem of interest in multiprogramming is partitioning the main memory space M among the active tasks. Specifically, at each moment of time t there will be a partition of memory

$$(7.1.1) \qquad \mathbf{Z}(t) = (Z_1(t), \ldots, Z_n(t))$$

where $Z_i(t)$ represents the set or block of pages of the ith active task; also†

$$(7.1.2) \qquad \bigcup_{i=1}^{n} Z_i(t) \subseteq M; \qquad Z_i(t) \cap Z_j(t) = \varnothing \quad (i \neq j)$$

In terms of (7.1.1), several problems present themselves: 1) Should $\mathbf{Z}(t)$ be a fixed or variable partition? 2) How should the blocks of $\mathbf{Z}(t)$ be determined? 3) If the size of $Z_i(t)$ is held fixed during some time interval, what policy should be used to determine fetches and replacements to $Z_i(t)$? As will be seen, it is necessary to define an intrinsic (machine-independent) measure of a

---

†The issues related to shared pages [$Z_i(t)$ and $Z_j(t)$ overlapping] will not be considered here.

program's demands for memory before answers to these questions can be obtained. The measure we shall use is known as the program's *working set*.

Unfortunately, the techniques of stack algorithms (Chapter 6) do not generalize in any useful way to multiprogramming. One reason for this is: If the memory space is permitted to vary, a priority algorithm will in general not be a stack algorithm in the sense that the top m entries of the stack would be in memory whenever the program is allocated m pages. As an example, consider a three-page program in this situation:

| | Time | |
	t	$t + 1$
Memory space	3	2
Page referenced	—	2
Priority list	(1, 2, 3)	—
Stack	(3, 2, 1)	(2, 3, 1)
Memory state	{1, 2, 3}	{1, 2}

The memory state S_{t+1} is obtained from S_t by deleting the lowest priority page; evidently S_{t+1} does not comprise the top two elements of the stack s$(t + 1)$. The only priority paging algorithm which will be a stack algorithm under variations in memory space allocation is the LRU algorithm, because its stack and priority list are identical at all times (cf. Chapter 6).

That the stack algorithm results do not depend on, or take advantage of, explicit properties of reference strings is a second reason they do not provide useful generalizations for multiprogramming. For these reasons, it is necessary to begin our treatment of multiprogramming with a discussion of the properties of *locality*, which are exhibited by practical reference strings, and to study how management algorithms can be designed to exploit this property and operate nearly optimally. It is not our intention to discuss program models per se (i.e., models of the mechanisms by which programs generate reference strings); our object is exposing the properties of multiprogrammed memory management procedures when applied to any reference strings satisfying locality, irrespective of what model describes the generation of those reference strings.

7.2. LOCALITY

Informally, the property of locality implies that a program tends to favor a subset of its pages during any time interval and that the membership of the set of favored pages tends to change slowly. This property has been observed repeatedly in experimental studies of program behavior [1–8] and it seems natural to include it as fundamental in our assumptions about program behavior. We can summarize the properties of locality in three statements:

L1. During any interval of time, a program concentrates references nonuniformly over its pages.

L2. Correlation between immediate past and immediate future reference patterns tends to be high, and correlation between nonoverlapping reference substrings tends to zero as the distance between them increases.

L3. Taken as a function of time, the frequency with which a given page is referenced tends to change slowly; i.e., it is quasi-stationary.

Of these three properties of locality, L3 places the strictest limitations on the applicability of the results. We have included it for three reasons. First, the majority of effective analysis techniques is limited to models for which assumption L3 is required. Second, it is possible to approximate certain aspects of nonstationary behavior by stationary models or by sequences of stationary models. Third, there is considerable evidence that the degree to which a program obeys L1–L3 can be enhanced by appropriately training programmers [2, 7, 9] or by appropriately distributing instruction and data code among pages [10]; thus it is possible in principle to influence programmers and compilers to develop programs satisfying the principle of locality.

The principle of locality is an abstraction of at least three phenomena observed in practice. First, programs tend to use sequential and looping control structures heavily and cluster references to given pages within short time intervals. Second, programmers tend to concentrate their attention on small parts of large problems for moderately long intervals, and simple alterations in algorithm strategy and data organization can magnify this effect by orders of magnitude [2, 7, 10]. Third, it is known from experience that programs may be run efficiently with only a subset of pages in main memory [7, 11, 12, 14].

It has been implied above that the properties of locality are highly desirable. For the more pronounced they are, the smaller are the main storage requirements of the program likely to be for efficient execution, and the more reliably is it possible to predict the memory requirements of a program based on observations of its immediate past reference string. For example, the working set model (to be discussed shortly), which is based directly on the assumptions of locality, is known to be viable in practice [6, 14]; the degree to which it is a reliable predictor of future memory demand increases as its adherence to L2 and L3 increases.

7.3. THE WORKING SET MODEL [3, 15, 16]

Consider an n-page program whose pages constitute the set $N = \{1, \ldots, n\}$. Neither the page size nor the manner of distributing address space words among pages are of concern here. A program's working set is, intuitively, the smallest subset of N that must be loaded in main memory to ensure a given level of efficiency in terms of page-fault rates.

7.3.1. Assumptions About Reference Strings

A program's reference string $r_1 r_2 \ldots r_t \ldots$ (over the set of pages N) can be regarded as a sequence of random variables, a discrete random process. The basic transition probabilities of interest are

$$(7.3.1) \qquad g_{ij}(t, x) = \Pr[r_{t+x} = j \mid r_t = i]; \quad i, j \in N, t \geq 1, x \geq 1$$

In the following discussion we shall make three assumptions about reference strings. First, we shall assume that the transition probabilities are *stationary*; i.e., the $g_{ij}(t, x)$ are independent of the origin of the interval $(t, t + x)$. (This is a more restrictive statement of locality property L3.) Of particular interest are the stationary *interreference densities* and *distributions*, respectively, determined from the $g_{ij}(t, x)$ as follows:

$$(7.3.2) \qquad f_i(x) = \begin{cases} g_{ii}(t, 1), & x = 1 \\ g_{ii}(t, x) - \sum_{k=1}^{x-1} f_i(k) g_{ii}(t + k, x - k), & x > 1 \end{cases}$$

$$(7.3.3) \qquad F_i(x) = \sum_{k=1}^{x} f_i(k)$$

Note that $f_i(x)$ is interpreted as the probability that an interval between two successive references to the same page i is of length x; it is analogous to the interarrival distributions used earlier in analyses of queueing systems.

Of the three assumptions, stationarity places the strongest limitation on the applicability of the results in practice. The limitations can be made clearer by the following considerations. According to the assumptions of locality, we may picture the program as making transitions from time to time among *localities*, a locality being some subset of N; the pages of the current locality are referenced with high probability. To be specific, suppose that the program, as it generates references $r_1 r_2 \ldots r_t \ldots$, passes through a sequence of localities $L_0 L_1 \ldots L_t \ldots$ in which $L_t \subseteq N$ and $L_t = L_{t-1}$ with high probability. If $L_t = L$ for $t_1 \leq t < t_2$, then $r_t \in L$ for all $t_1 \leq t < t_2$. Thus a reference string ω can be written as $\omega = \omega_1 \omega_2 \ldots \omega_i \ldots$ in which ω_i is a reference string generated over the ith distinct locality in the sequence $L_0 L_1 \ldots L_t \ldots$.

Now, one would expect that whatever nonstationarities exist in ω would depend primarily on locality; i.e., ω_i can be regarded as generated by a stationary stochastic mechanism. It follows that the stationarity assumption is in effect a restriction to one of a program's localities. Note that we could approximate a reference string $\omega = \omega_1 \omega_2 \ldots \omega_i \ldots$ by a sequence of models, each obeying the stationarity assumption, the ith model in the sequence being used to deal with the substring ω_i. If one attempts to apply our results to a given reference string segment containing many interlocality transitions, the results may not be meaningful inasmuch as they then pertain to program behavior averaged over many localities: The average behavior of many localities need not be representative of any given locality. In other words, the results are applicable locally in a reference string but not necessarily globally. Since our primary interest is understanding the behavior of the working set model as an adaptive estimator for use in memory management, this restriction will not be severe so long as the measurement intervals are comparable to or less than interlocality transition times. The foregoing ideas constitute the basis for the locality model [17], some aspects of which are considered in the Problems.

Our second assumption about reference strings is that each page is *recurrent*, i.e.,

$$(7.3.4) \qquad \sum_{x \geq 1} f_i(x) = 1$$

so that each page is referenced again, after a particular reference, with probability 1. Extensions including nonrecurrent (transient) pages are straightforward and will not be considered. The *mean interreference interval* for page i is defined to be

$$(7.3.5) \qquad \bar{x}_i = \sum_{x \geq 1} x f_i(x)$$

Since the above assumptions guarantee that the subsequence of times at which page i is referenced in $r_1 r_2 \ldots r_t \ldots$ is a renewal process, we may define the long-run probability of a reference to page i as†

$$(7.3.6) \qquad \beta_i = \frac{1}{\bar{x}_i}$$

We shall define the *overall interreference distribution* and *density* as, respectively,

$$(7.3.7) \qquad F(x) = \sum_{i \in N} \beta_i F_i(x)$$

$$(7.3.8) \qquad f(x) = F(x) - F(x - 1), \quad x \geq 1$$

where $F(0) \equiv 0$. According to our assumptions and (7.3.6), the mean overall

---

†As with similar arguments in Chapter 5, consider a long reference string of length t; the expected number of references to page i is approximately $t\beta_i$ and the mean distance between two of them is approximately $t/t\beta_i$. Asymptotically, we have (7.3.6).

interreference interval is

(7.3.9)
$$\bar{x} = \sum_{i \in N} \beta_i \bar{x}_i = n$$

The third assumption that we shall make about reference strings is *asymptotic uncorrelation;* i.e., r_t and r_{t+x} become uncorrelated in the limit $x \longrightarrow \infty$. This assumption is met by most physical processes; it is a statement that knowledge of the present is of little use in predicting the distant future. This assumption guarantees the ergodic property that time averages (over particular reference strings) converge to the corresponding ensemble averages. This assumption is a restatement of locality property L2.

7.3.2. Definitions

A program's working set at a given time should, ideally, be the current locality at that time. In the absence of prior information about the future reference string or about a program's localities, it is necessary to estimate the current locality. One possible way to do this defines a priority list $\mathbf{p}(t)$ and an integer $k(t)$ at time t and defines the working set to be the first $k(t)$ elements of $\mathbf{p}(t)$. A special case which has proved both amenable to analysis and viable in practice is defining the working set to be a set of most recently referenced pages.

A program's working set $W(t, T)$ at time t is defined to be the set of distinct pages referenced in the time interval $[t - T + 1, t]$, i.e., among r_{t-T+1} ... r_t. If $t < T$, $W(t, T)$ contains the distinct pages among $r_1 r_2 ... r_t$, and if $t \leq 0$, $W(t, T)$ is empty. The parameter T is called the *window size* since $W(t, T)$ can be regarded as the contents of a window covering the last T references of the reference string. This definition will provide a reliable estimator of current locality provided T can be chosen

1. Large enough so that the probability of a current-locality page's being missing from the working set is small, and

2. Small enough so that the probability of more than one interlocality transition's being contained in the window is small.

The *working set principle* of memory management asserts that a program may be active (eligible to receive processor service) only if its working set is in main memory. Stated as a replacement rule, it asserts that no active program's working set pages may be candidates for replacement. In particular, if the multiprogrammed memory is entirely filled with working set pages, it would be necessary to deactivate some program in order to create candidate pages for removal. This principle of memory management is sufficient to prevent thrashing, the collapse of system performance resulting from attempted overcommitment of main memory [4, 5].

The more the locality properties L1–L3 hold, the more likely will it be that T can be chosen to satisfy the two requirements given above; i.e., the more likely will it be that working set $W(t, T)$ can produce reliable estimates of current locality. Moreover, the better a program's locality properties, the longer will be the expected remaining holding time in the current locality; in this case a locality page will tend to have a shorter forward distance (time until next reference) than a nonlocality page, and managing memory according to the working set principle will tend toward optimality (replacing pages with longest forward distances as discussed in Chapter 6). Cases in which a working set policy is optimal or very nearly so are discussed in the Problems.

The *working set size* $w(t, T)$ is the number of pages in $W(t, T)$. In studying working set memory management, it is sufficient in most cases to characterize the stationary behavior of the process $w(t, T)$; the working set can be taken as the top $w(t, T)$ elements of the reference string's LRU stack at time t. We shall return later to the relation between working sets and the LRU paging algorithm.

Let $h(z, T)$ denote the probability mass function in the steady state of working set size, i.e.,

$$(7.3.10) \qquad h(z, T) = \lim_{t \to \infty} \Pr[w(t, T) = z]$$

[As will be shown shortly, $h(z, T)$ can be approximated by a normal distribution under general conditions.] The *mean working set* size is defined to be

$$(7.3.11) \qquad s(T) = \lim_{t \to \infty} E[w(t, T)] = \sum_{z=1}^{n} z h(z, T)$$

Now, since the definition of working set is based on observing the reference string post facto, the model cannot be used to predict the reference of a previously unreferenced page. It can, however, be used to assess the probability that a previously referenced page will return. To this end, we define the long-run *missing-page probability* $m(T)$ to be

$$(7.3.12) \qquad m(T) = \lim_{t \to \infty} \Pr[r_{t+1} \notin W(t, T)]$$

In systems using the working set principle of memory management, $m(T)$ will only be an upper bound on the page-fault probability experienced by a program, since a page may leave the working set and subsequently be referenced without leaving main memory in the meantime. An alternative definition of $m(T)$ can be formulated by defining the binary random variable

$$(7.3.13) \qquad \Delta(t, T) = \begin{cases} 1, & \text{if } r_{t+1} \notin W(t, T) \\ 0, & \text{otherwise} \end{cases}$$

whereupon

(7.3.14) $$m(T) = \lim_{t \to \infty} E[\Delta(t, T)]$$

7.3.3. Properties

Consider Fig 7.3-1, from which it is apparent that

(7.3.15) $$w(t + 1, T + 1) = w(t, T) + \Delta(t, T)$$

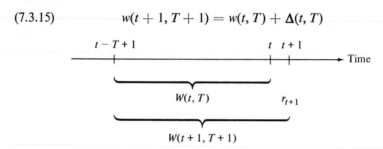

Fig. 7.3-1 Inclusion property of working sets.

Upon taking expectations and limits on both sides of (7.3.15), one finds that $s(T + 1) = s(T) + m(T)$. We have

(7.3.16) $$s(T + 1) - s(T) = m(T)$$

(7.3.17) $$s(T) = \sum_{x=0}^{T-1} m(x)$$

In words, these equations state that $m(T)$ can be regarded as the "slope" of the curve $s(T)$ versus T.

Example

Figure 7.3-2(a) enumerates working sets for a given 20-reference string and six values of T. An entry for given (t, T) is a column of numbers showing the membership of $W(t, T)$, ordered downward according to increasing backward distance. An entry (t, T) is marked with the symbol Δ if $\Delta(t, T) = 1$. The quantities $s(T)$ and $m(T)$ have been computed as time averages over the reference string and the results indicated. Figures 7.3-2(b) and (c) are plots of $s(T)$ and $m(T)$. Note that the relation $s(T + 1) - s(T) \leq m(T)$ holds here, equality not being achieved because (7.3.16) is based on the limit of infinite-length reference strings. The error between $s(T + 1) - s(T)$ and $m(T)$ for k-length reference strings is $\Theta(1/k)$ as seen in Problem 7-3.

Define the binary random variable $\alpha_i(t, T)$ to be 1 if and only if page i is in $W(t, T)$. Then

(7.3.18) $$w(t, T) = \sum_{i \in N} \alpha_i(t, T)$$

T	1 2 3 4 5 2 1 3 3 2 3 4 5 4 5 1 1 3 2 5	$s(T)$	$m(T)$

| 1 | 1 2 3 4 5 2 1 3 3 2 3 4 5 4 5 1 1 3 2 5 | 1.00 | 0.90 |

△ △ △ △ △ △ △ △   △ △ △ △ △ △   △ △ △

| 2 | 1 2 3 4 5 2 1 3 3 2 3 4 5 4 5 1 1 3 2 5 | 1.85 | 0.75 |
| | 1 2 3 4 5 2 1   3 2 3 4 5 4 5   1 3 2 | | |

△ △ △ △ △ △ △ △   △   △ △   △   △ △ △

3	1 2 3 4 5 2 1 3 3 2 3 4 5 4 5 1 1 3 2 5	2.50	0.75
	1 2 3 4 5 2 1 1 3 2 3 4 5 4 5 5 1 3 2		
	1 2 3 4 5 2 2 3 4 1 3		

△ △ △ △ △ △ △ △   △   △ △   △   △ △ △

4	1 2 3 4 5 2 1 3 3 2 3 4 5 4 5 1 1 3 2 5	3.10	0.65
	1 2 3 4 5 2 1 1 3 2 3 4 5˙ 4 5 5 1 3 2		
	1 2 3 4 5 2 2 1 2 3 3 4 4 5 1 3		
	1 2 3 4 5 2 1		

△ △ △ △ △   △ △   △ △   △   △ △ △

5	1 2 3 4 5 2 1 3 3 2 3 4 5 4 5 1 1 3 2 5	3.55	0.55
	1 2 3 4 5 2 1 1 3 2 3 4 5 4 5 5 1 3 2		
	1 2 3 4 5 2 2 1 1 2 3 3 3 4 4 5 1 3		
	1 2 3 4 4 4 2 2 4 5 1		

△ △ △ △ △ △   △   △ △   △   △ △

6	1 2 3 4 5 2 1 3 3 2 3 4 5 4 5 1 1 3 2 5	3.90	0.50
	1 2 3 4 5 2 1 1 3 2 3 4 5 4 5 5 1 3 2		
	1 2 3 4 5 2 2 1 1 2 3 3 3 4 4 5 1 3		
	1 2 3 4 5 5 5 1 2 2 2 3 4 5 1		
	1 1 3 4 4 4		

△ △ △ △ △   △ △   △   △ △

(a)

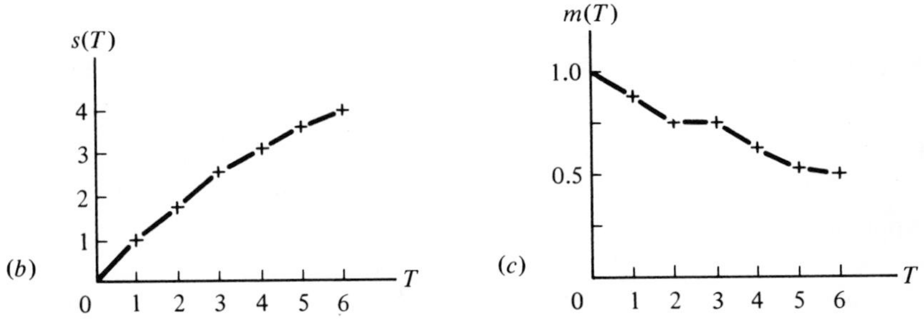

(b)

(c)

Fig. 7.3-2   Example.

For the expected value in equilibrium we have

$$s(T) = \lim_{t \to \infty} E[w(t, T)] = \lim_{t \to \infty} \sum_{i \in N} E[\alpha_i(t, T)]$$

Defining $\Pr[\alpha_i(T) = 1] = \lim_{t \to \infty} \Pr[\alpha_i(t, T) = 1]$ we have

(7.3.19) $$s(T) = \sum_{i \in N} \Pr[\alpha_i(T) = 1]$$

To obtain $\Pr[\alpha_i(T) = 1]$ we identify it with the probability that a page reference r_t selected at random in equilibrium falls within an interreference interval for page i whose elapsed time (number of references) does not exceed T. This is the so-called backward recurrence time problem described in Appendix B. As indicated there, the distribution of backward recurrence times is the same as that for forward recurrence times. Specifically, from Eq. (B.7), for the stationary distribution of backward recurrence times (see also Section 4.2.3 and Problem 4-12) we have

(7.3.20) $$R(T) = \frac{1}{\bar{x}} \int_0^T [1 - G(x)] \, dx$$

where $G(x)$ is the distribution function for the time intervals between successive events (renewals) and $\bar{x}$ is its first moment. In the discrete case at hand $\bar{x}$ is replaced by $\bar{x}_i$, $G(x)$ by $F_i(x)$, and the integral in (7.3.20) by a summation. Thus for $\Pr[\alpha_i(T) = 1]$ we have

(7.3.21) $$\Pr[\alpha_i(T) = 1] = \frac{1}{\bar{x}_i} \sum_{x=0}^{T-1} [1 - F_i(x)]$$

(This relation can be derived directly using precisely the same steps as in Appendix B.) Therefore

$$s(T) = \sum_{i \in N} \Pr[\alpha_i(T) = 1] = \sum_{i \in N} \sum_{x=0}^{T-1} \frac{1 - F_i(x)}{\bar{x}_i}$$

Reversing the order of summation and applying (7.3.6) and (7.3.7) we find

(7.3.22) $$s(T) = \sum_{x=0}^{T-1} (1 - F(x))$$

Applying (7.3.17) we find

(7.3.23) $$m(T) = 1 - F(T)$$

The importance of these results is that they establish the relation between interreference distributions, missing-page probability, and mean working set size.

The properties of $s(T)$ and $m(T)$ are summarized in Figs. 7.3-3 and 7.3-4. The curve $s(T)$ is bounded above by $\min\{n, T\}$; it is nondecreasing in T, and it is concave down, i.e.,

(7.3.24)
$$\frac{s(T-1) + s(T+1)}{2} \le s(T)$$

where (7.3.24) follows from the fact that $m(T)$ is nonincreasing.

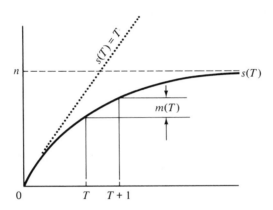

Fig. 7.3-3   Working set size.

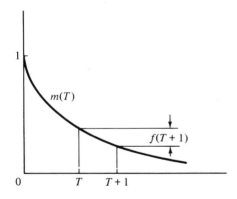

Fig. 7.3-4   Missing-page probability.

7.3.4.   Distribution of Working Set Size

It was stated earlier that, under general conditions, the distribution of working set size is approximately normal; i.e., the random process $w(t, T)$ is a stationary normal process. The conditions of locality, especially the asymptotic-uncorrelation condition, are sufficient to guarantee this. The assumption of a normal (Gaussian) process means that the density function $h(z, T)$ of working set size is given by the normal density

(7.3.25)
$$h(z, T) = \frac{1}{\sqrt{2\pi\sigma^2(T)}} e^{-(z-s(T))^2/2\sigma^2(T)}$$

where the mean is

(7.3.26)
$$s(T) = \int_{-\infty}^{\infty} zh(z, T) \, dz$$

and the variance is

(7.3.27)
$$\sigma^2(T) = \int_{-\infty}^{\infty} (z - s(T))^2 h(z, T) \, dz$$

In general, for an arbitrary set of n time points $t_1, \ldots, t_n$, the joint distribution of $w(t_1, T), \ldots, w(t_n, T)$ is jointly normal. In view of the enormous literature dealing with properties of normal processes, the assumption of normality can be crucial and can be exploited to great advantage in systems design. It is worthwhile, then, to investigate the conditions under which the normal approximation will be valid.

It is not essential in the following discussion to assume that $w(t, T)$ is stationary; quasi-stationarity will do. Good approximations can be obtained by replacing the mean $s(T)$ and variance $\sigma^2(T)$ with slowly time-varying mean $s(t, T)$ and variance $\sigma^2(t, T)$ in (7.3.25).

There are two immediate deviations inherent in the normal approximation: The distribution is defined for negative as well as positive values of working set size; and the distribution is continuous, whereas working set sizes can only be discrete values. The magnitude of the first deviation will be negligible for most parameter values $s(T)$ and $\sigma(T)$ of interest. The extent of the second deviation is kept small by dealing with programs whose working set size may vary over a sufficiently large number of values. Some experimental studies of working set sizes over reference strings generated by a model of locality show that the normal approximation can be remarkably good [18].

Assuming that the normal approximation is valid, we would require knowledge of the mean $s(T)$ and variance $\sigma^2(T)$ to completely characterize it. The analytic tools developed previously give us ways of calculating $s(T)$, but without detailed assumptions about the statistical dependencies among pages or among references it is not possible to determine $\sigma^2(T)$ analytically. Of course, in a practical situation, if the conditions for the validity of the normal approximation hold, it is necessary to measure only $s(T)$ and $\sigma^2(T)$. Even though the variables α_i of (7.3.19) are dependent, the linearity of expectation allowed us to express $s(T)$ as the sum of $E[\alpha_i(T)]$. The variance of working set size is given by

$$(7.3.28) \qquad \sigma^2(T) = \lim_{t \to \infty} E[w^2(t, T)] - s^2(T) = \sum_{i \in N} \sum_{j \in N} E[\alpha_i \alpha_j] - s^2(T)$$

Clearly, it is not possible to evaluate $\sigma^2(T)$ without assumptions about the covariance, which would follow from assumptions about the transition probabilities $g_{ij}(t, x)$ of (7.3.1).

To further justify the normal approximation let us express the working set size process in terms of a sequence of random variables $\theta(t, T)$, $t > 1$:

$$(7.3.29) \qquad w(t, T) = w(t - 1, T) + \theta(t, T)$$

According to the definition of working set, $\theta(t, T)$ can assume the values $-1, 0$, or $+1$. In terms of this sequence, the working set size at time t is

$$(7.3.30) \qquad w(t, T) = \sum_{k=1}^{t} \theta(k, T)$$

To apply the classic central limit theorem to (7.3.30), it would be necessary for the sequence $\{\theta(t, T)\}_{t \geq 1}$ to consist of independent random variables. This clearly is not so. The assumption that references are asymptotically uncorrelated, however, allows us to infer that $\theta(t, T)$ and $\theta(t + x, T)$ become uncorrelated as $x \to \infty$, and this is sufficient to allow a central limit theorem argument to be carried through. Let q be a given positive integer and observe that (7.3.30) can be written (for large t) as

$$(7.3.31) \qquad w(t, T) = \sum_{r=1}^{q} \sum_{k \geq 0} \theta(kq + r, T)$$

By choosing q sufficiently large, the correlation between successive terms in the subsequence $\{\theta(kq + r, T)\}_{k \geq 0}$ can be made arbitrarily small, so that

$$(7.3.32) \qquad w_r = \sum_{k \geq 0} \theta(kq + r, T), \quad r = 1, 2, \ldots, q$$

is approximated by a normal process. Then the working set size is

$$(7.3.33) \qquad w(t, T) = w_1 + \cdots + w_q$$

which, being the sum of (dependent) normal processes, is itself normal. Observe that the mean is asymptotically $s(T)$ but that we cannot specify the variance without assumptions regarding the correlations among the terms $w_1, \ldots, w_q$.

The argument of (7.3.29)–(7.3.33) is not a formal proof that $w(t, T)$ is approximately normal. A formal proof using an assumption more general than asymptotic uncorrelation can be found in [19]; the details are intricate and not particularly enlightening for our purposes. It is important to note that, when the asymptotic uncorrelation assumption is not met, the normal approximation to $w(t, T)$ may be poor; some of the programs cited in [20] do not have this property and have a nonnormally distributed working set size. Any program with a large, global loop may fail to satisfy this property and may also fail to have normally distributed working set size.

7.4. RELATION BETWEEN LRU PAGING
AND WORKING SETS

We noted earlier that the contents of the working set $W(t, T)$ can be determined by taking the top $w(t, T)$ entries of the program's LRU (least recently used) stack at time t; i.e., the LRU algorithm can be used to simulate the working set algorithm. This can be done by modifying the LRU stack so that, for each i, the ith entry is a pair $s_i = (j, t_j)$ in which j is the ith most recently referenced page and t_j is the time at which j was most recently referenced; given T, the working set size at time t is the largest integer z such that $s_z = (j, t_j)$ and $t_j \in [t - T + 1, t]$.

The LRU paging algorithm can also be simulated by the working set model. The basis for the simulation is that the contents of a p-page LRU memory is always the p most recently referenced pages, whereas the contents of a working set $W(t, T)$ is always the $w(t, T)$ most recently referenced pages. This suggests that the missing-page probability for a working set of average size p can be used to estimate the page-fault probability for a p-page LRU memory (cf. Fig. 7.4-1):

(7.4.1) $$F_p(\text{LRU}) \cong m(T_p), \qquad s(T_p) = p$$

Other properties of this relation are investigated in the Problems.

The following examples show how to apply and to extend the foregoing discussion to control fault probabilities within specified ranges.

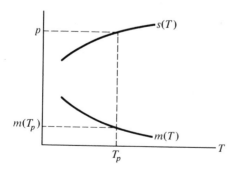

Fig. 7.4-1 Estimating LRU paging rate.

Example

Suppose that $m_1 > m_2$ and that it is desired to control T so that $m_1 \geq m(T)$ $\geq m_2$ with high probability. That is, it is desired to find a sequence of times $t_0 t_1 \ldots t_i \ldots$ and window sizes $T_1 T_2 \ldots T_i \ldots$ so that the working set is $W(t, T_i)$ for $t_{i-1} \leq t < t$ and $m_1 \geq m(T_i) \geq m_2$. One way of approximating this regime operates as follows. Let T_0 be an increment of window size. Let $t_i = t_{i-1} + T_i$ and let T_1 be given. Estimate the missing-page probability in (t_{i-1}, t_i) by

$$\hat{m}(T_i) = \frac{\text{number of returns to } W(t, T_i) \text{ in } (t_{i-1}, t_i)}{T_i}$$

and follow the decision rules

$$\text{if } \hat{m}(T_i) > m_1, \text{ then } T_{i+1} = T_i + T_0$$
$$\text{if } m_1 \geq \hat{m}(T_i) \geq m_2, \text{ then } T_{i+1} = T_i$$
$$\text{if } m_2 > \hat{m}(T_i), \text{ then } T_{i+1} = T_i - T_0$$

Example

We can approximate the decision rules of the previous example with LRU paging as follows. Let $t_0 t_1 \ldots t_i \ldots$ be the sequence of times at which page faults occur under LRU. A sequence of memory sizes $p_1 p_2 \ldots p_i \ldots$ will be defined so that LRU has p_i pages in memory in (t_{i-1}, t_i). Estimate the page fault probability by

$$\hat{F}_i = \frac{1}{t_i - t_{i-1}}$$

and follow the decision rules

$$\text{if } \hat{F}_i > m_1, \text{ then } p_{i+1} = p_i + 1 \quad \text{(add page to memory)}$$
$$\text{if } m_1 \geq \hat{F}_i \geq m_2, \text{ then } p_{i+1} = p_i \quad \text{(replace LRU page)}$$
$$\text{if } m_2 > \hat{F}_i, \text{ then } p_{i+1} = p_i - 1 \quad \text{(replace two LRU pages)}$$

7.5. FIXED VERSUS VARIABLE PARTITIONING
[18]

In this section we shall be concerned with applying the results of the previous sections to multiprogrammed memory management. The design problem of principal interest is the strategy according to which storage is partitioned among the active programs. Given that working set memory management is optimal or nearly so, in terms of controlling page-fault probability, the problem of partitioning storage among the programs demanding it remains to be solved. This problem appears to be at least as important in terms of its effect on system performance as the problem of selecting a page replacement algorithm.

The concepts of locality, especially as manifested via the working set model, will be exploited in a comparison of two basic strategies for partitioning storage: the *fixed partitioning* strategy, where the (maximum) degree of multiprogramming is fixed and storage is partitioned equally among the active programs, each active program being strictly confined to its own private block of the partition; and the *dynamic partitioning* strategy, where each program is allocated an amount of storage which varies dynamically in accordance with working set size. Most practical storage partitioning policies fall at or between these two extremes. It should be noted that the dynamic partitioning strategy is an implementation of the working set principle of memory management.

The primary argument advanced in favor of fixed partitioning is its simplicity of implementation and its low overhead. Intuitively, if the size of blocks in which programs are restricted is fixed but is sufficiently large to contain the working sets of programs most of the time, then the fixed partitioning scheme should perform acceptably.

On the other hand, if the block size is too small, performance may be affected adversely because unused space of unsaturated blocks cannot be reallocated and used to augment blocks operating in the overflow condition. It will be shown below that the performance of the fixed partitioning strategy may deteriorate significantly in comparison to dynamic partitioning for smaller block sizes; in such cases the improvement in system performance and capacity will exceed significantly the additional cost of implementing dynamic partitioning.

Let $w_i(t)$ denote the working set size of a given program; by our development in Section 7.3.4, $w_i(t)$ is normally distributed with mean $s = s(T)$ and variance $\sigma^2 = \sigma^2(T)$. Letting Φ denote the cumulative distribution of a normal random variable with zero mean and unit variance, the cumulative distribution for $w_i(t)$ can be expressed as

(7.5.1)
$$\Pr[w_i(t) \leq x] = \Phi\left(\frac{x - s}{\sigma}\right)$$

Consider an M-page memory in which n programs are to reside, and suppose that the independent working set sizes $w_1(t), \ldots, w_n(t)$ have the common parameters s and σ. (The last assumption is made out of convenience rather than necessity.) In the fixed partition case, each program will be allocated a space of b pages, where $M = nb$; in the variable partition case, each program will be allocated an amount of space equal to its working set size. For each case we shall define two measures: The *safeness factor* expresses the probability that no overflow condition exists, and the *exceedance* is the mean total amount of overflow. In comparing the two cases with respect to a given measure we shall find that the variable partition case always does at least as well as the fixed partition case, with dramatic differences appearing when the variance of working set size becomes large.

Consider the fixed partition case. The joint behavior of the n independent programs specifies at each time t a storage configuration

$$(7.5.2) \qquad \mathbf{Z}(t) = (Z_1(t), \ldots, Z_n(t))$$

in which

$$(7.5.3) \qquad Z_i(t) = \min\{b, w_i(t)\}, \quad i = 1, \ldots, n$$

The configuration $\mathbf{Z}(t)$ models directly a system in which programs operate concurrently and, with an appropriate change in time scale, processor sharing (cf. Section 4.4). Over longer periods of time it models multiprogramming systems in which a processor is multiplexed among the programs (as under a round-robin scheduling policy). It is implicit in the above that, with respect to individual blocks, a storage allocation procedure corresponding to the working set principle is effective; e.g., the LRU paging algorithm determines which part of a program occupies its block of the partition. In other words, according to the definition of $\mathbf{Z}(t)$, we have working set memory management to the extent that a maximum amount of working set for each executing program is maintained in each block.

A block of the partition will be considered safe at a given time if the working set of the corresponding program will fit. In terms of (7.5.3), block i is safe if $Z_i(t) = w_i(t)$. The fixed partition system will be considered safe whenever all the n blocks are safe simultaneously. Using $h(z, T)$ as the working set size density [see (7.3.25)] the safeness factor for this case is defined to be

$$(7.5.4) \qquad S_f = \left[\int_{-\infty}^{b} h(z, T)\, dz \right]^n = \Phi^n\!\left(\frac{b - s}{\sigma}\right)$$

where the integral is the safeness probability for one block and we have invoked the assumption of statistical independence among blocks. The functional behavior of S_f versus s is suggested in Fig. 7.5-1. The information of this figure can be summarized in the following statement: The fixed partition scheme gives acceptable safeness when variations in working set sizes are small (relative to mean values) and a block size b that is roughly 2σ in excess of the mean working set size is used. Under these conditions storage utilization is high but there is no appreciable increase in paging rate brought about by saturated (unsafe) blocks.

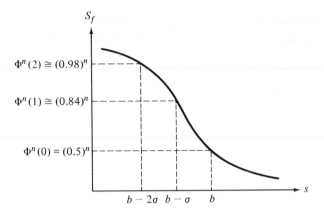

Fig. 7.5-1 Behavior of S_f.

A performance measure, the mean exceedance, from which page traffic can be estimated more directly is the mean amount of space required by the n working sets in excess of that provided. If we define

$$(7.5.5) \qquad X_i(t) = \max\{0, w_i(t) - b\}$$

then the mean exceedance for fixed partitioning is given by

$$E_f = E[\sum_{i=1}^{n} X_i(t)] = n \int_b^\infty (z - b)h(z, T)\, dz$$

Using (7.3.25) and simplifying we have

$$(7.5.6) \qquad E_f = \frac{n\sigma}{\sqrt{2\pi}} e^{-(s-b)^2/2\sigma^2} + n(s - b)\Phi\left(\frac{s - b}{\sigma}\right)$$

The safeness S_v and exceedance E_v for variable partitioning are defined as follows. Let S_v denote the probability that the sum of n normally distributed random variables, each with parameters s and σ, exceeds M. Since the sum of n independent normal random variables is itself normally distributed with mean ns and variance $n\sigma^2$, the safeness and exceedance can be expressed as

$$(7.5.7) \qquad S_v = \int_{-\infty}^{M} h_n(z, T)\, dz = \Phi\left(\frac{M - ns}{\sqrt{n}\,\sigma}\right)$$

and

$$E_v = \int_{M}^{\infty} (z - M)h_n(z, T)\, dz$$

where h_n is a normal distribution with parameters ns and $n\sigma^2$. This expression for E_v can be simplified to

$$(7.5.8) \qquad E_v = \sigma \sqrt{\frac{n}{2\pi}} e^{-(ns-M)^2/2n\sigma^2} + (ns - M)\Phi\left(\frac{ns - M}{\sqrt{n\sigma^2}}\right)$$

Figure 7.5-2 shows a comparison of S_f and S_v. There typically is a dramatic improvement to be obtained by variable partitioning when σ is large relative to the mean. Whenever

$$(7.5.9) \qquad\qquad\qquad \sigma \leq \frac{b - s}{2}$$

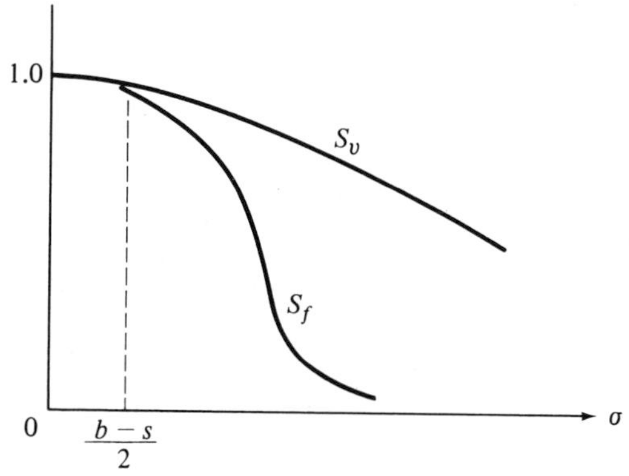

Fig. 7.5-2 Safeness factors.

the condition $b \geq s + 2\sigma$ holds and S_f and S_v are comparable. (It is easily verified that the two systems are asymptotically equivalent as $\sigma \rightarrow 0$.) The performance ratio S_v/S_f increases rapidly as σ becomes progressively larger than $(b - s)/2$.

Figure 7.5-3 shows the different memory sizes required by the two methods for a given level of exceedance, for a particular choice of parameters. For small M, E_f and E_v become asymptotically the same because all the blocks in the fixed case and all the memory in the dynamic case are saturated. As stated above, the region of most interest for fixed partitioning occurs when $b = s + 2\sigma$. A horizontal line is shown in Fig. 7.5-3 intersecting the E_f curve for $M = nb$ and $b = s + 2\sigma$. It is evident that the variable partition scheme requires about 30 percent less M for a given level of exceedance in this case, even though S_f and S_v will be comparable. This indicates directly the substantial economies possible under dynamic partitioning when the variation in working set sizes becomes relatively large.

Another important advantage of the dynamic scheme is its adaptability to variations in the working set size distribution, i.e., when the parameters s and σ are nonstationary [$s = s(t, T)$ and $\sigma = \sigma(t, T)$]. Performance of the

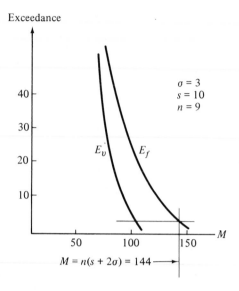

Fig. 7.5-3 Exceedances.

fixed partitioning scheme can degrade substantially during time intervals when the condition

$$b \geq s(t, T) + 2\sigma(t, T)$$

is violated. The dynamic scheme will not suffer to nearly the same extent.

The foregoing discussion deals with a method whereby the degree of multiprogramming was held fixed and the paging rate was allowed to vary. We can also consider a converse: Fixing the paging rate by retaining only total working sets in memory and allowing the degree of multiprogramming $n(t)$ to vary accordingly. The statistic $E[n(t)]$ is of interest in any such scheme. To evaluate it, define the binary random variable

$$(7.5.10) \qquad \gamma_k(t) = \begin{cases} 1, & \text{if } w_1(t) + \cdots + w_k(t) \leq M \\ 0, & \text{otherwise} \end{cases}$$

so that

$$(7.5.11) \qquad n(t) = \sum_{k=1}^{\infty} \gamma_k(t)$$

Therefore

$$(7.5.12) \qquad E[n(t)] = \sum_{k=1}^{\infty} \Phi\left(\frac{M - ks}{\sqrt{k}\,\sigma}\right)$$

In a practical implementation of this method one must be concerned with instability effects at the boundary M; e.g., if additional programs are activated exactly when overflow occurs, there can be considerable traffic of programs being activated and deactivated owing to statistical fluctuations of the sum of working set sizes about M. To avoid this situation, programs can be introduced only when free space exceeds by H the amount required to hold the working set; H will be a parameter of the allocation procedure. The values of (7.5.12) for memory size M and $M - H$ can be used as good estimates of bounds on $E[n(t)]$ in this case.

In practical implementations of dynamic partitioning methods, whether the degree of multiprogramming is held fixed or not, the average rate of upcrossings (memory overflows) is another measure of importance. Upcrossings are important because they represent moments when system overhead will be generated, overhead either to reduce working set sizes or to adjust the degree of multiprogramming. The analysis of the upcrossing problem has been treated in Problem 5-9.

PROBLEMS

7-1. This problem considers the implications of defining mean working set size $s(T)$ and missing-page probability $m(T)$ as time averages instead of ensemble averages (as was done in the text). Define

$$s_k(T) = \frac{1}{k} \sum_{t=1}^{k} w(t, T), \qquad m_k(T) = \frac{1}{k} \sum_{t=0}^{k-1} \Delta(t, T)$$

where $\Delta(t, T)$ is a binary variable equal to 1 if and only if $r_{t+1} \notin W(t, T)$.
Take

$$s(T) = \lim_{k \to \infty} s_k(T), \qquad m(T) = \lim_{k \to \infty} m_k(T)$$

Prove that the relations

$$s(T + 1) - s(T) = m(T)$$

$$s(T) = \sum_{x=0}^{T-1} m(x)$$

hold. Suppose that the program has n recurrent pages. Show that

$$\lim_{T \to \infty} s(T) = n$$

$$\lim_{T \to \infty} m(T) = 0$$

7-2. Let $\Delta(t, T)$ be defined as in Problem 7-1. Prove that $\Delta(t, T + 1) \le \Delta(t, T)$ and use this to conclude that $m(T + 1) \le m(T)$.

7-3. The definitions of Problem 7-1 assumed the time interval $t = 1$ to $t = k$. Suppose that we want to use instead the time interval $t = t_0 + 1$ to $t = t_0 + k$, where $t_0 \ge 0$ is arbitrary. Thus

$$s_k(T) = \frac{1}{k} \sum_{t=t_0+1}^{t_0+k} w(t, T), \qquad m_k(T) = \frac{1}{k} \sum_{t=t_0}^{t_0+k-1} \Delta(t, T)$$

Show that

$$s_k(T+1) = s_k(T) + m_k(T) - \frac{w(t_0 + k, T) - w(t_0, T)}{k}$$

$$\frac{s_k(T-1) + s_k(T+1)}{2} \leq s_k(T) + \frac{1}{2k}(w(t_0 + k, T-1) - w(t_0, T-1)$$

$$- w(t_0 + k, T) + w(t_0, T))$$

Show that $s_k(T)$ need not be concave downward unless $k \longrightarrow \infty$; consider, for example, the reference string

$$\omega = 1\ 2\ 3\ 4\ 5\ 2\ 1\ 3\ 3\ 2\ 3\ 4\ 5\ 4\ 5$$

where $t_0 = 5$ and $k = 10$. Show that $s_k(T)$ is concave down for $t_0 = 0$ since, then, $w(t_0, T) = 0$.

7-4. This problem investigates the relation between the LRU algorithm and the working set model. Define a variable window $T(t, p)$ to be the smallest T for which $w(t, T) = p$, where p is an integer; observe that $W(t, T(t, p))$ is precisely the topmost p elements of the LRU stack at time t. Define $g_p(x) = \lim_{t \to \infty} \Pr[T(t, p) = x]$. Define the time sequence $\{t_k(x)\}$ to be those t at which $T(t, p) = x$. Define the missing-page probability $m_p(T)$ over $\{t_k(x)\}$ as $m(T)$ is defined over all t. Define the mean value of T to be $T_p = \sum_{x > 0} x g_p(x)$.

a. Show that the fault probability for a p-page LRU memory is

$$F_p(\text{LRU}) = \sum_{x > 0} g_p(x) m_p(x)$$

b. Show that the overall missing-page probability for window size T is

$$m(T) = \sum_{i \in N} g_i(T) m_i(T)$$

c. Using parts a and b, show that (for an n-page program)

$$\sum_{x > 0} m(x) = \sum_{i \in N} F_i(\text{LRU}) = n$$

d. Show that there exists at least one value of p for which $m(T_p) \leq F_p(\text{LRU})$; i.e., the working set simulation of LRU leads to smaller missing-page probability.

e. Let $a_1, \ldots, a_n$ denote the LRU stack model distance distribution. Show that

$$m(T_i) - m(T_{i+1}) \leq a_{i+1}, \quad i \geq p$$

is sufficient to guarantee that $m(T_p) \leq F_p(\text{LRU})$. Show that $a_{i+1} = m(T_i) - m(T_{i+1})$ is not generally true.

7-5. It was mentioned that nonrecurrent pages (those for which $\beta_i = 0$) have no effect on the long-run mean working set size $s(T)$. To demonstrate this, state the definition of the interreference density $f_{ik}(x)$ over $r_1 r_2 \ldots r_k$ and let β_{ik} denote the fraction of these references to page i. Show that

$$\lim_{k \to \infty} \beta_{ik} f_{ik}(x) = 0$$

and use this to conclude that nonrecurrent pages do not contribute to

$$s(T) = \sum_{i \in N} \sum_{x=0}^{T-1} \beta_i (1 - F_i(x))$$

Let $\bar{x}_{ik}$ denote the mean interreference interval to page i among $r_1 r_2 \ldots r_k$. Suppose that page i is nonrecurrent, and prove that

$$\lim_{k \to \infty} \beta_{ik} \bar{x}_{ik} = 0$$

(It will be necessary to invoke stationarity to complete the proof.)

7-6. In the Problems of Chapter 6, it was shown that halving the page size while holding memory capacity fixed could cause increases in page-fault rate by factors in excess of 2. The same type of behavior can be observed in the working set model. Let $s_a(T)$ denote the expected working set size when the page size is 2^a words and $m_a(T)$ is the corresponding missing-page probability.

a. Show that $2s_{a+1}(T) \geq s_a(T) \geq s_{a+1}(T)$; i.e., halving the page size increases the working set size, as measured in pages, by a factor of no more than 2. Show that $2^a s_a(T) \leq 2^{a+1} s_{a+1}(T)$; i.e. the total number of words in the working set does not increase when page size is halved.

b. Let $\omega_1 \omega_2 \ldots \omega_n \omega_1$ be a sequence of cyclic permutations of $12 \ldots n$ such that the last $n - 1$ symbols of ω_i match the first $n - 1$ symbols of ω_{i+1}. The strings ω_i' and ω_i'' are the same as ω_i but over the pages $\{1', \ldots, n'\}$ and $\{1'', \ldots, n''\}$, respectively, where j' and j'' are the buddies constituting page j. Suppose that n is even and define the reference strings

$$\omega(a) = \alpha_k = (\omega_1' \omega_2'' \omega_3' \omega_4'' \ldots \omega_n'')^k$$
$$\omega(a + 1) = \beta_k = (\omega_1 \omega_2 \ldots \omega_n)^k$$

Show that, as $k \to \infty$,

$$\frac{m_a(T)}{m_{a+1}(T)} = n, \quad T = n - 1$$

Show also that, as $k \to \infty$,

$$\frac{m_a(2T)}{m_{a+1}(2T)} = n, \quad T = n - 1$$

(i.e., doubling the window size after halving the page size does not remove the anomaly).

7-7. Let us investigate further the effect of page size on missing-page rate. Let $m_i(T) = \beta_i(1 - F_i(T))$ be the missing-page rate of page i, so that $m(T) = m_1(T) + \cdots + m_n(T)$. Let $m_i^a(T)$ denote $m_i(T)$ for page size 2^a.

a. Show that $m_i^a(T) \leq m_i^{a+1}(T)$ is a sufficient condition for the intuitively desired result $m^a(T) \leq 2m^{a+1}(T)$. Letting i' and i'' denote the buddies constituting page i, this condition is equivalent to

$$\beta_j(1 - F_j(T)) \leq \beta_i(1 - F_i(T)), \quad j = i' \text{ or } i''$$

b. The condition of Part a need not hold, as was shown in the previous problem. That it need not hold even for the relatively well-behaved independent-reference model can be established as follows. Note that $m_i(T) = \beta_i(1 - \beta_i)^T$; show that $m_i(T)$ is maximum for $\beta_i = 1/(T + 1)$ and decreases in β_i for β_i larger than the maximum. Since the effect of cutting a page in half is decreasing the value of β_i for the two resulting buddies i' and i'', if $\beta_{i'}$ and $\beta_{i''}$ are both larger than $1/(T + 1)$, then $m_j^a(T) > m_i^{a+1}(T)$ for $j = i'$ or i''. Use this to conclude that $m^a(T)$ can exceed $2m^{a+1}(T)$.

7-8. Consider a program modeled by the independent reference model with page reference probability distribution $\beta_1, \ldots, \beta_n$. Define the set L_{m-1} to be those pages with the $m - 1$ largest values among the β_i. In the study of the optimal algorithm A_0 (Chapter 6) we showed that, in equilibrium, the pages of L_{m-1} are in memory at all times and that the page-fault probability per reference is

$$C(m) = \sum \beta_i - \frac{\sum \beta_i^2}{\sum \beta_i}$$

where all sums are over pages in $N - L_{m-1}$. Now, suppose that the probabilities associated with pages are permuted at time t (say, a new locality is entered) to define a new distribution $\{\beta_i'\} = \{\beta_i\}$. The page-fault probability at time $t + T$ can be expressed as $C(m) + g(T)$, where $C(m)$ is the same steady-state probability as above and $g(T)$ is a decaying transient corresponding to accumulating the pages of L'_{m-1} back into memory.

The transient $g(T)$ can be computed quite simply using working set arguments. Define the set $M = L'_{m-1} - L_{m-1}$ to be the pages missing from the steady-state memory configuration after the permutation of the reference probabilities. Show that $g(T)$ is the missing-page rate to the set $M \cap W(t + T, T)$ and conclude that

$$g(T) = \sum_{i \in M \cap W(t+T, T)} \beta_i'(1 - \beta_i')^T$$

Extend the argument so that $\{\beta_i'\}$ is an arbitrary new distribution that becomes effective at time t.

7-9. The (l, α) locality model is defined as follows [17]. A *locality* is any subset L of N containing exactly l pages. Localities L and L' are demand paging neighbors if $L' = L + x - y$ for some *exterior* page $x(x \notin L)$ and *interior* page $y(y \in L)$. Suppose that references $r_1 r_2 \ldots r_{t-1}$ and locality sequence $L_0 L_1 \ldots L_{t-1}$ have been generated. Then with probability $1 - \alpha$, x is chosen at random from the members of L_{t-1}; with probability α an (x, y) pair is chosen at random from among the members of $(N - L_{t-1}) \times L_{t-1}$. In either case $r_t = x$; in the first case $L_t = L_{t-1}$ and in the second case $L_t = L_{t-1} + x - y$. Observe that the holding time distribution in a given locality is geometric,

$$h(x) = (1 - \alpha)^{x-1}\alpha, \quad x \geq 1$$

so that the probability of an interlocality transition is α at any time and $1/\alpha$ is the mean holding time. Observe also that transitions occur only between demand paging neighbors. Consistent with the requirement that locality pages are favored, we assume that

$$\frac{1 - \alpha}{l} \geq \frac{\alpha}{n - l}$$

i.e., the probability of referencing an interior page is not less than that of referencing an exterior one.

For memory size $m \geq l$, let S_t be an m-page memory state. Let $C_k(S, L, t)$ denote the minimum cost of processing $r_{t+1} \ldots r_{t+k}$ under demand paging, given $S_t = S$, $L_t = L$, and that the references are generated by the locality model. Following the techniques of Chapter 6, show that (where $\bar{S} = N - S$ and $\bar{L} = N - L$)

$$C_0(S, L, t) = 0$$

$$C_{k+1}(S, L, t) = \begin{cases} \displaystyle\sum_{x \in \bar{S} \cap L} \frac{1 - \alpha}{l} C_k(S, L, t + 1) \\[2mm] + \displaystyle\sum_{x \in \bar{S} \cap L} \frac{1 - \alpha}{l} (1 + \min_{z \in S} C_k(S + x - z, L, t + 1)) \\[2mm] + \displaystyle\sum_{x \in \bar{S} \cap L} \frac{\alpha}{n - l} \sum_{y \in L} \frac{1}{l}(C_k(S, L + x - y, t + 1)) \\[2mm] + \displaystyle\sum_{x \in \bar{S} \cap L} \frac{\alpha}{n - l} \sum_{y \in L} \frac{1}{l} (1 + \min_{z \in S} C_k(S + x - z, L + x - y, \\[2mm] \hspace{8cm} t + 1)) \end{cases}$$

Prove the following:
a. $C_k(S, L, t) = k\alpha[(n - m)/(n - l)]$ if $S \supseteq L$ and the policy $S_t \supseteq L_t$ for all t is used.
b. For arbitrary S, the policy "replace nonlocality pages" is optimal.
c. A working set $W(t, T)$ with $T = 1/\alpha$ is a good estimator for L_t.

7-10. Consider the following extensions to the model of Problem 7-9: a) The probability of referencing an interior page x of L is $\beta(L, x, t)$. b) The probability of removing an interior page y from L given that a transition occurs and page x enters is $\gamma(L, x, y, t)$. c) $\alpha = \alpha(t)$, and $\alpha(t)$ is independent of $\alpha(t')$ whenever $t \neq t'$. Note that the page x entering a locality is still chosen at random from the $n - l$ exterior pages. Show that the condition

$$(1 - \alpha(t))\beta(L, x, t) \geq \frac{\alpha(t)}{n - l}$$

is necessary for the optimality of the policy "replace nonlocality pages," and that if $S \supseteq L$

$$C_k(S, L, t) = \frac{n - m}{n - l} \sum_{i=0}^{k-1} \alpha(t + i)$$

for this policy.

7-11. In the (l, α) locality model of Problem 7-9, let L_0 be an initial locality and $M_0 = N - L_0$. Let $r_1 r_2 \ldots r_t \ldots$ be a reference string and suppose that a_t is the number of elements of M_0 which have been referenced through time t. Notice that $a_0 = 0$ and that $a_t = a_{t-1} + 1$ only if a locality transition

$$L_t = L_{t-1} + x - y$$

occurs at time t, where x is in $M_0 - W(t - 1, t - 1)$ and W is a working set. Show that

(P7-11.1) $$E[a_t] = (n - l)\left(1 - \left(1 - \frac{\alpha}{n - l}\right)^t\right)$$

Recall that the expression for expected working set size of a k-page program in the independent reference model is

(P7-11.2) $$s(T) = k - \sum_{i=1}^{k} (1 - \beta_i)^T$$

Observe that (P2) is the same as (P1) when $k = n - l$, $T = t$, $\beta_i = \alpha/(n - l)$. Show that a_t is in fact the size of an appropriately defined working set.

7-12. We know that the mean working set size $s(T)$ is bounded above by $\min\{n, T\}$; indeed, this bound can be achieved for the reference string $12 \ldots n12 \ldots n \ldots$. This bound cannot, however, be achieved for the independent-reference model.

Suppose that the page reference probabilities in the independent reference model are $\beta_1, \ldots, \beta_n$. Show that

$$s(T) = n - \sum_{i=1}^{n} (1 - \beta_i)^T$$

and prove that $s(T)$ is maximum when $\beta_i = 1/n$ for each i, that is,

$$s(T) \leq n\left(1 - \left(\frac{n - 1}{n}\right)^T\right)$$

for this model.

7-13. Consider the following model for the working set size. For analytic convenience we suppose that the process operates in continuous time. Let λ denote the exponential arrival rate of pages into the working set; and suppose each page resides therein for a time exponentially distributed with parameter μ. Let π_k denote the equilibrium probability that k pages are in the working set, and show that π_k satisfies a Poisson distribution

$$\pi_k = \frac{\rho^k}{k!} e^{-\rho}, \qquad \rho = \frac{\lambda}{\mu}$$

with mean

(P7-13.1) $$s(T) = \rho$$

Assuming the times between successive references to the same page are independent and have distribution $F(x)$, and that the window size of the working set is T, show that the mean residence time of a page in the working set is

(P7-13.2) $$\frac{1}{\mu} = T + \bar{x}\left(\frac{F(T)}{1 - F(T)}\right)$$

From the analysis of Section 7.3, we expect that the missing-page rate is

(P7-13.3) $$\lambda = \frac{d}{dt} s(T) = 1 - F(T)$$

and that $\bar{x} = n$. The limitations of the model are 1) π_k must be small for $k > n$, which implies that ρ cannot be too close to n, 2) the residence times of pages must be at least T, which implies that T must be small compared to $1/\mu$, and 3) only certain interreference distributions $F(x)$ are consistent with Eqs. (P7-13.1–P7-13.3). Discuss these limitations more fully and characterize the distributions $F(x)$.

REFERENCES

1. BELADY, L. A., and C. J. KUEHNER., "Dynamic space sharing in computer systems." *Comm. ACM 12*, 5 (May 1969), 282–288.

2. BRAWN, B., and F. GUSTAVSON, "Program behavior in a paging environment." *AFIPS Proc. Conf.* (1968 FJCC), 1019–1032.

3. DENNING, P. J., "Resource allocation in multiprocess computer systems." M.I.T. Project MAC report MAC-TR-50, M.I.T., Cambridge, Mass. (May 1968).

4. DENNING, P. J., "Thrashing: Its causes and prevention." *AFIPS Conf. Proc.* (1968 FJCC), 915–922.

5. DENNING, P. J., "Virtual memory." *Computing Surveys 2*, 3 (Sept. 1970), 153–189.

6. DOHERTY, W., "Scheduling TSS/360 for responsiveness." *AFIPS Conf. Proc.* (1970 FJCC), 97–112.

7. SAYRE, D., "Is automatic folding of programs efficient enough to displace manual?" *Comm. ACM 12*, 12 (Dec. 1969), 656–660.

8. COFFMAN, E. G., JR., and L. C. VARIAN., "Further experimental data on the behavior of programs in a paging environment." *Comm. ACM 11*, 7 (July 1968), 471–474.

9. RANDELL, B., and C. J. KUEHNER., "Demand paging in perspective." *AFIPS Conf. Proc.* (1968 FJCC), 1011–1018.

10. HATFIELD, D. J., and J. GERALD., "Program restructuring for virtual memory." *IBM Sys. J. 10*, 3 (1971), 168–192.

11. BELADY, L. A., "A study of replacement algorithms for virtual storage computers." *IBM Sys. J. 5*, 2 (1966), 78–101.

12. LIPTAY, J. S., "The cache." *IBM Sys. J. 7*, 1 (1968), 15–21.

13. ODEN, P. H., and G. S. SHEDLER, "A model of memory contention in a paging machine." IBM T. J. Watson Research Center Report RG3053, Yorktown Heights, N.Y. (Sept. 1970).

14. OPPENHEIMER, G., and N. WEIZER. "Resource management for a medium scale time sharing operating system." *Comm. ACM 11*, 5 (May 1968), 313–322.

15. DENNING, P. J., "The working set model for program behavior." *Comm. ACM 11*, 5 (May 1968), 323–333.

16. DENNING, P. J., and S. C. Schwartz., "Properties of the working set model." *Comm. ACM 15*, 3 (Mar. 1972), 191–198.

17. DENNING, P. J., J. E. SAVAGE, and J. R. SPIRN., "Models for locality in program behavior." TR-107, Dept. of Electrical Engineering, Princeton Univ., Princeton, N.J. (Apr. 1972).

18. COFFMAN, E. G., JR., and T. A. RYAN., "A study of storage partitioning using a mathematical model of locality." *Comm. ACM 15*, 3 (Mar. 1972), 185–190.

19. ROSENBLATT, M., "A central limit theorem and a strong mixing condition." *Proc. Natl Acad. Sci. 42* (1956), 43–47.

20. RODRIGUEZ-ROSELL, J., "Experimental data on how program behavior affects the choice of scheduler parameters." *Proc. 3rd ACM Symp. on Op. Sys. Princ.* (Oct. 1971).

A TRANSFORMS, THE CENTRAL LIMIT THEOREM, AND MARKOV CHAINS

A.1. GENERATING FUNCTIONS

The sum

(A.1.1)
$$A(z) = \sum_{i=0}^{\infty} a_i z^i$$

defines a *generating function*† for the sequence $\{a_i\}$. If $\{a_i\}$ denotes a probability mass function (pmf), i.e., $a_i \geq 0$, $i \geq 0$, and

(A.1.2)
$$\sum_{i=0}^{\infty} a_i = 1$$

then $A(z)$ is more specifically a probability generating function. We are solely concerned with probability generating functions and hence the shorter term generating function will be used with this connotation understood. Clearly, under (A.1.2) the series (A.1.1) will converge for at least $0 \leq z \leq 1$. The variable z has no special significance; it is only the independent variable of a function representing a probability mass function.

The generating function has the properties

(A.1.3)
$$\lim_{z \to 0} A(z) = a_0$$

(A.1.4)
$$\lim_{z \to 1} A(z) = 1$$

Let X be a nonnegative integer-valued random variable such that

†The term *z-transform* is also used.

313

$\Pr[X = i] = a_i$ and $E(X^i)$ is finite for $i = 1, 2$. By differentiation of (A.1.1) we have

(A.1.5)
$$A'(z) = \sum_{i=1}^{\infty} i a_i z^{i-1}$$

from which

(A.1.6)
$$E(X) = \sum_{i=1}^{\infty} i a_i = \lim_{z \to 1} A'(z)$$

Differentiating again we have

(A.1.7)
$$A''(z) = \sum_{i=1}^{\infty} i(i - 1) a_i z^{i-2}$$

from which

(A.1.8)
$$\lim_{z \to 1} A''(z) = E(X^2) - E(X)$$

and

(A.1.9)
$$\lim_{z \to 1} A''(z) = \mathrm{Var}(X) + E(X)[E(X) - 1]$$

One of the principal advantages of generating functions is that the moments of X are frequently the most easily calculated from the generating function as shown in (A.1.6), (A.1.8), and (A.1.9). Examples can be found in Table A.1-1. Note that higher moments, when they exist, are found by further differentiations. In particular, we have the formula for the so-called *binomial moments*:

$$\lim_{z \to 1} \frac{d^k A(z)}{dz^k} = E[X(X - 1)(X - 2) \cdots (X - k + 1)]$$

The *convolution* of the two sequences $\{a_i\}$ and $\{b_i\}$ is defined to be the sequence $\{c_i\}$ given by

(A.1.10)
$$c_i = \sum_{j=0}^{i} a_j b_{i-j}$$

Let X and Y be two mutually independent nonnegative integer-valued random variables with the pmfs $a_i = \Pr[X = i]$ and $b_i = \Pr[Y = i]$. It can be seen that $\{c_i\}$ is the pmf for the sum $c_i = \Pr[X + Y = i]$. The following important result for the generating function $C(z)$ of $\{c_i\}$ is easily verified:

(A.1.11)
$$C(z) = A(z)B(z)$$

where $A(z)$ and $B(z)$ are the generating functions for $\{a_i\}$ and $\{b_i\}$, respectively. In computing the moments or in finding the form of the distribution of a sum of independent random variables it is often easier to work with (A.1.11) than with (A.1.10). Equation (A.1.11) extends in the obvious way to sums of more than two independent random variables. A special case of importance concerns the sum of n independent, identically distributed random variables $X_1, X_2, \ldots, X_n$. If $A(z)$ is the common generating function, then $A^n(z)$ is the generating function of the sum $S = X_1 + X_2 + \cdots + X_n$.

Table A.1-1 PROBABILITY DISTRIBUTIONS FREQUENTLY ENCOUNTERED IN THIS BOOK
(a) Discrete Distributions

Name	Probability Mass Function	Generating Function	Mean and Variance
Binomial $n = 1, 2, \ldots,$ $0 \le p \le 1$	$\binom{n}{j} p^j (1-p)^{n-j},$ $j = 0, 1, \ldots, n$	$[(1-p) + pz]^n$	np and $np(1-p)$
Poisson $\lambda > 0$	$\dfrac{\lambda^n}{n!} e^{-\lambda}, n = 0, 1, \ldots$	$e^{-\lambda(1-z)}$	λ and λ
Geometric $0 \le p \le 1$	$p(1-p)^n, n = 0, 1, \ldots$ or $p(1-p)^{n-1}, n = 1, 2, \ldots$	$p/[1 - (1-p)z]$ $pz/[1 - (1-p)z]$	$(1-p)/p$ and $(1-p)^2$ $1/p$ and $(1-p)p^2$

(b) Continuous Distributions

Name	Probability Density	Laplace Transform	Mean and Variances
Uniform over (a, b) with $0 < a < b$	$\dfrac{1}{b-a}, a < x < b$ 0, otherwise	$\dfrac{e^{-sa} - e^{-sb}}{s(b-a)}$	$\dfrac{a+b}{2}$ and $\dfrac{(b-a)^2}{12}$
Normal	$\dfrac{1}{\sqrt{2\pi\sigma^2}} e^{-(x-m)^2/2\sigma^2}$ $-\infty < x < +\infty$	†	m and σ^2
Exponential‡	$\lambda e^{-\lambda x}, x > 0$	$\dfrac{1}{1 + s/\lambda}$	$1/\lambda$ and $1/\lambda^2$
Special Erlangian (sum of n exponentials)	$\dfrac{\lambda}{(n-1)!}(\lambda x)^{n-1} e^{-\lambda x},$ $x > 0$	$\dfrac{1}{(1 + s/\lambda)^n}$	$n\lambda$ and n/λ^2

†The transform frequently employed for computing moments by differentiation (which is called the *characteristic function*) is given by $E(e^{iuX}) = e^{ium - u^2\sigma^2/2}$.

‡Clearly, the exponential distribution is defined by the special Erlangian distribution with $n = 1$.

A.2. LAPLACE TRANSFORMS AND THE CENTRAL LIMIT THEOREM

The role played by generating functions for discrete distributions is played by Laplace transforms for general distribution functions. Let X be a continuous nonnegative random variable with distribution function $F(x) =$

$\Pr[X \le x]$ and density function $f(x) = dF(x)/dx$. The Laplace transform of this distribution is denoted $F^*(s)$ and given by $F^*(s) = E(e^{-sX})$:

(A.2.1) $$F^*(s) = \int_0^\infty e^{-sx} f(x)\, dx$$

For the more general distributions (not dealt with in this book) $F^*(s)$ is expressed as the Stieltjes integral

(A.2.2) $$F^*(s) = \int_0^\infty e^{-sx}\, dF(x)$$

The moments are easily determined from the Laplace transform. In particular,

(A.2.3) $$E(X) = -\lim_{s \to 0} \frac{d}{ds} E(e^{-sX})$$

(A.2.4) $$E(X^2) = \lim_{s \to 0} \frac{d^2}{ds^2} E(e^{-sX})$$

and in general

(A.2.5) $$E(X^n) = \lim_{s \to 0} (-1)^n \frac{d^n}{ds^n} E(e^{-sX})$$

(Table A.1-1 contains illustrations of transforms used in the text.)

It is readily verified that the sum of two nonnegative independent continuous random variables X and Y with densities $f(x)$ and $g(x)$ has a density function given by the convolution

(A.2.6) $$h(x) = \int_0^x g(x - y) f(y)\, dy$$

but a Laplace transform given by

(A.2.7) $$H^*(s) = G^*(s) F^*(s)$$

In general terms, $E(e^{-s(X+Y)}) = E(e^{-sX}) E(e^{-sY})$, which follows from the definition of expectations and the independence of X and Y. Thus a convolution of densities becomes a product of transforms under the Laplace transform operation, just as a convolution of probability mass functions becomes a product of generating functions under the z-transform operation. As with generating functions this result extends to the sum of an arbitrary number of mutually independent random variables. Again a special case of importance is the sum of n independent random variables $S = X_1 + X_2 \cdots + X_n$ each with the distribution function $F(x)$. In such cases, which arise frequently in the study of waiting times in queueing systems, we have†

---

†For example, note the relation between the transforms of the exponential and Erlangian distributions in Table A.1-1.

(A.2.8) $$E(e^{-sS}) = [F^*(s)]^n$$

In connection with sums of random variables a result of great importance is the well-known central limit theorem. Let $X_1, X_2, \ldots, X_n$ be a sequence of mutually independent, identically distributed random variables, each with finite first and second moments. Let

$$S_n = X_1 + X_2 + \cdots + X_n \text{ and define } S_n^0 = [S_n - E(S_n)]/[\text{Var}(S_n)]^{1/2}.$$

A classic form of the central limit theorem asserts that as $n \to \infty$ the distribution of S_n^0 approaches the normal distribution with zero mean and unit variance. Symbolically,

$$\lim_{n \to \infty} \Pr[S_n^0 \leq x] = \frac{1}{\sqrt{2\pi}} \int_{-\infty}^{x} e^{-y^2/2} \, dy$$

At times it is very inconvenient to work with the distribution of the sum of arbitrarily (identically) distributed random variables; hence the so-called normal approximation provided by the central limit theorem becomes a highly useful simplification. Illustrations of this approximation will be left to texts in elementary probability theory; applications can be found in Chapters 5 and 7. However, it should be pointed out that the above result can be greatly generalized to include

1. Random variables with different distributions,
2. Certain classes of dependent random variables, and
3. Distributions for which the first moment does not exist.

Moreover, considerable work has been done on the problem of describing the error in the normal approximation for a given n.

A.3. MARKOV CHAINS

Consider the sequence of random variables $X_0, X_1, \ldots, X_n, \ldots$ and assume that each random variable can take on values in the set $N = \{0, 1, 2, \ldots\}$†. The sequence $\{X_i\}$ is said to be a *Markov chain* if for all n and all possible values of the X_i

(A.3.1) $$\Pr[X_n = j \mid X_0 = i_0, X_1 = i_1, \ldots, X_{n-1} = i_{n-1}]$$
$$= \Pr[X_n = j \mid X_{n-1} = i_{n-1}]$$

†Actually, we may assume any denumerable set of values for the X_i, but it will be a decided convenience to assume the set of nonnegative integers. All results are trivially rewritten for the general case.

i.e., the distribution for X_n is completely determined by X_{n-1} and independent of the behavior of $\{X_n\}$ prior to the $(n-1)$st step.

We say that the system being described by $\{X_i\}$ is in state j at the nth step if $X_n = j$. Correspondingly, the set N is called the *state space* of the Markov chain $\{X_i\}$. The distribution $\Pr[X_0 = j]$, $j \in N$, is called the *initial distribution*, and the conditional probabilities $\Pr[X_{m+n} = j \mid X_m = i]$, $n \geq 1$, are called the *n-step transition probabilities*. If $X_{n-1} = i$ and $X_n = j$, then the system is said to have made the transition $i \rightarrow j$ at the nth step. Knowing the initial distribution and the one-step transition probabilities enables us to determine uniquely the distribution for each X_n, $n \geq 1$.

In the applications of this book the chain index n is interpretable as a time parameter. For example, X_n may denote the number of people in a self-service elevator where the time parameter n indexes those time instants $(t_0, t_1, \ldots, t_n, \ldots)$ at which the number of people in the elevator changes. Alternatively, the t_i may represent the successive times at which the elevator reaches successive floors. The t_n are frequently referred to as the *epochs* of the Markov chain $\{X_n\}$.

The Markov chain $\{X_n\}$ is said to be *homogeneous* if the transition probabilities $\Pr[X_{m+n} = j \mid X_m = i]$ are independent of m (or the initial epoch t_m). We are concerned only with homogeneous Markov chains, and so we can write $p_{ij}^{(n)}$ for the above transition probabilities. The one-step transition probabilities are always written p_{ij}.

We say that state j is *reachable* from state i if for some $n > 0$, $p_{ij}^{(n)} > 0$. If every state of $\{X_n\}$ is reachable from every other state, then $\{X_n\}$ is said to be *irreducible*. All Markov chains treated in this book are irreducible. Reducible Markov chains can be analyzed by analyzing those Markov chains formed by considering those (maximal) subsets of the original state space which consist only of communicating states, i.e., states reachable from one another.

Suppose that the system is initially in state j and let $f_j^{(n)}$ denote the probability that the system first returns to (the occupancy of) state j at the nth step. The probability that the system ever returns to state j is clearly

$$(A.3.2) \qquad f_j = \sum_{n=1}^{\infty} f_j^{(n)}$$

If $f_j = 1$, state j is called *recurrent* (or *persistent*) and if $f_j < 1$, state j is called *transient*. State j is called *periodic* with period t if returns to state j can occur only at steps $t, 2t, 3t, \ldots$ and $t > 1$ is the largest integer with this property. Clearly, $p_{ij}^{(n)} = 0$ for all n not divisible by t.

If $f_j = 1$, then

$$(A.3.3) \qquad u_j = \sum_{n=1}^{\infty} n f_j^{(n)}$$

is the *mean recurrence time* of state j. We say that j is a *recurrent nonnull* (or *positive*) state if $u_j < \infty$ and a *recurrent null* state if $u_j = \infty$. All states of an irreducible Markov chain are either 1) transient or recurrent null states or 2) recurrent nonnull states. Their periods are always the same.

A probability distribution $\{\pi_j\}$ satisfying

$$(A.3.4) \qquad \pi_j = \sum_{i=0}^{\infty} \pi_i p_{ij}, \quad j = 0, 1, 2, \ldots$$

is called a *stationary distribution* for $\{X_n\}$. For finite (i.e., finite state space) Markov chains, (A.3.4) is frequently rendered in matrix notation. Let $\{0, 1, \ldots, k\}$ be the state space and let $\boldsymbol{\pi} = [\pi_0, \pi_1, \ldots, \pi_k]$. If $\mathsf{P} = ((p_{ij}))$ denotes the matrix of transition probabilities, then (A.3.4) may be written as

$$(A.3.5) \qquad \boldsymbol{\pi} = \boldsymbol{\pi}\mathsf{P}$$

If the initial distribution is the same as the stationary distribution, then $\Pr[X_n = j]$ is the same for all $n \geq 0$.

We have the following fundamental results.

Theorem A.1

In an irreducible, aperiodic Markov chain the limiting probabilities $\lim_{n \to \infty} \Pr[X_n = j] = \pi_j, j \geq 0$, always exist and are independent of the initial distribution. There are two possibilities:

1. The states are all transient or recurrent null states; in this case $\pi_j = 0$ for all j and there exists no stationary distribution.

2. All states are recurrent nonnull states; in this case $\pi_j = 1/u_j > 0$ for all j and $\{\pi_j\}$ is a probability distribution. This distribution is uniquely determined as the solution of the system (A.3.4) satisfying

$$(A.3.6) \qquad \sum_{j=0}^{\infty} \pi_j = 1$$

In this case $\{\pi_j\}$ is the unique stationary distribution and $\{X_n\}$ is said to be *ergodic*. (The states are also said to be ergodic.)

Theorem A.2

All states of a finite, aperiodic, and irreducible Markov chain are recurrent nonnull states.

Theorem A.3

An aperiodic and irreducible Markov chain $\{X_n\}$ with state space $\{0, 1, 2, \ldots\}$ possesses a unique stationary distribution if and only if there exists an absolutely convergent sequence $\{\pi_k\}$, not identically zero, satisfying (A.3.4).

B   RECURRENCE TIMES

Let $\tau_1, \tau_2, \ldots, \tau_n, \ldots$ be nonnegative random variables denoting the epochs of a recurrent (renewal) process for which the intervals $\tau_{n+1} - \tau_n$ ($n \geq 1$) are independently and identically distributed according to the distribution function $F(x)$ and the interval $(0, \tau_1)$ is independently distributed according to $F_0(x)$. The recurrent events may be arrivals in a queueing system, occurrences of machine failures, etc. For simplicity we shall assume that $F(x)$ possesses the density $f(x)$ and we shall let α denote the mean value.

For a given time $t \geq 0$ we seek the distribution function $R_t(x)$ for the time remaining until the occurrence of the next event. This time interval is called the *forward recurrence time* and, in the reliability context, the *residual life-time*. Now the forward recurrence time will be less than or equal to x if and only if $t < \tau_n \leq t + x < \tau_{n+1}$ for some $n \geq 1$. Thus

(B.1) $$R_t(x) = \sum_{n=1}^{\infty} \Pr[t < \tau_n \leq t + x < \tau_{n+1}]$$

But given $\tau_n = u$ the probability that $\tau_{n+1} > t + x$ is $1 - F(t + x - u)$, and therefore (B.1) may be written as

(B.2) $$R_t(x) = \sum_{n=1}^{\infty} \int_t^{t+x} [1 - F(t + x - u)]\, dH_n(u)$$

where $H_n(u)$ is the distribution function for the time of the nth event. Letting $H(u) = \sum_{n=1}^{\infty} H_n(u)$ we have on interchanging the summation and integration

(B.3) $$R_t(x) = \int_t^{t+x} [1 - F(t + x - u)]\, dH(u)$$

Next, we compute the function $H(u)$.

It can be seen immediately that $H_n(u) = \Pr[\tau_n \leq u]$ is simply the probability that the sum of the intervals $(0, \tau_1), (\tau_1, \tau_2), \ldots, (\tau_{n-1}, \tau_n)$ is less than or equal to u. Thus using Laplace transforms and the results of Appendix A we find

$$H_n^*(s) = F_0^*(s)[F^*(s)]^{n-1}$$

and therefore

(B.4)
$$H^*(s) = \frac{F_0^*(s)}{1 - F^*(s)}$$

It is now a decided convenience to define

(B.5)
$$F_0^*(s) = \frac{1 - F^*(s)}{\alpha s}$$

For in this case we have

(B.6)
$$H^*(s) = \frac{1}{\alpha s}$$

We shall see below that this choice of $F_0^*(s)$ is in fact what we want from the physical motivations of our problem. From (B.6) we find $dH(u) = du/\alpha$, which on substitution into (B.3) gives, after some simplification,

(B.7)
$$R_t(x) = \frac{1}{\alpha} \int_0^x [1 - F(y)] \, dy$$

This is the result we have been seeking. The expected value of $R_t(x)$ is easily computed (integrating by parts), and found to be the expression given in (4.2.27).

It can be shown[†] that with $F_0(x)$ arbitrary the limiting behavior of $R_t(x)$ as $t \to \infty$ is again given by (B.7). It is a routine matter to show that the Laplace transform of the distribution $R_t(x)$ is precisely (B.5). Thus in specifying $F_0(x)$ it is as if we had assumed that the process had been in operation for an infinite time and that the time origin was selected at random; i.e., the time origin is a point selected at random while the process is in statistical equilibrium. But since (in Chapters 4 and 5) we are after the equilibrium value of $R_t(x)$, our assumption for $F_0(x)$ is appropriate. Of course, it follows that it is only at this point that we are able to say that $R_t(x)$ as calculated here is precisely the $R(x)$ introduced in Section 4.2.

For a given $t > 0$ the *backward recurrence time* is defined as the time that has elapsed since the last event. Using a very similar analysis one can show that the distribution for backward recurrence times is identical to (B.7) assuming the same initial condition (or, again, considering only the equilibrium distribution).

[†]Cox, D. R., *Renewal Theory*. Methuen, London, 1962.

INDEX

A

A-schedule, 88
Access time, 3
Active task, 34
Address, 3
Address map, 16, 242
Address space, 16, 242
Address trace, 17 (*see also* Reference
    string)
Allowable transition (deadlock), 49
Alternating renewal process, 228
Anomalies:
    paging, 22, 251, 278
    scheduling, 12, 22, 107-112
Arrival process, 146-150
Arrival rate, 146
Assignment, 84
Associative memory, 18
Asymptotic uncorrelation, 290
Asynchronism, 2
Auxiliary memory, 3 (*see also* Disk
        memory, Disk models, Drum
        memory, Drum models)
    disk, 5
    drum, 4
    paging drum, 20

Available resource vector, 49

B

B-schedule, 95
Backward distance, 245
Backward recurrence time, 294,321
Balance equations, 155, 219
Binomial moments, 314
Block (of storage), 4
Block operation, 77
Buffers, 20-21, 224-230
    occupancy, 21, 228
    pooled, 20-21
    private, 20-21
    shared, 20-21
Buffer storage allocation, 224-230 (*see
        also* Partition)
    FIFO queue, 233
    fixed or variable partition, 226, 229
    low data rate input, 227-230
    nonzero readout times, 234
    occupancy, 228
    optimal cell size, 226, 232-233
    overflow probability, 229
    simple queueing model, 225
    upcrossings, 229-230, 234-235

Buffer storage allocation (*cont.*):
    zero readout times, 227-230
Bulk arrivals, 189, 225, 232
Busy form of waiting, 64
Busy period, 152, 189
Busy period distribution, 165-166

C

C-schedule, 121
Central limit theorem, 230, 297, 317
Chain of tasks, 46
Characteristic function, 315
Circular wait, 10, 46
Closed task system, 34
Coefficient of variation, 160
Communication deadlock, 74
Completion sequence (deadlock), 56
Completion time (scheduling), 11, 84
Complexity:
    of scheduling, 85, 87, 100
    of synchronization, 80
Computer system:
    characteristics, 2
    definition, 1
Concatenation of task systems, 34
Concurrency, 2, 7-15, 33
Concurrent programming, 7
Conditional waiting time, 152
Confluence of Poisson processes, 149
Congestion, 151
Console model, 238
Consumable resource, 74
Convolution, 314, 316
Critical path, 122, 138
Critical route, 138
Critical section, 60
Cyclic synchronization, 70
Cyclic task system, 35
Cylinder (disk), 5

D

D-schedule, 131

Deadlines, 85, 139
Deadlock, 10, 44-59
    avoidance, 55-59
    conditions for, 45
    detection, 53-55
    prevention, 51-53
Decomposition of Poisson process, 150
Degree of multiprogramming, 304-305
Demand paging, 243-244 (*see also*
        Paging algorithm)
Demand prepaging, 278
Departure process, 193
Determinacy, 10, 35-44
Determinacy, weak, 75
Determinate task systems, 35-44
Deterministic scheduling, 11-12
    A-schedule, 88
    anomalies, 12, 107-112
    B-schedule, 95
    bound on length, 96, 118
    bound on processors, 96, 119
    C-schedule, 121
    D-schedule, 131
    effectiveness, 115
    flow shop, 124
    general, 115
    history of, 12-15
    job shop, 124
    list, 106-112
    LPT, 100
    minimum completion time, 11, 84
    nonpreemptive, 86
    permutation, 130
    preemptive, 86, 112-123
    processor sharing, 114
    SPT, 135
Disable operation, 77
Disk memory, 5-6
    arm, 5
    cylinder, 5
    disk surface, 5
    seek, 6
    timing, 6

Disk memory (*cont.*):
  track, 5
Disk models:
  CSCAN scheduling, 237
  distribution of information on, 212, 231-232
  FIFO scheduling, 210
  FSCAN scheduling, 211, 215-218, 231
  NSCAN scheduling, 231
  queueing model, 198-200, 209-218
  SCAN scheduling, 211-215, 231
  SSTF scheduling, 210
Disk track, 5
Distance:
  backward, 245
  forward, 245
  LRU stack, 275
  stack, 255
Distributions:
  exponential, 147, 315
  Gaussian, 315
  geometric, 147, 315
  moments, 146, 314, 316
  normal, 315
  Poisson, 149, 315
  for sum of random variables, 314, 316
  table of, 315
  uniform, 315
Domain of task, 36
Drum memory, 4-5
  sector, 5
  timing, 5
  track, 5
Drum models:
  FIFO scheduling, 210ff
  precessing scheme, 207
  queueing model, 198-209
  SATF scheduling, 201ff
  saturated queues, 208
Drum track, 5
Due date scheduling, 139 (*see also* Deadlines)

Dynamic partition (*see* Partition)

E

Effectiveness of schedules, 115
Embedded Markov chain, 157 (*see also* Markov chain)
Empty task, 84
Enable operation, 77
Enqueue operation, 64
Equilibrium distribution, 155 (*see also* Markov chain, stationary distribution)
Equilibrium equations, 158 (*see also* Markov chain, stationary distribution)
Equivalent task systems, 41
Exception (*see* Exceptional condition)
Exceptional condition, 1, 9
  fault, 9
  interrupt, 9
  trap, 9
Execution sequence, 33
Exponential distribution, 147, 315
Extension problem
  for any stack algorithm, 265-267
  for LFU, 278

F

Fault, 9
Fault probability (*see* Page fault rate)
Fault rate (*see* Page fault rate)
FCFS (first come first served); (*see also* FIFO)
  disks, 210
  drums, 201-209
Feedback queue, 178
Fetch policy, 15, 243
FIFO (first in first out); (*see* Paging algorithm, Queue)

FIFO paging algorithm, 246, 251, 255
    259, 272-274, 278, 280-282
    anomaly of, 251, 278
Finishing time of schedule, 84
Finite source queue, 168
Fixed partition (*see* Partition)
Flow shop problem, 124
Flow time, 128-129
    weighted, 140
Foreground-background queue, 190
Fork operation, 77
Forward distance, 245
Forward recurrence time, 320
Functional task system, 35

G

Gantt chart, 84
Gaussian (normal) process , 228-230,
    234, 296, 300-303
General scheduling, 115
Generating function, 313-315
Geometric distribution, 147, 315

H

Handler task, 9
History array, 36

I

ith moment, 146
I/O (*see* Input/output)
Inclusion property (*see* Stack algorithm,
    Working set model)
Independent reference model, 268-275
    bounds on fault rate, 280-282
    bounds on working set size, 310
    limiting fault rate of A_0, 269
    limiting fault rate of FIFO, 274
    limiting fault rate of LRU, 272
    limiting fault rate of RAND, 282
    optimal algorithm A_0, 268
Independent tasks, 33
Indivisible operation, 9, 63, 69

Input/output (*see* Buffer storage
    allocation, Console model,
    Disk models, Drum models,
    Mutual exclusion, Producer-
    consumer problem, Queue,
    Queue network, Synchroniza-
    tion)
Interarrival distribution, 145
Interference of tasks, 38, 63
Interpretation of task system, 38
Interreference distribution, 288-289
Interreference interval, 288-289
Interrupt, 9

J

Job shop problem, 124
Join operation, 77

L

Laplace transform, 315-317
Largest processing time (LPT) schedule,
    100
Latency, 199
Lateness, 139
Least recently used (*see* LRU)
Level of task, 33
List scheduling, 106-112
Little's result:
    in deterministic schedule, 130
    in stochastic system, 164
Locality, 23, 286-287, 288-289
Locality model, 309-310
Locality transition, 288-289, 308,
    309-310
Lock operation, 77
Long term storage, 2
LPT schedule, 100
LRU (least recently used) paging
    algorithm, 24, 245, 253, 254,
    258, 262-264, 266, 271-273,
    275-282, 286, 291, 298-299,
    301, 306 (*see also* LRU stack

LRU paging (*cont.*):
    model, Stack algorithm,
    Working set model)
LRU stack model, 275-278, 282
  distance string, 275
  fault rate of LRU, 277, 282
  optimality of LRU, 276

M

M/D/1 queue, 203
M/G/1 queue, 157-161
M/M/1 queue, 152-157
M/M/*m* queue, 168, 195
Main memory, 3
Markov chain, 317-319
  epochs, 318
  ergodicity, 319
  homogeneous, 157, 318
  initial distribution, 318
  irreducible, 318
  mean recurrence time, 318
  recurrent state, 318
  state space, 318
  stationary distribution, 319
  transition probabilities, 318
Markov process (*see* Markov chain)
Markov property, 146, 317-319
Maximally parallel task system, 41
Maximum resource usage system, 58,76
Mean flow time, 11, 128-136
Mean interreference interval, 289
Mean residence time, 184
Mean response time, 173
Memory:
  auxiliary, 3
  blocks, 4
  cache, 248
  characteristics, 3
  devices, 3-7
  disk, 5
  drum, 4, 20
  main, 3
  pages, 4

Memory (*cont.*):
  slave, 248
Memory cells of task systems, 36
Memoryless property, 146
Memory management (*see also* Storage
    allocation)
  history, 16-24
  overview, 15
  policies, 15, 21-23
Memory overflow (*see* Buffer storage
    allocation, Upcrossings)
Memory space, 16
Memory state (*see* Paging algorithm)
Merging Poisson processes, 149
Method of stages (queues), 195
Missing-page probability, 291
Moment, 146, 314, 316
Moment generating function (*see*
    Generating function)
Multilevel queue, 178
Multiplexing, 2
Multiprogramming, 2, 285-286 (*see
    also* Partition)
  degree of, 304-305
  fixed or variable partition, 24, 285
  thrashing in, 24, 290
Mutual exclusion, 10, 59-67
Mutual synchronization, 71

N

Noninterfering tasks, 38
Nonpreemptive priority queues, 175-
    178
Nonpreemptive scheduling, 86, 150
Normal process (distribution); (*see*
    Gaussian process)

O

Occupancy of buffers, 21, 228
One-step transition probability, 157,
    203, 216, 317-319
Operating system, definition, 2

Optimal paging (*see also* Paging algorithm, Program models)
  forward distance criterion, 249
  principle of optimality, 252, 268, 276, 309
Optimal scheduling (*see* Deterministic scheduling)
Ordered resource usage, 52
Overflows (*see* Buffer storage allocation, Upcrossings)
Overlays, 15-16

P

P operation, 68
Page, 4
Page fault, 9, 17, 242
Page fault rate, 242, 246-248, 250
Page size effects, 279-280, 307-308
Paging algorithm, 21-33, 243ff (*see also* Stack algorithm)
  A_0 algorithm, 268
  anomalies, 251, 278
  B_0 algorithm, 245-254, 268
  cost, 246-248, 250
  demand, 243-244
  demand prepaging, 278
  extension problem, 265-267, 278
  fetch policy, 15, 243
  FIFO (*see* FIFO paging algorithm)
  forward distance criterion, 249
  LFU, 246
  LIFO, 246
  lookahead, 246
  LRU (*see* LRU paging algorithm)
  memory state sequence, 244
  nonlookahead, 246
  optimal, 22, 245-254, 268
  placement policy, 15, 243
  RANDOM, 259-260, 261
  replacement policy, 15, 243
Paging drum, 20
Parallel processes or tasks, 8
Parallel programming, 7

Parallel task systems, 34
Partial execution sequence, 34
Partial order of tasks, 33
Partition (of memory), 24, 285, 299-305 (*see also* Buffer storage allocation)
  dynamic, 300
  exceedance, 301
  fixed, 300
  safeness factor, 300
  variable, 300
Performance measures for queues, 151-152
Placement policy, 15, 243
Poisson distribution, 149, 315
Poisson process, 148-150
Pollaczek-Khintchine formula, 168, 193
Positional access, 3
Precedence graph, 33
Precessing drum scheme, 207
Predecessor task, 33
Preemption, 7 (*see also* Preemptive scheduling)
Preemptive scheduling, 112-113, 150
Primitive operations (parallelism), 64
  block, 77
  disable, 77
  enable, 77
  enqueue, 64
  fork, 77
  join, 77
  lock, 77
  P, 68
  remove, 64
  send, 68
  test-and-set, 76
  unlock, 77
  V, 68
  wait, 68
  wakeup, 77
Principle of optimality (*see* Optimal paging)
Priority algorithm (*see* Queue, Stack algorithm)

Priority queues, 175-189 (*see also* Queue)
Probability distributions (*see* Distributions)
Process, 1, 8 (*see also* Task)
    definitions, 8-9
    parallel, 8
Processor sharing, 13, 114, 172 (*see also* Queue)
Producer-consumer problem, 70, 72-74
Program behavior (*see* Program models)
Program models, 23-24
    independent reference, 250, 268-275 (*see also* Independent reference model)
    locality, 309-310
    LRU stack (*see* LRU stack model)
    working set (*see* Working set model)
Program restructuring for locality, 23

Q

Quantum, 169
Queue, 12-15, 145
    bulk arrivals, 189
    comparisons among, 186-189
    feedback, 178
    FIFO, 13, 153, 233
    finite queue limitation, 167
    finite source limitation, 168
    foreground-background, 190
    LIFO, 153, 193
    M/D/1, 203
    M/G/1, 157-161
    M/M/1, 152-157
    M/M/m, 168, 195
    multilevel, 178
    nonpreemptive priority, 175-178
    notation for, 153
    preemptive resume, 189
    priority, 13, 175-189
    processor sharing (PS), 13, 172
    random service, 153
    round-robin (RR), 13, 169-175

Queue (*cont.*):
    shortest elapsed time (SET), 13, 178-182
    shortest processing time (SPT), 177
    shortest remaining processing time (SRPT), 13, 182-186
    state dependent, 166-169
    tandem, 192
    two-level priority, 190
Queueing time distribution, 163
Queue network, 218-224
    central server, 222-224
    closed, 218
    cyclic, 218-219
    cyclic with I/O, 235-236
    open, 236
    stages of, 220

R

Random access, 3
Random arrivals, 149
Random process, 153
Range of task, 36
Recurrence times, 320-321
    backward, 321
    forward, 320
Reference string, 17, 242ff (*see also* Independent reference model, Locality model, LRU stack model, Program models, Working set model)
    backward distance in, 245
    forward distance in, 245
    interreference intervals in, 288
    random, 250
    recurrent page in, 289, 307
    reverse, 253
    stochastic, 243, 288
Regeneration points, 157
Release vector, 46
Remove operation, 64
Replacement page, 243
Replacement policy, 15, 243

Request vector, 46
Residence time, 184
Residual waiting time, 161, 320
Resources:
  consumable, 7, 74
  definitions, 3-7
  generalized, 7
  memory, 3
  processor, 3
  reusable, 7
  software, 1
Reverse reference string, 253
Reverse schedule, 137
Rotational latency, 199
Round-robin queue, 13, 169-175

S

Safeness:
  in mutual exclusion, 61
  in task systems, 50
SATF (shortest access time first),
    drums, 20, 201-209
Saturation condition, 160
SCAN (disk policy), 20, 211-215, 231
Scheduling (*see* Deterministic
    scheduling, Queue)
Sector, drum, 5
Seek time, disk, 6, 199
Semaphore, 68
Send operation, 68
Server, 145
Service mechanism, 150-151
Service time distribution, 145
Sharing, 2
Shortest access time first, 20, 201-209
Shortest processing time schedule, 135
Shortest seek time first, 20, 210
Sources for queues, 145
Speed independent task systems, 10, 35
SPT schedule, 135
SSTF, 20, 210
Stack algorithm (paging), 22, 251, 254-
    264 (*see also* LRU stack model)

Stack algorithm (*cont.*):
  characterization, 257
  cost function procedure, 263-264
  extension problem, 265-267, 278
  inclusion property, 254
  LRU case, 262-263, 275ff, 282,
    286, 298-299, 301
  priority algorithm, 22, 257-263
  stack, 254
  stack distance, 255, 275
  updating procedure, 260
Stages of queue network, 220
Stages of service, 192, 195
State dependent queue, 166-169
State sequence of task system, 34
Statistical equilibrium, 155, 203, 319
Steady state distribution, 155, 319
Stochastic process, 153
Stochastic service system, 14 (*see also*
    Queue)
Storage allocation (*see also* Buffer
    storage allocation, Multipro-
    gramming, Paging algorithm,
    Partition, Virtual memory)
  nonpaged systems, 241
Storage partition (*see* Partition)
Successor task, 33
Swapping time, 174
Synchronization, 10, 68-74
  cyclic task systems, 70
  graph, 74
Synchronization primitives, 68 (*see
    also* Primitive operations)
System of tasks (*see* Task system)

T

Tagged job, 170, 176, 180
Tandem queues, 192
Tardiness, 139
Task, 9, 31ff (*see also* Process)
Task chain, 46
Task system, 31-35
  active task, 34

Task system (*cont.*):
  closed, 34
  independent tasks, 33
  initial task, 33
  level of task, 33
  path length, 33
  precedence graph, 33
  state sequence, 34
  terminal task, 33
Terminal model (*see* Console model)
Test-and-set operation, 76
Think time, 173
Thrashing, 24, 290
Time slice, 169
Topological sorting, 77
Track, disk, 5
Track, drum, 5
Traffic intensity, 156
Transfer time, 199
Transition probability, 157 (*see also* Markov chain)
Trap, 9
Tree graph scheduling, 94
Two-level priority queue, 190

U

Uninterpreted task system, 38
Uninterruptible mode, 9, 77
Uninterruptible operation, 9
Unlock operation, 77
Upcrossings, 229-230, 234-235, 305
Utilization factor, 11, 156

V

V operation, 68
Valid execution sequence, 49
Value sequence, 37

Variable degree of multiprogramming, 304-305
Variable partition (*see* Partition)
Virtual memory (*see also* Paging algorithm, Reference string)
  address map, 16, 242
  address space, 16
  address trace, 17
  associative memory, 18
  memory space, 18
  organization, 16ff
  paged, 17-18, 242

W

Waiting time distribution, 162
Wait operation, 68
Wakeup operation, 77
Weak determinacy, 75
Weighted flow time, 140
Weight of a task, 85
Working set, 23, 286, 290
Working set model, 23, 287-299
  asymptotic uncorrelation, 290
  definition, 290
  estimating locality, 291
  inclusion property, 292
  interreference distribution, 288-289
  missing page probability, 291
  properties, 292-295, 305-306
  recurrent page, 289, 307
  relation to LRU, 291, 298-299, 301, 306
  window size, 290
Working set principle, 23, 290
Working set size, 291
  convexity, 295
  distribution, 295-298, 311